R. GENGHINI, *Digital new deal. The quest for a natural law in a digital society*

RICCARDO GENGHINI

DIGITAL NEW DEAL
THE QUEST FOR A NATURAL LAW IN A DIGITAL SOCIETY

Wolters Kluwer

Published by:
Kluwer Law International B.V.
PO Box 316
2400 AH Alphen aan den Rijn
The Netherlands
E-mail: international-sales@wolterskluwer.com
Website: www.wolterskluwer.com/en/solutions/legal-regulatory/permissions-reprints-and-licensing

Sold and distributed by:
Wolters Kluwer Legal & Regulatory U.S.
7201 McKinney Circle
Frederick, MD 21704
United States of America
E-mail: customer.service@wolterskluwer.com

ISBN 978-88-133-7238-5

e-Book: ISBN 978-94-035-4195-2
web-PDF: ISBN 978-94-035-4200-3

© 2021 Wolters Kluwer Italia S.r.l.
Originally published by Wolters Kluwer Italia s.r.l. with ISBN 978-88-133-7238-5

TABLE OF CONTENTS

FOREWORD

Dear Friends,

I'm a lawyer. Therefore I am not asking you just to believe me. Put me on the witness stand. Let me present my reasoning to you, cross-examine me, and then decide.

I have been working on this publication since 2004. I've changed my mind several times and only now am I convinced that I am asking the right questions needed to understand the decades of technological, legal and social change ahead of us.

At this stage of my research there can be no "passive readers"!

You must challenge my assumptions and my thoughts. I will listen.

All feedback is welcome and necessary to make this a reading and discussion tool with which we can shape knowledge together, in the same way it was shaped 2.000 years ago, through the dialectic process at the Platonic Academy.[1]

I can wait no longer! I need your feedback: Send me your comments at rg@digitalnewdeal.eu

Thank you, dear friends, for your patience with a project that, albeit immature and incomplete, should be of great importance in trying to understand our changing world!

Riccardo

---

[1] D. Sedley, "Academy", *The Oxford Classical Dictionary*, 3rd ed., p. 4.

INTRODUCTION

Flash back to **Christmas 1999:** While reading the millennium issue of **The Economist,** I had an epiphany. In an article called "**Road to Riches**",[2] some data from **Angus Maddison** was summarized in a graph, showing the increase in productivity of the "West".

When I saw the graph, I realized that **the productivity curve had to flatten**, so I prepared for this eventuality.

My investments began to pay off in 2006. My business thrived and eventually tripled in a market that was declining, if not collapsing.

The article in *The Economist* had fundamentally confirmed that the exceptional and exponential growth of wealth and knowledge in the past century was a sort of black swan. It was no coincidence that in May 2012, another article by Bagehot (yes, *The Economist* again!) summarized my thoughts: "The Nightmare Scenario" described a reality of austerity and spending cuts, debt, intermittent growth and relative decline.[3] Now it's 2020, and each of us can judge how prescient these articles were.

So, **have we entered into a (non-cyclical) crisis of the socioeconomic model of open, liberal, democratic societies?** Possibly yes. Possibly there is no solution other than to "reconsider reality starting from new theories" (Einstein). A lot of recent science fiction is about **redefining the parameters** – not just the boundaries of scientific knowledge and technological possibilities, but also the parameters of free will. Good examples include *The Host* and *Interstellar*.

And for the idea itself of law and social order: *Elysium, Oblivion, Divergent, The Maze Runner* or *The Hunger Games*.

Is the "Western world"[4] still able to offer a paradigm for social justice and peaceful, free, consensual order? My ambition is to ask tough questions and to collect the opinions of those who care to discover the path to a sustainable future. We will need some substantial changes in our rules and organisation. I will try to propose some of them.

---

[2] THE ECONOMIST, *The road to riches.*
[3] THE ECONOMIST, *The nightmare scenario.*
[4] "Western world" is an obsolete term because there are many Eastern and Southern nations that have become rich, democratic and open. A better term would be "OECD countries" or simply "OECD", in order to refer to the 34 nations that are currently members of the Organisation for Economic Co-operation and Development (www.oecd.org). The OECD's origins date back to 1960, when 18 European countries plus the United States and Canada joined forces to create an organisation dedicated to economic development.

My ideological biases are as follows:

I grew up in a **Christian** cultural environment. Still, I (try to) respect all religions and creeds, but prefer those where love and forgiveness have a cathartic moral significance.

I believe that **populism and autocracy/totalitarianism are based on exclusion**. They police inequality and injustice by keeping "the others" out – outside of borders, out of mainstream life … locked in … or OUT!

I believe that excluding is arbitrary and an act of unjustified violence. It produces a domino effect. Exclusion calls for violence and violence calls for exclusion. This isn't necessary, and it isn't the right way, as John Rawls has demonstrated in his fundamental "*A Theory of Justice*".

After the golden age of abundance (when we were hunter-gatherers and shared everything), scarcity has led to rules of exclusion and inclusion (family, property, tribe, state …) that are still upheld after 20,000 or 40,000 years. And it couldn't have been otherwise, considering the (slow?) evolution of our minds, of our language – considering the low productivity of human labour, the fragility of human societies – some of which have disappeared in the blink of an eye.

I sincerely dislike superficial hype about information technology. Still, I suspect that **IT may significantly change the inclusion/exclusion mechanism**, that it may offer an opportunity to improve the quality of life for all of us – those who live in the (still) rich world *and* those who live in developing countries – allowing us to share more, to exchange more.

But **as with all opportunities, there are also inherent risks** – risks of misunderstanding where the true innovation lies and how to use it. Printed books, radio, cinema, television and, ultimately, the Internet[5] have made knowledge more accessible, but also more easily manipulated.

As a lawyer, my ambition is to understand the rules that provide justice and peace for the next century and beyond. Good rules, in fact, last for a long time. The "*Ius Commune*" of the ancient Romans lasted for 1,500 years after the end of the Roman Empire, and its founding principles are still applied today, not only in Europe, but worldwide as "common law"[6] in the Commonwealth of Nations and the United States.

I believe many of our current laws will not last for another decade. What will come next?

I have devoted more than 15 years of research to this question by reading books covering subjects like linguistics (in particular semiotics), archaeology, anthropology, history, neurology, sociology, psychology, philosophy, economics and information technology. Law has been a minor field of research. Nonetheless,

---

[5] Steve Kent told me that Vint Cerf uses the capital initial for "Internet": Who am I to disagree?
[6] "Common law" is the English translation of "*Ius Commune*".

the whole analysis of the subject(s) is bound together by the aim of finding new founding (legal) principles for a new digital social agreement. It was a lawyer's mind that read through the vast literature, with absolutely no interest in becoming involved in any specialist or academic debate: Even a wrong assumption may lead to a good question as we seek to understand our course into the future!

In this work, I explain why I have chosen a certain theory about language or about human evolution, but I will not try to put an end to discussions that have been going on for decades (if not centuries). I possess neither the scientific knowledge nor the authority to do so. Simply, I have chosen, on a case-by-case basis, the most compelling line of reasoning for me. Maybe I was (am) too dumb to understand more sophisticated theories; however, in my research I can go only as far as my mind allows.

During my 15 years of study, I took the time to evolve, and I changed my assumptions, recognizing my prejudices. I didn't start writing because I felt that I had something to explain to others, but because I wanted to be able to ask the questions that are relevant to understanding our society – the questions that will allow us to construct a better future. This book (I hope) serves as a deep, meditated invitation to debate, to contribute, to build the future together.

I am also **trying to escape from the scathing condemnation of writing,** as Plato put in Socrates' mouth in the *Phaedrus*[7], "*You offer your pupils the appearance of wisdom, not true wisdom, for they will read many things without instruction and will therefore seem to know many things, when they are for the most part ignorant and hard to get along with, since they are not wise, but only appear wise*"[8].

With the current semiotics and technologies, I cannot escape the baleful fate of a lone writer, without some help of my readers.

My thoughts and my research are open to discussion, amendment, integration, extension, etc. Anyone who cares may contribute their knowledge and share their ideas. This book does not end the discussion; it opens it.

This shouldn't be a book or a blog. It should be inherently interactive and open to every contribution or criticism (see chapter 8.2).

Readers of my research should not be passive. They should partake in the outcome of the research, offering information, insights, doubts, questions and criticism. This is not an opportunity to gaze passively at some printed words (that pretend to tell a truth), but a chance to be actively involved in the creation and dissemination of new knowledge.

I don't want to be right. **My ambition is to find the right questions**. If the questions are right, the right answers will follow through deep, constructive debate.

---

[7] The online English version of the *Phaedrus* is available at http://classics.mit.edu/Plato/phaedrus.html. In the dialogue, Plato explains writing's origin by quoting the mythological dialogue between Theuth, god of writing, and the Egyptian King Thamus. http://it.wikipedia.org/wiki/Mito_di_Theuth.

[8] PLATO, *Phaedrus*, 274a-275b.

This work is a request for help. Students and scholars, please contribute with your ideas and information as you wish. This work is a living community of people who can comment, criticize, improve and amend the findings of the research over time.

I am excited to interact with you, and I will try to learn … and hopefully teach you a thing or two. I hope my active readers will be prepared to make the same marvellous journey.

Please contact me at rg@digitalnewdeal.eu with your ideas, criticisms, suggestions, references, and I will take due notice of them and include them as far as possible in the next edition of this book.

This work is dedicated to my children and their generation.

When I was their age, I was driven by the enthusiastic hope of improving life for everybody. But we were wrong in most of our assumptions, so we did not succeed. On the contrary, in the last 30 years our "Western" society has been savagely damaged; we are as indebted as if there had been a world war, with no winners, no moral high ground (or lessons taught) and thus no clear perspective on the future, and pandemics have come to stay.

The main error we have made is to think that anyone can disengage from the rest of the world, fencing off "the others" – an approach that is morally controversial and breeds totalitarianism, according to chaos theory.

I think my generation has to accept the blame for this state of affairs.

We are heading for a rough ride.

But life is nothing other than a journey, where the departure and the arrival are the same for all of us. The beauty of any journey lies in the ability to master the unexpected. So the journey ahead of us will be marked by a savage beauty!

I hope that this book will become one of your travel companions.

HOW TO READ THIS BOOK

In the first seven chapters, I try to work out some assumptions and definitions that need rethinking before we are able to reflect on our digital society in a way that isn't biased by outdated assumptions and definitions.

In the eighth chapter, I try to provide some conceptual categories and possible solutions to the unsolved challenges of our digital society.

One possible way to read this book is to start with chapter 8 and then go back to the previous chapters only if the reader does not understand (or agree with) the underlying assumptions.

Cognitive categories, proposals and possible legal principles are presented in chapter 8.

Whoever is principally interested in the main takeaways, should start there.

Anyone who is also interested in a critical and dialectical understanding of the ideas and proposals presented in chapter 8, should also read chapters 1 to 7, because there it should be possible to find any fallacies in my reasoning.

Chapters 1 to 7 are devoted to the analysis of our legal, social, anthropological reality. I try to correct some wrong assumptions that may mislead us as we seek to understand the risks that we face and the choices, and even opportunities, that are still open to us.

Whenever I use categories or refer to people in this book that are already likely to be familiar to the reader, rather than assuming that they are known, I will refer you to Wikipedia. Whenever I think it does not matter which precise definition is used, as with civil law, Roman law, the Vandals, the Union in the US Civil War or universal suffrage, I will refer you to Wikipedia.

But whenever I intend to refer to a specific interpretation of a term or category, I have quoted the scientific literature that has influenced my thoughts – as I have for "sign", "document"," human being", "justice", etc.

ABSTRACT

The structure of this book can be summarized as follows:

First, we will meditate on human nature and language. We believe that our uniqueness is self-evident. But we are wrong: Genetically, behaviourally, we are not so different from chimps or other evolved mammals. Also, language is no longer believed to be unique to mankind: Chimps change their utterances to match those of other apes, depending on where they live. Moreover, genetic engineering has gone so far that we will soon be able to engineer not just animals and plants, but human beings as well. This is certain, not simply the subject of dystopic science fiction novels like those of Philip K. Dick.

In the end, as far as we can tell, what really makes us unique is mankind's ability (and need) to tell stories! We cannot rule out the possibility that, even before my generation dies out, we will have story-telling machines and androids, thanks to artificial intelligence.[9] And there will be biological specimens identical to us that will not have been bred by parents, but generated in a laboratory.[10]

So we will need to find profound answers to these questions:

a) What is a human?

b) What is an animal?

c) and, Is a conscious being an object, just because it was fabricated (as opposed to naturally conceived)?

I try to offer a first answer to these questions in chapter 8.1.

Second, we will reflect on **the origins of law** and on how human rules are different (or not) from rules governing animal groupings (packs, herds, droves, flocks, hives, etc.). We will see that there are very **close connections between legal rules, language and the human way of life**. It is self-evident that, if language and the human way of life change, then the laws will also follow suit. Language and the law are the two tools that mankind has used to adapt nature to human life. Without either of them, there would not be such an evident and clear-cut difference between human and animal society. Without language or law, humans would still have to adapt to nature, instead of shaping it, and the principles governing human life would not have changed as frequently or quickly as they have. Other mammals still live in the same way they did 20,000 years ago. Humans have undergone an incredible evolution during that same time. This would be simply unthinkable without language and law.

Third, we will **reconsider the role of written and oral knowledge in human society**. It is simply untrue that all (good, true) knowledge comes from books and other written documents. Perhaps it has never been true that we learn mostly from written documents.

Fourth, we will study the fact that **slavery and forced labour have been very difficult to abolish**. It's been less than a century that we have lived in a world almost completely free of slavery. Regardless, almost 2,000,000,000 humans today live in extreme poverty: Their lives are not much better than the life of a slave. Innovation and industrialisation have lifted one-eighth of humanity out of poverty. Can the rest follow? Or will the gap grow wider and wider? Can we hope that digitalisation is already triggering a second new economy? How and on what basis?

---

[9] The Economist, *The Dawn of Artificial Intelligence*.

[10] The Economist, *Editing Humanity*.

Fifth, how has human law evolved from the Middle Ages until now? What evolutionary patterns can we recognize? Will they work in a digital society? It is quite evident, looking into the history of commercial law, that the merchants of the 11th century created rules for their trade in the same way that the "new economy" companies have in the past two decades, as they triggered the development of "e-commerce".

Sixth and **seventh,** we will try to define **what a digital society is**, while avoiding hype and banal descriptions. The precise definition of digital society is of paramount importance in understanding what rules will survive and what rules will die in the coming decades.

Eight, we will discuss a set of principles and rules that will "work" in a society highly impacted by digital language, digital media, digital documents, digital interactions and ultimately a digital economy and digital culture. Some of these (only partly new) concepts, are essential to preserving our open, democratic and pluralistic society. I see this work as a sort of "digital footnote" to the Federalist Papers, to enable them to survive in a digital society.

ACKNOWLEDGEMENTS

Most of what I know about cryptography and IT security, I learned from Andreas Pfitzmann, Steve Kent and Whit Diffie.

This book is the summary of about 15 years of studies and research.

Firstly, I would like to **thank my students** in the Course of Comparative Commercial Law at the Università Cattolica di Milano (2007-2017).

In particular my gratitude goes to following students for their specific contributions to this book:

chapter 1: Anna Pilo, footnote 49; Anna Maria Montrone, footnote 50; Marta Lantero, footnote 57;

chapter 2: Giada Perfumo, footnote 97; Irene Trezzi, Alessandra Capece, Annalisa Maestri, footnote 98;

chapter 3: Valentina Boga, to chapter 3.4.3; Riccardo Ryder, footnote 192; Mariamaddalena Landolfi and Giuliana Muraglia, to chapter 3.4.5; Maria Sole Bassi and Anna Tettamanti, to chapter 3.4.6; Elena Manzoni, to chapter 3.4.7;

chapter 4: Federica Palma, to chapter 4.1;

chapter 5: Elena Coloretti, to chapter 5.4.1.

Secondly, I want to thank all the members of the Technical Board "Electronic Signatures Initiative" (**TB ESI**) of the European Telecommunication Standards Institute (**ETSI**) and Vice Chairmen Nick Pope and Arno Fiedler, whose support over a more than a decade has shaped my view of eIDAS Digital Trust Services and Digital Identification as a centre of support for a free, pluralistic, digital society.

Furthermore, I had several **sparring partners**, who challenged my assumptions and ideas. In particular Reinhard Posch, and Herbert Leitold with whom I worked since 1999 on the protection profiles for signature creation devices (https://www.en-standard.eu/bs-en-419211-2-2013-protection-profiles-for-secure-signature-creation-device-device-with-key-generation/) and on the definition and features of the electronic identity. Jon Ølnes with whom I deepened my understanding of the technologic challenges of a "freedom device" protecting and managing our digital identities. Marit Hansen-Köntopp for inviting me in 2003 to join her research on identity management systems.

I would like to thank also Ludwig Kraft, Giuseppe Mascoli, Antonio Conte, Andrea Servida, Viky Manaila, Francesco Galgano, Natalino Irti, Giusella Finocchiaro, Cosimo Comella, Massimiliano Lovati, Andrea Valle, Leonard Rosenthol, Patrizia Sormani, Eleonora Giardino, Simone Fiore, Andrea Lisi, Giovanni Manca, Stefano Arbia, Michele Cermele, Stefano Cocchi, Giovanni Bussu, Nigel Williams, Matthias Schunter, Holger Krekel.

Since 2000 I had the opportunity to work with **Unit H4** of the European Commission's Directorate-General for Communications Networks, Content and Technology, in charge of eGovernment and Trust and the revision of EU Regulation 2014/910/EU (the so-called "eIDAS Regulation"). We had the opportunity for lengthy and deep discussions on the concept of the eID and its technological features, in particular with respect to the requirements of the General Data Protection Regulation (GDPR, EU Regulation 2016/679). So my special gratitude goes to Norbert Sagstätter, Dietmar Gattwinkel, Michal Hrbaty, Anders Gjoen, Carlos Gomez Munoz, Costas Kapsouropoulos and Bogdan Stefan. And Andrea Servida, of course.

Last but not least, I would like to acknowledge **my sons Niccolò** and **Leonardo,** for discussing with me the main concepts and bringing to my work the perspective of millennials. Moreover, Niccolò has helped with the legal searches and Leonardo with the spreadsheets, as well as with his extensive work on the footnotes and his deep philosophical studies.

Finally, my gratitude goes to Jody Summers and Anthony Deckoff for proof-reading the manuscript and improving my English.

Last but not least, I have to thank eWitness SA, that has fully funded my research since the beginning. Without that generous support, this work would have been impossible.

1   Human Language

Wovon man nicht sprechen kann,
darüber muss man schweigen.
(L. Wittgenstein) **Tractatus**
logico-philosophicus Abschnitt 7

1. Human Language

If we observe animals in their environment, we notice that their behaviour sometimes bears a resemblance to human legal rules:
1) Property: Some animals own and protect their dens.
2) Hierarchy: Some animal societies have specialized roles and rules that define responsibilities.
3) Territory: Some animal species mark and defend their territory.
4) Exclusive union: Some animals live in a closed, mutually exclusive union for a long time (even a lifetime).
Ultimately, what is the ontology of human law, and how does it differentiate itself from ethologic rules?
In this chapter we will see that "animal ethologic rules" and "human rules" are different in their essence:
a) Not only because of self-awareness: Self-awareness is increasingly accepted as a neurologic feature in the systems of some more-developed animal species (see chapter 2.1). Human self-awareness has a different quality at the neurological level, compared to animal self-awareness, but there is insufficient data to postulate an ontological difference between human and animal rules.
b) And not because humans are uniquely possessed (supposedly) of moral instincts (see chapter 2.4): Human morality has a different quality from animal morality; again, there is not sufficient information to postulate an ontological difference between human and animal rules.
The deep differences between human rules and animal rules are mainly related to:
1) the use and the function of language (see chapter 2.3)
2) and the aim of human rules, which have the scope to change nature, and in particular to transform scarcity into abundance. Animal rules mostly are about coping with natural phenomena, not about changing the way nature works.
Considering the most recent neurologic and ethologic discoveries on animal morality and self-consciousness, we can safely conclude that law is a purely human phenomenon. To enforce law requires a formalized and abstract language and the aim of "creating" a natural/social environment in which creatures can thrive. This is a feat that only human beings have been able to master thus far.
Digitalisation is clearly not only a change in the way information is shared, but also a radical change in the structure of the signs and sounds that humans use to communicate:
1) Binary code replaces signs traced on a surface, used by humans for more than a hundred thousand years.
2) Content and context are decoupled.
3) Content or text and their originators are decoupled.
4) Information no longer occupies a specific geographic position (since the arrival of ubiquitous computing. See chapter 6.1).
5) Textual communication is progressively meshed with other kinds of signs, such as icons, images, music and multimedia content.

6) Content generated without any human agency has become pervasive and difficult to distinguish from digital content generated by humans.

7) I, my identity, my words, my ideas are all on the same level in the digital dimension: They are found together "there", and meanwhile I am "here": Mind-body dualism is almost non-existent in the digital domain. Everything is an abstraction, everything is metaphorical.

Digitalisation presents the most radical change in the way humans communicate since the invention of words and verbal human communication.

In order to reason about the impact of digitalisation, we need to have a deep understanding of the structure, nature and working of human language.

Let us ask ourselves:

- Is human language able to describe reality in an objective manner, or is it more apt at creating and sharing some particular account of reality?

- If, as most theories sustain, human language is primarily a tool for shaping reality (See chapter 1.3), how much of human society will be affected by this change? In particular, we need to consider:

- The nexus between the structure of language (and human communication) and the rules of human society.

- The relation between the complexity of language and social inclusion. Civilisations with highly sophisticated languages, such as Egypt and China, have been markedly non-inclusive.

The debate on the origin of human language was abandoned in 1866, considered unsolvable. Famously, the Société Linguistique de Paris refused to admit any further papers on the subject.[11] Then, after more than a century, the subject was resumed – not because researchers are closer to a scientific proof of the origin of language, but because the theories on its origin provide a key for decrypting today's social reality.

That key lies in the analysis of how humans speak and document reality.

1.1. Definition of Human

Theories estimate that the human lineage may have diverged from that of chimpanzees about five million years ago and from that of gorillas about eight million years ago. However, a hominid skull discovered in Chad in 2001, classified as *Sahelanthropus tchadensis*, is approximately seven million years old and may be evidence of an earlier divergence. (There is little fossil evidence for the evolutionary divergence of the gorilla, chimpanzee and hominid lineages, which is why anthropologists are still disputing its exact timing.)

Current estimates of overlapping DNA sequences between functional humans and chimpanzees currently range between 95% and 99%. So even if there are obvious physiognomic differences between humans and apes, such differences are genetically explainable by means of phylogenetic evolution.[12]

---

[11] MITHEN S., *The Singing Neanderthal*, 4.

[12] Even consciousness may not be a uniquely human trait. In July 2012, during the "Consciousness in Human and Nonhuman Animals" conference in Cambridge, UK, a group of scientists announced and signed a declaration with the following conclusion:

The earliest member of the genus Homo, Homo habilis, evolved around 2.3 million years ago. The brains of these early hominids were about the same size as those of chimpanzees, yet Homo habilis walked on two legs and used stone tools.

During the next million years, brain mass grew. By the arrival of Homo erectus 1.8 million years ago, cranial capacity had doubled. Homo erectus was the first of the hominids to leave Africa. This species migrated throughout Africa, Asia and Europe for 500,000 years. One tribe of Homo erectus, sometimes classified as Homo ergaster, stayed in Africa and evolved into Homo sapiens.

In Wikipedia, "Human" is defined as follows:

"Humans are distinguished from other primates by their bipedal locomotion, and especially by their relatively larger brain with its particularly well-developed neocortex, prefrontal cortex and temporal lobes, which enable high levels of abstract reasoning, language, problem solving, and culture through social learning. Humans use tools to a much higher degree than any other animal, and are the only extant species known to build fires and cook their food, as well as the only known species to clothe themselves and create and use numerous other technologies and arts. The scientific study of humans is the discipline of anthropology.

Humans are uniquely adept at utilizing systems of symbolic communication such as language and art for self-expression, the exchange of ideas, and organisation. Humans create complex social structures composed of many cooperating and competing groups, from families and kinship networks to states. Social interactions between humans have established an extremely wide variety of values, social norms, and rituals, which together form the basis of human society. The human desire to understand and influence their environment, and explain and manipulate phenomena, has been the foundation for the development of science, philosophy, mythology, and religion."[13]

Western religions tell us that humans are ontologically different from animals. Our existential experience tells us otherwise. Whenever we live together with pets, they become part of our families. We talk to them; they communicate with us. We recognize their personalities. We understand their facial expressions and their emotions. We miss them when they pass. The same adaptation is true in reverse when a human is adopted by a pack of animals. More than 30 cases[14] studied by anthropologists have shown: such humans learn to use animal communication and may unlearn human language.

"Convergent evidence indicates that non-human animals have the neuroanatomical, neurochemical, and neurophysiological substrates of conscious states along with the capacity to exhibit intentional behaviours. Consequently, the weight of evidence indicates that humans are not unique in possessing the neurological substrates that generate consciousness. Non-human animals, including all mammals and birds, and many other creatures, including octopuses, also possess these neurological substrates." Koch, Christof, Stephen Hawking, Philip Low, Irene Pepperberg, Bruno van Swinderen, David B. Edelman, Edward Boyden, Diana Reiss, Donald Pfaff, Ryan Remedios, Harvey Karten, Franz X. Vollenweider, Naotsugu Tsuchiya, Melanie Boly, and Steven Laureys, *"The Cambridge Declaration of Consciousness"*. To listen to the presentations that discuss the issue of animal self-consciousness, go to http://fcmconference.org/.

[13] The definition copied in the text was available on 3 September 2020, Wikipedia.

[14] JARMAN M., *Encyclopedia Britannica*, "Feral children"; BIRDSONG D., *Second Language Acquisition and the Critical Period Hypothesis*, 74; TURKLE, S., *The Second Self*, 17, writes about the "Wild Child".

Western religions consider as human only beings who are fertilized by their natural fathers, carried in the womb of their mothers and born alive. Conversely, we have now arrived at a moment in history when a human (?) life can be generated without any coupling between male and female, but entirely through genetic engineering.[15]

Our aprioristic definition of "human" relates to the procreational process of a human being.[16] The most that anthropology and genetics can say today about the ontology of humans is that we are chimps living in packs who eventually learned to use their hands (two million years ago) and speak (about 50,000 years ago), while struggling to adapt to a hostile environment characterized by scarcity of resources.

Human language and animal communication are both made up of visual and acoustic signs. But they are fundamentally different, because our use of words and sentences allows a degree of abstraction in our communication that is unique.[17]

In order to find answers about the history of human communication, we have to ask ourselves if such differences are bigger or smaller than what differentiates a Homo sapiens from a Neanderthal or a genetically enhanced human from a "normal" human.[18] How vast do differences have to be for a genetically divergent being to be considered not human? At the time when Homo sapiens coexisted with Neanderthals, this was not just a theoretical question; it was a very practical one. But humans were as unprepared to deal with the concept then as they still are today!

When (human) writers create stories about humans who share the world with speaking and tool-using apes, the plot evolves into all-out war.[19] Is that really unavoidable?

---

[15] Albeit many conventions on human rights forbid it.

[16] A living entity generated by the (natural?) fertilisation of a (natural?) female human, through the (natural?) semen of a (natural?) human male. This may be overly restrictive as a definition, as it leaves the question open, what limitations would apply to human-looking beings that do not fit the definition? Simply that they cannot marry? Or rather, would they be outcasts that anybody can kill, like an animal?

[17] According to the current findings of biology, it is impossible, so far, to identify any level of semantic abstraction in communication between animals.

[18] For a dystopic vision of a society after eugenics, see the wonderful movie *Gattaca*, http://www.imdb.com/title/tt0119177/; the same subject is presented more trivially by *X-Men: Days of Future Past*, http://www.imdb.com/title/tt1877832/?ref_=fn_al_tt_2. The existential and ethical question of what are the consequences, of genetic differences on the rights of genetically "superior" or "inferior" beings, has become part of popular culture. Common sense is relieved by the conviction that it is just a theoretical question.

[19] Again, popular culture has dealt with the issue of where to place the border separating humans from apes: The successful 1963 novel by French author Pierre Boulle, *La Planète des Singes*, started a long franchise of movies and shows, http://www.imdb.com/title/tt0063442/, http://www.imdb.com/title/tt0133152/, http://www.imdb.com/title/tt1318514/, http://www.imdb.com/title/tt2103281/.

So today, we feel comfortable defining humans empirically,[20] not just through their genetic code, but also through their society and its rules. We communicate the intricacies of society through language. Thus, our complex, symbolic language is meant to define what human is.

If society and its language radically change (as they have in the last 20 years), the idea of what is a human being will be deeply affected by such changes. The way we communicate keenly influences the way we are human. Law and society currently have no grey zones on this issue. It is black or white. Humanity applies to humans, inhumanity to non-humans.

Humans have legal rights and cannot be owned, killed or eaten. Non-humans may be killed or eaten (unless they are a protected animal species).

Can we manage with such rules for the next 100 years? I doubt it.[21]

If what defines humanity is human language, then a radical change in the way we communicate is going to affect what may be considered human.

Riley v. California was a landmark case[22] in which the court unanimously held that the warrantless search and seizure of digital contents of a cell phone during an arrest is unconstitutional.

---

[20] Is there any *a priori* definition of human in religion? Apparently yes, as the only human-looking beings on modern earth are born by a woman fertilized by a human sperm. But what about a being with the human genome entirely generated in a laboratory? What about humans completed/enhanced by digital/mechanical components? What about eugenically enhanced humans?
Religion is fiercely against all these possibilities, because it poses questions that the holy scriptures do not even consider as a possibility. But they have become possible or they will become so not too far in the future. And then what? Shall we simply have the right to eliminate such replicants/skins/jobs/things as was possible with human slaves not long ago? The story "Do Androids Dream of Electric Sheep?", written in 1967 by Philip K. Dick, portrays a dystopic 2019 future. In 1982, (the year of Dick's death), the story was transformed into the blockbuster movie *Blade Runner*, by Ridley Scott. Philip Dick spent most of his career as a writer in near poverty, but since his death, 11 popular films based on his works have been produced, including:
Blade Runner, https://www.imdb.com/title/tt0083658/
Total Recall, 1990, https://www.imdb.com/title/tt2322772/?ref_=nv_sr_srsg_8, and 2012, https://www.imdb.com/title/tt1386703/?ref_=nv_sr_srsg_3
A Scanner Darkly, https://www.imdb.com/title/tt0405296/?ref_=nv_sr_srsg_0
Minority Report, https://www.imdb.com/title/tt0181689/?ref_=fn_al_tt_1
Paycheck, https://www.imdb.com/title/tt0338337/?ref_=fn_al_tt_1
Next, 2007, https://www.imdb.com/title/tt0435705/
Screamers, https://www.imdb.com/title/tt0114367/?ref_=fn_al_tt_1
The Adjustment Bureau, https://www.imdb.com/title/tt1385826/?ref_=nv_sr_srsg_0
Impostor, 2001, https://www.imdb.com/title/tt0160399/?ref_=fn_al_tt_2
Most of Dick's films deal with the issue of what is human, what is "me" and what happens if there is another entity identical to myself.
Christian religion was against slavery and contributed to bringing down the slave economy in Europe in the 5th century AD: Can it only consider human that which has been generated from a human womb?
Today, the religious/moral discussion is stalled on whether gays or divorcees can be part of the Christian (Catholic) community. It does not seem likely that we will able to deal with androids, artificial intelligence and genetically enhanced humans (anytime soon)!
[21] GRAY R., *The body parts which can be regrown in a laboratory*.
[22] US Supreme Court, Riley v. California, 573 U.S. 373 (2014).

More than likely, a mobile phone contains more personal information than any other situation protected by the Fourth Amendment; therefore a warrant is always required. This decision implicitly recognizes that a piece of information technology is part of our persona, even if not implanted in our body. Everybody uses their mobile phone as an extension of their memory; a cell phone carries the information that 20 years ago we would have memorized with our brains.

Has our mutation into cyborgs already begun?

The assumption that technology is something "outside" ourselves and "other" than us is misleading.

a) It is part of us because it is part of our language, of our social life, and because it is increasingly the tool through which we perceive reality (and exchange such perceptions with others).

b) It is part of us because we have delegated to a device some mental tasks that were performed by our brains before the age of ubiquitous computing.

c) Finally, it is part of us because it is possible to interact with some digital devices without using language or our hands; we simply plug such devices into our bodies. Today this possibility is restricted to health devices and experimental trials, but the idea of integrating machines into our bodies is no longer just science fiction.

When trying to define and regulate information technology, it is misleading to believe that we are regulating "something other than us" or "something that is part of the outside reality". The truth is that we are a trying to define and regulate something that is already part of us, and will become more so in the future. The quest for freedom (and proper regulation) of information technology is the quest to preserve our personal freedom in a digitalized society.

1.2. Definition of Sign

The definition of "sign" I prefer is "a change of reality induced by one or more events".[23] It is a compelling definition that approaches a deeper understanding

---

[23] My definition is based on the explanation of "sign" given in SEBEOK T.A., *Signs*, 3, and in M. FERRARIS, *Documentalità*, loc. 3330. Non-verbal communication, in particular within an organism, as when cells communicate or we memorize something in our brains, is ultimately just a physical change of reality. It is a broader definition than is usually accepted, because it does not include the requirement of a reference to something else, as postulated by Ferdinand de Saussure and the philosopher Charles Sanders Peirce. This reference to something else is quite weak in nonverbal communication between cells: It is simply deontologically postulated in order to preserve a logical distinction between signs and objects. An object "should not" be a sign: A chair is not a sign pointing to the act of sitting. It is just a chair, i.e., an object. But a chair can also be used as a sign: to mark the status of king (in which case a chair becomes a throne). Ferraris accepts that the line of distinction between a human sign and a human object is blurred and subjective and it depends on time and context. (For some people the chair is a goal post, for others the same chair is just a chair, in particular when the game is over, in FERRARIS M., *Documentalità*, loc. 837 and 3330.) A human object is just an object only when there is no more (memory of a) human society. **What matters to me in the context of this work is that there are no signs without a change of the physical reality.** Therefore, all forms of communication are ultimately a physical change of reality.

of language and communication as tools for reshaping reality. Communication changes reality; it is not abstract, a metaphysical event. It unavoidably implies a physical change of the physical reality.

Ever since Aristotle theorized a dualistic reality (the physical and the metaphysical reality), we have tended to assume that communication is mostly about the metaphysical dimension. This may be true, to a certain extent, in reference to human communication. But more than 99.99% of signs are not of human origin and are thus nonverbal. Most of them are generated by animals, or natural phenomena.[24] Even humans often communicate in a nonverbal manner. Now let's expand the concept to include the data protocols continuously exchanged between our mobile phones and GSM networks. Think of servers and computers connected on a TCP/IP network permanently exchanging packets and pings, even when unused.

It is misleading to consider human communication something ontologically different from any other form of communication. It is true that we are able to imagine alternate realities (and are therefore able to tell and write stories), but the essence of our communication remains in exchanging information and changing reality. Even if we are the only beings able to take a chair and transform it (socially) into a throne, a chair is still a chair.

In studying how digitalisation changes human society, we have to keep in mind that communicating implies a change in our reality.

Most likely, we are unaware of the change because of how books were (and are) published: They are printed in some factory, and the change of reality happens only there, in a large, dark printing room. Successively the book is wrapped and packaged, and copies are sent to bookshops, where they are bought and eventually read (alone in some drawing room, bed, armchair or deck chair). Not only was the author lonely while writing the book, but readers are isolated while reading it. The book's audience doesn't dream of talking to the author, high up in his or her unassailable castle of self-importance.

Today, we read other people's thoughts in the middle of the street, even during a conversation (or a meeting). Reading has become social. Much like reading scrolls of philosophy in a gymnasium in ancient Greece, we may read our cell phones in a theatre. Actually, neither in a gymnasium, nor in a theatre, are you supposed to be distracted by writings: They are both temples of oral tradition! In a sign, there may be something absolute and timeless, but interpretation depends upon the context. Therefore, the change of context changes the meaning of the sign. The same sign in a different context is ultimately a different sign.[25]

Writing as a social act is not the same as writing as a solitary act. Reading as a social act is not the same as reading as a solitary act. Today, there are reasons for printing a book or newspaper and reasons for not doing so. It depends on what kind of impact or interaction the author wishes to achieve. Poetry

---

[24] According to Miller and Spoolman, "there are about 14 million different animal species (without considering unicellular organisms), and humans are just one of them. But even nonliving entities produce signs, like atmospheric phenomena." T. MILLER G.T., SPOOLMAN S., *Environmental Science*, 62.
[25] WITTGENSTEIN, L., *Philosophische Untersuchungen*, 1-30.

is appropriate for printing. Even the printed page may be part of the significance. In poetry there is one voice speaking and one or more listeners. Poetry (at least in its current, established version, as an individual act of creativity) is not made to be interrupted. The flow of words and sounds generated by the author is a unilateral act that commands silence and passive attention. Static printed characters are perfect for (traditional) poetry.

News, scientific works and all other publications that are available for discussion and public scrutiny, are best published and distributed digitally. Historically, all human knowledge began through dialectic discussion, not through writing.[26] Printing on paper ends the conversation. Publishing in digital (interactive) format opens the discussion.[27]

Today, writing has the ability to change our social reality in real time. We are no longer lonely when writing and reading. And in doing so, we have created a new layer of reality. Our social reality is a fast-changing flow of ideas, of which we appreciate not only the "content" but also the uncoordinated, nondescript delivery.

Exactly the same words have a different meaning and impact depending on the context in which they are exchanged: face to face, on the phone, by text messaging, by WhatsApp, Facebook, Pinterest, by email, via Twitter, on a blog, in a handwritten mail, in a printed mail, in a newspaper or in a book.

This is why, I believe, Thomas Sebeok's work is so important: He has convincingly demonstrated and disseminated the thesis that all branches of semiotics are united in one single branch, known as "biosemiotics", which even includes the language of computers.[28]

An essential feature of life is the ability to produce signs which are perceived and interpreted by other living entities. Now, humans have created the first non-living entities (computers) that use and understand a language. Within biosemiotics, there are the sections of phytosemiotics (the genesis and understanding of the signs of plants), zoosemiotics (the genesis and understanding of the signs of animals), and human semiotics (the genesis and understanding of human signs, of which cyber-semiotics is a subbranch).

There is no ontological difference between human and animal semiotics; there is only a difference in the way signs are generated and understood.

In discussing the changes that digitalisation has introduced to our world, we can assume that all signs belong to the same family, no matter how they were generated: by humans, animals, plants or … machines!

The meaning of the same sign will be quite different depending on how it was generated and transmitted (by human being, animal or machine). Nonetheless, it remains a sign.

When we observe digital content, we sometimes don't know if it was generated by a human, an animal or an automated process, because the information was crafted and transmitted by some digital device. Furthermore, based on the

---

[26] THOMAS R., *Literacy and Orality in Ancient Greece*, 101.

[27] ONG, W.J., *Orality and Literacy*, 77.

[28] SEBEOK, T.A., *Signs*, 92 and 134.

way digital content is currently created, it can be almost impossible to trace the origin of the digital sign back to its author. At best, all traces stop at the device that generated the digital signs, and even that device will eventually make it impossible for the information to be traced back.

In just a few decades, human language has changed from being traceable (the owner of a voice, the author of a sign on parchment, etc.) to impossible to trace. Just 30 years ago, 99.99% of humans would use verbal communication almost exclusively, whereas today a relevant percentage of the daily communications of 99.99% of humanity is digitally recorded and leaves some kind of permanent trace.[29]

Leaving a permanent trace is not the prerogative of the educated elite anymore. Thirty years ago, the only people who left a trace where the "literati", who wrote (or published) something to share their thoughts with others at a distance.[30] Today, the only way to communicate at a distance, without leaving any trace, is to take paper and pen, write something, put it in an envelope, stamp it, and post it in the mail.

Verba manent, scripta volant.

Not many people have considered the implications of so many momentous changes … until now.

1.3. Communication and Language

The findings of the most respected semiotic studies[31] show that there is no ontological difference between signs, whether human or animal. The difference is morphologic, not functional.

As we have seen, animal communication is essentially made of (a static set of) signs that have no grammatical structure. Language is any univocal human system of signs that can be apperceived by other humans and interpreted.[32]

---

[29] Raising the issue of the moral importance of deleting information: MAYER-SCHÖNBERGER, *Delete: The Virtue of Forgetting in the Digital Age.*
[30] Analog phone calls were very hard to trace and impossible to record, unless you had physical access to the copper wires that were used for communicating!
[31] SEBEOK T.A., *Global Semiotics*, 1 and 31.
[32] Or in Saussure's words, "*Language is a system of signs expressing ideas (Locke argued the same) and hence comparable to writing, deaf and dumb alphabet, symbolic rites, forms of politeness, military signals, and so on. It is a social institution, but in various respects distinct from political, juridical and other institutions*", (Saussure, 1967:15-16 quoted in SEBEOK T.A., *Signs*, 5 and 127).
Cells "read" and react to chemical and/or physical agents. Plants do likewise. More complex living beings, with nervous systems, can read many more types of signals. The essential function of the nervous system of an animal is to receive signals (signs) from inside and outside its body, interpret them and react accordingly. Nervous systems are found in most multicellular animals, but vary greatly in complexity. The only multicellular animals that have no nervous system are sponges, placozoa and mesozoa, which have very simple body plans. At the cellular level, the nervous system is defined by the presence of a special type of cell, called the neuron, also known as a "nerve cell". Neurons have special structures that allow them to send signals rapidly and precisely to other cells. They send these signals in the form of electrochemical waves traveling along thin fibers called axons, which cause chemical neurotransmitters to be released at junctions

Compared to animal communication, human language offers the following differences:

1) It is dynamic, so potentially infinite, whereas the communication between animals has a limited and finite number of concepts that can be communicated.

2) It is productive, meaning that it allows humans to produce a vast range of utterances from a finite set of elements, and to create new words and sentences.

3) It employs grammatical and semantic categories, such as nouns and verbs or present, past and future tenses, which may be used to express complex and hypothetical or abstract concepts.

4) It is recursive: For example, a noun phrase can contain another noun phrase (as in "[{the chimpanzee}'s lips]") or a clause can contain another clause (as in "[I see {the dog is running}]").

5) It may be conveyed with different modalities (oral, written, digital).[33]

For a long time, **common wisdom** perceived language as co-essential to human nature, in such a way that **the use of language is a feature that distinguishes mankind from all other animals**.

According to these definitions of sign and language, we can safely conclude that:

a) The meaning of the (non-linguistic) sign is often the product of the activity of the reader/receiver; the originator of the signs may be unanimated or void of any consciousness, like a fire or a cell. Many organized systems of signs (semiotic systems) have no predefined meaning and cannot be an expression of any intention because there is no conscious will in generating them.[34]

b) The meaning of a linguistic sign is (socially) predefined: Some degree of learning is necessary to correctly understand it; experience – without any initiation – may not suffice.

Still, it is hard to find a biological-ontological difference between language and other systems of signs. The difference cannot be explained by adaptation and evolution, and thus is just an occasional, contingent difference.[35] In fact, the theory of convergent evolution fundamentally states that nature finds similar solutions to similar problems; so if language has been the solution to a survival issue for mankind, it cannot be excluded that other animal species facing

---

known as synapses. A cell that receives a synaptic signal from a neuron may be excited, inhibited, or otherwise modulated. The connections between neurons form neural circuits that generate an organism's perception of the world and determine its behaviour. Along with neurons, the nervous system contains other specialized cells called glial cells (or, simply, glia), which provide structural and metabolic support. From a morphological perspective, we can say that (almost) all animal species have a specialized, built-in system for reading and interpreting reality. Such specialized systems were not present in early monocellular forms of life on earth; now all of the more evolved forms of life have interpretive filters. SEBEOK T.A., *Signs*, 36 ff.

[33] It goes too far to assume that it is modality-independent; see TRASK R. L., STOCKWELL P., *Language and Linguistics: The Key Concepts*, 165.

[34] See chapter 3.3 on the ontology of documents.

[35] The *Planet of Apes* movies and TV series exploit the difficulty of isolating an ultimate ontological difference between humans and apes and portrays a reality where evolution (phylogenesis) is the only reason for the biologic difference between the two species – a literary masterstroke by the two screenwriters, Michael Wilson, and Rod Serling.

similar challenges could adopt some language as an evolutionary solution.[36] Many species, such as birds, whales and even bees and ants have developed more structured systems of signs to transfer information. Scientists may soon discover that animals, too, communicate using their own languages.

The field of evolutionary linguistics resurfaced in 1988, after being dormant for more than 120 years. It made its comeback in the "Linguistic Bibliography" as a subfield of psycholinguistics. In 1990, Steven Pinker and Paul Bloom published a paper, "Natural Language & Natural Selection", which strongly argued for an adaptationist approach to language origins.[37] Their paper is often credited with reviving interest in evolutionary linguistics. Today, a new scientific multidisciplinary approach to signs and language has increased the interest of major academic publishers: The *Studies in the Evolution of Language* series has been appearing in the Oxford University Press since 2001.[38]

Steven Mithen has critically organized the latest findings on the evolution of human language in *The Singing Neanderthals*, a book of great importance for understanding the social and cultural changes that are inherent in a digital society.[39]

The birth of language was the most important change in human evolution since the origin of mankind. Now that humans communicate with machines using the sheer power of thought,[40] it is imperative to understand what impact language has on the way we live and communicate. If we understand, we can conceive the changes that will affect our world in the coming decades. Will language be an impediment to the development of higher neural skills, for wordless communication between man and machine? In the future, what will hold higher value – linguistic or non-linguistic human communication?

In the digital environment, where it is nearly impossible to tell the difference between man and machine, computers are exploiting the opportunity using phishing attacks and emails carrying worms. Today we live in an environment where signs seem human, yet they may be merely recordings or machine-generated content, based on a set of algorithms.

In chapter 3 we will see why the interpretation of intentionally generated documents is quite different from the interpretation of other signs.

So in order to understand correctly any digital information conveyed to us, we must know its origin: human, fully automated or hybrid. We know how painful it can be when we wrongly interpret incoming messages! This is just the beginning: It may become worse before it becomes better.

---

[36] McGHEE G. R., *Convergent Evolution: Limited Forms Most Beautiful*, 322.

[37] PINKER S., BLOOM P., *Natural Language and Natural Selection"*, 13(4).

[38] See *Oxford Studies in the Evolution of Language*.

[39] MITHEN S., *The Singing Neanderthals: The Origins of Music, Language, Mind, and Body*.

[40] See at http://www.nature.com/news/toy-helicopter-guided-by-power-of-thought-1.13139. http://www.dailymail.co.uk/sciencetech/article-2335671/Helicopter-flown-using-power-thought.html. http://www.huffingtonpost.com/2013/06/06/mind-controlled-helicopter-incredible-flight_n_3396863.html.

Proper semiotic understanding of a message requires the proper understanding and use of six factors:[41]
a) message and code;
b) source and destination;
c) channel and context.

These elements are all mixed together in a digital communication; only in-depth analysis of the digital file(s) eventually allows to put each factor in its place.

Facebook looks like HTML text, but in actuality, what's displayed on your screen is more like a movie of a text. Few know the difference, and the consequence is that message and code, channel and context are irreversibly blended! But each of us sees a different landing page on most content aggregator portals, depending on his/her profile based on cookies and other hidden code.

Printed newspapers are (were) chosen by readers for their format and their editorial policies. Online newspapers (will) attract readers by showing them what they want to read. Nothing prevents an online newspaper from showing different news to different viewers, or even sharing different accounts of the same event, depending on the age, sex or political inclination of the reader.

The social function of newspapers has changed and will continue to change. Newspapers are losing their social function as aggregators of same-minded readers because of the technical properties of digital information. This aggregative function has been taken up by (some) bloggers and hits the public faster than print. A digital message identical to a verbal or a written message, with the same destination, still has a different code, source, channel and context, and therefore a different meaning.

1.4. The Singing Neanderthal

Steven Mithen, shortly after publishing *After the Ice* (2004), felt compelled to next publish *The Singing Neanderthals* (2006). His reason is striking:

"*I became acutely aware of my own neglect of music when writing my most recent book,* After the Ice. *That work included reconstruction scenarios for many of the prehistoric hunter-gatherers and early farming communities that existed between 20,000 and 5,000 BCE. Few of these felt realistic to me until I imagined music: people singing to themselves as they undertook some mundane task, communal singing and dancing at times of celebration and mourning, mothers humming to their babies, children playing musical games. The communities examined in* After the Ice *were all relatively recent, but the same is true of early Homo sapiens, the Neanderthals and even older ancestral species such as Homo heidelbergensis and Homo ergaster. Without music, the prehistoric past is just too quiet to be believed.*"[42]

In this work, I have chosen this theory of the evolution of language: from humming, singing and dancing, to words and verbal communication. Why?

Again, I don't try to solve longstanding disputes that will probably never be resolved, as verbal communication (before the digital age) left no traces.

---

[41] SEBEOK T.A., *Signs*, 3, 5 and 8.
[42] MITHEN S., *The Singing Neanderthals: The Origin of Music, Language and Body*, 4.

These are the reasons why I have chosen Steven Mithen as my favourite author for explaining the origins of verbal communication:

1) I was able to understand his theories. Other theories (such as Noam Chomsky's theory that all humans share the same underlying linguistic structure, irrespective of socio-cultural difference) are too difficult for me. They may be right, but I "don't get" them.

2) It is consistent with what we see happen with human babies: First they acquire the capability to understand rhythm, music and numbers, then they start to speak – as long as they do not grow among animals and have no contact with human society, like "feral children" who never learn to walk or speak.

3) It dramatically underpins the temporal coincidence of the evolution of verbal communication among *Homines sapientes* and the progressive extinction of the *Homines neanderthalensis*. Nobody theorizes that language was one of the causes of the extinction of the humming Neanderthals, but it is also true that few disputes that the two phenomena happened at the same time.

As long as scarcity was not an issue, human society was able to organize itself around songs, dances and choreographed rituals. But when scarcity was ferociously decimating humans, it became necessary to tell what is "mine" from what is "yours"; clearly a few utterances (words) were more effective than a dance.

A piece of land was no longer just land; it became my (or others') property. Invisible, yet absolutely real borders separated one parcel of land from another. And someone who worked my land was either a family member or a slave: Paid work is a quite recent legal invention that can be dated back no more than three millennia. Before then (for about 10,000 years), property was the only legal relation between a worker and his/her master. These early humans had yet to grapple with complex abstract thought, such as, "I pay you to rent to me your work capability for cultivating my land".

To pay requires money: 10,000 years ago, barter was the custom; there was no money.

The idea of a contract was devised more than 5,000 years later by the Sumerians, one of the world's earliest urban societies.[43]

Ten thousand years ago, human beings understood only the basics of "master/chief" and "property". Most likely they were used in their only possible combination, for structuring work on behalf of others. And so the worker became (a living) part of the property.

The law cannot go further than language permits.

1.5. Language: Why? The Human Consequences of Language

The question of why we speak is still unanswered, and I don't pretend to be able to solve such an old and arcane dispute. However, I believe that it is useful to indulge in the suspicion that **language** is not about improving communication, but **is an adaptive tool for conflict resolution**. So maybe we started

---

[43] For further explanation of the first type of contracts, see chapter 3.2.

to speak, not for mutual better understanding, but to be able to hunt, fight and solve disputes within our tribes without bloodletting.

The "mmmmh"[44] singing and dancing of Neanderthals was probably more deeply rooted and even better suited for showing feelings and emotions than music is today:[45] more emotional, more encompassing, more universal, more inclusive … and less apt for deception.

Verbal language has the ability to create abstract concepts enabling us to define and measure reality with rich nuances, beyond what human senses can perceive. For example, when someone says, "I am hotter than usual", we can instinctually verify the experience without using tools beyond sense and experience. But if we say, "I have a fever of 37.8 degrees centigrade", then a tool has been added to our reality, and we can no longer perceive the experience directly through our senses that the words are describing. The same concept applies to time, distance, weight and other measures that have been used by humans in order to define (some aspects of) reality for the last six millennia.[46] In the long run, the human ability to create tools and use them has literally created (not simply discovered) a (physical) world, beyond what we can sense. (Check your iPhone to confirm.)

Concepts like "fever" are a mixture of assumptions (What is the average temperature of a human? What is too high a temperature for a human? etc.) and measurements (body temperature) made with tools that register reality beyond our senses. The statement, "John has fever", truly represents reality only if the underlying assumptions are true: (a) The thermometer works properly, and (b) we properly perceive the thermometer.

In summary, our ability to create tools, combined with our language, has produced an inextricable mesh of objects, signs and words that is part of what we perceive as "real", completely oblivious to the fact that such a "reality" is instinctual. Think about time. Everyone would agree that one day is made of 24 hours (84,600 seconds) and a year of 365 days; but still, this is only approximately right (there are some days that include a "leap second",[47] and some

---

[44] For humming and singing as the pre-verbal communication of humans, see the previous chapter.

[45] Sir Nicholas Kenyon, in a recent interview with Peter Aspden, said about Simon Rattle, "It is as if his music-making goes beyond music, to elemental communicating with people", ASPDEN P., "Simon Rattle, Lightning Conductor".

[46] The origin of mathematics is broadly described by BOYER C., MEXBACH U. C., *A History of Mathematics*, 5.

I am aware that the late Wittgenstein was extremely critical of the idea that mathematics can usefully describe reality, rather than being a grammar of/for numbers and totally abstract, as he discussed in his lectures at Cambridge between 1939 and 1941, which a young Alan Turing attended: DIAMOND C., *Wittgenstein's Lectures on the Foundations of Mathematics*, loc. 2250. In fact he describes mathematics as a way to build roads in nature, not as a way to measure and proof nature.

[47] A "leap second" is a one second adjustment that is occasionally applied to Coordinated Universal Time (UTC) in order to keep its time of day close to the mean solar time. Without such a correction, time reckoned by the Earth's rotation drifts away from atomic time because of irregularities in the Earth's rate of rotation. Leap seconds are calculated and published by the International Earth Rotation Service (IERS), established in 1987 by the International Astronomical Union and the International Union of Geodesy and Geophysics, https://datacenter.iers.org/bulletins.php. It

years are bissextile). Nonetheless, we believe that the "leap second" (or the bissextile "leap" year) is the exception that confirms the rule. However, sometimes exceptions have been a sign that the rule was still approximate, or even wrong. For example, "Almagest" by Ptolemy was the universally accepted truth about the movement of the planets until the 1543 publication of *De revolutionibus orbium coelestium*, by Nicolaus Copernicus. The Ptolemaic theory needed some "exceptions" to justify its reconstruction of the movement of planets.

The ability of mankind to craft tools and to create words for them has created an "enhanced natural reality" not all that different from the current notion of "augmented reality" as defined in Wikipedia: "*Augmented reality is conventionally in real-time and in semantic context with environmental elements, such as sports scores on TV during a match. With the help of advanced AR technology (e.g., adding computer vision and object recognition) the information about the surrounding real world of the user becomes interactive and digitally manipulable. Artificial information about the environment and its objects can be overlaid on the real world*".[48]

Augmented reality (among other things) puts dynamic labels on natural reality, augmenting it.

This is precisely what words did to human social reality once humans started to speak: A landscape was not just a landscape anymore; it had become "my property" and "your property", "my tree" and "everybody's tree", and so on. When humans started to use words, natural reality was no longer enough. It had become enhanced through social concepts and rules that were connected to objects, people and everything that was part of human social life. Some Greek philosophers wondered if words were not part of some kind of parallel reality.[49] A thousand years later, words, for philosophers, still seem to hum

---

began operation on 1 January 1988. A leap second happened on 30 June 2012 at 23:59:60 UTC, on 30 June 2015, and more recently on 30 June 2016 (Wikipedia, 2020).

Consider how important "time" is as a social object: In order to make such a convention "scientifically true" and verified, an international organisation has been formed to monitor the movement of the earth through space so that we don't miss even one second out of 253,800 (i.e., three years).

[48] Wikipedia, *Augmented Reality*. But again, we can find this notion already in Wittgestein's lectures on the foundations of mathematics: DIAMOND C., *Wittgenstein's Lectures on the Foundations of Mathematics*, locc. 1032, 2250, 2267, 4118.

[49] In ancient philosophy there were two different schools of thought about the relationship between language and reality.

According to the **naturalistic approach**, language is the phonic representation of the essence of things. The **conventionalist approach** believes language is a human agreement; men arbitrarily assign certain sounds to real objects in order to communicate.

In an archaic belief, that there is no difference between the word and the thing it designates, reality and language merge: "*Nomen est omen*". Everything has an innate sound, a name that belongs to it, and that is the only one it can have. There is a necessary relationship between the sign and the object to which it refers. Moreover, words have the magic power to create and make things real. This explains why, for example, in the book of Genesis, God creates things simply by naming them. Or why certain primitive populations believed that knowing the name of something conferred domain to it. Naming is a unique ability that God gave to mankind in order to dominate the rest of creation and to build and identify concepts. In ancient Greece, we still find traces of this magic conviction: It is possible to gain power over a person by knowing their name, or it is necessary to know the real name of a divinity to invoke its power.

with the reverberation of some other world.[50]
It is interesting to note that today, people tend to consider cyberspace and the digital dimension as some kind of parallel reality. So after metaphysical reality, we now have augmented reality and even virtual reality.
What the early philosophers did with words and concepts, we do today with digital reality; we consider it to be "another reality". However, it is part of our

---

The naturalistic theory of language was questioned by Parmenides, who postulated that the experience of reality is deceptive and, as a consequence, so are its descriptions through words, which label illusory things. In Heraclitus' theory, the experience of reality isn't illusory, so its linguistic description may possibly be truthful. Words have knowledge value, but the fact that language changes, while the reality it describes remains the same, suggests that language and reality are two different things.

Plato criticized both theories, the naturalistic and the conventionalist, in the *Cratylus*, the first dissertation on language that deals with words' exactitude and their ability to reflect reality. For Plato, the name is perceived neither as a mere arbitrary label, nor as the phonic expression of the essence of real objects. Language is a subjective representation of reality. Its structure is different from the structure of reality; for this reason language is a necessary but not adequate tool to understand it. Aristotle partially agrees with Plato's thesis: Between language and reality there is an arbitrary relationship mediated by soul impressions, that is, the images of the objects produced in the subject's mind. The concept is the element of mediation between signs and reality.

We all know that during the Middle Ages there was selective preservation and copying of pre-Christian literature. As far as we know, pre-Christian philosophy ended with a strong preference for a dualistic vision of knowledge, where reality is (may be) beyond what words can represent.

[50] In Christian philosophy, mind-body dualism is preferred as an explanation of reality because it also reflects the dualism between God and humans. Three of the most relevant thinkers on this subject have been Saint Augustine, Spinoza and Kant.

Saint Augustine believed that dualism places a distinction between memory and God, which is reality. He focuses on how man can know God (reality), thanks to memory, which is the repository of all peoples' experiences and knowledge. He also reckons that the mind contains only images and representations of reality, but not things in themselves. Therefore, throughout the *Confessions*, Saint Augustine relies on memory, and he wonders whether God can be sought if he is not already known. The answer is that we can find God by reflecting on our own memory. According to the saint, the faculty of memory has a broader meaning; it is more than the ability to remember or the act of remembering. It encompasses all cognitive capacities. In short, memory is mind.

On the contrary, **Spinoza**, rejecting Cartesian mind-body dualism, stated that reality is a single substance with many attributes. In this way, he essentially denies that human beings have free will, explaining that this illusion is a result of our limited understanding of our own actions. His theory is known as "double-aspect theory", because it is based on the notion that the mental and the physical are simply different aspects of one and the same substance. For Spinoza, that single substance is God, which is the universal essence of everything that exists.

Finally, **Kantian dualism** of mind and reality consists in the idea that what we perceive is not merely objective; it is at least partly subjective. We assume that the perceptual function that the mind plays is passive, like a mirror, and doesn't alter the image of reality, but rather reflects it back to us. But according to Kant, this is not true. Our perception of reality might start with sensations of something outside ourselves, but by the time we perceive it, our mind has organized, categorized and arranged those raw sensations into our perception of reality. Therefore, what we perceive as reality is partially created by our minds. Furthermore, Kant distinguishes between phenomenon and noumenon. The former indicates our perception of reality, while the latter refers to "things in themselves", which are the objects of the external world as they actually exist. As a consequence, it is clear that man, according to Kant, can only know phenomena, while the external world is completely unknown to him, see Carreira J., *Kant and the Creation of Reality*; Rohlf M., *Immanuel Kant*; and Immanuel Kant, *Prolegomena to any Future Metaphysics That Will Be Able to Present as a Science*.

social reality, and we cannot separate our social reality from words, because without words and concepts, our social lives would be become something totally different. Without language, we would still be hunter-gatherers, or we would have gone extinct.

According to John Searle, the linguistic representation of reality is just another level of physical reality, manifesting itself (only) at neurological level; it is like the software that runs on the hardware.[51]

This explanation does not solve the issue of the ability of signs/words to correctly represent reality. We know our neurologic system can process input by the brain and the senses, but we cannot prove that the input into our neurologic system is true.

We all know that water can be so cold as to appear steaming hot, or that we may have hypothermia, so that cold water seems warm. Hot and cold are relative, but our body can only sense hot and cold; it cannot measure it. We are unable to measure reality only with our senses, and for this purpose, we invented and use tools. But language is not only used for "augmenting" nature, it has also been used for "augmenting" the usefulness of manmade tools. Humans have thus invented entire conventional systems, like numbers, geometry, algebra and the table of elements, for improving the usefulness of facts perceived and measured with tools. Any kind of "definition" – such as numbers, mathematics, physics and chemistry – is part of a system of a formalized knowledge, where the representation of reality is true, only so far as the axioms on which the system is based are also true. Such tools have created new concepts and thus new realities – many of which were previously hidden from our senses.

It is evident that 20,000 years ago, words had the same effect of creating an abstract/virtual/metaphysical reality that went well beyond the perception of natural reality/phenomena. Without language, any thermometer or other measuring tool would be useless and meaningless. A chair would never be a throne. Language makes it possible to build objects and to provide them with a unique, socially accepted meaning.

Language creates the reality of fever occurring at 40° centigrade (104° Fahrenheit); it does not find it in nature. The augmented reality of language allows us to know the names of mountain peaks, even when we see them for the first time. In their essence, words and digitalisation have accomplished similar things during two very different times in human history: They have added new meaning/information to (natural) reality, deeply transforming human society. This information brings us to two important sub-products of language:
- humans' existential need for storytelling[52]
- social reality.[53]

---

[51] Searle J. R., *Freedom and Neurobiology*, loc. 228, and Searle J. R., *Making the Social World*, 69.

[52] Gottschall J., *The Storytelling Animal*, loc. 1060, has popularised the conclusions drawn by Paul Ricoeur in his fundamental *Temps et Récit*, vol. 1 (1983), vol. 2 (1984) and vol. 3 (1985), Editions du Seuil (France), translated ed., University of Chicago Press.

[53] In my point of view, the best definition of social reality is provided in Searle J.R., *The construction of social reality*, 31.

1.5.1. Storytelling

Storytelling is one of our primary forms of communication with other people. It is a behaviour that involves the transmission of narratives among humans. Storytelling is one of the few human traits that remains universal across cultures and throughout history. Anthropologists find evidence of folktales everywhere in ancient cultures, written in Sanskrit, Latin, Greek, Chinese, Egyptian and Sumerian. Various bodies of evidence suggest that storytelling emerged tens of thousands of years ago at a point in time when humans still lived as hunter-gatherers. People in societies of all types share narratives, from oral storytellers in early tribes to the millions of writers churning out books, television shows and movies today.

Psychologists and neuroscientists have recently become fascinated by the human predilection for storytelling.[54] Their research indicates that storytelling is the goal of humankind. It concerns the exchange of representations of human experience and information sharing among people belonging to the same social context.

Storytelling requires cooperation, expanding an individual's knowledge base exponentially by giving them access to the experiences of other individuals. For this reason, narration is the most important cognitive process we use to explain the reality in which we live.

Storytelling allows humans to identify and conform themselves to certain models and specific standards. It sets the socio-cultural base of a group, and that is the reason why we can't define the concept of "culture" without including the art of "telling a story". Harvard University evolutionary psychologist Steven Pinker explained that living in a community requires keeping tabs on who the group members are and what they are doing, and storytelling seems to be the best way to spread such information.[55] Indeed, to this day, people spend most of their conversations telling personal stories and gossiping. A 1997 study by the anthropologist and evolutionary biologist Robin Dunbar found that social topics (i.e., gossip, among others) accounted for 65 percent of speaking time among people in public places, regardless of age or gender.[56]

The "theory of mind" or "mindreading" is something humans have developed in their evolutionary process in order to interrelate with others.[57] It consists of a suite of capabilities that enables us to (1) understand that other human beings have mental states (e.g., beliefs, feelings, desires), (2) interpret others' mental states, and (3) make predictions about others' behaviour based on their mental states. In other words, mindreading enables us to think about how others might respond to our actions.

---

[54] Salmon C., *Storytelling: La machine à fabriquer des histoires et à formater les esprits*, 10; Ricoeur P., *Time and Narrative*, Vol. 2, 153; Gottschall J., *The storytelling animal: How stories make us human*, loc. 23.

[55] For the anthropologic and evolutionary role of arts and entertainment, see Pinker S., *How the Mind Works*, 521 ff.

[56] Dunbar R. I., *Gossip in Evolutionary Perspective*, 8(2).

[57] The theory of mind can be traced back to Descartes in cognitive philosophy. But only recently, it has been grounded systematically by Dennet D., *Content and Consciousness*.

This theory has to be considered an integral part of storytelling: The raconteur must be able to attribute the mental ability of comprehension to the audience. In this way, sharing stories potentially offers the storyteller ways to improve the ability of manipulation.[58]

Jonathan Gottschall thinks that storytelling is increasingly seen as an essential survival skill.[59] He notices that people spend more of their lives in the storylands of television, novels, dreams, daydreams, social networking and YouTube-gazing, etc., than they do in the real world.[60] Therefore, according to Gottschall, a new kind of human is emerging: the "*Homo fictus*" or fiction man. Such a man is emerging to complement the traditional human model, Homo sapiens. This new type of being acknowledges that humans are creatures of emotion as much as logic, and that facts and arguments move us most when they are embedded in good stories.[61] Gottschalk's "experiment" to show our natural inclination to create stories, is striking in its effect: https://www.youtube.com/watch?v=s4kXLK1dWc0.

---

[58] HARARI Y. N., *Sapiens, a Brief History of Mankind*, 23-25, 58, and literature cited at p. 541.

[59] GOTTSCHALL J., WILSON D. S., WILSON E. O., CREWS F. E., *The Literary Animal*, 93. The subject of storytelling is quite fashionable among philosophers and anthropologists. Among others, there are the following noteworthy publications: TURNER M., *The Literary Mind*; BOYD B., *On the Origin of Stories*; and ZUNSHINE L., *Why We Read Fiction*.

[60] GOTTSCHALL J., *The Storytelling Animal*, loc. 54.

[61] Most anthropologists agree that storytelling persisted in human culture not only because it promotes social cohesion among groups, but also because it serves also as a valuable method to pass on knowledge to future generations.

Besides this, according to SCALISE SUGIYAMA M., *On the Origins of Narrative*, 7(4), storytelling offers a means of criticizing antisocial behaviour: A character's behaviour can be openly condemned by other characters in the story and, implicitly or explicitly, by the narrator as well. This sends a message to the audience that persons engaging in such behaviour will incur the wrath of the group. Variations on this tactic include the use of monster stories to frighten children into obedience: In these stories group disapproval is replaced by a terrifying monster that carries off children who misbehave. Although group living has its advantages, it also presents a formidable challenge: The interests of group members often come into conflict. For example, a parent's goal (e.g., marry daughter to headman) might conflict with a child's goal (e.g., marry the man of her choice).

Thus, there are times when an individual can benefit from persuading others to modify their goals and behaviour such that they serve his/her interests. For example, advertisers have long taken advantage of narrative persuasiveness by sprinkling likable characters or funny stories into their commercials. A 2007 study by marketing researcher Jennifer Edson Escalas of Vanderbilt University found that a test audience responded more positively to advertisements in narrative form, as compared with straightforward ads, which encouraged viewers to think about the arguments for a product, see ESCALAS J., *Self-Referencing and Persuasion*, in *Journal of Consumer Research*, 33(4).

Narration can't be excluded from our daily life stories. Listening to stories amplifies an individual's ability to generate plans: The more experiences an individual has to draw upon, the greater the range of possible future scenarios he/she can assemble. Listening to stories also serves to increase an individual's range of responses to events/actions and consequences/reactions, which may provide emotional input useful for the calibration of relevant decision-making mechanisms. That is why storytelling is often used, for example, in schools, as an educational tool, and even in the business world. As far as the former is concerned, storytelling is an educational resource that has the unique capability of letting the students interact as listeners or as storytellers themselves. In both cases, storytelling promotes student skills in listening, reading and comprehension. Students participate

As we have seen in chapter 1.3, according to Sebeok's findings, there is no clear-cut distinction between human and animal communication, because they share several traits, particularly when human communication doesn't rely exclusively on the written or spoken word.

Yet when it comes to storytelling, we cannot doubt that humans have no equivalent in the animal world.[62]

As Gottschall pointed out, storytelling requires the desire to believe in a fictional account of reality, even knowing that it is pure fiction, like a fairy tale or a novel. When we are children, we project ourselves into the fictional lives of soldiers, explorers, nurses, doctors, fathers and mothers – training ourselves to fill social roles through play and fantasies.

This dimension is exclusively human, as it is our ability or need to choose a character that is "us" and present it consciously (or subconsciously) to others. The fundamental change in the way that stories are created today is that they may be collectively produced and shaped by social media, using clusters of (automatically, unintentionally) registered images, sounds and texts.

At the origins of oral tradition, tales about reality were the (conscious and intentional) accounts of many individual storytellers. Today, social media makes it possible for a collective, documented account of events to spring up unconsciously through the chronological juxtaposition of digital registrations made by anonymous, untraceable people, sometimes having a direct impact on the progress of events. This is precisely what happened during the "Arab Spring", where the unfolding of facts and the collective recording and broadcasting of them went hand in hand.[63]

---

in the oral presentations of the stories themselves. Stories essentially are dramatic activities that encompass the nonverbal communication of body language, gestures and facial expressions. Therefore, the students absorb these elements mostly without their being an item of specific focus. As far as the business field is concerned, it seems that stories are the best way for CEOs "to motivate people to reach certain goals" says Robert McKeen (a screenwriting lecturer), interviewed by BRONWYN F., *Storytelling That Moves People*, in *Harvard Business Review*. McKeen thinks that the best way to persuade and to motivate a person is by telling a compelling story. In a story you not only weave a lot of information but you also arouse your listener's emotion and energy. It begins with a situation in which life is relatively in balance. But then there is an event that throws life out of sorts. The story goes on to describe how, in an effort to restore balance, the protagonist's subjective expectations crash into an uncooperative objective reality. This is the way, according to McKeen, businesspeople should imagine and project a company's future, trying to anticipate possible future events. He adds that a good storyteller has to be a realist, because in his opinion, civilized humans are sceptics, and scepticism is another principle of the storyteller. The sceptic always seeks to discern what's really going on. Furthermore, by telling the truth, you are more likely to get people behind you. To conclude, McKeen asserts that storytelling takes intelligence and demands life experience, because self-knowledge is the root of all great storytelling. He is also convinced that sometimes great storytellers are great leaders too: They are sceptics who understand their own masks as well as the masks of life, and this understanding makes them humble. They see the humanity in others and deal it with them in a compassionate, yet realistic way.

[62] HARARI Y. N., *Sapiens, a Brief History of Mankind*, 21.

[63] This was also the case of a viral video (https://www.youtube.com/watch?v=Y4MnpzG5Sqc) about a warlord named "Kony"; opinions are still bitterly divided on its truthfulness (see

Newspapers and publishers were once able to influence our perception of events (think of the journalism and propaganda during the two world wars, the Korean and Vietnam wars). Now we face a multitude of (sometimes) anonymous footage whose origin and authenticity (and ultimately, responsibility) are not verifiable, but are still (to us) more "real", more "believable", than what we read (often much later) in the "official" news.

Behind this innovation of news in the form of stories lies one of the trickiest and most interesting recent changes in human society: the difference between information collected and spread through (unintentional and unverifiable) posting of events, as compared to information intentionally presented by documents with a given (traceable and verifiable) author. The concept needs to be properly understood, in order to preserve our pluralistic democracies and the rule of law (see Chapter 8.2 and its subsections).

1.5.2. Social Reality

Social reality is a sort of by-product of storytelling.

Nobody knows (or fully understands) the vast system of rules and acts that, when combined, create a society. Most people also don't really know the exact meaning of words like money, marriage, property, contract and constitution. Still they try to abide by them. Why, if they don't really know the meaning?

Let's exclude for a moment that we do it for the same reasons for which bees and ants follow the rules of their hives. Let's exclude that in the end we all behave like a pack of wolves, respecting a kind of pecking order.

It is obvious that we choose to follow the rules of our society, even if it is not easy to prove it scientifically, to or explain why.

The most comprehensive explanation for this peculiar human behaviour is language and, in particular, storytelling. This was noted by John Searle in his epistemological research on the theory of knowledge and the making of social reality.[64] In several of his books, particularly *Making the Social World: The Structure of Human Civilisation*,[65] Searle concludes that social reality is made up of concepts that are intangible, but humans accept them as tangible.[66]

What is property? How can I tell if it's property, or if someone is the real proprietor of something?

We know that property laws vary, and marriage rights are not respected or enforced everywhere. The process to establish them is long and fragile. Each setback can annihilate the process, which consequently has to be restarted from scratch.

In order to enforce property rights, at the origin of mankind it was necessary to defend them by brute force (Cain and Abel; Romulus and Remus; etc.).

___

Wikipedia, Kony 2012). Still 100 million people around the world in 2012 believed that there was something happening in reality that needed a prompt response!

[64] SEARLE J. R., *The Construction of Social Reality*, 90; and SEARLE J. R., *Mind, Language and Society: Philosophy in the Real World*, 75.

[65] SEARLE J. R., *Making the Social World*, 123.

[66] SEARLE J. R., *Making the Social World*, 90.

Subsequently, the violation of property became a religious taboo, and infringement on those rights had dire consequences (death or exile). Evolution sped up, and now property has become a good to be swapped, exchanged, traded, dematerialized, securitized and flash-traded.

A social object describes any name that is understood in context by almost all people, even by those who disagree with it or would like to abolish it. Most social objects that become embedded in our synapses have a long history. There must be a lot of storytelling, or active usage, before something becomes a real social object. Usage is faster: Google was quick to become a social object.[67] To describe the genesis and evolution of social objects, it would be necessary to write one or more books on the subject; so we again refer to the findings of Searle. According to him, because we name and understand social reality through words, in the end it is impossible to see the difference between physical reality and metaphysical reality.

A telling example of this difficulty can be seen in a dialogue between an Italian soldier in Afghanistan and an elder tribesman. The Italian (despite having majored in law) fails to be able to explain the notion of "state". This dialogue was reported by the military man himself. Let's call him Italo and the tribesman Sayed.

Sayed: "Why are you here?"

Italo: "We want to help you to build a free state."

Sayed: "What is a state?"

Italo: "It's an organisation of people that guarantees and enacts just rules for everybody."

Sayed: "So does our tribe."

Italo: "But a tribe is a different thing from a state."

Sayed: "Tell me why and how."

Italo: "Well, the state has a set of given, objective rules produced by lawmakers, an administration that enforces them, and a judiciary that resolves the legal disputes."

Sayed: "Our tribe has the council of the eldest that legislates, people in charge of enacting the law and others who are judges."

Italo: "But a state is much more complex and vaster than your tribe; it also has schools and hospitals and social security..."

Sayed: "We do have in our tribe doctors and teachers, and we help the poor and the weak."

This dialogue went on and on for days and weeks. Poor Italo didn't succeed in explaining the difference between state and tribe, for one simple reason. For Sayed, our concept of "state" was already covered by his concept of "tribe". So Italo should have explained to Sayed how to forget his concept of "tribe" and why to substitute it with our concept of "state". The only obvious difference that

---

[67] SEARLE J. R., *The Construction of Social Reality*, 90; and Searle J. R., *Mind, Language and Society: Philosophy in the Real World*, 75. See SEBEOK T.A., *Signs*, 146, the creation of social objects without the use of language and institutions: For example, the wall that surrounds a village marks the boundaries of the village, even when it has decayed.

Sayed could have easily accepted is that in our (large) states, we are (generally) anonymous. There is not the same level of direct personal control and knowledge that you find in a small community, like a tribe. Probably Sayed would not have acknowledged any advantage to a bigger system. And he would be right in thinking so. In Europe there are several tiny states, like Lichtenstein, San Marino and the Vatican, that are barely larger than a tribe in size or population! The substitution of the tribe by the state is usually the outcome of a long social and military process, evolving over centuries (if not millennia). The military effort of NATO and its allies in Afghanistan will not succeed in teaching Afghans to shift their loyalty to the state (and away from the tribe).

To substitute the concept of his tribe with our state in Sayed's mind (or vice versa) is not something that can be achieved by talking, or not even by winning a war. You have to rewrite history.

This is precisely what the study of history is about: It is a (pseudo)scientific account of events that in the end explains and morally justifies the current social order. It makes us certain that a state is better than a tribe (even if we cannot explain why).

We feel as uncomfortable about the Chinese or Russian way of teaching history as they do with ours, because history is (almost) always written with the assumption that "where we are, we must be, even if a better world is conceivable". Grimm's or Andersen's storytelling had exactly the same assumption and used fantasy narratives to make the point that current moral and social values must be defended.

The Chinese and Russian states and societies rightly assume they have a legitimate legacy, and therefore prefer an account of events that justifies their legitimation. We do the same in Europe, Japan, the USA, etc.

Let's imagine for a moment that in 2014, Europe had become a terrible, digital, Orwellian, dystopic society. Big Brother is always watching, prying into the private lives of everybody, ensuring that they abide by the law, work and pay all their taxes, as in Suzanne Collins' *The Hunger Games*.[68] Today's predicaments would be a clear sign for tomorrow's historians that a better social order had to take shape. In the future, when democracy and liberty are restored, after a revolution of the Districts against the Capitol, historians will again provide a different storytelling of the events, this time from the perspective of the future society. History is the reason why Sayed was unable to understand Italo and vice versa. Italy could not be ruled by tribes today, much as today's Afghanistan struggles to be ruled by a central state. In their attempts to understand of each other, their frame of reference for social order was the end-station of history.

Another interesting example of the making of social objects can be found in euro banknotes. It is impossible to know if a banknote is printed by Greece or Germany, but on the contrary, it is possible to tell the origin of euro coins. Why the different treatment of banknotes and coins?

The answers are found in the eurozone crisis: Few in 2009-2011 and in 2014-2015 would have accepted banknotes from Greece, Portugal, Ireland, Spain or

---

[68] See the film's description at Wikipedia, *The Hunger Games*.

Italy. The fact that it was impossible to determine their origin saved the euro. While nobody is really afraid to lose the value of a few coins, banknotes are a totally different matter.[69]

If people had started to look at the backs of euro banknotes to verify their origin, nobody would have been able the save the euro, not even "Super Mario".[70] So, in the case of the euro, it was manifest that its engineers considered the possibility of trouble, and for security's sake they anonymized the banknotes. They deleted the link between a nation and its money on the banknotes, even if it was impossible to decouple the currency from its surrounding economic and legal systems. What we are experiencing in Europe today is the consequence of that "technocratic" choice. Even if we don't trust the Greek or Italian state, we are forced to use their currency, because it is identical to the German or Dutch. Without the imaginative decision to hide the origin of the notes, the euro would have fallen apart.[71] We have to ask ourselves, in an Information and Communication Technology (ICT) society, "Could it have worked better?" Probably, because there is no such thing as "too much information"! Even so, there is no silver bullet to decide how much information is truly needed.

On the other hand, this deceptive approach is a terrible obstacle to making a new currency a social object that can supersede incumbent currencies, like the Deutsche mark or Italian lira.

The necessary quality of a social object is that it not be questioned, but is accepted at face value.

The euro has been questioned a lot lately, precisely because it is hard to tell what its face value is.

Euro banknotes are intentionally deceptive and untraceable, in order to minimize the impact that a single eurozone nation can have on the common currency. It is a currency without history, trying to be rootless and anonymous.

Not a good start to becoming a social object.

It took several millennia for concepts like law, right, property, contract, marriage, money, etc., to become unquestioned, as social objects must be. Now we see our social reality through the lenses of such concepts.

Changes in our understanding of social objects like law, democracy, right, are momentous for a society, because they bring considerable instability and insecurity.

In 1804 and 1807, Napoleon introduced his civil and commercial codes. In less than 10 years they were adopted by (imposed on) all countries that were under

---

[69] Interestingly the *Frankfurter Allgemeine* recently published an article disclosing how to recognize where the banknotes were issued in Europe.

[70] I am referring to Mario Draghi, the chairman of the European Central Bank at the peak of the eurozone crisis.

[71] Please note that I am not against the euro. Actually, I love(d) the idea. But the idea of money without origin is interesting, because, for technical reasons, it reduces the freedom of choice of citizens. There was a similar problem in the U.S. 150 years ago, but it was a consequence of the ease of counterfeiting banknotes printed by one state reserve. Consequently, the greenback was introduced, a banknote that was identical in all states, so it was no longer possible to tell if it was printed in Virginia or, say, Colorado.

Napoleonic rule. The codes' most important innovation was that they allowed the state to rule on civil and commercial law, which until then were traditional, customary laws. The standing regimes were pleased with this innovation, which gave them more power than even the monarchs they succeeded.

Thus the absolute monarchies restored by the Congress of Vienna were even more powerful than they had been before the French Revolution. For the first time, they were able to rule on matters of civil and commercial law.

The name of property was unchanged, but its meaning was radically different because, after the Napoleonic Code, it was exposed to the whims of the absolute monarch. Before the Napoleonic Code, property was a natural, God-given right, with which no monarch could tamper. It was administered by customary justice, based on rules dating back millennia to Roman law.

After Napoleon, continental Europe had a codified right granted by the national law. Suddenly, the legislative power could decide to abolish or curtail property.[72]

Some 30 years later, the nations of continental Europe were lacerated by violent protests surrounding the introduction of constitutional guarantees. The riots of 1848, which toppled more than one monarchy, were triggered by the new legislative powers of the monarchs, which lumped bourgeoisie and lower classes together. Additionally, they impacted the legislative process with rigid constitutions and democratic elections. History books tell the story as a fight for democracy, for new rules giving more power to legislative bodies. This is surely true, but not the whole truth. What motivated the revolutionaries of 1848 was that the additional legislative powers given to absolute monarchies could impact the status quo. The desperate violence of 1848 went beyond democratic idealism: There was a concrete fear that rights that had been intangible for millennia could be curtailed by new laws. If a monarchy was able to dispose of property by law, then it was necessary to have a constitution to guarantee that some rights would be genuinely untouchable, even by the law.

It was a change in the effective meaning of natural rights – which had existed until 1804 by customary law (*Ius Commune*, i.e., common law) – that triggered violent social unrest, followed by a spate of extremely bloody global wars in the second half of the 19th and first half of the 20th centuries.

It took nearly 100 years of modern warfare for the balance of power in Europe to stabilize, under modern democratic constitutions that have since fostered internal social stability and mutual trust between European states.

Continental Europeans, after the French Revolution and Napoleonic rule, had to learn (through pain and suffering) how to govern under a new social order – replete with new laws, guarantees and rights. (A whole batch of new social objects!) They accomplished what the Britons had with the Glorious Revolution

---

[72] The abolishment of property is possible only if it is a right granted by national law and not by common law. In fact, wherever parliaments have abolished property, as in communist countries, there was no common law. Fascism and communism haven't arisen (thus far) under common law legal systems. To abolish property, you really must believe that property is sanctioned by national law and not by natural law!

of 1688, which stabilized the United Kingdom and its social/legal system. As a young country, the U.S. overhauled its antiquated systems with the Civil War in 1861, when it imposed the social/economic model of the Union over a Confederacy that was still inextricably bound to slavery.

In the first half of the 19th century, the meaning of a series of words representing fundamental social objects changed: the (social) meaning of the word "citizen" (revolutionized by the French and American constitutions), of "person" (through the abolishment of slavery), of "law" (as a consequence of the Napoleonic Code), of "nation" (no longer impersonated by the king, but by the generality of its people), of "right" (from natural rights to legislative rights). Moreover, because the monarchy now had the right to change natural law through legislation, a new idea was born: the idea of a (strong) "constitution" to replace the control function of natural law over the monarchy. Many constitutions (in particular, the U.S.) recognize that there are "inalienable rights" that not even the legislature can tamper with: life, liberty, property, and the pursuit of happiness, etc.

It cannot be just coincidence that when legislation was enabled to change natural rights, there was strong social and political pressure to formulate a piece of national legislation that recognized and enshrined such natural rights as inalienable.

Compromise is impossible when it comes to the meaning of a social object. In the end, one meaning must prevail.

So after Napoleon made legislation omnipotent on the continent, the intangibility of natural rights, established by a millennium of custom, had to be replaced with something even more omnipotent than legislation: the concept (social object) of inalienable rights,[73] enshrined by a constitution (a piece of legislation binding the monarch and the legislature).

If some people prefer a weak currency and others a strong one, if some people are prepared to work for their currency and others want it to be a tool for their ends, no compromise is possible. For the same reason, religious conflicts are violent and endless, because, with respect to the meaning of God, compromises are impossible (as long as you are not an atheist or someone who believes that religion is not an essential part of social reality). As they are, if "electoral fraud" is understood as a fact and not as an interpretation of facts…

We now know that our language creates social reality, generates the rules of our social reality, and crafts the meaning of what we understand as social reality.

Language is not just a descriptive tool; it forges, influences and protects a given social order. The partisan freedom fighters of today's history books were the terrorists and fanatics of their day.

---

[73] It is well known that the concept was theorized by Thomas Hobbes in the *Leviathan* and expanded in John Locke's *Two Treatises on Government,* Book II - Of Civil Government, chapters II to V. Less known is that John Locke was the secretary of Anthony Ashley Cooper, 1st Earl of Shaftesbury, involved in drafting the laws of the Colony of Carolina (a feudal monarchic colony at the time) and personally involved with his investments in the slave trade.

Throughout human history, there has been a "natural selection" of the story told about social reality. That is the subject of the powerful novel *The Name of the Rose*.[74]

At this point in our discussion, we understand that the information we have (and even that we don't have) shapes an image of our reality that is hard to change without deep (personal or social) disruption.

We know that today, there are many more sources of information and story-telling than in the past. This means that

a) either the image of our social reality is more nuanced/fragmented (with unanswered questions), or

b) we tend to take refuge in "cultural silos", which accept the account of social reality that we have already absorbed (with a great deal of help from digital technologies that consistently allow us to remain "among us").[75]

If we understand how we produce social reality through language and thoughts, then we probably understand that language cannot be "neutral". It may be "invisible" in how it shapes our understanding, but not neutral. It is one of the tools that we need to make social reality happen.

A world of human societies that live in their own cultural silos – that is the subject of *Gulliver's Travels*.[76] It is an absurd world, not a role model for our future. But the digitalized world is becoming increasingly intolerant of cultural differences. In the paper-based "literary society", the "authors" and the "journalists" were all part of the hegemonic social class, either by birth or through co-optation. The facts and stories they referred to were shared by all of them. Diverging opinions were on the interpretation of the facts, not on the facts. Eventually, different facts were deemed as relevant, but disputes on the truthfulness of an event were quite uncommon, within a given social and political context. You don't see different facts reported in Italian newspapers; they report more or less the same facts. This is also true in Germany and everywhere else. It's when you compare newspapers of different nations that you see that different facts are reported.[77]

---

[74] Eco U., *Il nome della rosa*, 514.

[75] The reference is to how search engines and social media work: In order to be successful, they tend to show us a selection of (social) items that will be liked by us. The consequence is that if we search something unusual for our (search engine) profile, that piece of information becomes even harder to find. Search engines are gerrymandering human life, creating digital enclaves where each of us has the feeling of being "mainstream". This explains the increased impact of the extremist fringes of society: Search engines, digital platforms, browsers and apps, all facilitate finding those who are likeminded: each of these digital tools have a (mostly nondescript) policy according to which that they choose what we can see and what we cannot; what is "safe", and what is not: according to their general conditions of service, we are bound to trust them, blindly. For literature on the subject, see chapter 8.4.4.

[76] Swift J. D., *Gulliver's Travels Into Several Remote Nations of the World*.

[77] Most striking (for German-speaking readers) is to compare the television news broadcasts of "Aktuelle Kamera" of communist East Germany with the "Tagesschau" of West Germany. It was as if the two Germanys were located on two different planets! Rarely did they ever report the same events. For decades, German state broadcasters have repeatedly shown the same footage, and rightly so. I don't think there is a single German today who is not clearly and deeply aware

Closing the first chapter, we may summarize our findings:

1) The genetic, biologic distinction between human and not human is quite weak.

2) Human communication is significantly different from animal communication when not only words, but also social reality, comes into play.

3) Language (and storytelling in particular) shapes human social reality.

4) Human language has changed (and still changes) human perceptions of physical reality in several ways.

5) Changes in language and how we use it directly affect social rules.

(How digitalisation has changed the meaning of today's social objects or has created new social objects will be discussed in chapter 8.)

---

of how manipulative the (mass media) account of reality can be! For example, the fall of the Berlin Wall was reported by "Aktuelle Kamera" on 9 October 1989 as "New regulatory disposals for foreign travel".

2

Origins of Law

si in ius vocat, ito. ni it,
antestamino. igitur em capito

Duodecim Tabularum Leges
(Tabula I) 451-450 A.C.

2. Origins of Law

If we observe animals in their environment, we notice that their behaviour sometimes bears a resemblance to human legal rules:
1) Property: many animal species own and protect their dens
2) Hierarchy: some animal societies have specialized roles and rules that define responsibilities
3) Territory: many animal species mark and defend their territory
4) Exclusive union: many animal species live in a closed, mutually exclusive union for a long time (even a lifetime).
Ultimately, what is the ontology of human law, and how is it different from ethologic rules?
In this chapter we will see that "animal ethologic rules" and "human rules" are different in their essence:
a) not only because of self-awareness: Self-awareness is increasingly accepted as a neurological feature in the systems of some more-developed animal species (see chapter 2.1). Human self-awareness has a different quality at the neurological level, compared to animal self-awareness, but there is insufficient data to postulate an ontological difference between human and animal rules.
b) and not because only humans are (supposedly) capable of moral instincts (see chapter 2.4): Human morality has a different quality from animal morality; again, there is insufficient information to postulate an ontological difference between human and animal rules.
The deep differences between human rules and animal rules mainly relate to:
1) the use and function of language (see chapter 2.3), and
2) the aim of human rules, which have the capacity to change nature, and in particular to transform scarcity into abundance. Animal rules mostly involve coping with natural phenomena, not changing the way nature works.
Considering the most recent neurologic and ethologic research on animal morality and self-consciousness, we can safely conclude that law is a purely human phenomenon. To enforce law requires a formalized and abstract language and the aim of "creating" a natural/social environment in which creatures can thrive. This is a feat that only human beings have been able to master thus far.

2.1. Self-awareness (as cooperation, empathy, justice)

Since the time of Descartes and Locke, the studies of philosophy, psychiatry and neuroscience have debated the notion of self-consciousness.[78] Issues of importance in the philosophy of consciousness include whether the concept is fundamentally coherent; whether consciousness can ever be explained mechanistically; whether non-human consciousness exists – and if so, how can it be recognized? How does consciousness relate to language? Studies in artificial

---

[78] For an actual definition of self-conscience, refer to: GALLUP G. G. JR., *Self-recognition in primates: A comparative approach to the bidirectional properties of consciousness*, in *American Psychologist*, 32(5).

intelligence explore whether consciousness can be understood in a way that does not require a dualistic distinction between mental and physical states or properties, and whether it may ever be possible for machines like computers or robots to be conscious.

Still, it cannot be denied that if a living being follows some rules, with no consciousness (like plants or monocellular organisms), these rules (and the following of them) have a different quality than humans abiding by the law.

The mainstream view of self-consciousness sees neurological behaviour control systems as having co-evolved with more capable sensory systems. The idea is that consciousness emerged as a by-product of increasing biological complexity, evolving from non-conscious precursors and composed of non-conscious components.[79]

Research into animal intelligence and animal emotions has taken its place in the agenda of disciplines ranging from evolutionary biology and cognitive ethology, to psychology, anthropology, philosophy, history and religious studies. There is tremendous interest in the emotional and cognitive lives of animals, and there are daily revelations that confound some of our assumptions about animal characteristics.[80] The idea that humans are the only living beings with an adequate neurological substrate to be conscious of themselves is no longer universally accepted.[81] A group of neuroscientists issued the following declaration in 2012: *"The absence of a neocortex does not appear to preclude an organism from experiencing affective states. Convergent evidence indicates that non-human animals have the neuroanatomical, neurochemical, and neurophysiological substrates of conscious states along with the capacity to exhibit intentional behaviours. Consequently, the weight of evidence indicates that humans are not unique in possessing the neurological substrates that generate consciousness. Non-human animals, including all mammals and birds, and many other creatures, including octopuses, also possess these neurological substrates"*.[82]

More recent ethologic studies show that animals have distinctive moral abilities.[83] All this considered, when we look at more developed living beings, it can be very hard to differentiate between animals and humans when it comes to following rules:

1) What is the difference between an ant in an anthill and a human being in the Middle Ages who believed in a pyramidal social order – that the king was

---

[79] Zelazo P. D., Moscovitch M., Thompson E., *The Cambridge Handbook of Consciousness*, loc. 333; William Seager, *A Brief History of the Philosophical Problem of Consciousness*, loc. 333.

[80] Bekoff M., Pierce J., *Wild Justice*, loc. 22.

[81] Animals are capable of creating alliances and coalitions among themselves and are also capable of compromise, reducing their own individual liberty to promote the community in a group; see Bekoff M., Pierce J., *Wild Justice*.

[82] Koch Christof, Stephen Hawking, Philip Low, Irene Pepperberg, Bruno van Swinderen, David B. Edelman, Edward Boyden, Diana Reiss, Donald Pfaff, Ryan Remedios, Harvey Karten, Franz X. Vollenweider, Naotsugu Tsuchiya, Melanie Boly, and Steven Laureys, *The Cambridge Declaration of Consciousness*, 2.

[83] Bekoff M., Pierce J., *Wild Justice*, loc. 1369 ff.

chosen by God and that there existed a natural order of things that could not be changed or subverted?

2) What is the difference between a human society and a pack of wolves? From time to time, wolves establish a new leader, similarly to the case when humans were hunter-gatherers.

The capacity to assess and adopt intentions and to make judgments about whether a particular course of action is morally justified is unique to humans and represents a break from our animal past. The prefrontal cortex, the area of the brain responsible for judgment and rational thought, is more highly developed in humans than in other animals. With judgment and rational thought (what is often called reason), we gain self-consciousness about the grounds of our action and gain a corresponding capacity for self-governance and conscious control. The capacity for normative self-government and the deeper level of intentional control that goes with it are probably unique to human beings. It is because animals lack this capacity for reflective self-control, that we don't hold them responsible. We don't hold them morally culpable for following their strongest impulses.[84]

We can no longer deny that some animals show traits of morality, exhibiting clusters of cooperation, empathy and justice,[85] even when observed in their natural habitat (where imitation of humans can be ruled out). According to the latest findings, there isn't an antinomy between humans and animals. It's not the case that humans have been provided with morality and judgment, while animals are totally void of any morality. Ethology and social neuroscience show that animals operate on a continuum of increasing self-awareness, cooperation, empathy and even justice.[86]

This first pre-condition for the development of legal rules is shared by humans and higher forms of animal life. Not only science (ethology and neurology), but also common sense acknowledges that some animals have an intrinsic moral ability. Consider higher mammals, like dogs, apes, whales, dolphins and elephants, whose actions can and often do emotionally move every one of us.

Neurology has disproved the contention that women are morally and intellectually inferior to men. Biology is moving in the same direction.[87]

---

[84] BEKOFF M., PIERCE J., *Wild Justice*, loc. 1721 ff.

[85] BEKOFF M., PIERCE J., *Wild Justice*, loc. 1696 ff.

[86] BEKOFF M., PIERCE J., *Wild Justice*, loc. 1710 ff.

[87] I must remark that Roman and Middle Ages law considered women irrational and unable to control themselves, and therefore put them under the tutelage of their husbands (or of their closest male relative, if unmarried). They were affected by *"levitas animi, infirmitas, fragilitas, debilitas, imbecillitas, simplicitas"*, which can be roughly translated as "moral carelessness, infirmity, fragility, debilitation, stupidity, simplicity". At that time, women were deemed to be human, but devoid of the most important psychological trait of humans!
We can read in the statutes of Rome in the 16th century that women were not allowed to enter any legal agreement without the consent of a curator:
"De contractibus sine solemnitate non valituris: Volentes autem fraudibus obviare, ne mulieres ex earum simplicitate et puberes etiam masculi, qui adhuc imperfectae aetatis existunt defraudentur: Statuimus ut pacta de non petendo, refutationes, quietationes, donationes, quae a quibuscumque mulieribus, vel minoribus viginti annis maculi, sive sub patria potestate, sive sui iuris existentibus fient, nullius sint roboris, vel

2.2. Scarcity[88]

The ice ages decimated the fauna on earth. Humans miraculously survived. In order to survive they became nomadic, on a quest for a less hostile environment.[89] The history of human migrations is long. According to anthropological studies, the different waves of migration could have been set in motion by two major causes:

1) Major shifts in the world's climate, such as the Ice Age, caused the near extinction of the human race.[90]

2) The dropping of the sea levels allowed our ancestors to journey to new lands. Some 70,000 years ago, after the last Ice Age, the first great population expansion extended beyond Africa.[91] About 40,000 years ago, humans crossed the Bosporus from modern-day Turkey, and reached Europe by navigating the Danube River.[92] Evidence of these migrations has been found in the genetic background of modern Europeans. Analysis of the gene pool and DNA patterns suggests that two major events in prehistory significantly affected European genetics:

1) The initial peopling of the continent by hunter-gatherers during the Palaeolithic Age some 40,000 – 50,000 years ago.[93]

2) A wave of migration by Near Eastern farmers during the Neolithic Age.[94]

---

momenti, nisi duobus coniunctis proximioribus adibiti, quorum non intersit, etiam medio iuramento approbantibus, non esse in praeiudicium earumdem mulierum vel minorum; et si sub patria potestate existant, vocentur ex linea materna, et nihilominus praesentia patris interveniat: et si aliqui coniuncti non existerent, cum curatoris legitimi auctoritate ac semper cum iudicis competenti decreto, causa in scriptis illi expressa, insinuata ac plene cognita, contrahere deberent: et iuramentum praestitum, censeatur dolo et metu extortum, et nihil operetur". Pope Gregory XIII, Statuta Urbis Romae, 151, quoted by FECI, S., La capacità di agire (Italia, sec. XII-XIX); SANFILIPPO C., Istituzioni Di Diritto Romano, 62.

[88] PERLÈS, C., Review of First Farmers: The Origins of Agricultural Societies, by Peter Bellwood, in Journal of Field Archaeology, 31, 109-110.
More readings on the subject:
http://news.nationalgeographic.com/news/2001/11/1112_overkill_2.html.
CURNOE D., Climate change, doomsday and the inevitable extinction of humankind; ALLAN D., Ecological Role of Prehistoric Humans; HENDRY L., First Britons;"; RICHARDS M.P., A Brief Review of the Archaeological Evidence for Palaeolithic and Neolithic Subsistence, 56.

[89] BOLUS M. AND CONRAD N. J., The Late Middle Palaeolithic and Earliest Upper Palaeolithic in Central Europe and their Relevance for the Out of Africa Hypothesis, 29-40; MELLARS P., Why Did Modern Human Populations Disperse from Africa ca – 60,000 Years Ago? A New Model, 9381-9386; and TATTERSALL I., Human Origins: Out of Africa, 16018-16021.

[90] MITHEN S., After the Ice, 89; STUART A.J., The extinction of woolly mammoth and straight-tusked elephant in Europe, 171-177; WEISDORF J.L., From Foraging to Farming.

[91] The earliest people to colonize the Eurasian landmass likely travelled across the Bab-al-Mandab Strait separating present-day Yemen from Djibouti. Back 60,000 years ago, there was land that connected India and Borneo. Humans trekked rapidly along the coast to India, and reached Southeast Asia and even Australia within 20,000 years. Around 50,000 years ago, a second group set out on an inland trek, heading toward (what is now) the Middle East and southern Central Asia. This tribe was poised to colonize the northern latitudes of Asia and Europe.

[92] ROBERTS A., The Incredible Human Journey, loc. 3770.

[93] BARRAS C., Mystery Invaders Conquered Europe at the End of Last Ice Age.

[94] RINCON P., Making of Europe Unlocked by DNA.

Archaeological findings of ancient settlements from 40,000 years ago establish that Europe was first colonized during the Palaeolithic Age. Historical markers then trace a retreat to Southern Europe, due to a new glacial period (20,000 years ago), followed by renewed expansions to Northern Europe.[95] In this epoch, the American continent first showed traces of colonisation.[96]

Around 20,000 years ago, during the Last Glacial Maximum, the sea levels dropped by more than 300 feet. This exposed a land bridge that connected the Old World to the New, joining Asia to the Americas, allowing tribes to rapidly expand into the Americas. This migration was so rapid that, within 1,000 years, the Amerind indigenous peoples of the Americas had made it all the way to the tip of South America.[97]

After the last ice age (i.e., starting from about 12,000 B.C.), humans in the Mediterranean area experienced scarcity of food. According to one theory, scarcity was a consequence of overhunting; others see it mainly as a consequence of climate change.[98]

As long as large game was available, sharing the spoils was the most rational thing to do: Collective hunting made it easier to catch prey. Once the game was killed, it had to be eaten before it rotted. Mankind learned how to preserve meat around the seventh millennium B.C.,[99] when the first non-nomadic

---

[95] RINCON P., *DNA study deals blow to the theory of European origins*.

[96] KITCHEN A., MIYAMOTO M.M., MULLIGAN C.J., *A Three-Stage Colonisation Model for the Peopling of the Americas*.

[97] There are two contrasting theories about how the Americas where colonized:
1) The Bering land bridge theory (from Asia to Americas by land).
2) The coastal migration theory (from Northwest Asia along the northern Pacific coastline of North America by sea).
According to the Bering land bridge theory, the first humans to migrate from Asia to the Americas crossed over a land bridge (Beringia) during the last ice age (from approximately 110,000 to 12,000 years ago). Homo sapiens migrated into North America through a gap between the Laurentian and Cordilleran glacial ice sheets.
Clans of this period went through two stages of growth, separated by a long period of population stability. The Amerind ancestors likely left the Asian continent prior to 40,000 years ago and experienced a gradual population expansion as they moved into Beringia.
Conversely, the coastal migration theory affirms that the first Americans migrated from Northeast Asia along the northern Pacific coastline of North America using primitive boats and rafts. As they migrated southward, they could have stopped in ice-free refuges, becoming the first people to colonize the coast of the American continent. These Amerinds moved inland as the glacial ice sheet melted and opened up access routes to North America. A recent theory also supports the idea that the first Americans came from Siberia to North America by a coastal route.
Back 60,000 years ago, as the coasts of Alaska and Northern Canada were deglaciating, coastal corridors opened. These may have been used by our ancestors to expand to the south. When the route was blocked by ice sheets reaching the coast, they probably used small boats to go further. Traces of this coastal dispersal have been found in the genetic makeup of Indian American populations throughout the Americas, from North to South. http://www.transpacificproject. com/index.php/transpacific-migrations/.

[98] MITHEN, S., *After the Ice Age*, 197 and 232.

[99] WAYLAND BARBER E., *The Mummies of Ürümchi*. CARUSI C., *Il sale nel mondo Greco*, VI a.C.-III BC; and KURLANSKY M., *Salt: A World History*.

human civilisations started to appear in China and the Mediterranean. Hunter-gatherers appeared some 600,000 years ago and were the most common social organisation of humans until about 12,000 years ago.[100]

It was during the Neolithic Revolution that mankind introduced a new means of survival: agriculture.[101] The Neolithic Demographic Transition saw the wide-scale shift of many human cultures from a lifestyle of hunting and gathering to one of agriculture and settlement. This gave Homo sapiens the ability to support an increasingly large population. Permanent settlements, cities and civilisations grew.

Simultaneously, plant domestication and livestock farming spread across the landscape, making resources more available and accessible. Before the cultivation of plants and the domestication of animals, man was a hunter and gatherer of whatever food sources he could find in his local environment. Hunter-gatherers did not live differently from packs of wolves or hyenas, or a pride of lions. Imitation was a sufficient behaviour to transmit knowledge and establish the pecking order within a group (based on health and strength) and thus the sharing of shelter, food and beverages.[102]

The early farmers learned that some soils were more productive than others; they also learned that continuous cultivation of the same land resulted in reduced yields. The first fertilizers, or soil amendments, were discovered by trial and error. They yielded unpredictable results that needed to be re-examined and modified. Agriculture and the use of soil amendments started through independent developments in Mesopotamia in the river basins of the Tigris and Euphrates, and in the Nile Valley.

The creation and transmission of such knowledge is all but impossible through imitative behaviour. Moreover, an agricultural society requires an established notion of "mine" and "yours", and specialisation of skills and roles that is

---

[100] The Cambridge Encyclopedia of Hunter-Gatherers says, *"Hunting and gathering was humanity's first and most successful adaptation, occupying at least 90 percent of human history. Until 12,000 years ago, all humans lived this way. Following the invention of agriculture, hunter-gatherers were displaced by farming or pastoralist groups in most parts of the world. Only a few contemporary societies are classified as hunter-gatherers, and many supplement, sometimes extensively, their foraging activity with farming and/or keeping animals"*.
Other interesting materials on scarcity and agricultural revolution:
JORDAN D.K., *The Neolithic: Essay 1*; JORDAN D.K., *The Neolithic: Essay 2*; JORDAN D.K., *The Neolithic: Essay 3*; KRAUTKRAEMER J., *Economics of Natural Resource Scarcity*.
[101] DIAMOND, J., *Guns, Germs, and Steel: A Short History of Everybody for the Last 13,000 Years*, (ch. 9, "To Farm or Not to Farm", pp. 109 ff.) argues very convincingly that the switch from foraging to agriculture was not a given and presents many cases where foragers decided not to become farmers. Diamond also convincingly shows how farming societies experienced social and health issues unknown by foragers, which pushed them to enslave neighbouring populations. Finally he convincingly argues that the social/legal rules of most resident farmers were built on human exploitation – a point shared by FLANNERY, K., MARCUS, J., *The Creation Of Inequality*, 91, which underlines that some foragers found a way to create hereditary inequality, and some successful agricultural societies remained egalitarian, even after thousands of years of farming.
[102] HARARI Y., N., *Sapiens: A Brief History of Humankind*, 40, where we read the size of human groupings and the complexity of their rules is directly proportional to their ability to transmit larger chunks of information.

inconceivable without the use of (human) language. The constructive function of language (which creates a reality, more than describing it) becomes evident if we look at the agricultural human society of the Neolithic: Without the use of language it would not have worked out (see chapter 1.3).

This change in in the social structure of humans began about 10,000 years ago, when humans learned how to cultivate crops and to domesticate animals. Rather than adjusting to their environment through biological evolution like most other organisms, humans developed themselves through cultural adaptation, using their intellectual and social skills to "improve nature" and adapt it to their survival needs. Language was needed to change reality; the use of language just to adapt to nature would have been a bit of overkill![103]

To permanently change how nature works – i.e., creating complex new tools for working the earth, cross-breeding plants to make them more productive and resistant, etc. – it was essential to develop the ability to create and disseminate knowledge. The old way of passing it to the next generation through experience, trial and error had become obsolete. Human language made it possible to transfer knowledge without needing to observe and memorize the actions of the tutor. For the first time on earth, it became possible to learn something without experience; we could comprehend concepts by recognizing abstract descriptions of rules and procedures. This abstraction is the essence of human language. It does not show reality or events; it reconstructs them in a purely hypothetical and theoretical context. Through human language, you can know things, without ever having seen them.[104]

Early on, philosophers became aware of this miracle: Humans, through language, had created a parallel reality that was in its essence normative, because it was populated by hypothetical actions and rules about how things should or must work. Its main purpose was to shorten the human learning process. You didn't have to wait years to experience a flood or for a mad bear to attack the village. Such rare events were shared through narration. Humming and dancing, wouldn't do the trick!

Language is the tool through which humans began to acclimate reality to their needs, overturning the adaptive process. Humans became the first animals to change reality to fit it to their needs.

The most significant results of the Neolithic Revolution were: **language**, **law**, agriculture, population growth, specialisation, trade, **government** … and new diseases.[105]

2.3. Language

Scarcity without language would only generate fighting for the control of limited resources. Only the fittest would survive. In evolutionary theory, scarcity can have two outcomes:

---

[103] MITHEN, S., *After the ice age*, 212.

[104] HARARI Y. N., *Sapiens: A Brief History of Humankind*, 40.

[105] DIAMOND, J., *Guns, Germs, and Steel: A Short History of Everybody for the Last 13,000 Years*, 211 ff.

1) adaptation

2) extinction.

Animals are threatened by extinction when food is scarce. The weakest among them die. Eventually, their total number declines to the point of extinction. Every day, certain species become extinct because they cannot adapt quickly enough. Humans have adapted, they have even changed their metabolism from carnivorous to omnivorous. Language was essential to this specific outcome of the adaptive process. It was essential to defining new procedures for survival, new roles … and, in the end, a new social order.[106]

---

[106] HARARI Y., N., *Sapiens: A Brief History of Humankind*, 21.

The history of language follows a pattern. The first attempts at writing and expressing feelings mostly took the form of **drawings** or graphic symbols. Studies conducted by Ferraris and Marshack on the Palaeolithic era (200,000 BC) suggest a connection between inscriptions on artifacts and an early form of language. Research shows that some images carved on artifacts were used in different ways and contexts. Artifacts were marked with geometric patterns, creating intentional zigzag images that have clearly posed problems of interpretation. According to Marshack's research, these patterns and images may be an early form of non-representational symbolic markings, indicating some sort of linguistic expression used by Neanderthal man. As Marshack notes, we also have evidence that in the Mousterian era (35,000 – 30,000 BC), there were a variety of symbol systems, and the images carved on some artifacts may have had a phenomenological reference, expressing awareness of the natural world. These symbols document the capability of abstraction, probably related to linguistic competence, rather than to simple tool-making.

Ideograms can be considered the next step in the history of language. They are graphical symbols directly representing ideas or objects, instead of using letters conventionally arranged in words or speech sounds. The name of the concept represented is closely identified with the simplified picture. In the past, they were mostly used to represent the idea of a living being or an inanimate object. Nowadays, the term "ideogram" is used to describe logographic writing systems (such as Chinese or Egyptian).

Logograms stand in contrast to phonograms, which are syllabic signs used to represent primary oral sounds. They represent phonemes and determinatives. Studies have distinguished hundreds of phonemes used in different languages, accents and dialects. Logographic signs are graphemes and may represent a word or a morpheme (part of a word). They are visual symbols representing words. A single logogram can be used in different languages to represent words with similar meanings.

Pictograms first appeared around 9000 BC in various ancient cultures throughout the world and are commonly believed to be the first form of writing. They consist of fragmented drawings or illustrations representing simple ideas or objects, such as "man", "fire", "tree".

There is no known connection between the drawing and the word used in the spoken language to identify the same object; the drawing was used to recall an image or picture of the concept itself, not the word or name associated with it. These drawings were somehow combined in order to form stories or songs, and they were mostly etched into monuments. Egyptian hieroglyphics emerged from the preliterate artistic tradition and combined three kinds of glyphs (i.e., symbols): phonetic glyphs, logographs and ideograms. This writing system was used to represent stylized but perfectly recognizable elements. At first, the Egyptians wrote on a paper-like material made from compressed papyrus fibres, using a brush made from reeds. They called their writing "words of the gods" because they believed that a god had invented writing. As writing became more widespread among the Egyptians, popular, simplified forms and higher, priestly forms of writing hieroglyphs, called demotic and hieratic, developed. Hieratic was a form of sacred writing and was considered tricky to read and understand by Greco-Roman authors. Because of the different written "dialects", some of the stories represented by hieroglyphs were misinterpreted as allegorical. Ancient Egyptians believed in an afterlife. They presumed that if their name was written on their tomb, their life and

Let me be clear about one point: I am not trying to make the argument supporting the evolutionary theory of language. Whatever its origin – genetic (according to Chomsky's theories) or evolutionary (according to Mithen's concepts) – in looking at human history, we can recognize the influence of language in our evolution.[107]

---

fame would continue after death. Words were thought to be so powerful that they were sometimes used to make a person disappear from history, simply by scratching out their name and picture. "Scribe" was the name given to those who knew how to read and write hieroglyphs. These people were highly respected, and it was a great ambition to be educated to become a scribe. There were very few scribes, as it required 12 years of hard training. The discovery of the Rosetta Stone in 1799 provided the key to our modern understanding of Egyptian hieroglyphics. This tablet represented the same text in three different scripts: hieroglyphs, demotic and Greek, allowing scholars to decipher the previously untranslated ancient Egyptian language.

One of the world's earliest systems of alphabetic writing was invented by the Sumerians more than 5,000 years ago (3500 – 3000 BC). This form of writing, called **cuneiform** (from Latin for "wedge-shaped"), originated because of the need to find a means of accounting and record-keeping (especially in the fields of public administration, private legal and sales documents, contracts, inventories, religious texts and school texts). These early signs were pictograms, but they could also be used to represent the sound of the spoken words related to the same idea or object. Sumerians used clay as their writing surface because it was recyclable, yet durable if baked. Reeds were used (as wedge-shaped styli) to inscribe marks on the clay surface. Later, inscriptions were carved on stones, using stone-cutting tools. Cuneiform signs most frequently **represented syllables**, which made this form of writing very flexible. As a matter of fact, cuneiform is a script, not a language. It can be used to express any language, in spite of having been developed to write Sumerian. The Law Code Stele of Hammurabi was written in cuneiform signs.

References: MARSHACK A., *Some Implications of the Palaeolithic Symbolic Evidence for the Origin of Language*, 289-311; FRIEDRICH J., *Decifrazione Delle Scritture E Delle Lingue Scomparse*; KATAN J.N., MINTZ B., *Hieroglyphs: The Writing of Ancient Egypt*; VAN DE MIEROOP M., *Cuneiform Texts and the Writing of History*.

[107] Scholars debate whether language is an innate part of our biology which evolved over time, or the result of our experiences, with a leading role in defining our view of the world around us. Steven Mithen, *The Singing Neanderthals* **theory**: Mithen categorizes this kind of communication as holistic, multimodal, manipulative and musical ("hmmmm"). Music and dance were the communication tools used by Neanderthals to organise their social lives and transmit knowledge. Noam Chomsky: His **generative grammar theory** hypothesizes the existence of neural mechanisms, or switches, which allow children to develop language. Those mechanisms work like a computer program, called a language acquisition device (LAD). The human brain experiences a "fertile time", when it's more capable of learning (and can be filled with data and knowledge). Called the "sensitive phase", it lasts only a few years. If left empty and unchecked, the brain won't be able to learn things as easily afterward. The development of language is similar to the growth of a child's body. It needs both verbal and nutritional nourishment to thrive and grow strong. The idea of an innate body of knowledge (generative grammar theory) possessed by every user explains why children successfully acquire language and how the quality of their learning is impacted by the environment they live in and the quality of the linguistic stimuli they receive. Quality and quantity of linguistic stimuli impact the linguistic knowledge that children will attain at the end of their studies: CHOMSKY N., *The Study of Mind*; CHOMSKY N., *Linguistic Contributions to the Study of Mind*; CHOMSKY N., *Language And Mind*. Official website: http://www.chomsky.info/.

BARSKY R.F., ZELLING HARRIS, *From American Linguistics to Socialist Zionism*; BLOOMFIELD L., *An Introduction to the Study of Language*.

The **Sapir-Whorf Hypothesis**: Edward Sapir studied the differences between different languages. He focused on habits, social hierarchies, traditions and customs of people from different countries.

Instead of evolving through our physical strengths and becoming stronger Neanderthals, we became smarter and more communicative, losing body hair and muscles. We became *Homines sapientes*. Without (new) rules, without new procedures, without a new definition of reality (of food, property, roles, etc.), humans would not have evolved on this path. We would not have been able to change nature (and thus physical reality) to fit our needs for survival. Over the past 5,000 years we have transformed nature around us. We have changed ourselves more than nature has changed us. We have created a human society. The importance of language in our society is unmistakable.

Without language, it would only have been possible to use up natural resources successively, according to some ranking or a (naturally) given order (as in a pack of wolves or an anthill), until each of the scarce resources had been exhausted. Humans didn't do that. They "augmented" nature – increasing soil fertility, strengthening the resistance of crops, domesticating and breeding animals, creating secure shelters and secure agglomerates of shelters (villages), agglomerates of villages (tribes) and agglomerates of tribes (states), and so on. Language was necessary to establish the human skills needed to improve nature and reality to make it fit the needs of humans, after millennia of hunger and starvation.[108] Language improved reality, not only through agriculture and architecture, but also through social engineering. After having "augmented" nature, it was still necessary to efficiently divide scarce resources among all members of a community, without too much fighting or dying. A better division of scarce resources requires the ability to negotiate rules without getting into a fight. Only humans can do that, through language. Animals have either an order

---

Sapir's pupil, Benjamin Whorf, hypothesized that language can influence people's mentality. In fact, comparing people from different countries, he found out that all of them had different cognitive processes and mentalities. All humans have the same cognitive potential, but language can create cognitive differences. For example, Eskimos are more experienced about snow than any group on the planet; that is why they have the most words to describe snow in all its forms. Language impacts not only thought, but also other behaviours not related to the linguistic area.
CARROLL J.B., *Language, Thought and Reality*; LEE P., *The Whorf Theory Complex*; Lucy J.A., *Language Diversity and Thought*; CHANDLER D., *The Sapir-Whorf Hypothesis,* online extract.
ADLER G. J., *Wilhelm von Humboldt's Linguistical Studies,* 1-47.
PINKER S., *Language as an adaptation*: Pinker considered language as an instinct, an innate ability which marks our superior intellect, rather than a mere human invention, such as writing or metalworking. Language, especially speech, can be extremely spontaneous. Children can create a new word spontaneously, even without adults correcting them. Pinker believed that language is universal and that people who belong to the same social system share it. It doesn't matter if the speakers are fully or partially educated, because every form of language has a systematic set of rules. For example, when children from different cultures lacked a culturally transmitted language, they would develop a language on their own. In another case, when children with different culturally transmitted languages were thrown together, they developed some kind of "lingua franca" on their own to communicate.
PINKER S., *Language as an Adaptation to the Cognitive Niche.* PINKER S., *The Language Instinct: How the Mind Creates Language.* DARWIN C., *On the Origin of Species by Means of Natural Selection,* 5-28, 39-82, 131-154. COSMIDES L., TOOBY J., *Cognitive Adaptations for Social Exchange,* in COSMIDES L., BARKOW J., TOOBY J., *The Adapted Mind: Evolutionary Psychology and the Generation of Culture,* loc. 2904.
[108] MITHEN, S., *After the Ice Age,* 21, 22, 35.

that can be changed through challenge and fight (as in animal packs), or rules that are simply unchallenged (as in anthills and hives). Human language served dual functions: to transmit knowledge for "augmenting" nature and to negotiate rules for a flexible division of scarce resources.

As John Searle brilliantly demonstrates, language goes far beyond achieving knowledge or better mutual understanding: It is about creating a social reality.[109] In its most concise and revealing definition,[110] a sign (and thus language) is a modification of reality.

Language offers the ability to modify and even create reality, beyond just describing it.

In the beginning, humans probably weren't aware that we were changing nature. In our language, many concepts (in particular measurements) are abstractions that we cannot perceive through our senses. We were simply building new things – homes, roads, harbours. We were unaware that we were radically changing nature. Our mental focus was (and sadly still is) on human society. Nature is just a background. Language has always been about transcending nature and physical reality, about changing and improving reality.

With sophisticated early languages like Greek and Latin, it was already a hopeless task to tell the difference between the meaning of a word and the physical reality behind it. Consider this example: In the 5th century B.C., humans distinguished between three kinds of persons: citizens (having all rights), aliens (having just some rights), and slaves (who were not the subjects of rights, but the objects of them).

Knowing that a human being is a slave changes the way we look at that human being. Why would we segregate them and treat them as property if we did not believe that slaves were somehow different from us? Humanity thrived for 15,000 years on the distinction between citizen and slave. Only in the last century have we abolished the concept that humans can be mere objects of rights. The first "Universal Declaration of Human Rights" was voted on by the United Nations on 10 December 1948, with 48 nations in favour and eight abstaining.[111] This was the first time that it became legally sanctioned that all humans have rights.

The main difference between a free person and a slave lies in the meaning of the word "slave" and in the ability of language and society to distinguish different kinds of persons – those who are subjects from those who are objects.

2.4. Morality and Law

Morality (religion) predates law in all human societies. Even animal groupings have a code of conduct.[112] It has long been assumed that the law needs some kind of underlying morality as a source of legitimacy. When humans where

---

[109] SEARLE J. R., *Making the Social World*, 61 ff.
[110] SEBEOK T.A., *Signs*, 3, and *Global Semiotics*, 1.
[111] United Nations, *"The Universal Declaration Of Human Rights"*.
[112] FLANNERY, K., MARCUS, J., *The Creation Of Inequality*, 54.

foragers, they had a moral code and a cosmology that underlined the morality of the social order of their tribe.

Such moral values invariably include:

1) generosity
2) sharing
3) reciprocating gifts
4) homicide is taboo
5) winning is important
6) respect for elders
7) honour.[113]

The philosophy of law today agrees that the law needs to be ethical, but at the same time it tries to extricate the legitimacy of the law from any given moral code. In order to do so, there needs to be a clear distinction between moral rules and legal rules. There are two major ways to argue this difference: legal positivism and natural law theories.

For legal positivism, morality differs from law for ontological reasons: Law has a formalized system of sanctions for enforcing compliance with the rules.[114] It is an easy and clear-cut distinction.

Under natural law theories, some rights are inherently part of the legal rules (i.e., the right to live, to have property and to be free, according to John Locke); so the effort to tell the difference between legal and moral rules is quite messy. Natural law assumes that certain rights or values are inherent in, or universally cognizable, by virtue of human reason or human nature. A theory of natural law claims to be able to identify conditions and principles of practical right-mindedness, of good and proper behaviour among persons and in individual conduct.[115]

One difference between law and morality is the coercive nature of law – primarily by way of punitive sanctions, secondarily by way of preventive sanctions.[116] But for natural law theorists, the distinction is insufficient, because law without morality or justice is just empty authority.[117] But under natural law theories, law requires more than just the enforcement of rules. It must also fulfil four intrinsic properties that, if missing, would degrade what is supposed to be law to an arbitrary exercise of power:[118]

1) Law brings definition, specificity, clarity and thus predictability to human interactions using a system of rules and institutions so interrelated that rules define, constitute and regulate the institutions. In turn, those institutions create

---

[113] FLANNERY, K., MARCUS, J., *The Creation Of Inequality*, 56.

[114] KELSEN H., *Pure Theory of Law*, loc. 1148 ff.

John Rawls, a prominent legal positivist, has elaborated a theory of justice to prove that law has an intrinsic moral value, without depending on any particular moral theory. See RAWLS J., *A Theory of Justice*. The 1999 revised edition incorporates changes that Rawls made for translated editions.

[115] FINNIS J., *Natural Law and Natural Rights*, 18.

[116] FINNIS J., *Natural Law and Natural Rights*, 265.

[117] Meanwhile, for legal positivists, any system of rules that is enforced qualifies as law.

[118] FINNIS J., *Natural Law and Natural Rights*, 267-271.

and administer the rules, settle the questions about their existence, scope, applicability and operations.

2) Law has a working postulate (so fundamental that it is scarcely ever identified and discussed) that any legal rule or institution (e.g., contract, settlement, corporation) which has been validly created remains valid in force or in existence in contemplation of law until it is determined otherwise according to its own terms or under some valid act or rule of repeal. All legal entities have the quality of persistence through time.

3) The rules of law go beyond regulating the creation, administration and adjudication of such rules and the constitution, modification and termination of institutions. Law decides the conditions under which a private individual can modify the application of the rules (whether in relation to himself or to other individuals). That is to say, individuals may perform juridical acts which – if performed in accordance with the rules in place at that point in time – count as making a contract, entering a marriage, forming a trust, incorporating a company, issuing a summons or entering a judgment. The rule of law allows the individual to act freely and provides proper legal relevance to his actions.

4) Law brings precision and predictability into the order of human interactions by a special technique: the treating of past acts (whether of enactment, adjudication or any other exercise of public and private "powers") as giving, *now*, sufficient and exclusionary reason for acting in a way "provided for" *then*. In other words, it provides words with normative power if exchanged between two or more people (contracts, agreements) or if ritually published (laws and decrees).

What matters here, is that both definitions of law presuppose the use of human language. For legal positivists, the "formalized system" of rules requires the use of human language. So does the natural law theory, which requires definitions, specificity, clarity and institutions.

So both schools of thought – the philosophy of law and legal positivism – agree that the main difference between law and morality lies in the formal use of language.

In moral philosophy, the use of language is mainly about demonstrating the moral foundations. It is focused exclusively on providing proper definitions and illustrating how moral rules apply to human reality. Words are not used to build systems of institutions and procedures, or to assess whether, in a specific case, the rules have been respected or violated.

In a legal system, the use of language is almost exclusively about making the rules and enforcement mechanisms effective. Institutions and procedures are conjured up through words, in a way that makes it possible to judge (by the finding of specific facts) if, in a specific case, the rules have been followed, to define the consequences of the facts that have been proved, and ultimately, also to enforce such consequences, if they are not accepted spontaneously by the parties involved in the judgement.

Moral philosophy is about what is right.

Law is about properly defining the rules and the consequences of breaching such rules, and creating procedures and institutions that are effective at judging and enforcing judgements.

Moral philosophy is about "why" and "what". For morality, justice is the ultimate goal.

Law is about "how". For the law, justice is due process, under the (potential) supervision of a competent authority.

The language of morality is prescriptive. The language of law must also be effective.

2.5. Property as the first rule: a slave economy

About 12,000 years ago, when large animals had become almost extinct, the human population resorted to agriculture in the Middle East (Mesopotamia), China and Central America.

Early Neolithic villages show evidence of the ability to process grain. The Near East was the birthplace for the cultivation of wheat, barley and peas. There is evidence of the cultivation of figs in the Jordan Valley as long as 11,300 years ago and cereal (grain) production in Syria approximately 9,000 years ago.

During the same period, farmers in China began to farm rice and millet, using manmade floods and fires as part of their cultivation regime. Fibre crops were domesticated as early as food crops. China domesticated hemp, while flax was the product of the Near East, and cotton was developed in both Africa and South America. The use of soil amendments – including manure, fish, compost and ash – began early and thrived independently in several areas of the world, including Mesopotamia, the Nile Valley and Eastern Asia.

Squash was grown in Mexico nearly 10,000 years ago, while maize-like plants (derived from wild teosinte grasses) were seen around 9,000 years ago. The development of teosinte and Zea grasses into modern corn was slow, it was not until about 5,800 years ago that it was cultivated into what we know today as maize. After being introduced, it gradually spread across North America, becoming the main crop of Native Americans at the time of European exploration. Beans were domesticated around the same time.

Squash, maize (corn), and climbing beans together formed the "three sisters" nutrition foundation of many native populations in North and Central America. Combined with peppers, these crops provided a balanced diet for much of the American continent.

Grapes were first grown for wine in the southern Caucasus approximately 8,000 years ago, and by 3,000 B.C. they had spread to the Fertile Crescent, the Jordan Valley and Egypt.

Agriculture extended to Europe slightly later, reaching the northern corners from the East around 4,000 B.C.

If we look at human societies 9,000 years ago (7,000 B.C.), when mankind started to build stone walls, we will see that all human cities looked almost identical.[119] Their similarities are so striking that it would be impossible to tell if we are in Mesopotamia, China or Central America, based on archaeological findings alone. Human urban agglomerates all look the same.

---

[119] FLANNERY, K., MARCUS, J., *The Creation of Inequality*, loc. 164.

Considering what we know about human migrations,[120] we are pretty sure that this was not a consequence of direct cultural influence. Too few specimens of Homo sapiens migrated too many millennia before the appearance of any trace of stone-walled urbanisation.

Today, we believe that the human race, after it ceased to roam around as hunter-gatherers, solved identical adaptation problems in identical ways.[121] When anthropologists studied the evolution of several hunter-gatherer societies extant in the 19th and 20th centuries A.D., they found that all of them abolished the taboo forbidding hoarding first. Subsequently these cultures began to enforce property rights, in particular horticultural property,[122] long before any more articulated social structure was established among the clan. Property ownership marks the landmark change in social rules between nomadic hunter-gatherers and sedentary farmers. In other words, property predates the state.

Slavery was rare (and socially and economically marginal) in known societies of hunter-gatherers or foragers.[123] With this in mind, it is safe to assume that slavery and agriculture were connected from their origins until the (second) agricultural revolution of the 18th century A.D., when Industrial Age machines were deployed to improve the productivity of agriculture and proved to be much more fruitful than human labour had ever been.

I offer two ways to understand slavery in its anthropologic origins:

1) The coexistence of Homo sapiens and Homo neanderthalensis.

2) At the time of the shift from hunting-gathering to agriculture, language did not provide appropriate concepts to organize work in the fields.

Homo neanderthalensis was stronger, unable to speak and (probably, therefore) less intelligent than Homo sapiens.[124] So it was unable to formulate the more sophisticated processes and rules required to address social issues and the pressing issue of food scarcity.

---

[120] See chapter 2.2.

[121] DIAMOND, J., *Guns, Germs, and Steel: A Short History of Everybody for the Last 13,000 Years*, ch. 14 ("From Egalitarianism to Kleptocracy"), p. 289 ff.

[122] FLANNERY, K., MARCUS, J., *The Creation of Inequality*, p. 91 ff.

[123] FLANNERY, K., MARCUS, J., *The Creation of Inequality*, p. 61 ff. For DIAMOND, J., *Guns, Germs, and Steel: A Short History of Everybody for the Last 13,000 Years*, in chapter 14 ("From Egalitarianism to Kleptocracy"), p. 315 ff.: "*Where population densities are high, as in regions occupied by states or chiefdoms, the defeated (…) have nowhere to flee, but the victors now have two options for exploiting them while leaving them alive. Because chiefdoms and state societies have economic specialisation, the defeated can be used as slaves, as commonly happened in biblical times. Alternatively, because many such societies have intensive food production systems capable of yielding large surpluses, the victors can leave the defeated in place but deprive them of political autonomy, make them pay regular tribute in food or goods, and amalgamate their society into the victorious state or chiefdom. This has been the usual outcome of battles associated with the founding of states or empires throughout recorded history*", such as the Roman or Spanish empires.

[124] In chapter 1.5 we learned that the ability to master language extends the human (social) reality and allows us to name (i.e., understand) facts that cannot be perceived simply through the senses. Moreover, we have seen that language allows us to transmit knowledge without the need of direct experience and practice: Abstractions made possible by words can transmit more information, implying the full potential of abstract thinking and understanding (a more complex intellective feature than imitative behaviour).

There are only indirect traces of coexistence and interbreeding between Homo sapiens and Homo neanderthalensis,[125] and it is quite difficult to formulate an explanation for the extinction of the Neanderthal and the successful adaptation of the Homo sapiens.[126]

In a speaking human society, Neanderthals had to go extinct, because their social reality had ceased to exist. They were wordless, unspeakable – an animal society compared to the social reality of Homo sapiens.

Language took away the legitimacy of the speechless humans, transforming them into humanoids, just as apes are to us today.[127]

Language makes us (feel) superior to other animals, as we have seen in chapter 2.3.

I like the hypothesis that the origin of slavery is rooted in the inability of the Neanderthals to speak. Creatures of lesser intellect were bound to physical work and became objects of property. This hypothesis shows how close we are to finding a rational explanation for treating other humans like beasts (if not like inanimate objects) – no matter whether Neanderthals, unbelievers, Negroes, boat people, aboriginals or migrants. We have been able to find (through the use of language and "reasoning") a reason why some rights are reserved for a blessed minority or why some people are human and others just animals.[128]

It is an intriguing hypothesis that Homo sapiens was able to impose on Homo Neanderthalensis a new social order – providing an account of it, rooted in myths and religion, theorising it functionally, explaining it. Maybe the extinction of Homo neanderthalensis was a consequence of the strength of a specific account of reality, and not just of better hunting and military skills.[129] Animals

---

[125] GREEN R.E.et al., *A Draft Sequence of the Neanderthal Genome*, 713; ZIMMER C., *In Neaderthals' DNA, Ancient Human May Have Left Genetic Mark*.

[126] But few doubt that there must be some correlation: FLANNERY, K., MARCUS, J., *The Creation of Inequality*, 5; HARARI Y., N., *Sapiens, a Brief History of Mankind*, 5. I don't have adequate knowledge to support or reject any of the theories for the extinction of Neanderthals (interbreeding or replacement, discussed in the literature cited). What is relevant to this research is that human history is littered with recurring genocides, whose political oversimplification is "the evolution of the species", and this not only in the *Nationalsozialistische Rassenhygiene* laws [*Gesetz zur Verhütung erbkranken Nachwuchses* (GzVeN), 14 July 1933 (RGBl. I S. 529), inspired by the United States' programs of forced sterilisation, and especially by the eugenics laws enacted in California], but also in the storytelling of "human evolution", from apes to what we are now. The German Law for the Prevention of Hereditarily Diseased Offspring, enacted on 14 July 1933, allowed the compulsory sterilisation of any citizen who, according to the opinion of a "Genetic Health Court", suffered from a list of alleged genetic disorders and required physicians to register every case of hereditary illness known to them, except in women over 45 years of age.

[127] MITHEN, S., *The Singing Neanderthals*, 246 ff.

[128] "Thus, food production, and competition and diffusion between societies, led as ultimate causes, via chains of causation that differed in detail but that all involved large dense populations and sedentary living, to the proximate agents of conquest: germs, writing, technology, and centralized political organisation": DIAMOND, J., *Guns, Germs, and Steel: A Short History of Everybody for the Last 13,000 Years*, ch. 14 ("From Egalitarianism to Kleptocracy"), p. 319.

[129] HARARI Y., N., *Sapiens, a Brief History of Mankind*, 15 and 40 f.: The cognitive revolution of Homo sapiens, made him able to transmit larger quantities of information about the world and social

do not fight against reality; even humans don't do it. Most human societies provide an account of reality that makes their given social order "superior" to others. Human societies are ethnocentric.[130] The more complex the given social order, the greater is the need to postulate superiority. Human foragers (the least structured human society, extending barely beyond the family and organized in clans, at most) believe that each human group has different origins and different ancestors; foragers adjust to their neighbours, rather than try to change them.[131]

With this in mind, it is intriguing to imagine that when Homo sapiens started to speak and to justify the superiority of its social order, Neanderthals tried to adapt ... up through enslavement and finally extinction.[132]

This has not been proven, but it is an unsettling hypothesis that will never lose its potency. There will always be people (like Hitler, Stalin and several of today's warlords and religious fanatics) theorizing about others who do not deserve to live in peace because of their race, origin, colour or belief. Slavery among Christians was abolished in the Middle Ages. But for humans who did not share the same religion (and thus the same moral values), slavery was tolerated until the 19th century.

There is another completely different, yet equally provocative explanation for slavery in the society of the speaking humans. Language, at its origin (and thus the human ability to design reality), was not as sophisticated as it is now.

A million years of hunting and gathering plus a few thousand years of agriculture in a settled society did not provide sufficient evolutionary time to yield articulated ideas such as "to work for another person" or "to lease one's time to another person". The most ancient known examples of contractual agreements date back to the third millennium B.C.,[133] and not to 9,000 to 12,000 years ago, when farming began.

Before humans were able to understand an agreement as a source of law, humans already had a clear conception of property and of social hierarchies. Going back 9,000 years, the only way to explain the concept of "working for another person" was to base it on the idea of one person owning the other. The notion of being owned (or owning someone) is as ancient as the social roles

---

relations and to communicate about things that do not exist (such as tribal sprits, nations, limited liability, companies and human rights). All this allowed cooperation between very large numbers of strangers and the rapid innovation in social behaviour that marks human history.

[130] FLANNERY, K., MARCUS, J., *The Creation of Inequality*, 123 ff.

[131] FLANNERY, K., MARCUS, J., *The Creation of Inequality*, 88.

[132] FLANNERY, K., MARCUS, J., *The Creation of Inequality*, 5.

[133] The oldest documented contractual agreement in human history is a fragment of a small tablet discovered in Shuruppak (modern Fara), a city in southern Mesopotamia. There is no date on it, but the format and the cuneiform signs place it in the Early Dynastic 3rd period (c. 2600-2500 B.C.). The document records several objects and the name of the owner, likely confirming an exchange of gifts as part of a contract. (A digital copy of the table's fragment is available at the online archive of UCLA, Tablet Entries).

and moral values that we know exist even in the most archaic and primitive societies of foragers or hunter-gatherers.[134]

This idea is so ingrained in human society that, even now, serfdom has been abolished only by the wealthiest and most evolved legal systems; it still exists where agriculture is the main economic activity.[135]

Do we have the linguistic skills to understand immaterial things such as "intellectual property", "software", "electronic signatures", "digital identities", "digital privacy", "digital freedom"? Do we, after just a few decades?

One may doubt it ....

In early human societies, the focus was on producing food (later also goods and tools), so it was practical to rationalize that some humans were bound to work for others without any compensation – but just for some indirect benefits (shelter and food).

Now that we live in a society where the focus is on exchanging services[136] and information, what could slavery look like? If the slave of the material economy toils in the fields and in the transformation of commodities into goods, what does the slave in the information and communication (ICT) society do?

I would guess that the slave of the ICT society gives away (personal) information (and provides services) for free and in return receives some indirect benefits, like access to a website, participation in a social network, access to other information and services. The most loyal customers (slaves?) receive some discounted direct benefits, like discounts on the purchase of products or services.

The rewards for online customers in the ICT society and the rewards for the slaves of yore are quite similar: indirect, in-kind benefits. For the slaves of the material economy, the in-kind benefits are in goods; for ICT slaves, they are in information and services.

---

[134] Moral values, religion and social roles are the first rules of human society: FLANNERY, K., MARCUS, J., *The Creation of Inequality*, p. 21, 211, and passim.

Similarly also, DIAMOND, J., *Guns, Germs, and Steel: A Short History of Everybody for the Last 13,000 Years*, ch. 14 ("From Egalitarianism to Kleptocracy"), p. 289 ff.

[135] HARARI Y., N., *Sapiens, a Brief History of Mankind*, 92, defines the agricultural revolution (around 9500-8500 B.C.) as "history's biggest fraud": *"Foragers knew the secrets of nature long before the Agricultural Revolution, since their survival depended on an intimate knowledge of the animals they hunted and the plants they gathered. Rather than heralding a new era of easy living, the Agricultural Revolution left farmers with lives generally more difficult and less satisfying than those of foragers. Hunter-gatherers spent their time in more stimulating and varied ways, and were less in danger of starvation and disease. The Agricultural Revolution certainly enlarged the sum total of food at the disposal of humankind, but the extra food did not translate into a better diet or more leisure. Rather, it translated into population explosions and pampered elites. The average farmer worked harder than the average forager, and got a worse diet in return. The Agricultural Revolution was history's biggest fraud."*

DIAMOND, J., *Guns, Germs, and Steel: A Short History of Everybody for the Last 13,000 Years*, 110, also stresses that the agricultural revolution didn't benefit everybody and was the beginning of a society of castes that, in some regions, extends to the present day.

[136] The service industry in OECD economies is about 70% of gross domestic product. In rich nations it is close to 80% of GDP; the world average is about 60%: https://www.cia.gov/library/publications/resources/the-world-factbook/fields/214.html.

Somehow our role in the ICT society resembles that of chickens in a chicken farm: We involuntarily provide throughout our lives the goods that are commercially exploited by others. But this is not how we perceive it. We somehow believe that we get more than we give away.

And probably so did slaves 5,000 years ago: They were simply incapable, as we are today, of even dreaming of a different organisation of reality.

We will see in chapter 1.4 that the slave trade flourished until the 19th century, because unpaid human labour was more productive than any other way of producing goods. Technological innovation, and in particular industrialisation and machine tools, freed the slaves. Without such innovations there would have been no abolitionist movement in the United Kingdom or the United States.[137] They were abolitionist because they could afford to be. A century earlier, in 1772, public opinion in England was divided about the Somerset case, ruled on by the Lord Chief Justice of the King's Bench, William Murray, 1st Earl of Mansfield. In his ruling one can read, *"The setting 14,000 or 15,000 men at once free loose by a solemn opinion, is much disagreeable in the effect it threatens."*[138] It became a landmark ruling, but in its reasoning, it is more than ambiguous. Lord Mansfield formally denied that his ruling had as a consequence the freeing of thousands of slaves in England.[139] Still, many contemporaries and succeeding generations accepted the accounts of the journals, in particular the Boston Gazette and Middlesex Journal, which incorrectly reported the conclusion of the case.[140]

The ruling of Lord Mansfield in the Somerset case is considered a landmark ruling against slavery. Reading it, one realises how hesitant the judge and, thus, the law were about freeing slaves. Ultimately the law freed the slaves, but not before technological innovation had dramatically increased the productivity of human labour, making slavery uneconomical.

So we may conclude that our condition, as involuntary and unpaid producers of raw materials for the ICT society, can be upended only by technological innovations, not just by (data protection) laws.

2.6. The natural consequences of property: the natural evolution of law

At the beginning of settled life, there was property. Property was known long before there was a formalized state or legal system. It dates back to the origins

---

[137] In the Civil War, the industrialized North of the United States was abolitionist and the agricultural South was in favour of slavery.

[138] WATSON A., *Lord Mansfield; Judicial Integrity or its Lack; Somerset's Case*, 226; HEWARD E., *Lord Mansfield*, 73; and NADELHAFT J., *The Somersett Case and Slavery*, 193; these studies of the Somerset case discuss the concerns of public opinion and of merchants about the consequences of a ruling against slavery.

[139] NADELHAFT J., *The Somersett Case and Slavery*, 193.

[140] NADELHAFT J., *The Somersett Case and Slavery*, 194.

of human society:[141] Hunter-gatherers and foragers have (almost without exception) a moral code against greed and accumulation.[142]

The first contract in Roman law was the "*sponsio*", which was a verbal agreement. Later, lawyers invented rules that made it possible to transfer property for a limited period of time (usufruct/lease). As language evolved, contracts grew to include the leasing of objects and, finally, to the lease of work (*locatio operae*).

Fundamentally, the different contracts and rights were a derivation of the sales agreement:

1) First, the concept of property was limited in time,
2) then in geographic extension,
3) and finally, in its nature.

It became possible to transfer rights that were minor or essentially different from property, just temporarily or for a given scope of time.

Language reaches its greatest creative potential when used for legal purposes. If we watch a person handing over an object to someone else, we cannot sense the legal implication of such a handover. It may be a donation, a restitution, a sale, a lease, a bailment, a borrowing, etc. Only through linguistic elaboration on the meaning of the handover can we understand its purpose and implications.

In law, language does not just represent reality; it creates its own reality. Legal evolution requires changes in the meaning of words and, with that, their social acceptance. Law evolves with humanity, redefining itself and what humanity stands for.

As long as human life and society were mostly about physical objects (whose use and possibility of being shared were limited by their physical characteristics), property was (rightly and aptly) the archetype of all rights: exclusive, perpetual, and enforceable against everybody. Property assumes, as a matter of fact, the impossibility of unlimited sharing. It must be defendable against illicit use, or it is worthless.

Now, humans deal with (digital) objects that, through ubiquitous computing, inherently allow for unlimited sharing. Is property still the cornerstone of all rights?

And if not, what is the new archetypal right?

For some, it is unlimited open sharing (as in the hunter-gatherer's society). This is the take of the open-source community.

For others it is the lease: limited in time and extension. This is the take of those who believe that a proper reform of intellectual property rights will do the trick, finding a better, more nuanced balance between the exclusive rights of the intellectual property rights owner and the rights of the public. Here,

---

[141] LEE R.B. and DALY R., *The Cambridge Encyclopedia of Hunters and Gatherers*, loc. 731; FLANNERY, K., MARCUS, J., *The Creation of Inequality*, 23 and 56.

[142] LEE R.B. and DALY R., *The Cambridge Encyclopedia of Hunters and Gatherers*, loc. 765

the model looks similar to the rules governing common pastures and fishing grounds in archaic societies.[143]

A more balanced approach would be to combine ownership and openness, as the Creative Commons organisation has done – simplifying and rationalizing the regulation of intellectual property rights (IPRs), and creating a taxonomy of open (and less open) IPRs[144].

One thing is certain: Property is not the cornerstone of the natural law of a digital society.

In chapters 8.1 and 8.5 we will see that the starting point of a natural law of a digital society is the digital identity.

---

[143] It is somehow odd that the model for future digital rights would be derived from a system that is peculiar to poor and static social enclaves.

[144] Creative Commons.

https://emperorx.bandcamp.com/album/10000-year-earworm-to-discourage-settlement-near-nuclear-waste-repositories

3. Orality vs. Literacy

We live in a world where written documents have long been the main tool for recording and disseminating knowledge. Books have been "real culture", and movies, comics, videos and, of course, the Internet are "superficial", ephemeral, or "pseudo-cultural". Today, children may hide from their parents when they play videogames (or watch TV), just as their great-grandparents had to hide to read romantic literature (Dumas, Proust, Verne …). Today's scholars, scientists and parents are all worried about the risks of not reading enough and the consequences of playing too many videogames.

The syllogism "knowledge = written" already dates back half a millennium. Look at Raphael's fresco "The School of Athens" (1509-1511)[145] in the Vatican: It depicts the most famous Greek philosophers, most of them living in the time of oral tradition, and some of them (Socrates and Plato) deeply averse to teaching and learning through writing.

Yet Raphael, in order to make their wisdom unmistakable, puts in their hands scrolls and writing instruments. The fresco dates just 70 years after the invention of the printing press!

To properly understand these issues, let's first look at oral tradition and what written culture consists of.

Then we'll analyse how much of our knowledge comes from written documents and how much from things that we hear or see (as in the time of oral tradition). Finally, we should try to avoid aprioristic moral judgments on what is "right" or "good": Good and right depend on the reference model.

Let's look at how culture and role models presently[146] "work" in human society.

---

[145] Wikipedia, "*The School Of Athens*".

[146] If our reference model is the world as it was, our judgment is biased, because in essence we are dreaming of reversing developments that have already changed human society. If the reference model is some moral *a priori*, we will provide answers that are not satisfying to those who do not

In a hunter-gatherer society, the "great hunter" is the role model. In an aristocratic/oligarchic pre-industrial society, the military hero is the role model. In mercantile society, the role model is the merchant, and so on.

Who are the role models of a digital society? A pony-tailed, junk-food-eating hacker? Mark Zuckerberg? Steve Jobs? Vince Cerf? Edward Snowden? You name it .... The fact is that we don't know for sure.

Let's take an in-depth look at how knowledge is created and disseminated in a digital society, before stating what is good or bad knowledge, or what's the preferred way to acquire and disseminate knowledge. This way of looking at things opens surprising new perspectives.

A great deal of our knowledge still comes from "hear-seeing". The Internet has made the border between written and oral almost unrecognizable, so that sometimes we mix them up. Is an SMS a written text or a verbal communication, muted and "subtitled" on a phone screen? If I record a message that is transformed into text by an application for the hearing impaired, is it written or verbal? And what if I write a text and it is spoken to the addressee by a machine? What is it: written or verbal? And what of a text with images and sounds? Or pictures in motion overwritten by a text?

Before jumping to any conclusions, we must carefully analyse commonplace items, to find if there is some truth in them, or if they are misleading. If we examine oral history, we learn that it belongs to a particular mindset that is obliterated as soon as one becomes (even moderately) literate. On the other hand, if we study literacy, we understand that most of our knowledge is still conveyed to us by oral means. Still, **literacy has had a profound impact on human society**, allowing for a progressive increase in the abstraction of our social reality.

First, in **oral societies**, there was property.[147] You could almost see it and almost touch it. You could mark it. The oath followed as a means to the peaceful exchange of property. Subsequently, in **literate societies**, abstractions of the idea of property started to become tradable: usufructs, leases, mortgages, etc. After that, the concept of credit was used in legal transactions: that is, the legally enforceable expectation of being presented with some object. Later, it became one's right to expect a precise behaviour on the part of the debtor, and one had the right to become proprietor of something (be it an object or the outcome of a behaviour). Still more abstract was a possibility - established in the Middle Ages – to trade in papers representing credits (of money, goods or services). After that, it became possible to incorporate an entire enterprise on

---

accept any moral *a priori*, like utilitarians and materialists. If we choose a moral reference model that is not shared by an overwhelming majority (like Christendom, Confucianism or Kant's moral imperatives), it will simply make any judgment subjective, fallacious and practically useless.

On the other hand, a reference model is not valid simply because it is shared by a vast majority. The vast majority supported Hitler, Stalin and Mussolini (and many other past and present vicious dictators). This did not provide them with any moral legitimation. It simply allowed them to wield unrestricted power, until it was too late to stop them.

We will address the thorny issue of justice in chapter 5.5, "Justice in the 21st Century".

[147] See chapter 2.4.

a piece of paper, with limited liability shares, as first issued by the Dutch East Indies Company in 1601.

At this point, it's obvious that **the levels of abstraction are potentially unlimited**, so that even derivatives and other structured financial services can be securitized.[148] Securitisation is the financial practice of pooling various types of contractual debt, such as residential mortgages, commercial mortgages, auto loans or credit card debt obligations (or other non-debt assets which generate receivables), and selling their related cash flows to third-party investors as securities, which may be described as bonds, pass-through securities, or collateralized debt obligations (CDOs). Investors are repaid from the principal and from interest cash flows collected from the underlying debt and redistributed through the capital structure of the new financing. Securities backed by mortgage receivables are called mortgage-backed securities (MBS), while those backed by other types of receivables are asset-backed securities (ABS).

The oral society swore oaths to close agreements, while the literate society recorded verbal agreements in written documents. Once this became custom, the legal practice fragmented the content of the contractual agreement into different utilities that can be negotiated separately and are represented by another piece of paper: letters of credit, promissory bills, shares, futures. A new tier of documentation is added every time a new layer of abstraction is appended to the documents: documents that represent (parts of) documents that represent (parts of) documents … that represent (parts of) documents.

Humanity has needed about 6000 years to establish property and the legal validity of the written agreement under the rule of law, which are the first three layers of any legal system. In the following 2000 years, we have added several dozens of additional layers of abstractions (money, companies, trusts, obligations, credits, letters of credit, etc.). **With information technology, the layers of legal abstraction have ballooned almost infinitely, and well beyond the human ability to understand or manage them.**

3.1. The Oral Society

What, exactly, is orality?

Walter J. Ong devoted his life to the study of orality. His *Orality vs. Literacy*[149] is a masterpiece, describing vividly how the way we communicate influences the way we think and understand reality.

According to Ong,[150] "primary orality" refers to thought and its verbal expression within cultures that remain "totally untouched by any knowledge of writing and print".

---

[148] The definition of "securitisation" can be found at Wikipedia, "*Securitization*". Critics have suggested that the complexity inherent in securitisation can limit investors' ability to monitor risk, and that competitive securitisation markets with multiple securities may be particularly prone to sharp declines in underwriting standards. Private, competitive mortgage securitisation played an important role in the U.S. subprime mortgage crisis.

[149] ONG, W.J., *Orality and Literacy*.

[150] ONG, W.J., *Orality and Literacy*, 11.

"Residual orality" refers to thought and its verbal expression in cultures that have been exposed to writing and print, but have not fully "interiorised" the use of these technologies in people's daily lives.

Is there any culture that has fully interiorised writing?

Drawing on hundreds of studies, ranging from anthropology to linguistics and the study of oral tradition, Ong summarizes 10 key aspects of the "psychodynamics of orality". While these key aspects are subject to continuous debate, his list remains an important milestone. Ong draws his examples from both primary oral societies and societies with a very high "oral residue". Let's address Ong's most relevant revelations:

1) **Formulaic styling.**[151] To retain complex ideas requires that they be memorably packaged for easy recall. To effectively solve the problem of retaining and retrieving carefully articulated thought, you have to do your thinking in mnemonic patterns, shaped for ready oral recurrence. Your thoughts must come into being in heavily rhythmic, balanced patterns, in repetitions, alliterations or assonances, epithetic and other formulaic expressions. Serious thought is intertwined with memory systems.[152]

2) **Additive rather than subordinative**. Oral cultures avoid complex "subordinative" clauses. Ong[153] cites an example from the Douay-Rheims version of Genesis (1609–10), noting that this basic additive pattern (in italics) has been identified in many oral contexts around the world: "*In the beginning God created heaven and earth. And the earth was void and empty, and darkness was on the face of the deep; and the spirit of God moved over the waters. And God said ...*"

Demonstrating how oral modes of communication tend to evolve into literate ones, Ong additionally cites the New American Bible (1970), which offers a translation that is grammatically far more complex: "*In the*[154] *beginning, when God created the heavens and the earth, the earth was a formless wasteland, and darkness covered the abyss, while a mighty wind swept over the waters. Then God said ...*"

3) **Aggregative rather than analytic**. Oral expression brings words together in pithy phrases that are the product of generations of evolution: the "sturdy oak tree", the "beautiful princess" or "clever Odysseus". This does not apply specifically to poetry or song; rather the words are brought together out of habit during general communication. "Analysing" or breaking apart such expressions adds complexity to communications and questions received wisdom.

Ong cites an American example, noting that in some parts of the United States with heavy oral residue, it is still considered normal or even obligatory to use the adjective "glorious" when referring to the "Fourth of July".

4) **Redundant or "copious"**. Speech that repeats earlier thoughts or thought-pictures, or shines a different light on them somehow, helps to keep both the speaker and the listener focused on the topic, and makes it easier for all to

---

[151] ONG, W.J., *Orality and Literacy*, 33.
[152] ONG, W.J., *Orality and Literacy*, 129.
[153] ONG, W.J., *Orality and Literacy*, 36.
[154] ONG, W.J., *Orality and Literacy*, 38.

recall the key points later. "Oral cultures encourage fluency, fulsomeness, volubility. Rhetoricians were to call this *copier*."[155]

5) **Conservative or traditionalist**. Because oral societies have no effective access to writing or print technologies, they must invest considerable energy in basic information management. Storage of information, being primarily dependent on individual or collective recall, must be handled with particular thrift. It is possible to approximately measure oral residue "from the amount of memorisation the culture's educational procedures require."[156]

This creates incentives to avoid exploring new ideas[157] and particularly to avoid the burden of having to store them. It does not prevent oral societies from demonstrating dynamism and change, but there is a premium on ensuring that changes cleave to traditional formulas and "are presented as fitting the traditions of the ancestors."

6) **Close to the human lifeworld**. Oral cultures take a practical approach to information storage. To qualify for storage, information must usually concern matters of immediate practical concern or familiarity to most members of the society. Long after the invention of writing, and often long after the invention of printing, basic information on how to perform a society's most important trades was left unwritten, passed from one generation to the next as it always had been – through apprenticeship, observation and practice. Primary oral culture is little concerned with preserving knowledge of skills in an abstract, self-subsistent corpus.[158]

By contrast, only literary cultures have launched phenomenological analyses, abstract classifications, ordered lists and tables, etc. Nothing analogous exists in oral societies.

7) **Agonistically toned**. Writing fosters abstraction that disengages knowledge from the arena where human beings struggle with one another. It separates the known from the knower.[159] "Agonistic", for Ong, means "combative". Ong actually advances a deeper thesis with this point. Writing and, to an even greater extent, printing, he argues, disengage humans from direct, interpersonal struggle. Products of "the highly polarized, agonistic, oral world of good and evil, virtue and vice, villains and heroes", the great works of oral literature from Homer to Beowulf, from the Mwindo epic of the Congo to the Old Testament, are extremely violent by modern standards. They are also punctuated by frequent and intense intellectual combat and tongue lashings on the one hand, and effusive praise (perhaps reaching its height among African praise singers) on the other.

8) **Empathetic and participatory**, rather than objectively distanced.[160] For an oral culture, learning or knowing means achieving close, empathetic, communal identification with the known,[161] "getting with it". Writing separates the

---

[155] ONG, W.J., *Orality and Literacy*, 40.
[156] ONG, W.J., *Orality and Literacy*, 41.
[157] ONG, W.J., *Orality and Literacy*, 41.
[158] ONG, W.J., *Orality and Literacy*, 42.
[159] ONG, W.J., *Orality and Literacy*, 42.
[160] ONG, W.J., *Orality and Literacy*, 45.
[161] HAVELOCK E. A., PLATO, *Preface to Plato*, 145-146.

knower from the known and thus sets up conditions for "objectivity", in the sense of personal disengagement or distancing.

Ong cites a study of community decision-making from 12th century England.[162] Writing already had a long history in England, and it would have been possible to use texts to establish, for example, the age of majority of the heir to an estate. But people were sceptical about texts, noting not only the cost of generating and managing them, but the problems involved in preventing tampering or fraud. As a result, they retained the traditional solution: gathering together "mature, wise seniors of many years, having good testimony", and publicly discussing the age of the heir with them, until agreement was reached. This hallmark principle of orality, that truth emerges best from communal process, resonates today in the jury system.

9) **Homeostatic**. By contrast with literate societies, oral societies live very much in the present, which keeps itself in equilibrium (or homeostasis) by sloughing off memories which no longer have present relevance.

Oral cultures of course have no dictionaries and few semantic discrepancies. The oral mind is uninterested in definitions.[163] Words acquire their meaning only from their always-insistent actual habitat, which is not, as in a dictionary, simply other words, but includes also gestures, vocal inflections, facial expressions, and the entire human, existential setting in which the real, spoken word always occurs. Word meaning always come out of the present, though past learning has, of course, shaped the present meaning in many and varied ways, no longer recognized.[164]

10) **Situational rather than abstract**. Oral cultures tend to use concepts in situational, operational frames of reference that are minimally abstract, in the sense that they remain close to the living, human world. Pre-Socratic Greeks thought of justice in operational, rather than formally conceptualized, ways.[165] Studies of illiterate and moderately literate individuals conducted by A.R. Luria in Uzbekistan from 1931 to 1932 provide some findings that are of great interest:

a) Illiterate (oral) subjects identified geometrical figures by assigning them the name of objects, never abstractly as circles, squares, etc.; moderately literate subjects (like primary school students), identified geometric figures by categorical geometric names[166].

b) Illiterate subjects group objects around existential and practical groupings, and don't grasp or memorize abstract distinctions like "tools" and "objects to be worked on by tools"; they all belong to the category "work".[167]

c) Illiterate subjects do not operate with formal deductive procedures at all. This is not to say that they cannot think, or that their thinking is not governed

---

[162] ONG, W.J., *Orality and Literacy*, 92-94.
[163] ONG, W.J., *Orality and Literacy*, 45.
[164] ONG, W.J., *Orality and Literacy*, 46.
[165] HAVELOCK E.A., *The Greek Concept of Justice*; ONG, W.J., *Orality and Literacy*, 48.
[166] LURIA R. A., *Cognitive Development*, 32 ff.; ONG, W.J., *Orality and Literacy*, 49.
[167] LURIA R. A., *Cognitive Development*, 54 and 67 ff.; ONG, W.J., *Orality and Literacy*, 50.

by logic; but they do not fit their thinking into pure logical forms, which they find uninteresting (because it is unrelated to practical reality).[168]

d) Illiterate subjects resist any request for a definition of even the most concrete objects: "Why should I try to define a tree? Everyone knows a tree!"[169]

e) Illiterates had difficulty articulating self-analysis. Self-analysis requires a certain demolition of situational thinking. It calls for the isolation of the self, around which the entire world swirls for each individual. Illiterates had trouble removing themselves from the centre of every situation enough to allow the centre, the self, to be examined and described.[170]

In describing the characteristics of orality, we have used the words of Walter J. Ong, because they are compelling in the way they describe the "oral mind". In reading them, it becomes quite obvious how (printed) paper has shaped our minds and our ability to perceive and understand reality. It also provides a hint of how many things will change (or have already changed) in our minds, when we read or watch digital content or interact "live" with distant people (or machines).

Simply, we learn from Ong that our "oral brain" is completely different from our "literate brain", which forces us to consider the distinctive features of the human "digital brain".

3.2. The Literate Society

We believe that we learn through written texts (textbooks, syllabuses, manuals, etc.). This belief is quite misleading. Schools and universities are still modelled on the Greek gymnasium, where the master taught his pupils by engaging in dialogues with them. Textbooks should (in theory) only help in rehearsing a lesson and are not meant to be a substitute for it.

Furthermore, a great deal of our knowledge of the world in which we live comes from the radio, television and other multimedia channels. Today, with YouTube and other sharing services, we even have "broadcasting on demand". And finally, the most important decision-making processes legally or socially codified today (cabinet meetings, parliamentary sessions, board meetings, assemblies, family gatherings), still require[171] that people convene synchronously in a single place, to discuss and to deliberate "together", "face to face". To properly grasp the impact of digitalisation, one must understand how orality has mutated; it is still alive, and it interacts with the dissemination of knowledge via written text.

---

[168] Luria R. A., *Cognitive Development*, 108 ff.; Ong W. J., *Orality and Literacy*, 51.

[169] Luria R. A., *Cognitive Development*, 90 ff.; Ong W. J., *Orality and Literacy*, 52.

[170] Luria R. A., *Cognitive Development*, 136 ff.; Ong W. J., *Orality and Literacy*, 53.

[171] ... well... at least until the Covid-19 pandemic: judicial trials and even legislative sessions have been held remotely or by proxy, for reducing social contacts and limit the spreading of the virus. With very few exceptions (some Parliaments and the German notaries) legislation has recognized everywhere the functional equivalence of virtual meetings to physical face to face meetings, at least temoprarily.

How many people read (and how many understood) Karl Marx's *Das Kapital*[172] (*Kritik der politischen Ökonomie*), a work spanning three tomes and over 2,500 pages? How many fought and died for the ideas of communism? The ideas embraced by communism (and so also those embraced by democracy or fascism or, most evidently, Christendom) are spread (mostly) by word of mouth and not (only) by the reading of primary sources.

The consequences of writing in human society have been extensively studied by scholars. Writing establishes what is called "context-free" language[173] or "autonomous" discourse.[174]

It takes only a moderate degree of literacy to make a tremendous difference in thought processes, as demonstrated by Luria's study of illiterate and somewhat literate persons.[175]

Like the oracle or prophet of the oral tradition,[176] the book relays an utterance from a source, the one who really "said" or wrote the book. The author might be challenged if only he or she could be contacted, but the author cannot be contacted in any book. There is no way to refute the text directly. After a total and absolutely devastating refutation, the book still says exactly the same thing as before. This is why "the book says", is tantamount to, "it is true". This also offers one reason why books have sometimes been burnt.[177]

Even before printing, the act of writing itself encouraged a sense of poetic closure. By isolating a thought on a written page, detached from any interlocutor, delivering an utterance (in a sense) autonomous and indifferent to attack, writing presents utterance and thought as uninvolved with all else, somehow self-contained and complete.[178]

By contrast, manuscripts, with their glossaries and marginal commentary (which was often worked into the text in subsequent volumes) carried on a dialogue outside their own borders. They stayed closer to the give and take of oral expression. The reader of a manuscript is less closed off from the author, less absent, than the reader of a printed books. Print is curiously intolerant of physical incompleteness.[179]

In the strictest sense of the word, writing, as the technology that has shaped and powered the intellectual activity of modern man, was a very late development in human history. Homo sapiens has been on earth for some 50,000

---

[172] MARX K., *Das Kapital*. In 1867, the first edition of the book was published with a printing of 1,000 copies; the second was 3,000. Each successive printing involved between 1,000 and 10,000 copies. See Karl Marx Online Archive, *Alcuni Dati Sulla Fortuna Del 'Capitale' Di Marx*.

[173] HIRSCH E. D., *The Philosophy of Composition*, 21-23 and 26.

[174] OLSON D. R., *On the language and the authority of textbooks*, 186-96.

[175] LURIA R. A., *Cognitive Development*, 29 ff.; ONG, W.J., *Orality and Literacy*, 49.

[176] The Delphic oracle was not responsible for her oracular utterances, for they were the voice of the gods; the oracle was just the channel, not the source. ONG, W.J., *Orality and Literacy*, 77.

[177] ONG, W.J., *Orality and Literacy*, 78.

[178] ONG, W.J., *Orality and Literacy*, 129.

[179] ONG, W.J., *Orality and Literacy*, 130.

to 75,000 years.[180] The earliest script, or true writing, discovered thus far, was developed among the Sumerians in Mesopotamia around 3500 B.C.[181]

Writing is a skill (a technology) that was developed and perfected by highly hierarchical human societies.[182] So writing was probably used as a tool to make something objective and, at the same time unobjectionable. It was particularly relevant for the ruling elite, not for the masses.

Perhaps the most legendary account of a struggle for written laws comes from Roman history: the Secessiones Plebis (494-493 B.C.; 451-449 B.C.; 445 B.C.; 376-371 B.C.), protests staged by the commoners to demand more equal justice and written laws. This led to the first written codification of civil laws, the *duodecim tabularum leges*, in 450 B.C. The moral purpose behind it was that written rules could not be manipulated to the advantage of the ruling aristocracy.

Nonetheless, in a world where fewer than 10% of people were able to read, where parchment and vellum were rare and extremely expensive (costing many times more than a computer today), writing was mostly a tool for the authorities. Commoners could not afford to pay for written documents and were generally incapable of reading them.

Most people are surprised, and many distressed, to learn that essentially the same objections commonly levelled against computers were brought up by Plato in the *Phaedrus*[183] and in the *Seventh Letter*[184] against writing. "Writing", Plato has Socrates say in the *Phaedrus*, "is inhuman. Pretending to establish outside the mind what in reality can only be in the mind. It is a thing, a manufactured product."

The same is said today about computers.[185]

If you ask a person to explain his or her statement, you can get an explanation; if you ask a text, you get back nothing except the same, often stupid, words that called for your question in the first place. In the modern critique of the computer, the same objection is often stated, "Garbage in, garbage out."[186]

Plato's Socrates, in keeping with the antagonistic mentality of oral cultures, also holds a grudge against writing. His philosophy argues that the written word cannot defend itself as well as the spoken word. Real speech and thought always exist in a context of give and take between living beings. Writing is passive, and out of it may come an unreal, unnatural world.

Last but not least, the author can hide behind a text. You never really know who wrote a text, just as you also cannot be sure that a text shown to you is not a forgery.

It cannot be disputed that a written text is ontologically unilateral, one-to-many. It is broadcasting on paper. It's a unilateral bully pulpit: No dialogue is

---

[180] LEAKEY R. E. LEWIN R., *People of the Lake: Mankind and its Beginnings*, 141 and 168.

[181] ONG, W.J., *Orality and Literacy*, 82.

[182] See chapter 2.3.

[183] PLATO, *Phaedrus*, 274-7.

[184] PLATO, *Seventh Letter*, 341b–345c.

[185] ONG W.J., *Orality and Literacy*, 78.

[186] Defenders of "Big Data" believe that huge amounts of data can produce some deeper understanding of social phenomena. It is a contentious subject, criticized by those skeptical of Big Data, as you will read in chapter 7.3.

possible, no mutual understanding, no feedback. Writing (on paper) is intrinsically authoritarian.

All these objections found in Plato against written texts have been used to criticize the use of computers. Some of this criticism is still reiterated now, even as computing has become part of our social reality and an essential part of how we express ourselves, as pervasive as talking and even more than writing.

Information technology today, if properly designed, could combine the advantages of writing (an objective text) with those of orality (dynamic communication and open dialectical discussion). It could, but it doesn't.

So as an author, I am stuck here on the other side of a book, unilaterally presenting my "knowledge". But it would be much better to have an open discussion, considering the topics at hand. In chapter 8.2 we will analyse the new semiotics (and IT features) needed for to achieve truly interactive written communication.

3.3. Ontology of Documents. (Digital) Traces, Recordings, Inscriptions, Documents

We live in a literate society, but there is not much you can find in the way of an ontological definition of "document". Legislation and literature mostly rely on some unproven assumptions.

It is necessary to have a proper definition of document if we want to have all the cognitive tools that are needed to understand the changes that digitalisation has brought, and will bring, to our society.

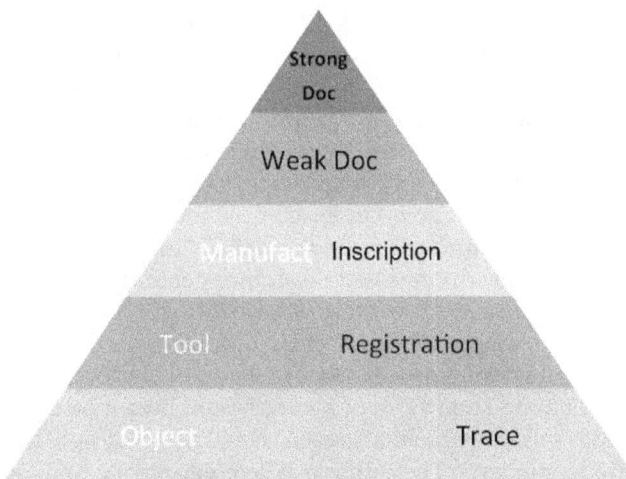

I think that the best ontological definition of documents is found in *Documentality: Why It Is Necessary to Leave Traces (Commonalities)*, by Maurizio Ferraris.[187]

---

[187] First published in 2009 as FERRARIS M., *Documentalità: Perché è necessario lasciar tracce*. Translated into English by Richard Davies and published by Fordham University Press in December 2012 as FERRARIS M., *Documentality: Why It Is Necessary to Leave Traces (Commonalities)*.

Documents are at the top of a layered pyramid of signs. On the left side, we have the escalation of objects towards documents, and on the right side we have the escalation of signs towards documents. At the apex, documents and objects merge: a banknote or a passport are at the same time objects and documents. Marcel Duchamp's *Bicycle Wheel* is an object and a document.[188]

At the bottom of the pyramid on the side of signs, we have the **trace.**[189] This is a sign that has been generated by events, with no meaning, intention or purpose. In information technology, the only example of a trace is the trace left by deleted data in a memory device.

At the next level, we have the **recording,**[190] in which a trace is generated on a medium that is (ontologically) designed to retain the trace over time – like the recordings made by a running camera or a microphone, or like something that is passively memorized by the brain. Recordings must be accessible to at least one person. They are not created with a specific meaning or purpose; they simply exist on a medium that is designed for the purpose of recording facts. The difference between a trace and a recording is the functional nature (or intrinsic meaning) of the medium: A wall shows the trace of a flood; on a hydrometer, the same trace is a recording. In the digital environment, recordings are all digital data generated by a given information technology system, without the aim of being seen by anyone other than the system administrator (and only eventually).

At the next level we have **inscriptions,**[191] where the recording is ontologically accessible to more than one person: Inscriptions are recordings that are made specifically for the purpose of being read by more than one person. The intention of the author is both to make the inscription and to make it accessible. An inscription has no inherent semantic aim. The author of the inscription does not want anything more than to leave a sign and make it available to at least one more person. The intention behind leaving the sign differentiates inscriptions from recordings. In the digital environment, inscriptions are organized data that is stored together to provide information not only to the system administrator, but also to other authorized individuals (like auditors, experts, etc.). Their most common form are so-called "audit trails".

Documents are inscriptions that the author generates in order to convey a specific semantic message.[192] If there is a further aim of having a socially recognized effect, then we may speak of legal documents (or strong documents). If the aim of the document is simply to convey specific information to at least one additional person (think of an encrypted love message), with no socially recognized consequence whatsoever, then we may simply speak of documents (or weak documents). The difference between strong and weak documents is of huge social importance. Strong documents may have to be generated in a formal context; they may have to use language that is formally accepted by

---

[188] Wikipedia, *Bicycle Wheel*.
[189] FERRARIS M., *Documentalità*, loc. 4539.
[190] FERRARIS M., *Documentalità*, loc. 4645.
[191] FERRARIS M., *Documentalità*, loc. 3518.
[192] FERRARIS M., *Documentalità*, loc. 5019.

the social context (in order to avoid ambiguity); they may need to possess an author who is defined or definable; they may need to possess a recipient who is defined or definable; and they may need to fulfil specific formal requirements. But most importantly of all, the meaning of a strong document is determined by its social context, and its individual intention may become just one of the factors that determines its final meaning.[193]

In the digital world, texts, images and sounds may be generated at random, in an uncontrolled manner, and still look precisely like text, image or sound that has been intentionally generated.

It is possible to tell the difference between a digital recording (or inscription or trace) and a digital document only if trustworthy information about the generation process is available. Currently, in the digital environment, we have such detailed information when recordings are generated, but not when documents are generated. The explanation for this oddity is that the designers of word processing software have replicated the analogue typewriter, expanding its functionalities, without considering the radical differences between a paper sheet typed mechanically and the generation of a text file. In the analogue world, documents were typed or written by hand, under no particular control or supervision. So word processors (which replicate an enhanced typewriter) don't include any reliable audit trail function.

In the analogue world, recordings could be generated only by machines (video cameras or other recording devices, automated stamps, etc.).[194] In an analogue world, it was easy to distinguish recordings from (human-generated) documents: A typed sheet of paper could not be a recording (before the invention of the Xerox copier), while audio and video recordings were always recordings, with the easily recognisable (and copyright-protected) exception of artistic productions (e.g., movies, TV and radio shows, music recordings), which were documents. In the analogue world, humans could not generate recordings. Whenever someone personally copies or writes something down (even using a computer), or if they sing or dance, it is never a recording. It is ontologically an intentional activity, which, as a consequence, generates inscriptions or documents – never recordings.

As we have shifted into a fully digital environment, things have become radically different: It is all but impossible to tell apart registrations and documents just by looking at them. In the digital environment, even what we call "documents" are a mixture of recordings generated automatically (size, date, format of the file, etc.) with what we intentionally write. If anybody opens a PDF or Word file as a .txt file, they would see hundreds of lines of text automatically generated by the software. Therefore, even proper digital documents are a mixture of documents and recordings (normally hidden from and unknown by the author of the digital document).[195]

---

[193] There is a striking symmetry between Ferraris' document of dualism weak vs. strong and Sebeok's dualism of language and speech.

[194] GENGHINI R., *La forma notarile digitale*, 19.

[195] GENGHINI R., *La forma notarile digitale*, 7.

If we go digital and want to produce strong documents and sign them, we have to take into account the complexity of the systems that handle digital information. When the final outcome is a paper document, the complexity of information technology systems may have some unwanted consequences (like cut-and-paste errors, or the increasing length of legal documents, which have become more difficult to read and understand); but in the end, a sheet of paper is still signed (making it the only original document). The signature on paper means, among other things, that the signer takes full responsibility for the complexity of the tools used to generate the paper document, which is the only original and so, it is assumed, has been read and verified in paper form by the signatory. By controlling the printouts, the signatories bear full responsibility for the transformation of the complexity of the IT systems used to generate the paper document into the static simplicity of the paper document.

A digitally signed document is a whole different story, because the signatories have only indirect control of the digital document – through the complexity of some IT system. They never see or touch it, as with paper documents.

Considering the lack of direct control over signed digital documents, it is essential to have trustworthy IT environments, where digital data is made objective and verifiable, as would be the case on paper. Let's call these environments "**Virtual Signing Rooms**". The Virtual Signing Room is not simply a digital platform for presenting and signing digital files, of which there are many, such as AdobeSign or DocuSign. It is a system that acts as an electronic witness, providing a digital trail for how the digital document has been generated and signed.[196]

First of all, the Virtual Signing Room must compensate for the fact that digital documents aren't directly perceived by the signatories (whereas on paper, they can read the signs marked on the paper with their eyes). In digital documents, the authors have to rely from the beginning (to the bitter end) on the trustworthiness of the information technology systems they have chosen to craft (and read) the document.[197]

Secondly, the Virtual Signing Room must also compensate for the fact that at the moment of signing, further complexity arises. The digital signature process requires that the authors have faith in the correct functioning of several additional pieces of technology.[198]

---

[196] GENGHINI R., *La forma notarile digitale*, 75.

[197] LANDROCK, P., PEDERSEN, T., *WYSIWYS? What you see is what you sign?* in *Information Security Technical Report*, vol. 3, no. 2, 1998, 55-61; SCHEIBELHOFER, K., *Signing XML Documents and the Concept of What You See Is What You Sign*.

[198] What follows are the technologies involved in signing a digital file or document. Most of them have been standardized by the European Telecommunication Standards Institute (ETSI) and are publicly available:

First, the cryptographic algorithms for generating the signatures must be robust in order to avoid forgery. There are several papers on the security of signature algorithms. Here I cite just one that is particularly relevant in Europe, ETSI's TS 119 322 "Algo Paper", ETSI, Electronic Signatures and Infrastructures.

Then, the function for calculating the "unique identifier" of the file to be signed must be "collision resistant". This means that it must be empirically true, that for one file there is one and only one hash.

Without a properly designed Virtual Signing Room, we have a situation in which the control of the author(s) of a digital legal document is even more precarious than signing the box of a video or a CD containing the recording of a legal agreement between interacting parties (or a unilateral declaration of the will of the author). The lack of direct control over the true content of what is presented for signature[199] and the lack of direct control over the signature generation process have consequences: Without proper configuration of a Virtual Signing Room, only "weak documents" (according to the definition of Ferraris) may be digitally signed.[200] And weak documents aren't much of a proof, even when signed!

If not correctly understood, the claim that digital signatures are equivalent to handwritten signatures would mean that when we sign anything, even if it is just a recording or an inscription, we have entered a signed legal contract that we cannot repudiate. In other words, the law would be stating that it is okay to sign a CD or a DVD box in order to generate a legal document, even if we cannot be sure of what is recorded on the CD or DVD.

But it doesn't. The law assumes that the digital signature is being put on a strong document, not on a box that contains some unspecified information about the closing of an agreement. The law does not assume that we might just as well be signing a recording, an inscription or any other kind of weak document.

A digital signature on a recording cannot be functionally equivalent to a handwritten signature, because the content of a recording isn't an intentional act; it is a mere fact. To properly understand the law, when it states that a digital signature has the same value as a handwritten one, we must recognize the unstated, but obvious, requirement that a strong document has been signed. Before digital signatures, we never put our handwritten signature on a recording.

I hope the following example clarifies the difference between a document and a recording: Let's consider the meeting of a board of directors. The five directors discuss the items on the agenda and make decisions. Everything is videorecorded. The five directors then digitally sign the recording.[201] Finally the chairman of the board and one of the directors, acting as secretary, write the minutes for the meeting, reporting on the decisions taken, and digitally sign them.

The security of the signature creation device, for which there is a CEN Standard (CEN CWA 14169) and also Protection Profiles approved by the Senior Official Group for Information Security (SOGIS): https://www.sogis.eu/.

The security of the signature creation application: ETSI EN 319 102-1 and TR 119 100.

The security of the data to be signed: ETSI TR 0019100.

The secure preservation of the signed document, ETSI EN 319 512.

The proper preservation of the digital signatures beyond the time of expiration of the signature certificates and of the signature keys, ETSI EN 319 512.

[199] What we address here is the WYSIWYS issue.

[200] GENGHINI R., *La forma notarile digitale*, 81.

[201] If it is a board of people used to work together, they may address issues and facts in a way that only they can understand, like saying "we enact the second decision with the usual procedure" or "we provide the power of attorney to the same manager as last time", and so on. Taking decisions and documenting them are two distinct activities, that need different wordings.

Which of the two signed files is the document that serves as proof of the decisions made by the board of directors?

The first file, with the videorecording, is richer in information (one may say "more authentic"), but being just a recording, it may not convey unambiguously the decisions taken, because they are embedded in comments, discussions, changes of mind, which will make the recording difficult to interpret. Eventually we may have to watch five hours of recording in order to filter out the five relevant sentences representing the decisions.

The second file, intentionally written by the chairman and the secretary, filters the facts, focusses on the relevant and final decisions, using formalised language and a formalised structure. It may be less complete, even less "authentic", but it is intentional and it provides only (and all) the (legally) relevant facts, information and statements about the board's meeting.

If the chairman and secretary were to generate a third file, cutting and pasting the videorecording so that the file contains only the decisions taken and all other relevant information, we wouldn't have a recording anymore, we would have a strong (video) document, intentionally generated, with the same evidential value as the second file.

I think that this example clarifies the different function and meaning of recordings and documents, in particular the important correlation between intentionality and significance.

A recording can only document a fact that happened, and only indirectly captures the intentions of the people whose words or actions were recorded. In contrast, a document always represents the stated intentions of its author(s). But digital documents aren't perceived or generated by the authors in the same way as paper documents. Information technology must eliminate this gap if we want digital documents to have the same evidential value as paper documents. To objectivise digital documents, the Virtual Signing Room should therefore memorize not only the signed document but also the audit trail of the document's generation process. Only when all these features are in place does a digital legal document have same informational and evidential value of a signed piece of paper. Without the transparency of a Virtual Signing Room, a digital contract is worth much less, because it is impossible to know if it is a strong or a weak document ... because it is impossible to know for sure if it was intentionally generated and signed ... because it lacks the objectivity of a paper document.[202]

The law says that the digital signature is equivalent to the handwritten signature – not that a recording is the same as a document or that a digital file is equivalent to a piece of paper.

We will discuss how to make a digital document equivalent to a paper document (or even more trustworthy) in chapter 8.2. There we will also see that in the digital environment, under certain circumstances, a signed, sealed (and/or timestamped) recording may provide sufficient legal proof of a digital transaction, particularly in highly standardised transactions.

---

[202] GENGHINI R., *La Forma Notarile Digitale*, chapters I.2 and IV.

3.4. A Short History of Strong (Legal) Documents

Strong documents, as we have seen in the previous chapter, are documents that are created intentionally, with a clearly defined social function. Often, strong documents serve such an effective social function, that they create "social objects" (as defined in chapter 1.5.2): Think of money, shares, tickets, birth certificates, etc.

A short history of strong documents is important at this point in this work, because in order to understand how our social and legal reality changes with digitalisation, we need a proper understanding of how strong documents worked before digitalisation. This will help us explore what is really changing (and has already changed) recently.

In following the evolution of strong documents, we can recognize a clear progression. First, oral rules and jurisprudence were the only known law. Written laws followed many centuries later; they became widely accepted, despite a high rate of illiteracy and difficulty in confirming the authenticity of documents. Still, there was and still is a clear difference between a written document that simply records facts (*Notitia*)[203] and a written document that substantiates an agreement (*Charta*).

Once our brains accepted the fact that one's will could be properly represented and safely stored on a piece of written parchment (around the 10th century A.D.), humans became more creative and daring. The written text was no longer just a way to substantiate and preserve a declaration of will in a legally binding form, i.e., to signify the transfer of property, or to regulate its temporary use, or to regulate a contract for work. Documents became themselves objects of contracts, and contracts became objects to be shared or exchanged. This was the birth of the receivable note: letters of credit and promissory notes. There is a high level of sophistication in such abstractions: "In this piece of paper, 10 gulden are incorporated and will be paid only to the due holder." Once this concept was socially and legally accepted, endless levels of abstraction became possible.

About 500 years after the social acceptance of written contracts, the next level of abstraction created the limited liability share – letting you buy a piece of an enterprise, without becoming an entrepreneur, without risking all your assets, and without the obligation of remaining a partner in that venture. Look at how many layers of abstraction are involved in the socially accepted idea that a shareholder can share the profits from a limited liability company, where the goods traded by the company are turned into dividends for the shareholder. In order to make this possible, all the following abstractions have to work together smoothly:
- the contracts and commercial relations between the shareholders and the enterprise (legal abstractions of the exchanges of goods traded by the enterprise with its counterparts)

---

[203] This is, more or less, the signed DVD box from the example in the previous chapter: a means of proof, not a document.

- the enterprise as a legal entity fully separated from its shareholders (and other stakeholders), that is, the limited liability company (a legal fiction, because the limited liability company does not exist in nature, but is a legal abstraction)
- the shareholders: a legal fiction that implies that if one owns a share, then one owns a part of the enterprise
- the share: an abstract concept (or eventually a piece of paper) that represents the ownership of an abstract legal entity, such as the company
- the management: a legal fiction that implies that certain people (the managers) act exclusively on behalf of another (legal) person (i.e., the company) and that all consequences of their actions fall upon the company
- the decision of a meeting of the shareholders to approve the balance sheet: a legal fiction according to which, if the shareholders are duly convened to discuss the balance sheet reported to them by the management of the company, and if such discussion ends with approval, the company will have recorded profits (or losses). The profits are eventually passed on to the shareholders. Losses are kept inside the company and do not affect directly either the shareholders or the management.

In 500 years, humanity has evolved from beginning to accept that a piece of paper is equivalent to the act of expressing verbal consent to a legal agreement, to accepting complex multilayer abstractions, that make it possible for one to enter a contract in India with the East India Company, while some other people share the profits from such acts of trade in London or Amsterdam, with limited liability for the economic risk and no liability at all for any crime that might be committed. As the concept of the contract became more abstract and as social acceptance grew for the idea that a piece of paper can incorporate (not simply represent) the declaration of the mutual consent of the contracting parties, it was just a matter of time before we arrived at almost unlimited levels of abstractions, as with ABSs (asset-backed securities), packed into CDOs (collateralized debt obligations), and all the other derivatives and securities that have become so complex that few are able to understand and manage them properly.[204]

There is a threshold involved in using written text, when it starts to become unreadable for humans, but is still readable by computers. When this point is reached, mixing digital documents and written documents creates a toxic mixture with long-lasting noxious consequences, not much less dangerous or costly than nuclear fallout. If we compare the cost of the 2008 financial crisis unleashed by the securitisation of subprime loans with the damage done by the meltdown of the Fukushima reactor, this becomes evident.

It is clear that without information technology, derivatives and complex securities would be simply impossible.

In my understanding, securities and derivatives are legal and economic structures created in a native digital language, referring (mostly still) to paper-based (or even oral) contracts. The mixture of these ontologically different semantics in a single business case or legal instrument makes them inherently toxic, as we will see in chapter 3.4.7.

---

[204] For a wonderful history of derivatives, see: TETT, G., *Fool's Gold*.

3.4.1. Sacred Scriptures

The sacred scriptures were among the first strong documents.

The ancient Greeks and Romans had oral religions, with no written texts. Their traditions were made possible by a caste of priests who were confined to hieratic places where religious knowledge was administered only by the people belonging to the priest's caste.

Architecture and visual artifacts are present in each sedentary civilisation, serving to create a proper environment for practicing religious rituals and thus transmitting religion.[205]

Still, most religions practiced today have developed sacred scriptures.[206] If we consider how Walter J. Ong described the properties of written documents,[207] it's pretty obvious why religions (and in particular monotheistic religions) have chosen writing as a way to keep records of the fundamental teachings of their theology. As we realized in chapter 3.2, a book has all the semiotic qualities that suit it perfectly as a way to make God's voice heard:

1) It is inhuman.

2) It exists outside of any specific context.

3) It never changes, no matter what the reader says or thinks.

4) It does not listen, waver, blink or shut off, whatever the readers do.

5) It is immanent.

The schism between Catholics and Lutherans in the 15th century can be understood from a different perspective, precisely that of the written vs. the oral tradition of the faith. Catholics didn't want to publish the Bible in print, either in Aramaic or in a Greek or Latin translation. This was because the word of God was not to be interpreted by anyone. Through the weekly rite of Mass,

---

[205] On the general issue of the relationship between architecture and social rules, see PARKER PEARSON M. RICHARDS C., *Architecture and Order: Approaches to Social Space*, loc. 216, with additional bibliographic references. For specific references to religious architecture, see WESCOAT B. D., OUSTERHOUT R. G., *Architecture of the Sacred*, loc. 292.

[206] The oldest known religious texts are the Pyramid texts of Ancient Egypt, which date to 2400-2300 B.C. The earliest known example of the Phoenician alphabet is the inscription on the sarcophagus of King Ahiram of Byblos (at the Sumerian Temple Hymns). The Epic of Gilgamesh from Sumer, originating as early as 2150-2000 B.C., is also one of the earliest literary works that includes various mythological figures. The Rigveda of Hinduism is believed to have been composed between 1700–1100 B.C., making it possibly the world's oldest religious text still in use. The oldest portions of the Zoroastrian Avesta are believed to have been transmitted orally for centuries before they found written form, and although widely differing dates for Gathic Avestan (the language of the oldest texts) have been proposed, scholarly consensus floats at around 1000 B.C. The majority of scholars agree that the Torah's composition took place over centuries. Since the late 19th century, there has been a general consensus about the documentary hypothesis, which suggests that the five books were created in 450 B.C. by combining four originally independent sources, known as the Jahwist, or J (about 900 B.C.); the Elohist, or E (about 800 B.C.); the Deuteronomist, or D, (about 600 B.C.); and the Priestly source, or P (about 500 B.C.). The first scripture printed for wide distribution to the masses was the Diamond Sutra, a Buddhist scripture. It is the earliest recorded example of a dated, printed text, bearing the Chinese calendar date of 11 May 868 A.D.

[207] See chapter 2.4.

God's word is spread and kept unchanged over the centuries.[208] It is the living word. The Church (as a living body of people) is the only possible intermediary between God and a believer.

Lutherans, on the contrary, were convinced that everyone capable of reading should read the Bible in order to access the word of God directly and that we shall not have any intermediary between us and God.

Catholics were in favour of the oral tradition of faith, while Lutherans were in favour of a Christian religion disseminated through writings. This difference of opinion generated a century of religious wars and persecutions in Europe.

3.4.2. Written Laws

The Code of Hammurabi was the Babylonian legal code of Mesopotamia, dating back to about 1772 B.C. It is one of the oldest deciphered writings of significant length in the world. The sixth Babylonian king, Hammurabi, enacted the code, and partial copies exist on a human-sized stone stele and various clay tablets. The code consists of 282 laws, with scaled punishments, prescribing "an eye for an eye, a tooth for a tooth" (*lex talionis*), which were graded depending on social status, i.e., slave vs. free man.[209]

Rome's original Law of the Twelve Tables (*Leges Duodecim Tabularum* or *Duodecim Tabulae*) is lost. We know about its existence through other written documents from Roman lawyers. The Twelve Tables served as the ancient foundation of Roman law. They formed the centrepiece of the constitution of the Roman Republic and the core of the *mos maiorum* ("custom of the ancestors").[210]

If we think back to the semiotic properties of oral tradition and of written documents, as discussed in chapters 3.1 and 3.2, we will come to a deeper understanding of why written laws have been adopted over time:

1) An oral society has a changing set of rules that adapt to the needs of the present and to the qualities of the people involved and finds its equilibrium (homeostasis) in the dialectical contraposition of the interested parties. This is the reason why the apex of the Roman legal system was the decision of the

---

[208] Sebeok theorised that the best way to keep information unchanged over 10,000 years would be an "atomic priesthood". See also POSNER R., *Und in alle Ewigket: Kommunikation Über 10.000 Jahre*, ch. 6.2.

[209] Nearly one-half of the code deals with matters of contract, by establishing (for example) the wages to be paid to an ox driver or a surgeon. Other provisions set the terms of a transaction, by establishing the liability of a builder of a house that collapses, or of a property that is damaged while left in the care of another. A third of the code addresses issues concerning household and family relationships, such as inheritance, divorce, paternity and sexual behaviour. One nearly complete example of the code survives today, on a diorite stele in the shape of a huge index finger, 2.25 m. (7.4 ft) tall.

[210] The Twelve Tables came about between 451 and 449 B.C., as a result of the mythical social struggle between patricians and plebeians, when Rome had about 30,000 citizens. After the expulsion of the last king of Rome, Tarquinius Superbus, the Republic was governed by a hierarchy of magistrates. The Twelve Tables were drawn up on 12 ivory tablets (Livy says bronze) which were posted in the Roman Forum, so all Romans could read and know them. It was not a comprehensive statement of all laws, but a sequence of definitions of various private rights and procedures. The family and various rituals for formal transactions are acknowledged as preexisting by the Twelve Tables.

Tribunal (as it is still in common law systems): The presence of antagonizing interests, actively represented by the conflicting parties, is fully consistent with the oral mind[211] and with the "here and now" approach to knowledge in an oral society.

2) When a social structure becomes more complex and more people are affected by it (say 50,000 people), personal acquaintance becomes unimportant. The rules cannot be traced back to a person whom we personally trust. They become general and abstract. They are trustworthy only if they are formulated in a way that allow general and abstract application. This requires that such rules be put down in writing.

Thus the apparent reason for the adoption of written laws in Rome was the resolution of social conflicts among the ruling elite or between the ruling elite and the commoners. But if we consider that it is impractical (if not ultimately impossible) to regulate a complex social system involving tens of thousands of people with oral rules alone, we may understand the deeper reasons for the adoption of written laws in a society of illiterates. When human society is not held together by personal bonds and individual trust, general and abstract rules become necessary, and their sheer quantity and complexity require a new way to record them, making them accessible, verifiable and enforceable.

When the republic was founded in 509 B.C., the Roman censuses recorded a population of 30,000. By about 270 A.D., the republic, including the city of Rome itself and its immediate surroundings, had already 187,000 inhabitants.[212] It is evident that, at that point in time, personal bonds between the citizens of Rome were not the norm anymore. They had to trust people they had never seen or heard of before. At that point in social evolution, trust could be founded only upon proper rules and procedures, which, in order to be trustworthy, had to be general, abstract, verifiable and knowable. These are semiotic qualities missing in verbal communication and oral tradition, as we saw in chapter 3.1. They are also missing when we share information on today's social networks (see chapters 7.4 and 8.2).

3.4.3. Written Contracts: Tabulae Cerae, Scribae and the Digital Signature

In the previous chapter, we looked at the deeper ontological reasons why a larger state has a compelling need for written documentation of the laws.
But why written contracts?
At that time, the proportion of the Roman population that was able to read was estimated at between 10% and 15%.[213]

---

[211] The law in oral cultures is enshrined in formulaic sayings and proverbs (e.g., "An eye for eye, a tooth for a tooth"), which are not mere jurisprudential decorations, but themselves constitute the law. A judge in an oral culture was often called on to articulate sets of relevant proverbs, out of which he could produce equitable decisions in cases under formal litigation. Ong, W.J., *Orality and Literacy*, 35.

[212] Gabba, E., Schiavone, E., *Storia di Roma*, vol. IV, 26.

[213] Harris W. V., *Ancient Literacy*, p. 78.

A written document for an illiterate is threatening: He cannot dispute it, because he cannot understand or verify it. This is unlike witnesses, whom he can refute, interrogate, contradict. The illiterate facing a written text is helpless, and all his words become powerless in contradicting a written document. He would be acting against a fact: *protestatio contra factum nihil relevat.*[214]

This was why, even in literate Roman society, there was a widespread and long-lasting mistrust of written documents. They were therefore considered a secondary source of legal information about interpersonal agreements long after laws had been put down in writing.

The incredible thing is that, in the 5th century B.C., the Romans already had to solve the issue of WYSIWYS (What You See Is What You Sign)[215] – an issue that was also hotly debated at the end of the 20th century as a new concern arising from the use of digital signatures. In Roman times, the agreement was not put down in writing by the parties themselves, but through a scribe. The parties could not verify the content of the writing on their own (because in 90% of the cases they were illiterate), so they had to rely on witnesses, who also signed the agreement. And there was no such thing as graphology!

This is not the only similarity between Roman contracts and digital contracts. The second striking similarity is that the document itself was easily tampered with. Wooden tablets covered by a thin layer of wax were the most easily forgeable document that we can imagine, other than the digital (text) file.

The Roman solution for protecting contracts was to seal them. On the outside of these sealed documents they placed a summary of the contract and the signatures of the parties and witnesses,[216] something resembling the function of the hash of a digital file.

Technically, the ancient Romans employed the same solution used today for the signature of digital files. Today a mathematical seal is applied to an easily forgeable document, put into a digital envelope called "PKCS#7".[217]

At the end of the Roman Empire, the use of written documents had spread and was increasing in relevance.[218] It was only a matter of time before it became

---

[214] It has no (legal) relevance to deny facts.

[215] LANDROCK, P., PEDERSEN, T., *WYSIWYS? What you see is what you sign?* in, *Information Security Technical Report,* vol. 3, no. 2, 1998, 55-61; SCHEIBELHOFER, K., *Signing XML Documents and the Concept of What You See Is What You Sign.*

[216] MEYER E.A., *Legitimacy and law in the Roman world: tabulae in Roman belief and practice,* 145.

[217] Being involved in the standardisation of electronic signatures, I am 100% positive, that none of the engineers designing the PKCS#7 format was aware (before I told them) of the Roman practice of sealing the waxed tables. I find it incredibly telling that 2,000 years later the same solution has been found again, for the same problem, in a completely different human/social/technical context. Despite its name, the digital signature differs morphologically from today's conception of a handwritten signature, despite serving an equivalent legal function. The digital signature is a mathematical seal, with no biometric information whatsoever; the handwritten signature is a biometric sign with no sealing capability whatsoever. Both have the legal and social meaning of validating and approving a document.

[218] By the 2nd century B.C., written contracts were a viable way to record oral agreements. The use of written memoranda became a custom both for the Romans, who "traditionally consigned their most important transactions to [specific] tablets" called *tabulae cerae,* and (much earlier) in

mandatory for all commercial agreements to be reported in written form. It became law that contracts must be documented in writing, or they would not be considered binding.

After the fall of the Roman Empire, the legal infrastructure necessary for all these written contracts consisted of a network of reliable, long-term archivists. This network was provided, starting from the Carolingian era, by notaries.

Can you believe that the vast majority of written agreements signed in front of a notary since the 15th century are still preserved today?

Without this network of legal archives spanning Europe, written contracts would have been far less important. Not only were most people illiterate, but paper was extremely expensive and very difficult to preserve in the buildings of that time; very few rooms had proper heating or ventilation.

What made paper more relevant than oral agreements was the successful long-term preservation of (almost all) such papers. This we learn from papyrology and ancient diplomacy – that availability and preservation are of paramount importance in the history of written documents.[219] This is also, and will continue to be, true for digital documents, as we will see in chapters 8.2 and 8.5.

3.4.4. *Charta* vs. *Notitia*

We have seen how the author is hidden by a written text;[220] so a document may be drafted by one of the parties or by a third party.

If a document is drafted by a third party, it is essential to know if he is acting on behalf of the parties or if he is just a scribe recording the event of the agreement, without being involved in any other way.

When the editor of the document is acting as one of the parties (or on behalf of both), the document substantiates the agreement; it is not just a proof of it. In this case we have a *charta*.

Mesopotamian society, where Babylonian legal custom required "every transaction to be evidenced by a writing", in order to guarantee the observance of the terms of the contract. Mesopotamian law knew a variety of written contracts, from rentals and loans, to marriage and divorce, the purpose of which was to regulate public and private life. (A woman married without a written marriage contract wasn't considered married.)

However, the Roman and Mesopotamian societies weren't the first or only ones to use literal contracts in their legal systems. The ancient Egyptians and Greeks employed written contracts in order to record or document private agreements prior to the Hellenistic period. As in Mesopotamian law, the written instrument was seen as a proof of the oral agreement. Through the study of ancient papyri, it is known that well-established forms of written agreement (sales, leases, loans) were developed in the demotic tradition from the middle of the 7th century B.C. Furthermore, historians and papyrologists have discovered that, during the 3rd century B.C., a new method of documenting private oral contracts developed, which allowed the document to be registered in a local registry by scribes who acted as notaries. These public notary scribes (called agoranomoi) replaced the ancient Egyptian system of recording private contracts in the presence of 16 witnesses. The transition from a tradition of oral agreements to the habit of literal contracts was a response to the need to confirm that the terms of the deed were observed by both parties.

[219] THOMAS, R., *Literacy and Orality in Ancient Greece*, 132 ff.

[220] See chapter 1.2.

When the editor of a document is not personally involved in the exchange of declarations of the parties, and is simply keeping a record of certain events, in this case we have a *notitia*.[221]

The *charta*[222] was born in the Middle Ages.

---

[221] A *notitia* records the fact of the agreement. The *charta* incorporates the intentional declarations of the will of the parties. This distinction is symmetrical to the distinction made by Maurizio Ferraris between recording and document (see chapter 3.3). The *notitia* differs from the ontological definition of recording, because it is the outcome of an intentional act of writing (and not of an automated recording). It has in common with the recording the fact that the scribes did not represent their own intentions, but were recording the intentions of others.

[222] After the 2nd century A.D., the *charta* became the most used form of document. Faith in the document was no longer proven by the seals on the document, but by the signatures of the author and the action of the witnesses. It is generally called *charta* or *chartula*, *scriptura* or *instrumentum*. The *charta* can be objective in form, stemming from a chirographist, or subjective, stemming from the epistle.

In the chirographic form, the document begins with the declaration of the author (*praescriptio*) followed by the *rogation*, and continues by giving notice of the legal office.

In the epistle, the author of the action speaks in first person: *promitto, dono, vendo, cedo tibi*, announcing at the end the name of the person who was in charge of writing the document (*rogatio*). In one or the other form of the document, the legitimacy was bestowed by the writing, and therefore the *rogatio*, with the author's signature, was essential, since it provided the opportunity to compare the person's handwriting with other documents. The signatures of the author of the action or the witnesses increased the legitimacy of the document; however if the author was unable to write, he could be substituted by someone else; the witnesses would serve to personally sign the document.

After Justinian I, the *tabellione* had to notify the parties and witnesses that he had written the act. The *tabellione* read the text to obtain approval by the author of the action to which he gave the *charta*. The author, in turn, gave it to the receiver to symbolically confer the transference of the property. Then, the receiver handed it back to the notary, who requested the signatures of the author of the action and the witnesses. In the end the notary signed it himself with the *completio* formula (*Ego C. scripsi, post traditam complevi et absolvi*). The *completio* formula appeared for the first time in documents of the 6th century and entered common use not only in all Byzantine territory, but also in the Tuscan-Roman and Longobardic areas. With this formula, the *charta* acquired a probationary and constitutional value, since the judicial office came into play and the document was validated by the formalities of the *traditio chartae*.

The two forms of *charta*, stemming from the chirographist and the epistle, became known to the barbarians who lived just outside the empire's boundaries. However, with the breaking up of the empire, each population lived according to its own laws, so the records lost their unifying characteristics. In Italy at the beginning of the 8th century, there were three documental territories: The Longobardic integrated French-Germanic law with the Roman signature. From Central Italy through Naples and Amalfi, the Roman forms remained unchanged. In the Byzantine and Arabic South of Italy, other forms were introduced. Besides Latin, there was the Greek form, and in Sicily an Arabic one. Even documents from the same territory had significant differences based on the diversity of the laws. Regarding language, documents were generally written in Latin until the modern age. However, documents in Greek and Arabic were found in the South of Italy and in Sicily. Towards the 7th century, another type of document was created beside the *charta*, called the *notitia* or *breve*. While the *charta* was a constitutional act, the *notitia* was a document that gave proof of a legal office which was in operation prior to the act. *Notitiae* were used for various matters, but not for transference of property. There was a distinction between judicial *notitiae* (meaning verdicts) and extrajudicial *notitiae*. They usually begin with the *Notitia Dignitatum* (or *breve, brave Memoratorium*), "*qualiter presentia bonorum hominum quorum nomina subter leguntur*". The date is written at the end

While *charta* is an act of incorporation, the *notitia* is an act that need only provide proof of a transaction finished prior to documentation. *Charta* is the cornerstone of the whole Roman-barbarian system of obligatory contracts, such as agricultural contracts. In contrast, *notitia* represents oral legal acts, such as the sale of goods or services; for this reason, it is a document with a probative value.

Summarizing, *charta* could be an objective document originated by a chirographist, or a subjective document originated as an epistle. Writing gives probative value to *charta*. Since the time of the Roman *rogatio* (legislative bill), the name of the writer has been fundamental in order to compare the writing with other documents written by the same person.

The *charta* is a document of value by itself. The expeditor notifies, by means of the document, that he accomplishes the disposition defined in the document – for example, transference of ownership, pronouncing of sentence, an appointment. Such documents were destined to be preserved as persistent evidence of the validity of the disposition that was introduced by means of the *charta*.

The *notitia*, on the other hand, is principally a document of no value by itself, as an instrument of decision. A *notitia* only offers information about a valid disposition that has taken place beforehand.[223]

3.4.5. Promissory Bills (Letters of Credit)

Promissory bills and letters of credit incorporate credit on a piece of paper. So a credit is no longer inherent in a contractual agreement, but becomes a utility represented by a piece of paper, which circulates with that piece of paper.

So the credit is no longer the legal consequence of an agreement between two or more parties; it has become abstract and an object in itself.

The letter of credit is one of the oldest forms of transporting money, and was used internationally by merchants. Before the invention of the letter of credit, there was only one kind of money: coins. A letter of credit enabled the deposit of a sum of gold to a banker in exchange for a credit title, which contained a payment order.[224]

("*factum est hoc anno …*"). The texts are defined by "*interfuerunt ibi testes*". The notary's signature is without the *completio* formula, but usually uses the words "*Ego C. hoc breve scripsi*".

[223] HÜBNER R., *A History of Germanic Private Law*, 568. PULSIANO P., *Medieval Scandinavia: An Encyclopedia*, 137. NICOLAJ G., *Il documento privato nell'Alto Medioevo*, 153-19. PURPORA G., *Sulle origini della Notitia Dignitatum*, 347 - 357.

[224] Available documents trace the origin of credit letters to ancient Eastern civilisation, which had an early banking system. The earliest letters of credit were used in ancient Egypt and consisted of a cuneiform tablet as the bill of exchange or letter of credit. Egypt had a pioneering role in world civilisation, developing trade and institutions (temples) that performed banking functions.
Similar devices were also used in Greece. The first known bankers were from Athens. They were called the *trapezitai* and sat in the open market behind their tables or *trapezai*. They stood out because the activity of changing money needed people with specialized knowledge. The *trapezitai* worked as creditors and borrowers, but they also issued letters of credit to travelers who didn't want to carry money with them for fear of theft.
In Imperial Rome, there was a strong banking system; bankers were known as *argentarii*, so named because of the huge amount of money accumulated in Rome. One of the functions of the *argentarii*

The advantages of using letters of credit as payment were many. Not only did they assure security after the exchange was made, but they also provided a prearranged sum of money. Moreover, the merchants weren't compelled to travel carrying huge sums of money. They could take letters of credit abroad without engaging in a real money transfer. This was a great achievement for the banks of Genoa, Venice and Florence in their work as credit corporations across Europe.

Along with letters of credit came another invention: the commission – a sum of money that had to be paid to employ the letters of credit. Thus the role of the bankers came into play, and trading became much easier for the merchants. Merchants became bankers. Even the Pontificate had merchant-bankers, called *campsores domini papae* (money-changers from the Pope).

There were close connections between the banking system and the merchants' activity. In fact, merchants improved the payment and credit systems to make trade easier. This is how paper (a contract) started to replace silver or gold coins.

3.4.6. Shares

Shares are, ultimately, pieces of paper representing a percentage of the stock of a company – in other words, an abstract portion of an enterprise. Shares, therefore, represent another increase in the level of abstraction made possible by written legal documents.

Shares made it possible not only to own an abstract portion of an enterprise (a possibility going back to Roman law), but to transfer it to others, by means of a piece of paper!

A joint stock corporation is formed from the capital paid in by investors, who receive in return shares in that company. The shares entitle the investor to dividends from the company's profits proportional to the number of shares held.[225]

---

was the *Receptum argentarii*, a relative of the modern letter of credit. The collapse of the Roman Empire and the barbarian invasions eradicated the banking system as well as the trade exchanges. The only operations remaining were those relating to the manual exchange of money. Credit was considered illegal by the Catholic Church; it was practiced only by Jews, to whom the ecclesiastical prohibition was not applied.

It was not until the late in the 12th century that the banking system and trade in Genoa, Florence, Venice and other European cities were reestablished. The banking system included such activities as bank deposits, mortgages and money exchange. A letter of credit was introduced in 1171 by the Bank of Venice to simplify nonlocal business transactions and to make the transfer of capital easier. The oldest known letter of credit dates back to 1207 and reads, "In the year 1207 Simone Rubens banker claims he received L.34 in Genoa coins, with 32 coins, 8 of which, Simone Rubens, his brother, has to give in silver marcs to whomever will show this paper, in Palermo." The letter of credit served a double function: It was both a credit device and a money transfer device. Merchants, during their travels, could obtain a refund of their money in a different currency and a different country.

For further information, see Mugasha A., *The Law of Letters of Credit and Bank Guarantees*, 37; Sosnowski R., *Origini della lingua dell'economia in Italia: dal XIII al XVI secolo*.

[225] *Encyclopedia Britannica*, "East India Company". The East India Company is an example of an early joint stock company. The British and Dutch East India Companies were founded by merchants, who wanted to share costs and risks, with the support of the government, in order to promote trade and colonize new territories. The company had investors who contributed capital

The East India Company had all the characteristics of the contemporary limited liability company – such as long duration, patrimonial autonomy (a limited risk in its investment), an organisation that reserved the management to an authority administrator, and the division of capital in parts, or shares. The share was tradable, so every shareholder had a way to leave the company – by selling their shares.

The joint stock companies enjoyed commercial, tax and political privileges. They had thousands of shareholders, not only belonging to the upper classes, but also to subordinate social categories (craftsmen, servants, clerks, etc.).[226] The sale and purchase of stock in the joint stock companies was inherently

---

and derived profits from the activities of the company on the basis of the number of shares held. The East India Company was highly successful in raising capital almost from its beginning. In 1613, it raised £429,000 to finance four voyages, and in 1617 it raised £1.7 million to finance seven voyages. At this point, it had 934 shareholders and 36 ships. At the end of the 18th century, the company was considered one of the most powerful fleets in the world.

Investors had the right to choose whether or not to invest in a particular voyage. Since stock markets weren't established, this strategy offered a form of exit option. In the absence of a stock market, an investor wishing to sell shares and exit the company completely had to find a buyer through personal contacts and have the transaction approved by the company. There were around 40 such transactions approved each year in the early years of the East India Company. The initial investors in the company expected a relatively quick return, so the first 12 voyages were financed independently. When the ships returned after a voyage that took, on average, 16 months, the proceeds were distributed and new capital was raised for the next voyage. But from the mid-17th century the voyages and the colonies were financed through the joint stock. See also BARROW, I., *The East India Company, 1600–1858*, 4.

[226] LIPTON P., *The Evolution of the Joint Stock Company to 1800: A Study of Institutional Change.* After the Glorious Revolution of 1688, Great Britain saw a boom in joint stock companies, both incorporated and unincorporated. This boom was closely interrelated to the development of stock markets and the growth of trading in the shares of both types of joint stock companies. One indication of the rise of widespread share trading was seen when papers began to publish share prices in 1692. All the institutional structures characterizing an effective modern stock market – professional brokers, established brokerage fees, available price information and a variety of tradable securities – evolved through commercial practice, with little or no legal encouragement.

The invention of the limited liability company was aimed at collecting money from speculators, and the mere possibility of making such risky bets, transformed into financial speculators people from all social classes, even the lowest.

The popularity of share trading and the perception held by most Members of the English Parliament that share speculation was undesirable can be seen from the passing of several acts that attempted to regulate brokers and share traders. These statutes were the precursors of the Bubble Act (1720), which established that organisations that "presumed to act as a corporation" or issued transferable shares were public nuisances. It made them illegal and imposed criminal liability for breaches of the act. The Bubble Act passed in a period of intense, undesirable speculation in joint stock "bubble" company shares. After the Bubble Act, there was a boom in shares that lasted until the late 18th century.

The EIC and other colonial companies were precursors of the 19th century European *société anonyme*, but their structures were also quite different. Originally, EIC shareholders weren't paid with money, but with goods procured during the voyage. Reports made at the end of the overseas voyage and the shareholding records could easily hold different values.

speculative. In the mid-17th century, most of the subscribers for shares aimed to sell them at a profit, not to wait for the distribution of profits.[227]

The Napoleonic Commercial Code of 1807[228] introduced the first regulated type of *société anonyme*. The *société anonyme* is so called because shareholders were protected by anonymity, even though permission to establish the company was given by the government. The *société anonyme* is characterized by perfect patrimonial autonomy, because its juridical personality is set apart from the shareholders' possessions.

The Napoleonic commercial code, therefore, ratified and transformed, as a general principle of commercial law, the 200-year-old special exception that bestowed by decree the privilege of limited liability upon just some companies with shares. Nowadays, the difference between joint stock corporation and *société anonyme* is merely formal, depending on the country and the language.

From 1807 on, the limited liability company spread to all European legal systems, due to its ability to fund and operate very large and risky enterprises.

3.4.7. Futures and Other Contracts on Contracts

In finance, a futures contract ("future") is a contract between two parties to buy or sell an asset for a price agreed upon today (the future price), with delivery and payment occurring at a future point (the delivery date). Because it is a function of an underlying asset, futures contracts are considered a derivative product. Contracts are negotiated at futures exchanges, which act as a marketplace between buyers and sellers. The buyer of the contract is said to be "long", and the party selling the contract is said to be "short".[229]

The history of futures contracts can be traced to the 17th century, when Dutch merchants sold tulip bulbs that had just been planted or that they were going to plant. This speculation caused the demand for tulip bulbs to increase considerably and consequently their price rose.

However, it was only in the mid-19th century that the Chicago Board of Trade created the first specialized market for future contracts. Early futures contracts were negotiated in the markets for the commodities that they represented.

Derivatives, futures, securitisations, are all legal agreements that have, as their object, other legal agreements, and so on, through several layers of abstraction. Today, these kinds of contracts present a dense mixture of oral, written and digital agreements that are all but impossible to extricate, once they have been put together. In 2014, the European Central Bank (ECB), in cooperation with

---

[227] The first voyages had made handsome profits (155%, but sometimes declining to just 20% after the first two years), but the East India Company also invested heavily in non-liquid assets (such as fortifications, harbours, factories), so the liquid profits of the voyages didn't represent the entire economic value of their outcome. Barrow, I., *The East India Company, 1600–1858*, 4.

[228] Code Napoléon.

[229] FEDERAL RESERVE BANK OF CHICAGO, *Understanding Derivatives*.

some leading European banks, started a program for end-to-end digital securitisation, in order to reduce the systemic risk of inextricable derivatives.[230]

Digitalisation brings great advantages in the field of securitisation. Every paperless asset, if managed in a proper environment, would provide in real time its actual capital value, its risk profile and other relevant information – without making it necessary to refer to various paper documents that are normally impossible to access. By providing each credit card account, each mortgage and each corporate credit with its own transparent and trustworthy digital identity, we could achieve abstraction and complexity at the same time, as well as the real possibility of verifying the underlying assets.

In my understanding, we are seeing a new phenomenon here: The complexity of legal abstractions and the speed at which they evolve has outpaced the human ability to understand the abstractions and make them part of our social reality.

So, the task of transforming creative abstractions into identifiable categories, has shifted from general society (the agora, the market, the court, the stock exchange) to some technocratic organisations. But nobody seems to care. Even if such technocratic organisations have the technical ability to address such complex abstractions, still they possess certain ontological flaws that may poison the outcome of their work:

1) They have no democratic or legal legitimacy. They are the expression of the very same interests that are supposed to be regulated or rationalized.

2) In trying to bend financial and commercial innovation into some generally recognized taxonomies they ultimately tend to hinder innovation.

When we think of the priests of ancient civilisations, we instinctively see them as inherently old-fashioned, conservative and static. On the contrary, if we look to such technocratic outfits as CoGESI or the Internet Engineering Task Force (IETF) or the European Telecommunications Standards Institute (ETSI), we are instinctively consider them as part of a dynamic, modern infrastructure. Well, from a strictly functional point of view, they have the same role as the priests of ancient cultures. The social function with which they have been entrusted is to fairly manage knowledge that is inaccessible and incoherent to the large majority of people.

I really don't know if there is (in theory or in practice) a better way to deal with the legal and technical complexity of today's society. I don't know if today's

---

[230] The initiative was named the Contact Group on Euro Securities Infrastructure (CoGESI). Its papers and efforts work toward greater standardisation and formalisation of securities, in order to avoid opacity. "Collateral eligibility and availability: Follow-up to the report on 'Collateral eligibility requirements – a comparative study across specific frameworks'":
https://www.ecb.europa.eu/pub/pdf/other/cea201407en.pdf?62198014e6401011996555ea1c0edc8a
https://www.ecb.europa.eu/pub/pdf/other/collateralframeworksen.pdf and https://www.pressreleasepoint.com/euro-securities-infrastructures-cogesi.
These initial efforts became policy rules on 31 May 2017 when the General Secretariat of the Council of the European Union issued issued a Report of the FSC Subgroup on Non-Performing Loans (EF 113 ECOFIN 481), https://www.consilium.europa.eu/en/press/press-releases/2017/07/11/conclusions-non-performing-loans/.

society can avoid the high priests of technology. What makes the current technocratic method of handling complexity dangerous, is that most people take it for granted, regarding these entities either as evil institutions or as a force for good.

I don't know if these technocratic bodies have become social objects and an essential part of our society. I myself am part of them, and still I don't know if they should be. In about 20 years in ETSI, several times I had to resist the effort to dress a political or legal issue, as a technologic matter.

The most recent and relevant case are digital identities for physical and legal persons (websites, apps). The question is, what functions shall they have, what fundamental rights shall they consider and protect; not how to make them interoperable or most widely adopted. We have already, as we will see, in chapter 8, widely (universally) adopted "digital identities": But they do not consider and respect our fundamental rights, they don't have the legal and functional properties that digital identities need in an open, democratic, pluralistic society (and market). In fact, they are functional in preserving and enacting existing (technologic and economic) monopolies, handling each of us as an object and not as a subject (see chapter 8.1, and, in particular, 8.1.4).

The only thing that I am sure of, is that in order to be a positive part of our complex society, such technocratic entities should be able to recognize and process interests and issues that may not be represented by their participants. One way to achieve this is to keep them open to contributions from all stakeholders, as ETSI for sure is, because all legal entities, even very small enterprises and no-profit organisations are allowed to participate for a small yearly fee and, on top of that, it has cooperation agreements with several organisations representing specific interests, including consumer protection.

Technocratic outfits (that want to have a different social role of high priests of yore) need to be transparent and participative: They need to interact with stakeholders, making them aware of the impact of the technocratic regulations they are working on.

Ultimately, I believe that digitalisation can help to held technocratic outfits accountable – but only if we develop the proper formats and semiotics for open and free online interaction (see chapters 8.2 and 8.5).

The New Economy

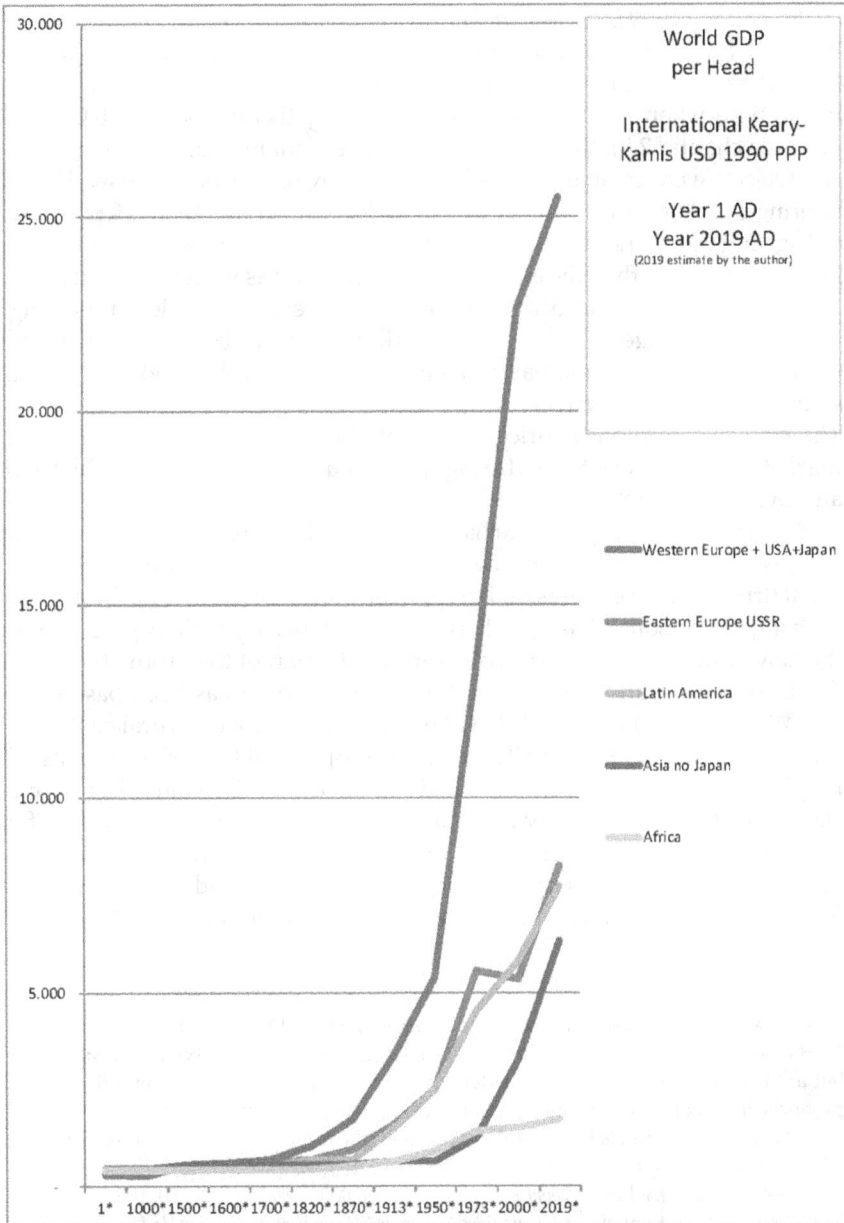

World GDP per Head

International Keary-Kamis USD 1990 PPP

**Year 1 AD
Year 2019 AD**
(2019 estimate by the author)

Legend:
- Western Europe + USA+Japan
- Eastern Europe USSR
- Latin America
- Asia no Japan
- Africa

Y-axis: 30.000, 25.000, 20.000, 15.000, 10.000, 5.000

X-axis: 1* 1000* 1500* 1600* 1700* 1820* 1870* 1913* 1950* 1973* 2000* 2019*

4. The New Economy

"Little of significance happened until 20,000 B.C. – people simply continued living as hunter-gatherers, just as their ancestors had been doing for millions of years. They lived in small communities and never remained within one settlement for very long. A few cave walls were painted, and some rather fine hunting weapons were made; but there were no events that influenced the course of future history, that which created the modern world.
"Then came an astonishing 15,000 years that saw the origin of farming, towns and civilisation. By 5000 B.C. the foundations of the modern world had been laid and nothing that came after – classical Greece, the Industrial Revolution, the atomic age, the Internet – has ever matched the significance of those events."[231]

In the time when most humans were hunter-gatherers (600,000 B.C. to 12,000 B.C.; see chapter 2.2), there was (almost) no economy and, most likely, no slavery. Objects were created and exchanged mostly on a personal basis. The idea of offering a tool or a jewel to the highest bidder would have been offensive enough to trigger a fight. The practice of barter does not necessarily imply an open market for goods, and thus the existence of an economy as we understand it today.[232] Before humans practiced agriculture, there were legal rules protecting and enforcing exchanges. There was no market for goods, because items were only exchanged on a personal basis, while commodities (like food) were normally shared and used collectively.

The concepts of money, price, impersonal exchange, and thus the idea of a market, came into existence during the agricultural revolution of the Neolithic and Bronze Ages.[233]

With agriculture, the goods exchanged among humans were mostly commodities (seeds, vegetables, fruits, shells, etc.). These exchanges did not imply a personal (trust) relationship, as had previously been the case among foragers for the exchange of personal items (such as weapons, tools or jewellery).[234] Slaves under the new system were considered a commodity, part of the production process.

For most of human history since then, the economy has been based on slavery. We are taught in school that slavery was abolished several centuries ago. This is only half true. Formally, with the adoption of Christianity as its official religion, the Roman Empire banished the slavery of Christians; but in practice, slavery was rooted out only a few decades ago. Only in the second half of the 19th century was slavery outlawed in the United States and the British Empire. France abolished it in its colonies in 1794, in the aftermath of the French Revolution and the *Déclaration des Droits de l'Homme et du Citoyen de 1789*.[235]

---

[231] MITHEN, S., *After the Ice: A Global Human History, 20,000 - 5000 B.C.*, p. 15.

[232] HARARI, Y.N., *Sapiens: A Brief History of Mankind*, 222; Harari writes about an economy of barter, but at the same time admits that "barter is effective only when exchanging a limited range of products. It cannot form the basis for a complex economy." GRAEBER, D., *Debt: The First 5000 Years*, 21 ff.; Graeber reconstructs barter as a legal custom that is not as ancient as has been presumed.

[233] FLANNERY, K., MARCUS, J., *The Creation of Inequality*, 16 f.

[234] MITHEN, S., *After the Ice: A Global Human History, 20,000 - 5000 B.C.*, 57, 80, 102.

[235] Conseil Constitutionnel, *Déclaration des Droits de l'Homme et du Citoyen de 1789*.

Religious scholars agreed by around the 11th century that slavery was ultimately incompatible with Christianity. The next step was a difficult task – figuring out how to replace slave labour with other kinds of work and production. This was so difficult that the first universally recognized document declaring slavery illegal everywhere in the world was approved only 70 years ago. The *Universal Declaration of Human Rights* was accepted by vote at the United Nations on 10 December 1948; 48 nations voted in favour of abolishing slavery, while eight abstained.[236]

In the 18th and 19th centuries, when slave labour was an accepted practice, Europe's colonies provided a boost in capital and liquidity for the parent country, which was then invested in the agricultural and industrial revolutions (achieved most successfully by the British and Dutch).

In 1898, 33 years after it abolished slavery, the United States supported the Philippine Revolution against Spain, which led to the colonisation of the Philippines. After the revolution, the main crops that had been cultivated in the Confederate States with slave labour – tobacco and cotton – were extensively planted in the Philippines. New slaves were needed to replace the freed Americans. The formal abolition of slavery did not really improve the living conditions of peasants or other low-skilled laborers until the first half of the 20th century.

If we look at economic evolution from a millennial perspective, and in particular, if we look at the data gathered by Angus Maddison, some unexpected questions arise, which we will analyse in this chapter:

- When did the slave-labour economy really end, giving birth to a new economic system?

- Are we bound to grow economically forever? Or should we consider the Agricultural Revolution (18th century), the Industrial Revolution (19th century), the Post-Industrial Revolution (20th century) and the Digital Revolution (21st century) as "singularities": exceptional, unpredictable, non-recurring events?

- In all "rich" countries, growth has become sluggish. Is it because wealth reduces the incentives for hard work? Or are there other factors at play?

- Is our wealth sustainable, or have we reached a tipping point?

All these questions are relevant to understanding the digital society and economy of today.

First, they are relevant because the important changes in how wealth is created and exchanged present a double-edged sword: Some gain from the changes, others are harmed, and so we eventually resist change. Innovation almost never distributes wealth evenly.

Second, they are relevant because it is simplistic to believe that information technology is all about generating growth; it may also serve to enable us to make better use of available resources – particularly if we have reached a tipping point and the growth that we consider normal shows itself as a non-recurring singularity that has begun to ebb since the end of the last century.

---

[236] United Nation, *Universal Declaration of Human Rights.*

4.1. Social and Economic Consequences of the Abolition of Slavery

In the 1st and 2nd centuries, the Roman Empire was at its peak. It was a political entity that stretched from the Scottish border to Egypt, with a population of 20 million in Europe, 20 million in Western Asia and 8 million in North Africa. With the progressive abolition of slavery[237] and the breakup of the Roman Empire, the European population shrank dramatically, starting in the 4th century.

By the Carolingian Age (7th century), the minting of gold had ceased. The lending of money at interest was prohibited. There was no longer a class of professional merchants. Many Oriental products (papyrus, spices and silk) were no longer imported. The circulation of money was reduced to a minimum. Laymen could neither read nor write. Taxes were no longer collected regularly. The towns were merely fortresses. We can say, without hesitation, that this was a civilisation that had regressed to a purely agricultural stage; its social fabric no longer required commerce or credit.[238]

The main changes between the 1st and 10th centuries were:

a) the collapse of a large and cohesive political unit, which was replaced by a fragmented, fragile and unstable polity

b) the disappearance of urban civilisations and the predominance of self–sufficient, relatively isolated and ignorant rural communities, where a feudal elite extracted an income in kind from a servile peasantry

c) the virtual disappearance of trading links between Western Europe, North Africa and Asia.

As early as the 6th century A.D., slavery in Europe was replaced by serfdom, a system that proved better suited to the emerging feudal, agricultural economy.[239] Still, slavery in medieval Europe was so common that the Roman Catholic church repeatedly sanctioned it, after dithering on the issue for centuries. Still, the kings of Spain and Portugal were granted the right by Pope Nicholas V (in the papal bull *Dum Diversus,* 1452) to reduce any "Saracens, pagans and any other unbelievers" to perpetual slavery, legitimizing the slave trade in the context of war.[240] Large-scale slave trading was confined to the southern and eastern regions of early medieval Europe. The Byzantine Empire and the Muslim world were the preferred destinations for these slaves. Pagan Central and Eastern Europe (along with the Caucasus and Tartary) were other destinations. Viking, Arab, Greek, and

---

[237] In the year 1 A.D., European GDP was US$11.115 million, calculated in Geary-Khamis 1990 purchasing power parity (PPP) value; in 1000 A.D., it was US$10.165 million: MADDISON A., *The World Economy*, 241; MADDISON A., *The West and the Rest in the World Economy: 1000–2030*.

For a short description of the consequences of the end of the Roman Empire and of the slave economy, see also HEUMAN, G., BURNARD, T., *The Routledge History of Slavery*, 32, which highlights that between 100 A.D. and 500 A.D., slaves began to decrease in number.

The World Economy, *Europe's decline from the first to tenth centuries;* The World Economy, *The Contours of World Development.*

[238] PIRENNE H., *Mohammed and Charlemagne*, p. 86; CURT, E., *Rome's 5th Century Grain Supply.*

[239] HEUMAN, G., BURNARD, T., *The Routledge History of Slavery*, 32.

[240] Religious Tolerance, *Christian Support of Slavery.* BIOT E., *Sull'Abolizione della Schiavitù antica in Occidente*, 266 ff.

Jewish merchants were all involved in the slave trade during the early Middle Ages. The trade of European slaves reached a peak in the 10th century, following the Zanj Rebellion, which dampened the use of African slaves in the Arab world.[241] The slave trade and slave labour were central features of the (Western) economy (and the colonies). The abolition of slavery in Great Britain in the 18th century and in the United States in the 19th century shifted the balance of economic activity toward capital-intensive agriculture and industry.[242]

It is unquestionable that the wealth produced by slave labour was essential to gathering the capital needed for large investments in (industrial) agriculture and industry. In fact, the agricultural and industrial revolutions were triggered by two successful colonialist states, Great Britain and the Netherlands. Slavery produced the wealth needed to invest in innovation and to shift the balance from human labour to machine tools.

Thus the first "new economy" was the slave-free economy that took up the better part of the 20th century. Is the digital economy another "new economy"? Let us ponder whether the digital economy deserves to be called "new", and if so, let's be clear on why it is so.

4.2. The Great Divergence: Mercantilism, Colonialism, Industrialisation. Where Do We Come From?

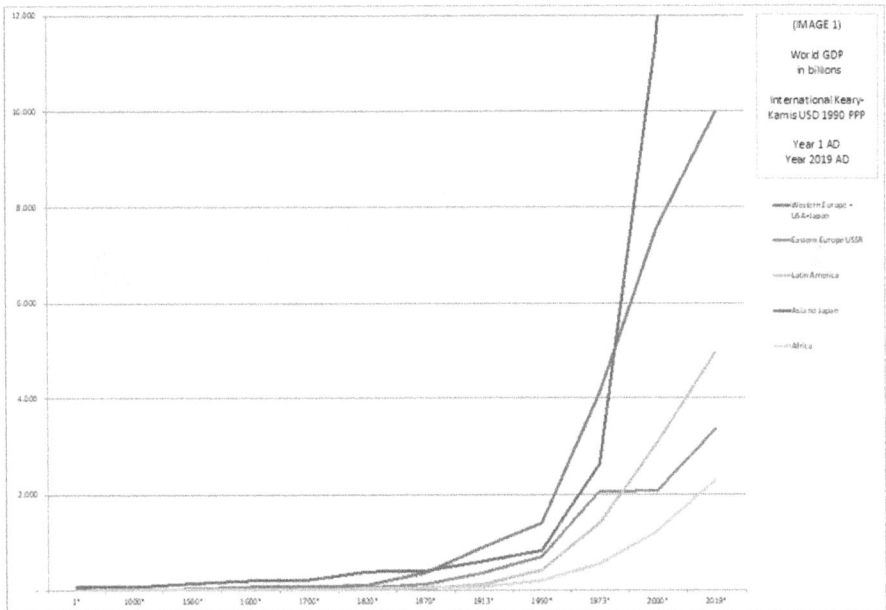

It is understandable that we consider "normal" that which has been the standard for the last 150 years. But if we look at the same phenomena from a millennial perspective, then our "normal" may look like an exception.

---

[241] Liquiserach, *Slavery in medieval Europe, Barbary slave trade*.
[242] HEUMAN, G., BURNARD, T., *The Routledge History of Slavery*, 180.

The world's gross domestic product (GDP), as calculated by Angus Maddison in Geary-Khamis dollars in 1990, on a purchasing power parity (PPP) basis, was about $100 billion in 1 A.D. In 2000, it was more than $25 trillion, an increase of 250 times. The increase from $100 billion to $600 billion took approximately 1,820 years. The increase from $600 billion to $25 trillion took 180 years. In the subsequent 20 years, further 7 trillion (in Geary-Khamis 1990 US dollars) have been added to the World GDP. The rate of GDP increase over the last 200 years was 400 times greater than in the previous 1,800 years (see image 1).

What has changed over the last 200 years?

One important factor in this change has been population growth. In the last 200 years, the population has grown 10 times faster than in the previous 1800 years. From 1 A.D. to 1820 A.D., the population increased fivefold, from 165 million to 1 billion. From 1820 A.D. to 2020 A.D., the population increased eightfold, from 1 billion to 7.8 billion (see image 2), with 1.8 billion added just in the last 20 years.

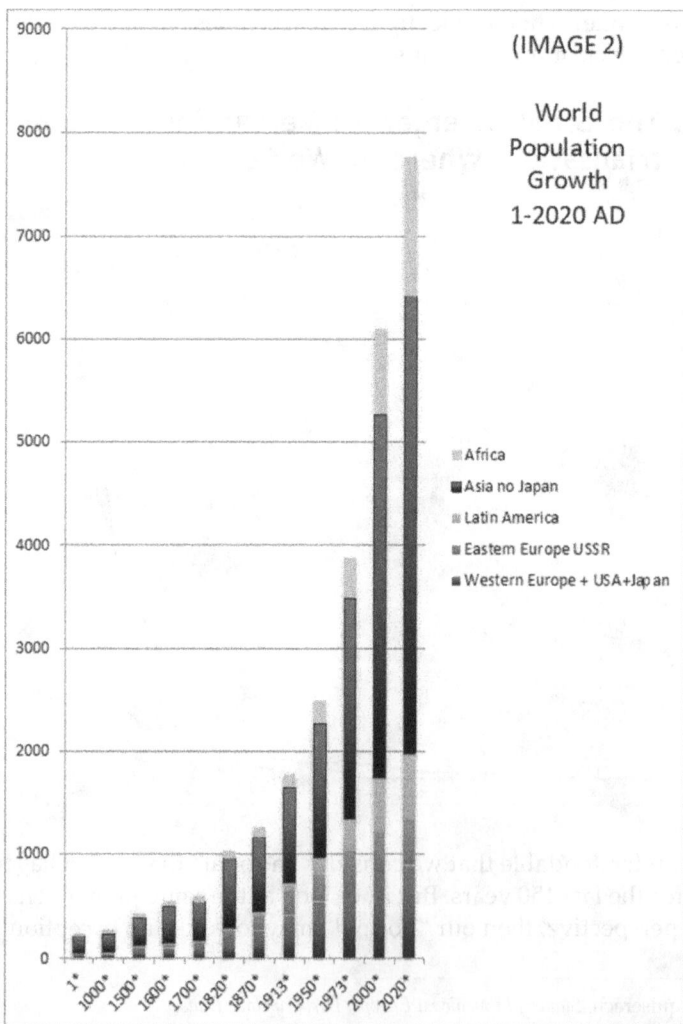

(IMAGE 2)

World Population Growth 1-2020 AD

Legend:
- Africa
- Asia no Japan
- Latin America
- Eastern Europe USSR
- Western Europe + USA+Japan

What else has changed in the last 200 years that can explain a 5,000% increase in world GDP at 1990 PPP?[243].

The obvious answer is that the Industrial Revolution has been transforming the world since 1820. But the Industrial Revolution has not acted evenly or synchronously over the globe. Some nations were eager to embrace it, while others could not or chose not to.[244] The nations that did not embrace the Industrial Revolution were generally unprepared to embrace the social consequences of industrialisation, or they tried to domesticate its side effects, by erecting moral, social and ethical hurdles to industrialisation. Some nations have not built strong industries and remain poor.

To build national industries, true industrialists were needed. Bureaucrats, shopkeepers and merchants preferred to carry on in the usual way of doing business. From their perspective, the past way of life was more effective and more lucrative, depending on low investment with the highest possible return. It focused mainly on exploitation and regulation (such as slavery or colonialism), on informational asymmetries and scarcity.[245]

The deployment of capital-intensive production systems and mass labour required a radical change in the use of capital, as well as a new social class with a new mindset. That was what happened in the United States during the second half of the 19th century. The Industrial Revolution brought about new rules, a new aesthetic and the birth of new ethics. The ethics and aesthetics of the British gentleman (detached, indifferent, self-sufficient, impractical) were superseded by the ethics and aesthetics of the engaged, professional, effective businessman. A social class with a new mindset overtook the existing ruling classes (the aristocracy, shopkeepers, artisans, the military and merchants), who had formed the backbone of society for millennia.

The British Empire (and parts of its Commonwealth) started industrialisation, but the traditional mindset of the British – the conservative social structure of the aristocracy and professional military – were quite alien to unrestrained industrialisation, and eventually it was contained. In the U.S., industrialists

---

[243] In nominal terms, world GDP in 2019 was US$ 135 trillion, according to the World Bank.

[244] Kuran, T., *The Long Divergence,* analyses how Islamic law held back the evolution of a society which, in the 11th century was the most advanced in the Mediterranean region. His most relevant findings are as follows:
- The Islamic partnership lacked the sophistication of the Roman *societas* or the *societas mercatorum* (Kuran, ch. 4). The rules of the *societas mercatorum* favored the accumulation of capital in the *societas*, putting the interests of the enterprise above the interests of the partners. In Islamic law, the interests of the partners were considered more important than those of the partnership and its creditors, so it was illiquid and depended entirely on its partners.
- The corporation, absent in Islamic law, was introduced in Europe in 1601 with the Dutch East India Company (ch. 6).
- Credit markets operated without banks (ch. 8).
- Trade isolationism (ch. 11) dominated at the beginning of the 20th century, with the abrogation of bilateral trade deals (capitulations).
- Islamic courts were perceived as biased against non-Muslims (ch. 12).

[245] Flannery, K., Marcus, J., *The Creation of Inequality,* explains wonderfully, from prehistory to the end of slavery, how inequality was shaped by social and legal rules.

became the first local aristocracy, the first ruling class. Even today, the United States is a living monument to the triumph of industrialisation.

Why did Asia,[246] Africa and Latin America[247] lag behind? Colonialism certainly held back the industrialisation of the colonies in the 19th century. But colonialism alone cannot explain why industrialisation did not occur on four-fifths of the globe during the 20th century.

As a matter of fact, many efforts were made in Asia, Africa, Eastern Europe and Latin America, mostly to no avail. Industrialisation was a success only in open societies. The more "open" a nation was to foreigners and to social change, the more it benefitted from industrialisation. It is no coincidence that the United States (a British ex colony) has benefitted the most from industrialisation. In contrast, industrialisation failed where societies oppressed change and innovation. In communist or populist or autocratic regimes, huge investments in infrastructure and industrial assets were wasted.[248]

Germany, Japan and, to a lesser extent, France and Italy successfully followed the path of industrialisation, following the two forerunners, the U.S. and U.K. In all these nations, the rising classes established a new mindset, new rules, new ethics and new aesthetics: libertarianism, utilitarianism, impressionism, realism, existentialism, rationalism, irrationalism, socialism, cubism, nudism, expressionism, etc.[249]

Some scholars explain the social openness of Europe in the last 15 centuries by citing the coexistence of temporal power (monarchs) with spiritual power (the Pope). But the Pope, in the end, was just another emperor of the epoch. He ruled a nation and was presumed to have a moral right to decide who should rule as king in other nations (by crowning them).

Certainly the dualism between religious power and temporal power in Europe was unique and distinct from other great societies (i.e., the Arabian, Indian and Chinese).[250] However, the importance of Roman law and its evolution through the mercantile class should not be underestimated. Roman law survived the collapse of the Roman Empire by 1500 years, lasting until 1804, when Napoleon repealed it with his "Civil Code". In the Middle Ages, by transforming Roman law, merchants created the *lex mercatoria* ("law merchant"): For more than six centuries (from the 11th century to 1804), merchant tribunals functioned in parallel with state tribunals. Nonetheless, their authority was rarely questioned by private citizens or even by absolutist states.[251]

---

[246] PARTHASARATHI, P., *Why Europe Grew Rich and Asia Did Not: Global Economic Divergence, 1600–1850*.

[247] POMERANZ, K., *The Great Divergence: China, Europe, and the Making of the Modern World Economy*.

[248] ACEMOGLU, D., ROBINSON, J.A., *Why Nations Fail: The Origins of Power, Prosperity and Poverty*: for the Soviet Union, 144, 384; China, 292 ff.; India, 264 f.; Argentina, 323; Sierra Leone and other sub-Saharan nations, 329 ff. and passim.

[249] ACEMOGLU, D., ROBINSON, J.A., *Why Nations Fail: The Origins of Power, Prosperity and Poverty*: Germany, Austro-Hungarian Empire, 216 ff.; France, Italy, 294 ff., Japan, 290 ff.

[250] ZAKARIA F., *The Future of Freedom*, loc. 1758. For ACEMOGLU, D., ROBINSON, J.A., *Why Nations Fail: The Origins of Power, Prosperity and Poverty*, 67 ff., economic and political success are the consequence of inclusive institutions, while nations fail if ruled by autocratic, extractive institutions.

[251] GALGANO, F., *Lex mercatoria*, 83.

The law merchant was technocratic – evenly and strictly applied all over Europe. Consider the court scene in Shakespeare's *The Merchant of Venice*, written around 1599, which describes the workings of the "Supremo Tribunale della Quarantia" in Venice in the 16th century.[252] The law merchant protected and enhanced the accumulation of capital at the expense of the individual rights of the entrepreneur. It required merchants to be solvent and, even better, rich. So it was no coincidence that many of them became richer even than entire states.[253]

It is common sense to say that the success of the "Western" nations was the success of individualism. But there is a great deal of approximation in this assumption. In fact, the law merchant was not individualistic at all. The law merchant protected the enterprise (*mercatura*) and its creditors, at the expense of the merchant. All merchants involved in an enterprise had to be personally and fully liable for all debts of the enterprise. No exceptions.[254] Silent partners were fully responsible for all the obligations of the merchant with whom they were associated. A merchant who cooked his books was punished with long prison terms. If he also went bankrupt, then he was put to death. The personal creditors of the merchant had no recourse to the assets of the enterprise; the property of the merchant was fully pledged to the workings of the merchant's enterprise.[255]

These rules protected the community of merchants and all their relying parties. They protected the extension of trade, the expansion of credit, the increase in the assets of the enterprise. They protected the accumulation of capital and the economy – not the single merchant!

In comparison to the *lex mercatoria*, Arabic law was much more individualistic. It allowed the merchant to leave his enterprise at any moment and to protect his property from the thereto connected risks and liabilities.[256]

The rapid progress of Western Europe in the 19th century followed a long preparation, during which the European nations became more tolerant, open and individualistic. They respected collective interests and rights that were nurtured and represented by several legal entities: companies, foundations, other non-profit organisations, and last but not least, several different branches and legal entities of the states themselves.[257]

In a difficult time like the present, we cannot take for granted that what happened over the last 20 centuries was all inevitable. We have to understand the reasons that placed the "Western" world on the road to riches. We have to ask ourselves how it was possible that Europe, which was dirt poor after the fall of the Roman Empire, was able to recover after the abolition of slavery and the collapse of the slave-based economy. Europe not only recovered, but became more prosperous than the other great civilisations of the world.

---

[252] SHAKESPEARE, W., *The Merchant of Venice*, Act IV.

[253] KURAN, T., *The Long Divergence*, loc. 2052.

[254] GALGANO, F., *Lex mercatoria*, 43, 47, 54.

[255] GALGANO, F., *Lex mercatoria*, 125.

[256] These are the findings from KURAN, T., *The Long Divergence*, loc. 1152.

[257] ACEMOGLU, D. AND ROBINSON, J., *The Narrow Corridor: How Nations Struggle for Liberty*, 466.

Western Europe was impoverished in the 5th century – with a much lower per-capita income than the poorest African nations today. At the turn of the first millennium A.D., Europe's per-capita income was one-third lower than the average for the rest of the world at that time (Asia, Africa and Latin America; little is known of North America and Australia in that era.). Today, Africa, Asia and Latin America have about one-fifth of the GDP per person of Europe or the U.S. (see image 3), even though, in the last 180 years, per-capita GDP increased three times in Africa, eight times in Asia and more than 10 times in Latin America and Eastern Europe.

After the long "Dark Ages" between the end of the Roman Empire and the year 1000, the "West" (at that time, just Western Europe) kept growing, inventing, innovating. But only with industrialisation did per-capita income increase exponentially.

This same pattern holds true for the rest of the world. We finally see industrialisation impacting Latin America and Eastern Europe after 1870.

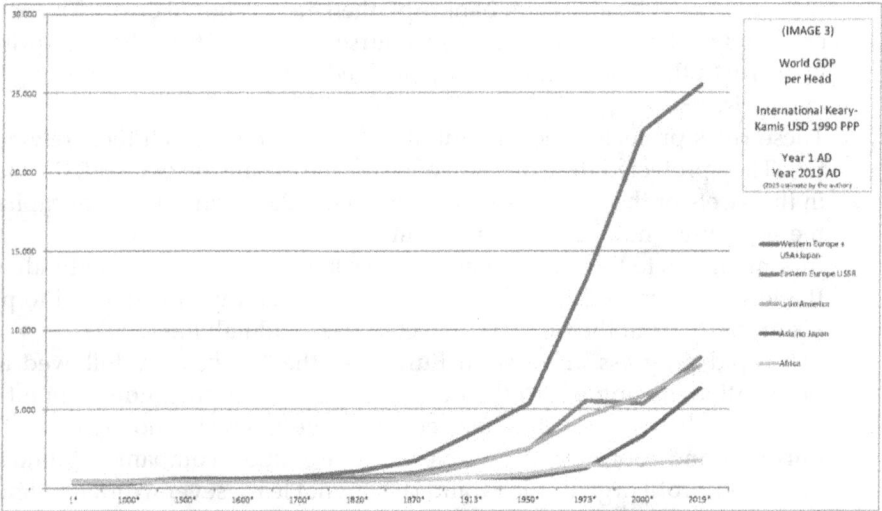

(IMAGE 3)

World GDP per Head

International Keary-Kamis USD 1990 PPP

Year 1 AD
Year 2019 AD

Western Europe + USA+Japan
Eastern Europe USSR
Latin America
Asia no Japan
Africa

Now look at Asia – how it has risen since 1950. In Africa in the second half of the 20th century, there was a more modest increase in personal income, which has plateaued in this millennium.

Industrialisation has solved a structural problem, which countries need to tackle in order to become affluent. The problem is the curse of the low productivity of labour. How many crops can a peasant produce by scraping the earth with his bare hands? Can he feed a family of 10? The obvious answer is that he cannot. Slavery was the socially engineered solution to that problem. In the 7th millennium B.C., slavery existed in all human societies around the world – Mesopotamia, Central America and Asia. Ironically, none of these civilisations had any knowledge of the existence of the others.[258]

---

[258] FLANNERY K., MARCUS J., *The Creation Of Inequality*, 91 and passim.

The most effective way to feed everybody was for the person who owned the land and the expensive tools necessary for cultivation also to own the people on the land. Even Western Europe restarted its economy by reintroducing slavery in its colonies, even though the practice was banned by the Christian religion.[259] Slave-powered agriculture represented a radical change to the socioeconomic relationships of hunters-gatherers, who had roamed the earth freely and fiercely for the previous 50,000 years.

Industrialisation was another radical change, and it proved to be a much better way to increase wealth than slavery or mercantilism. Industrialisation treated the cause of poverty (scarce productivity), and not the symptoms (low income, and thus a low rate of accumulation). All the rules that had been introduced to regulate trade and consumption from the 11th century onward traced their moral and practical justifications to scarcity.[260]

Industrialisation made abundance possible, and therefore led to global markets, global rules and lower barriers to commerce.

Few of those who today advocate trade barriers are aware that China[261] and India[262] originally became poor because they shut down foreign trade. Britain and the Netherlands overtook Spain and France in the 17th century because they favoured trade and industry, not mercantilism.

Knowing where we come from is of great importance, because it shows us the (highly linear) path the "West" has taken to become the world power that it is today. It also shows us the direction we are now heading – our social direction, cultural direction, economic and political direction.

In one sentence – the success of the "West" is characterized by its willingness to be culturally open and technically innovative, allowing social change nurtured by the growth of industry, and with it, the rise of a class of industrialists who solved the problems of scarcity and the low productivity of labour.[263]

But something has recently changed. In 2012, because of a congressional stalemate, the United States was headed toward a technical default on its public debt. Since 2012, Spain has asked for a massive bailout for its banks; Greece has technically been in default; Ireland and Portugal have been bailed out; Italy and France look quite shaky – all because of high public debt.

Growth after the Great Recession of 2008-2012 has slowed the OECD economies, as well as many developing countries.

---

[259] HEUMAN, G., BURNARD, T., *The Routledge History of Slavery*, 216.

[260] GALGANO, F., *Lex mercatoria*, 77.

[261] For an analysis of why China became impoverished, ACEMOGLU, D., ROBINSON, J., *The Narrow Corridor: How Nations Struggle for Liberty*, 200-221, 230. The Chinese states were totalitarian, until the communist revolution led to another form of totalitarianism. The economic miracle in China was the consequence of the adoption of a different economic model by Deng Xiao Ping in 1978, with a less top-down approach and more freedom of initiative granted to individuals; since 2001, the rules of capitalist corporate governance have also been applied to state-owned enterprises. ZHANG, X., *Integration of CCP Leadership with Corporate Governance*, 55-63, in part, 57 f.

[262] For an analysis of why India became impoverished, ACEMOGLU, D., ROBINSON, J., *The Narrow Corridor: How Nations Struggle for Liberty*, 236 ff. The caste system forced India to become increasingly inward-looking, ultimately isolating itself from any form of trade in goods and ideas.

[263] FRIEDMAN, B.M., *The Moral Consequences of Economic Growth*, 52 ff.

Interest rates in Europe and the U.S. have been minimal for many years; now they are negative. This means that in order to keep money in a safe central bank account, one must pay interest (instead of receiving interest on deposits)! And now, the Covid-19 pandemic and a constitutional crisis in the United States, the land of the free.

Where are we heading?

4.3. The Great Turnaround: Where is the "West" Heading?[264]

I was asked by my children, "Why can't states get more credit? They're so much richer than families."

Instinctively, I almost answered, "Yes, they are." But before answering, I looked up a few numbers, just to be sure. Here are the numbers:

The OECD has an average GDP per capita of about $43,000.[265]

The average price paid by a home buyer in Western Europe is between $150,000 and $180,000 at 2009 PPP.

Consequently, homebuyers obtain mortgages for which the principal typically ranges from a minimum of 350% to a maximum of 420% of their yearly income. So why can't states borrow money in the markets, since their GDP/debt ratio varies from 70% to 200%?

The answer is easy, but not obvious: Would a bank lend $150,000 to a family that plans to spend its money as follows:[266]

- 4% for capital investment
- 18% for healthcare
- 47% for the support of elderly family members
- 6% for interest expenses
- 25% for running expenses

NEVER EVER!!!

In fact, the average OECD family with a mortgage spends its income this way:[267]

- 10% for capital investment (in the house)
- 25% for food and other goods (furnishings, clothing)

---

[264] For a reasoned analysis of a possible new social contract, an essential reading is SHAFIK, M., *What We Owe Each Other: A New Social Contract*.

[265] https://stats.oecd.org/index.aspx?queryid=61433. Note on the units used: in national currency, in current prices and constant prices (national base year, previous year prices and OECD base year 2015); for comparative purposes, in US$ current prices and constant prices, using exchange rates, and for the GDP by expenditures (in absence of specific PPP series), GDP PPPs for all series, except actual individual consumption where a specific PPP is used; expressed in millions and in indices. For the euro area, the data in national currencies for all years are calculated using fixed conversion rates against the euro.

[266] LENZI, S., ZOPPÈ, A., *Composition of Public Expenditures in the EU*, briefing, European Parliament, Economic Governance Support Unit (EGOV) Directorate-General for Internal Policies PE 634.371, June 2020. In their table, expenditures are related to total GDP of the EU. In my example, the percentage is related to average total government spending in the OECD, or 42% of GDP: OECD, "General government spending (indicator)", 2020, doi: 10.1787/a31cbf4d-en (accessed 8 November 2020).

[267] OECD, "Household spending (indicator)", 2020, doi: 10.1787/b5f46047-en (accessed 8 November 2020).

- 11% for services (communications, utilities, recreation, culture, education, hotels, restaurants)
- 9% for transportation (car and public transportation)
- 2% for healthcare
- 8% for interest expenses
- 35% for taxes (the OECD average in 2009; but taxes can be as much as 50% of GDP in some states, as in France).

This means that 68% of a family's disposable income goes to the purchase of goods. About 33% of a family's purchases are durable goods (house, car, furniture, white goods, TV, computers, etc.), compared to 4% of state expenditures. In 1910, these countries spent 12.5% of GDP, devoting about 30% of this expenditure to the purchase of durable goods (infrastructure), much like the modern family. Today, the state spends an average of 45.6% of GDP and devotes just 4% to building infrastructure.[268]

Countries today display the spending pattern of a homeless family, consuming almost 90% of earnings. The homeless do not have access to credit. Poor people can obtain credit, eventually, if there is the concrete prospect of a significant increase in earnings or, as in microfinance, if credit can spur investment and consequently earnings.

It's obvious that a paradigm shift is needed. In the last 100 years, the amount of money collected by government in absolute and relative terms has relentlessly increased. In 2020, public spending reached unprecedented levels. Changes seem unavoidable, for three main reasons:

1) It is difficult to imagine that any government could account for a share of GDP larger than 50%, so there is not much room to increase the state's share of the pie. It is recommended by many economists to keep taxation under 35%,[269] so at some point, the state's share of GDP will likely shrink.

2) Productivity in OECD countries is slowing down; thus, growth in personal income and in general wealth is slowing down.

3) The dependency ratio in OECD countries will change dramatically in the next 35 years: In 2050, there will be more than 75 dependent persons for every 100 working persons (see image on next page). Today it is about 55 to 100. That amounts to an increase of nearly 50% over the next 35 years.[270]

---

[268] Vito TANZI, V., SCHUKNECHT L., *Public Spending in the 20th century: A Global Perspective.*

[269] Several papers have been published by OECD researchers on the topic: OECD, *Taxation Working Papers No. 26. Tax Design for Inclusive Growth* (2008); OECD, *Taxation Working Papers No. 38: Corporate Effective Tax Rates: Model Description and Results from 36 OECD and Non-OECD Countries* (2018); OECD, *Taxation Working Papers No. 2: What is a "Competitive" Tax System?* (2011).

[270] The dependency ratios quoted here and the graph are found on p. 12 of the Communication [COM(2015) 429 final] from the Commission to the European Parliament, the Council, the European Economic and Social Committee and the Committee of the Regions, titled "*Draft 2015 Joint Report of the Council and the Commission on the implementation of the renewed framework for European cooperation in the youth field (2010-2018)*". Updated data from Aug. 2020 can be found at Eurostat, *Population structure and ageing,* substantially confirming the data of the EU Commission Joint Report.

If nothing changes, in 2050 no less than 60% of GDP will be for welfare. To cover that, the average tax contribution will have to exceed 60%, or no less than an additional 10%.

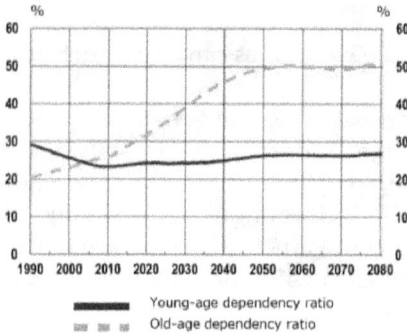

Note: The old-age-dependency ratio is the ratio of the number of elderly people at an age when they are generally economically inactive (i.e. aged 65 and over), compared to the number of people of working age (i.e. 15-64 years old). The young-age-dependency ratio is the ratio of the number of young people at an age when they are generally economically inactive, (i.e. under 15 years of age), compared to the number of people of working age (i.e. 15-64).

Young-age dependency ratio
Old-age dependency ratio

Source: Eurostat [demo_pjanind] [proj_13ndbims]

So the answer I gave to my children was:
"No, the state is borrowing much less than a family with a mortgage. But it is evident that its spending pattern is unsustainable. Less than 10% of the money borrowed goes into improving its infrastructure (assets); most of the rest is passed over to needy people. Who would help the needy with borrowed money? A saint or a fool."
What are the implications of current social expenditures in OECD countries?
Today, Europe has about 450 million inhabitants. The number of people younger than 15 is usually used as the basis to calculate the young-age dependency ratio. Today that ratio is 23%.[271] The number of people aged 65 or older provides the basis for the old-age dependency ratio. Today that ratio in the EU28 is 33%. There are 33 people over age 65 for every 100 people of working age (as defined above).
If we add the number of young people (in 2019, those aged 0-19 numbered 23% of the working population) to the older population (in 2019, those above 65 numbered 33% of the working population), we have a resulting total dependency ratio of about 56%. That means that in the EU28, there are 56 (young or old) dependents for every 100 working people. This is about 1.8 working-age people for every dependent person.
In 2050 in the EU 28, the young-age dependency ratio will be 27%, and the old-age dependency ratio will be 50%.[272] That comes to 77 dependents for every 100 working people. In 2050, the ratio of old people to working-age people in the EU28 will increase from 1:2 to 3:4 – a dramatic shift. The demographic pyramid in the EU (and in most of the OECD countries) is capsizing.
What is important to know is that if we compare this trend with Japan, the U.S., Canada or Australia, there are significant differences, but still the overall

---

[271] Eurostat, *Being Young in Europe Today*.
[272] Eurostat, *"Old-age dependency ratio increasing in the EU"*, indicates that in 2100 the old-age dependency ratio will be 61%.

trend is the same.[273] The total (old-age + young-age) dependency ratio in the U.S. in 2050 is projected to be somewhere in the mid-60% range – a bit better than the EU28, but still a significant increase. China is much worse, because of its one-child policy, which will lead to a quadrupling of old-age dependent people in the next 40 years – an explosive situation if not dealt with.

From OECD research, we learn that social expenditures (including healthcare) were roughly 30% of GDP in the OECD countries in 2013, with interesting differences between Europe and the U.S.:[274]

Table 3.1. Total tax revenue as % of GDP

	1985	1990	2000	2007	2010	2013	2015	2017	2018	2019p
Australia	20.8	28.1	30.5	29.5	25.3	27.1	27.9	28.5	28.7	..
Austria	33.8	39.3	42.3	40.5	41.0	42.6	43.1	41.8	42.2	42.4
Belgium[1]	30.8	41.4	43.8	42.9	42.9	45.0	44.1	43.8	43.9	42.9
Canada	26.0	35.1	34.7	32.5	31.0	31.1	32.8	33.1	33.2	33.5
Chile	..	16.9	18.8	22.7	19.6	19.9	20.4	20.2	21.1	20.7
Colombia	..	11.3	15.7	19.3	18.1	20.0	19.9	19.0	19.3	19.7
Czech Republic	..	..	32.3	34.1	32.2	33.7	33.1	34.4	35.0	34.9
Denmark[1]	29.1	44.4	46.9	46.4	44.8	45.9	46.1	45.8	44.4	46.3
Estonia	..	..	31.0	31.0	32.9	31.5	33.1	32.6	32.9	33.1
Finland	30.0	42.9	45.8	41.4	40.6	43.4	43.5	42.9	42.4	42.2
France[1]	33.7	41.2	43.4	42.5	42.1	45.4	45.3	46.1	45.9	45.4
Germany	31.7	34.8	36.4	35.4	35.5	37.0	37.3	37.8	38.5	38.8
Greece	17.1	25.2	33.4	31.8	32.0	35.7	36.4	38.6	38.9	38.7
Hungary	..	..	38.8	39.4	37.2	38.6	38.9	38.3	37.5	35.8
Iceland	25.7	30.4	36.0	38.8	32.3	34.5	35.4	37.6	37.2	36.1
Ireland	24.5	32.4	30.8	30.8	27.7	28.9	23.4	22.8	22.7	22.7
Israel	..	..	34.8	34.2	30.7	30.8	31.2	32.5	30.9	30.5
Italy	24.6	36.3	40.5	41.6	41.7	43.8	43.0	41.9	41.9	42.4
Japan	17.6	28.2	25.8	27.5	26.5	28.9	30.7	31.4	32.0	..
Korea	..	18.4	20.9	23.7	22.4	23.1	23.7	26.4	26.8	27.4
Latvia	..	..	29.1	28.3	28.7	29.4	30.0	31.4	31.2	31.2
Lithuania[1]	..	..	30.8	30.0	28.4	28.8	28.7	29.6	30.2	30.3
Luxembourg[1]	26.4	33.5	36.9	36.2	37.5	38.2	37.0	37.6	39.7	39.2
Mexico	..	12.1	11.5	12.0	12.8	13.3	15.9	16.1	16.2	16.5
Netherlands	30.5	39.7	36.9	35.7	35.7	36.1	37.0	36.7	36.8	39.3
New Zealand	24.5	36.2	32.5	33.9	30.3	30.5	31.6	31.6	32.9	32.3
Norway	29.4	40.2	41.7	42.0	41.8	39.8	38.4	38.8	39.6	39.9
Poland	15.7	..	32.9	34.8	31.4	31.9	32.4	34.1	35.2	35.4
Portugal	15.7	26.5	31.1	31.8	30.5	34.0	34.4	34.1	34.8	34.8
Slovak Republic	..	..	33.6	29.2	28.1	31.0	32.7	34.2	34.3	34.7
Slovenia	..	..	37.7	38.1	37.8	37.2	37.3	37.1	37.4	37.7
Spain	14.3	31.5	33.1	36.4	31.3	33.1	33.8	33.9	34.6	34.6
Sweden	30.9	49.0	48.8	45.1	43.1	42.7	42.9	44.3	43.9	42.9
Switzerland[1]	16.5	23.7	27.6	26.2	26.6	27.0	27.6	28.4	28.0	28.5
Turkey	10.8	14.5	23.5	22.9	24.7	25.2	25.0	24.7	24.0	23.1
United Kingdom	30.1	32.9	32.8	32.8	32.1	32.1	32.4	32.8	32.9	33.0
United States	23.6	26.0	28.3	26.8	23.5	25.6	26.2	26.7	24.4	24.5
Unweighted average										
OECD Average[2]	24.8	31.1	33.3	33.2	31.9	33.0	33.3	33.7	33.9	33.8

.. Not available
Note: Full time series can be accessed at http://oe.cd/full-time-series.
1. The total tax revenue has been reduced by the amount of any capital transfer that represents uncollected taxes. The capital transfer has been allocated between tax headings in proportion to the reported tax revenue, except for Belgium, where the capital transfers were subtracted directly from the specific taxes to which they relate.
2. 2019: calculated by applying the unweighted average percentage change for 2019 in the 35 countries providing data for that year to the overall average tax to GDP ratio in 2018.

StatLink https://doi.org/10.1787/888934209856

We also know from the OECD[275] that, in 2019, average taxation (on personal income, company income, capital gains, social security and consumption) in OECD countries was about 33.8% of GDP (see chart on previous page), with the lowest taxation in Mexico (16.5%) and the highest in Denmark (46.3%).

---

[273] THE ECONOMIST, *Old-age dependency ratios.*
[274] ADEMA, W., LADAIQUE, M., *How Expensive Is the Welfare State"*, OECD Social, Employment and Migration Working Papers, 92(1).
According to OECD data, the U.S. has social expenditures of 16.3% of GDP, and healthcare expenditures that equal 16.4% of GDP, for a combined total 32.7% of GDP. IMMERVOLL, H., JENKINS, S.P., KÖNIGS, S., *Are Recipients of Social Assistance 'Benefit Dependent'?*, OECD, *Social, Employment and Migration Working Papers*, 162(1).
OECD, *Health at a Glance 2015*, in *OECD Indicators.*
[275] OECD, *Revenue Statistics 2015.*

The share of current taxes on income, wealth, etc. in OECD countries has remained stable since 2007, despite efforts to reduce the tax bill.

Looking to single OECD economies like Germany, Italy, France and the U.S., we can see that social expenditures (including healthcare) make up the absolute majority of public spending (i.e., more than 50%), topping 60% in some cases (Germany, Italy,[276] France).[277]

German Chancellor Angela Merkel had an interview with the *Financial Times* on December 17, 2012, in which she hinted at the need to cap social spending. Chancellor Merkel stated that only 7% of the world's population lives in Europe, producing 25% of global GDP and spending about 50% of global social expenditures. So the welfare of about 450 million people tops the welfare of the remaining 7.2 billion (800 million of whom are residents of the U.S. or other OECD economies!).

In 2014, OECD (and EU28) tax revenue streams were split as follows:
- about one-third from VAT and similar taxes, like import tolls
- about one-third from income (personal and enterprise)
- about one-third from social security contributions.

Table 1.2. Tax structures in the OECD area, selected years (unweighted average as % of GDP)

Per cent

	1965	1990	2000	2007	2010	2015	2016	2017	2018
Total tax revenue	24.8	31.1	33.3	33.2	31.9	33.3	34.0	33.7	33.9
1000 Taxes on income, profits and capital gains	8.7	11.8	11.7	11.9	10.4	11.1	11.1	11.4	11.5
of which:									
1100 Taxes on income, profits and capital gains of individuals	6.6	9.3	8.5	8.0	7.4	8.1	8.0	8.1	8.1
1200 Taxes on income, profits and capital gains of corporates	2.1	2.4	3.2	3.6	2.7	2.8	2.9	3.0	3.1
2000 Social security contributions (SSC)	4.5	7.1	8.4	8.3	8.7	8.8	9.0	8.9	9.0
3000 Taxes on payroll and workforce	0.3	0.3	0.4	0.3	0.3	0.4	0.4	0.4	0.4
4000 Taxes on property	1.9	1.7	1.7	1.8	1.7	1.9	2.3	1.9	1.9
5000 Taxes on goods and services	9.4	9.9	10.8	10.7	10.6	10.9	11.0	11.0	10.9
of which:									
5111 Value added taxes	0.4	5.1	6.3	6.5	6.4	6.7	6.7	6.8	6.8
5121 Excises	3.5	2.6	2.8	2.6	2.6	2.5	2.6	2.5	2.4
6000 Other Taxes	0.1	0.3	0.2	0.2	0.2	0.2	0.2	0.1	0.1

Note: Percentage share of major tax categories in GDP. Data are included from 1965 onwards for Australia, Austria, Belgium, Canada, Denmark, Finland, France, Germany, Greece, Iceland, Ireland, Italy, Japan, Luxembourg, the Netherlands, New Zealand, Norway, Portugal, Spain, Sweden, Switzerland, Turkey, United Kingdom and United States; from 1972 for Korea; from 1980 for Mexico; from 1990 for Chile and Colombia; from 1991 for Hungary and Poland; from 1993 for the Czech Republic and from 1995 for Estonia, Israel, Latvia, Lithuania, the Slovak Republic and Slovenia. The figures for the 2016 OECD average includes the one-off revenues from stability contributions in Iceland.
Source: OECD (2020), "Revenue Statistics: Comparative tables", OECD Tax Statistics (database), DOI: http://dx.doi.org/10.1787/data-00262-en.

StatLink https://doi.org/10.1787/888934209609

All this considered, we understand that social expenditures (including healthcare) comprise the vast majority of public outlays in the OECD and are covered partly by social contributions and partly by taxes.

What do we learn from these statistics?

We learn that **it will be impossible to increase overall taxation (and/or contributions) in order to cover the dramatic increase in the dependency ratio**

---

[276] MAZZOTTI F., *Nota Sull'Analisi Della Spesa Sociale In Italia.*
[277] Der Tagesspiegel, *Sozialausgaben steigen um 33 Milliarden Euro.*

expected over the next 35 years. Therefore, in the near future we will be forced in the OECD to **reduce public expenditure per head**. Social expenditures (including healthcare) are about 60% of the public outlay, so it will not be possible to keep the current level of welfare and healthcare, even when reducing every other kind of public expenditure.

Table 1. Public social expenditure in OECD countries: levels and composition, 2007 [1] [2]

	Total	Cash	Income-tested	Old age	Survivors	Incapacity related	Health	Family	Active labour market prog.	Unemployment	Housing	Other social policy areas
	in % of GDP			in % of total spending								
Australia	16.4	7.3	5.6	28.7	1.2	13.4	34.8	15.2	1.8	2.4	1.8	0.6
United Kingdom	20.4	9.9	5.0	27.9	1.0	12.3	33.8	16.2	1.5	1.0	5.4	1.0
Ireland	16.7	8.9	4.3	18.5	4.8	10.7	35.1	17.3	3.6	6.0	1.9	2.4
France	29.7	17.1	4.1	37.2	6.0	6.0	29.2	10.1	3.0	4.7	2.7	1.0
Iceland	15.3	5.6	4.0	15.2	0.0	14.6	37.7	23.2	0.0	1.3	4.0	4.0
Canada	16.8	8.7	3.6	21.8	2.4	5.3	41.2	6.5	1.8	3.5	2.4	15.3
Netherlands	21.1	10.1	3.6	25.1	0.9	14.2	33.2	9.0	5.2	5.2	1.9	5.2
New Zealand	18.6	9.6	3.3	22.8	0.5	14.7	38.0	16.3	1.6	1.1	4.3	0.5
Germany	25.1	14.5	3.3	33.9	8.4	8.4	30.7	7.2	2.8	5.6	2.4	0.8
Portugal	22.7	15.0	2.7	40.4	7.0	9.2	29.4	5.3	2.2	5.3	0.0	1.3
Spain	21.3	12.8	2.6	30.4	8.9	11.7	28.5	6.1	3.7	8.4	0.9	1.4
Greece	21.6	14.1	2.2	46.8	9.3	4.2	27.3	5.1	0.9	2.3	2.3	1.9
Slovenia	19.5	12.8	1.9	42.3	7.7	10.8	28.9	5.2	1.0	1.5	0.0	2.6
Austria	26.3	17.4	1.9	40.8	7.3	8.8	25.6	9.9	2.7	3.4	0.4	1.1
Switzerland	18.5	10.7	1.7	33.9	2.2	16.1	30.1	7.0	3.2	3.2	0.5	3.8
Denmark	26.5	12.6	1.6	27.7	0.0	16.3	28.4	13.3	4.9	7.2	2.7	2.7
Hungary	23.0	14.6	1.5	36.4	6.1	11.7	22.6	14.7	1.3	3.0	3.9	0.4
Norway	20.5	10.0	1.4	29.8	1.5	20.5	27.3	13.7	2.9	1.0	0.5	2.9
Finland	24.7	14.2	1.4	34.1	3.3	14.6	24.0	11.4	3.7	6.1	0.8	2.0
Belgium	26.0	16.6	1.4	27.3	7.3	8.8	26.9	10.0	4.6	11.9	0.4	2.7
Italy	24.7	16.7	1.2	47.6	9.5	6.9	26.8	5.7	1.6	1.6	0.0	0.0
United States	16.3	7.9	1.2	32.5	4.3	8.0	45.4	4.3	0.6	1.8		3.1
Sweden	27.3	12.8	1.1	32.8	1.8	19.6	23.7	12.4	4.0	2.6	1.8	2.2
Slovak Republic	15.7	9.4	1.0	34.2	5.1	9.5	32.9	11.4	1.3	2.5	0.0	3.2
Poland	19.7	14.2	0.9	43.9	10.1	12.1	22.7	5.6	2.5	1.5	0.5	1.0
Israel	15.5	9.0	0.9	28.6	4.5	18.8	26.0	13.6	1.3	1.9	0.0	5.2
Mexico	6.9	2.2	0.8	16.2	2.9	1.5	38.2	14.7	0.0		14.7	11.8
Korea	7.7	2.8	0.8	24.4	3.3	7.4	45.8	7.0	1.7	3.3		10.2
Czech Republic	18.1	11.4	0.7	36.5	3.9	12.7	30.9	10.5	1.1	3.3	0.6	0.6
Luxembourg	20.3	12.2	0.6	23.8	8.4	13.4	29.7	15.3	2.6	4.6	0.5	2.0
Japan	18.7	10.5	0.6	45.8	6.9	4.3	33.5	4.3	1.1	1.6		1.6
Chile	10.4	5.7	0.4	46.2	6.5	6.6	30.1	8.6	2.2	0.0	0.0	0.0
Turkey	10.5	6.3	0.3	48.1	11.5	1.0	39.4	0.0	0.0	0.0		
Estonia	12.7	8.2	0.1	40.2	0.8	14.7	29.9	12.6	0.8	0.9	0.0	0.8
OECD - Total	19.2	10.9	3.7	32.4	5.1	10.6	29.3	10.1	2.3	3.6	3.0	3.5

1. Data are in descending order of spending on income-tested cash transfers relative to GDP. They are before tax and account neither for the tax treatment of social benefits nor for tax expenditure (such as tax deductions for children), although tax credits that are paid in cash are included. The OECD also calculates net spending data which address these issues (see link in the sources).
2. Blank entries indicate that data are not available. The following income-tested spending items are included in the 'income-tested' category: spending on 'other contingencies - other social policy areas', income-tested spending on the unemployed (e.g. unemployment assistance), income-tested support payments to elderly and disabled, other income tested payments (family cash transfers). It does not include specific housing subsidies, spending on Active Labour Market Policies, or income-tested medical support.

It will be necessary to find a balanced solution[278], in which:
1) GDP will increase.
2) The absolute value of taxes will increase.
3) The absolute value of social and healthcare expenditures per person will decrease.
It is unlikely that in the next 50 years productivity will increase enough (and, with it, income and GDP) to sustain the current level of public expenditure.[279]

---

[278] SHAFIK, M., *What We Owe Each Other: A New Social Contract*, 188 ff. comes to similar conclusions, to which I refer. Information technology may be a tool for finding a new solution for pensions and social security, that are still regulated on the legal fiction that some money is saved somewhere for covering social expenditure. If there aren't any funds put aside for pensions and social security, they should be paid out of the overall taxation, without pretending there are some nonexistent provisions.
[279] PIKETTY, T., *Capital in the Twenty-First Century*, considers that high taxation on income has failed to deliver redistribution and proposes a global tax on wealth and higher inheritance taxes: loc. 5824 and 6537. SHAFIK, M., *What We Owe Each Other: A New Social Contract*, 163 ff. is more optimistic and believes that social policy may increase productivity of labor.

Figure 7.3. **Health expenditure as a share of GDP, 2018 (or nearest year)**

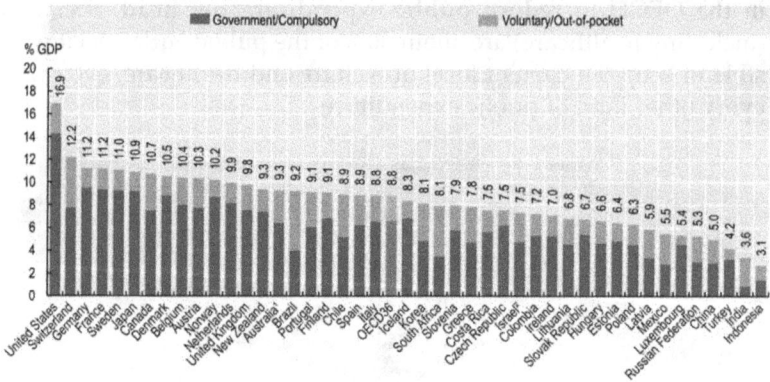

■■ Government/Compulsory   ▓▓ Voluntary/Out-of-pocket

% GDP

16.9 12.2 11.2 11.2 11.0 10.9 10.7 10.5 10.4 10.3 10.2 9.9 9.8 9.3 9.3 9.2 9.1 9.1 8.9 8.9 8.8 8.6 8.3 8.1 8.1 7.9 7.8 7.5 7.5 7.5 7.2 7.0 6.8 6.7 6.6 6.4 6.3 5.9 5.5 5.4 5.3 5.0 4.2 3.6 3.1

United States, Switzerland, Germany, France, Sweden, Japan, Canada, Denmark, Belgium, Austria, Norway, Netherlands, United Kingdom, New Zealand, Australia¹, Brazil, Portugal, Finland, Chile, Spain, Italy, OECD36, Iceland, Korea, South Africa, Slovenia, Greece, Costa Rica, Czech Republic, Israel², Colombia, Ireland, Lithuania, Slovak Republic, Hungary, Estonia, Poland, Latvia, Mexico, Luxembourg, Russian Federation, China, Turkey, India, Indonesia

Note: Expenditure excludes investments, unless otherwise stated.
1. Australia expenditure estimates exclude all expenditure for residential aged care facilities in welfare (social) services. 2. Includes investments.
Source: OECD Health Statistics 2019, WHO Global Health Expenditure Database.

StatLink ▨▤▧ https://doi.org/10.1787/888934016816

The OECD 2015 Revenue Statistics[280] clearly show that, over the last 50 years, taxation levels have been inversely proportional to GDP growth. In 1965, average OECD taxation was 25.5% of GDP, and the growth rate was solidly above 4%. From 1975 to 2007, the average taxation increased by almost half, and growth in the OECD is sluggish or non-existent, mainly for two reasons:
a) because of the accumulated debt in OECD countries
b) because the steep increase in overall taxation has reduced the ability of citizens and enterprises to accumulate, invest and spend.
For more detailed consideration of the optimal rate of taxation on GDP, read the OECD paper of November 2011 on the subject, *"What is a 'Competitive' Tax System?"*[281]
The OECD demographic pyramid is poised at a cusp, and it is unsustainable at the current pace of social expenditure. People feel left behind because nobody told them that the promises made in past decades were hollow at best. Soon there will be an unsustainable lack of proportion between what a single OECD citizen is asked to give to the state and the benefit they receive in exchange. This system needs to be reformed, because it will certainly produce more anger and unrest in the coming years, and **it is delegitimising democracy**.
But this will not be easy, particularly after 2020, which saw a dramatic increase in welfare expenses during the Covid-19 pandemic, increasing the sense of entitlement of many and raising the expectations for how far welfare can go.
Still, far too many citizens of OECD countries have the unsettling feeling that the reciprocity of the social pact is biased and slowly unfolding, to their detriment.[282] Political institutions (governments and parliaments) seem unable to design a sustainable tax policy or to find a sustainable redistribution

---

[280] OECD, *"Revenue Statistics 2015"*.

[281] MATTHEWS S., *What Is a "Competitive" Tax System?*

[282] PIKETTY, T., *Capital in the Twenty-First Century*, passim.

model; non-governmental organisations increasingly dictate the technological, economic, political and social agenda to national governments. The reason for this is that governments prefer to present hard choices as technical necessities and not as political decisions, for fear of losing popular support.

This practice of disguising politics as something technical is harmful and is weakening democracy in the OECD countries.[283] If the system "necessarily" excludes the vast majority of citizens[284] based on choices that "must be" technical[285] and cannot be political, then the citizens, for good reason, react against the system.[286] Populism and the radicalisation of politics ensue.

The main purpose of politics is to manage security and redistribution in a fair and sensible way. These cannot be "sold" to the voters as technical decisions.[287] The damage to trust and social cohesion may be long-lasting.

In this book I address the issue of how written text on paper (chapter 3.2) and in digital (chapter 8.2.1) can radicalise the political debate and has supported (is supporting) populism. But politics and politicians that disguise political choices as technical choices, share the responsibility for the success of populism.

---

[283] ZAKARIA, F., *Ten Lessons for a Post-Pandemic World*, 74.
[284] PIKETTY, T., *Capital in the Twenty-First Century*, passim.
[285] PIKETTY, T., *Capital and Ideology*, loc. 1036.
[286] PIKETTY, T., *Capital in the Twenty-First Century*, loc. 10093 and passim.
[287] PIKETTY, T., *The Economics of Inequality*, 100.

5

The New Law
Beyond Natural Law: Constitution, Freedom, Pluralism, Social Security

Déclaration des Droits de l'Homme et du Citoyen de 1789
Les Représentants du Peuple Français, constitués en Assemblée Nationale, considérant que l'ignorance, l'oubli ou le mépris des droits de l'Homme sont les seules causes des malheurs publics et de la corruption des Gouvernements, ont résolu d'exposer, dans une Déclaration solennelle, les droits naturels, inaliénables et sacrés de l'Homme, afin que cette Déclaration, constamment présente à tous les Membres du corps social, leur rappelle sans cesse leurs droits et leurs devoirs; afin que les actes du pouvoir législatif, et ceux du pouvoir exécutif, pouvant être à chaque instant comparés avec le but de toute institution politique, en soient plus respectés; afin que les réclamations des citoyens, fondées désormais sur des principes simples et incontestables, tournent toujours au maintien de la Constitution et au bonheur de tous.
En conséquence, l'Assemblée Nationale reconnaît et déclare, en présence et sous les auspices de l'Etre suprême, les droits suivants de l'Homme et du Citoyen.

Art. 1er. - Les hommes naissent et demeurent libres et égaux en droits. Les distinctions sociales ne peuvent être fondées que sur l'utilité commune.

Art. 2. - Le but de toute association politique est la conservation des droits naturels et imprescriptibles de l'Homme. Ces droits sont la liberté, la propriété, la sûreté, et la résistance à l'oppression.

Art. 3. - Le principe de toute Souveraineté réside essentiellement dans la Nation. Nul corps, nul individu ne peut exercer d'autorité qui n'en émane expressément.

Art. 4. - La liberté consiste à pouvoir faire tout ce qui ne nuit pas à autrui: ainsi, l'exercice des droits naturels de chaque homme n'a de bornes que celles qui assurent aux autres Membres de la Société la jouissance de ces mêmes droits. Ces bornes ne peuvent être déterminées que par la Loi.

Art. 5. - La Loi n'a le droit de défendre que les actions nuisibles à la Société. Tout ce qui n'est pas défendu par la Loi ne peut être empêché, et nul ne peut être contraint à faire ce qu'elle n'ordonne pas.

Art. 6. - La Loi est l'expression de la volonté générale. Tous les Citoyens ont droit de concourir personnellement, ou par leurs Représentants, à sa formation. Elle doit être la même pour tous, soit qu'elle protège, soit qu'elle punisse. Tous les Citoyens étant égaux à ses yeux sont également admissibles à toutes dignités, places et emplois publics, selon leur capacité, et sans autre distinction que celle de leurs vertus et de leurs talents.

Art. 7. - Nul homme ne peut être accusé, arrêté ni détenu que dans les cas déterminés par la Loi, et selon les formes qu'elle a prescrites. Ceux qui sollicitent, expédient, exécutent ou font exécuter des ordres arbitraires, doivent être punis; mais tout citoyen appelé ou saisi en vertu de la Loi doit obéir à l'instant: il se rend coupable par la résistance.

Art. 8. - La Loi ne doit établir que des peines strictement et évidemment nécessaires, et nul ne peut être puni qu'en vertu d'une Loi établie et promulguée antérieurement au délit, et légalement appliquée.

Art. 9. - Tout homme étant présumé innocent jusqu'à ce qu'il ait été déclaré coupable, s'il est jugé indispensable de l'arrêter, toute rigueur qui ne serait pas nécessaire pour s'assurer de sa personne doit être sévèrement réprimée par la Loi.

Art. 10. - Nul ne doit être inquiété pour ses opinions, même religieuses, pourvu que leur manifestation ne trouble pas l'ordre public établi par la Loi.

Art. 11. - La libre communication des pensées et des opinions est un des droits les plus précieux de l'Homme: tout Citoyen peut donc parler, écrire, imprimer librement, sauf à répondre de l'abus de cette liberté dans les cas déterminés par la Loi.

Art. 12. - La garantie des droits de l'Homme et du Citoyen nécessite une force publique: cette force est donc instituée pour l'avantage de tous, et non pour l'utilité particulière de ceux auxquels elle est confiée.

Art. 13. - Pour l'entretien de la force publique, et pour les dépenses d'administration, une contribution commune est indispensable: elle doit être également répartie entre tous les citoyens, en raison de leurs facultés.

Art. 14. - Tous les Citoyens ont le droit de constater, par eux-mêmes ou par leurs représentants, la nécessité de la contribution publique, de la consentir librement, d'en suivre l'emploi, et d'en déterminer la quotité, l'assiette, le recouvrement et la durée.

Art. 15. - La Société a le droit de demander compte à tout Agent public de son administration.

Art. 16. - Toute Société dans laquelle la garantie des Droits n'est pas assurée, ni la séparation des Pouvoirs déterminée, n'a point de Constitution.

Art. 17. - La propriété étant un droit inviolable et sacré, nul ne peut en être privé, si ce n'est lorsque la nécessité publique, légalement constatée, l'exige évidemment, et sous la condition d'une juste et préalable indemnité.

5. The New Law

We have now covered the evolution from hunting-gathering to the slave economy, and then to the industrial and post-industrial economy.

In this chapter we will have a look at the evolution of law from the end of the Roman Empire to modern times.

In 13th century Europe, the invention and deployment of capital-intensive enterprise became the most important economic change since the abolition of slavery and, earlier, the invention of tools. This momentous change needed new rules, new concepts and a new social structure.

Law evolved from a system of "natural rules". These rules needed no special justification because they sprang from a natural order sanctioned by God and by ancestral tradition, developing into a system of rules that serve to enact justice.[288]

There is a striking parallel between the evolution of law and the socioeconomic evolution from hunter-gatherers (adapted to the rules of nature) to the industrial and post-industrial city dwellers (who "adapt" nature to the needs of mankind). When nature dictated the rules to mankind, human law was inspired by natural law; the more mankind imposes its rules on nature, the more the law springs from human society.

The evolutionary and anthropologic implications must be considered if we are to fully understand why we developed language, social structure and a social reality.[289] The evolution of law, like the evolution of language and, ultimately, of the human brain, is driven by practical, but also by moral and religious considerations, as we read in history books.

The evolution of human values and the human environment play an important role in defining the rules (customary, legal and moral) that govern us.[290] In looking at the possible impacts of digitalisation, we cannot ignore any of these rules, because digitality has become part of our environment, of our language and, thus, of our values.[291]

Today, particularly in civil law nations, people believe that the law is a consequence of the state, and not the other way around. This conviction is flawed. As we saw in chapter 3, jurisprudence is the law-making tool of an oral society. The personal bonds between citizens engender trust in the judicial institution that "speaks the law" with formulaic utterances applied to specific cases.

This system of producing rules through decisions is so powerful that judicial proceedings all over the world are still oral, and only cases brought to the supreme courts are (mostly) decided in writing.

The law precedes the state, historically, anthropologically, semantically, semiotically and even logically: A state cannot be born if there are no legal rules already in place. Anthropologic studies have shown that all known living

---

[288] Galgano, F., *Lex mercatoria*, 34.
[289] Searle, J., *The construction of social reality*, loc. 981.
[290] Lee R. B., Daly R., *The Cambridge Encyclopedia of Hunters and Gatherers*.
[291] Ong, W.J., *Orality and Literacy*, loc. 3154.

human societies have some form of law, even small tribes of hunter-gatherers living in a Stone Age or Bronze Age society.[292]

So why do many of us believe exactly the opposite? It's because of democracy, as we understand and live it today. Most of us believe that the legitimacy of the laws depends on their enactment by legitimate governments, elected by legitimate parliaments, legitimately elected in fair elections. Nothing wrong with that. But it is not enough to explain the legitimacy of the law.

If we are right to believe that democratic elections are a panacea for all social and political problems, it would mean that the rule of law has stood for not much more than a century or two. If we stop and think critically, we realize that, in effect, we are superciliously looking down our noses at all of the ancient civilisations – Egypt, Greece, Rome, as well as the Middle Ages, the Renaissance and the absolute monarchies of the 11th to 19th centuries. We only have a little empathy for the age of Enlightenment, because we somehow feel it relates directly to our world today.

On the other hand, we travel to admire the wonderful monuments and artifacts that all of these past civilisations created, quietly accepting that today's societies seem incapable of achieving such splendour. Some of us believe that the splendour was possible only because societies were exploitative and unjust, and conversely, our society today is more inclusive, and we pay a just price for that.

Is it really so?

Communist regimes abolished almost all forms of property and constrained the opportunities for individuals to control their own lives. Any form of personal achievement was regarded as a taking of wealth or opportunities away from others, rather than a contribution to the greater good. Life was a zero-sum game.[293]

After less than a century, all communist and socialist states have failed, and communism exists in name only, but clearly not in actuality. Even in North Korea, some form of property ownership and enterprise is now allowed.

Formally, the communist system possessed some legitimacy. Elections were held; the tyranny of the majority was considered a positive good, serving to preserve the "dictatorship of the proletariat",[294] with the goal of creating a new order and the new man. Communist regimes were legitimate, but the people of the 20th century never really stood behind them.

Fascist tyrannies of the 20th century were even less durable, because they strove to recreate a glorious past (the Roman Empire, or *das Deutsche Kaiserreich*), instead of working toward a newer and better future. So many things had changed irreversibly – language, law, custom. The human brain makes

---

[292] NADER L., *The Anthropological Study of Law.*

[293] POPPER, K., *The Open Society and its Enemies*, 293 and 327.

[294] The term was coined by Joseph Weydemeyer in an article of 1 January 1852, titled "Dictatorship of the Proletariat" in a German-language newspaper, *Turn-Zeitung*, in New York. Subsequently, it was used by Lenin and Stalin to describe the intermediate status of the society between capitalism and communism and to justify their ironclad communist tyranny as necessary to achieving a classless society.

different associations when assessing an absolute ruler of the 20th century, rather than one of the 17th century. Politics, law and even Goebbels' subtle propaganda, could not really turn back the minds, the language, the self-perceptions of our grandparents living in the first half of the 20th century.

The failures of idealists trying to establish a new order, or to re-establish an ancient order, prove that neither the state, nor a Führer, nor even an elected parliament are (or can be) the ultimate and sole custodians of legitimacy. There is something "more" than the rule of the majority, "more" than a hierarchy of rules.[295]

But what is this "more"? We will try to come to some conclusion on the subject of justice in the 21st century at the end of this chapter, after making a quick examination of the evolution of the law in the last millennium.

Your author has confessed that he is a practicing lawyer. Therefore, we will discuss "justice" not as an issue of moral philosophy, but as a practical issue.[296] Law is all about solving practical issues, with solutions that are just.

To define, in practical terms, the word "justice", we will make two important assumptions.

The first assumption is that, when the first legal rules arose in human evolution, they served as a **limitation on the full, unrestrained animal freedom** that we possessed before that time. Before that moment, killing one's own siblings[297] and eating them would have been acceptable in a necessary fight for survival.

Since then, "need" has ceased to be a valid moral justification. The day the first rule appeared was the day the human race placed the means above the end; this was a major step in the evolution to what humanity has become. Christianity, Islam, Judaism, Buddhism, Confucianism, Hinduism, all agree on this one, fundamental, moral-absolute imperative: **Never use another human being as means to an end**.

The second fundamental assumption is that **legal and social rules are an essential part of what defines humanity** (see chapter 1) from an anthropological and ontological point of view.

So let's take an approach that (if possible) is satisfactory from two different perspectives:

1) It is compatible with as many moral theories as possible,

2) and it is attainable in practice.

The conclusions we will reach in this chapter do not represent innovative new ideas about justice. Still, I must first state what I consider "just", in order to allow my active and engaged readers to understand and critique the rules that I propose for a digital society.

---

[295] *"It is the greatest happiness of the greatest number that is the measure of right and wrong"*, BENTHAM J., A fragment on government, in The History of Political Thought; BURNS, J. H., *Happiness and Utility: Jeremy Bentham's Equation.*

[296] This is similar to the approach taken by Amartya Sen in The Idea of Justice: "Justice for institutions that legislate or enforce the law, is a totally different issue, compared with the issue of justice for common practices and of unregulated human activity." SEN A., *The Idea of Justice*, VII.

[297] Think of Abraham and Isaac, Cain and Abel, or the myth of Romulus and Remus; in each of them, a higher rule justifies the sacrifice of a son or brother.

Let us analyse the legal mechanisms that have evolved over the last millennium – from feudalism to post-industrial society. Some of them are incredibly familiar to us, even if we barely notice them. Some of them are still contributing to changes in our society, but not always in a way that will guarantee freedom or justice in the future. Therefore, in the last chapter of this book, I will propose some legal principles that should govern a digital society, in order to avoid the possibility of our epoch turning into a new "Dark Ages", between the Written Age and the Digital Age.

5.1. The Roman Law and its Evolution: the Law Merchant

Europe between the 2nd and the 6th centuries imploded.

It lost more than one-third of its population, and per-capita incomes collapsed.[298] Warrior tribes invaded Europe, pillaging and vandalizing the remnants of the Roman Empire. One of the first such tribes were actually the Vandals,[299] the source of the term "vandalism".

The people of Europe retreated into fortified citadels and ceased to travel. Commerce all but stopped. The economy became a subsistence economy of products locally farmed and produced.

Europe was a failed continent, where armed bands of warriors held sway, and the civil population fled war and famine as best they could.

It wasn't until around the 10th or 11th centuries that income per person began to match the levels under the Roman Empire in the 1st century A.D.[300]

What changed in Europe in the 11th century is that the alien invasions ceased, and some level of state authority was re-established. The population was no longer forced by war and wanton violence to stay put in their citadels. It became possible again to travel and trade.

The more daring individuals left the rigid, hierarchical organisation of the fiefs and began to repopulate the ancient Roman cities that had been abandoned during the barbaric invasions of the 4th to the 11th centuries. The Roman cities had been abandoned because of the network of roads that connected them. This system extended more than 400,000 kilometres, of which over 80,500

---

[298] MADDISON A., *The World Economy: A Millennial Perspective* (Development Centre of the Organisation for Economic Co-operation and Development, 2001); SCHEIDEL W. AND FRIESEN S. J., *'The size of the economy and the distribution of income in the Roman Empire'*, 61–91. The description of demographic in classic period and in middle age is explained by Wikipedia at Wikipedia, *Classical demography* and Wikipedia, *Medieval demography*.

[299] See Wikipedia, *Vandals*.

[300] ACEMOGLU D., ROBINSON J. A., *Why Nations Fail: The Origin of Power Prosperity and Poverty*, 150. In 1990-1992 the Greenland Ice Core Project drilled down through 3.000 meters of ice, covering about 250.000 years of human history. One of the major findings of this project and others preceding it was that there was a distinct increase in atmospheric pollutants, starting around 500 BC. Atmospheric quantities of lead, silver and copper then increased steadily, reaching a peak in the 1st Century AD. Remarkably, this atmospheric quantity of lead is reached again only in the 13th Century. These findings show the intensity of Roman mining. When compared to what happened before and after, this upsurge in mining is a clear indicator of economic expansion and of the implosion of economy in the first millennium in Europe.

kilometres were paved in stone.[301] The roads were built not only for trade, but also for military use.[302] Consequently, invading armies could march along the Roman roads with all necessary supplies and weapons and arrive swiftly at the cities targeted for attack.

Between the 4th and 11th centuries, it became too dangerous to live in most Roman cities, including Rome, which was besieged and sacked in 410 A.D. by the Visigoths, led by Alaric, and in 455 A.D. by Genseric, king of the Vandals. In the following 500 years, Rome was taken several more times by invaders, up to its final sack by the Normans in 804. Its population shrank from 1,500,000 in the 1st century A.D. to just 40,000 when sacked by the Normans.[303] It was not until the 1950s that Rome reached the same population it held in the 1st century A.D. In the Early Middle Ages, life in Europe was far more dangerous than during World War II or in any failed state today.

The Roman legal, social and economic system, when it imploded in Europe during the Early Middle Ages (476-1000 A.D.), had lasted almost a millennium. It was, together with the Chinese Empire, one of the largest, richest states in human history, prior to the British Empire. The income of an average worker under Emperor Diocletian (301 A.D.) was almost the same as that of an Italian worker of the 17th century.[304] The history of how Europe climbed out of poverty, becoming the richest and most economically and socially developed region of the world from the Late Middle Ages until the present day, makes for a compelling read and has been extensively researched.[305]

What is less known is that legal innovation triggered the revival of Europe.[306] Technological innovation followed about five centuries later.[307]

All of the rights of our everyday lives – property, contracts, marriage, leases, employment contracts – originated in a time of oral justice and oral agreements, long before the establishment of written laws or written agreements.[308] Prior to the invention of social security,[309] a democratically elected parliament never created anything as important as the system of contracts, rights and obligations of private and commercial law. Private and commercial laws in the Western world (Europe and the Americas) evolved directly from Roman law. In the 19th century, these legal innovations were exported to Africa[310] and Asia. They "naturally" expanded, and in the end, even communist China had to

---

[301] GRANT M., *History of Rome*, 264.

[302] GABRIEL R. A., *The Great Armies of Antiquity*, 9.

[303] F. GREGOVIUS, *Storia di Roma nel Medioevo*, Roma, vol. 1, 278; GIORGIO SPINI, *Storia dell'Età Moderna*, vol. I, 121.

[304] ACEMOGLU, D., ROBINSON, J.A., *Why Nations Fail: The Origins of Power, Prosperity and Poverty*, 178.

[305] ACEMOGLU, D., ROBINSON, J.A., *Why Nations Fail: The Origins of Power, Prosperity and Poverty*, 180 ff.; PIRENNE H., *Mohammed and Charlemagne*, 86.

[306] GALGANO, F., *Lex mercatoria*, 83.

[307] ACEMOGLU D., ROBINSON, J.A., *Why Nations Fail: The Origins of Power, Prosperity and Poverty*, 190.

[308] See chapters 3.2 and 3.6 on the establishment of written laws. Property, usufruct, contracts, obligations, all pre-date written laws that were established in Rome around 450 B.C.

[309] See chapters 5.4.3 and 5.4.4.

[310] On Islamic legal pluralism, see KURAN, T., *The Long Divergence*, loc. 3583.

adopt these laws in order to support its economic expansion with effective rules and functioning institutions.[311]

In the first millennium, the law in Europe was mostly public law, addressing the organisation of the state (the military, justice, crime, taxes). Public law was an expression of the absolute power of the monarch, and it was subject to change with every new regime.[312]

Private law in the first millennium was considered "natural law", beyond the reach of any legislative authority. This concept has remained unchanged since that time. Private law mostly involved regulating property.[313]

The legal innovation that began at the end of the Early Middle Ages was a wondrous process because it created a new legal system, the Law merchant (*Lex Mercatoria*), at a time when law was deemed to be eternal and unchangeable. It is important to understand this process, because it is still ongoing today. To understand it allows one to understand some aspects of the present legal evolution.[314]

The legal innovations underlying eBay, Google, Facebook and cloud computing are, in their essence, very similar to what the merchants did in the 11th century in order to establish the Law merchant. But they also have some extremely relevant differences,.

Let's see how.

5.2. The Merchants: Outcasts and Outlaws at the Turn of the First Millennium

War and insecurity drastically reduced the opportunities for trade between the 5th and 11th centuries.[315] Many of the merchants who resumed trading were people fleeing from the fiefs and their hierarchical subsistence economy. As long as there were invading armies and robbers beyond the walls of the manor, it was a reasonable choice to trade freedom for protection. But when the invasions ceased and the only threat was the occasional robber, the idea of regaining lost freedoms became enticing again.

The boldest left the fiefs, breaking a contract and an oath: Whoever left the fief, ending homage and fealty, could be punished by death.[316]

So the first merchants put themselves outside of the reach of the law. They were literally outlaws. Knowing this makes it seem even more incredible that

---

[311] ZHANG, X., *Integration of CCP Leadership with Corporate Governance*, 55-63, in part. 57 f.

[312] GALGANO, F., *Lex mercatoria*, 77.

[313] GALGANO, F., *Lex mercatoria*, 54.

[314] GALGANO, F., *Lex mercatoria*, 273 ff.

[315] The opinions of historians are split among those who assume that trade was reduced but did not stop altogether, and those who believe that trade virtually halted for half a millennium. ACEMOGLU, D., ROBINSON, J.A., *Why Nations Fail: The Origins of Power, Prosperity and Poverty*, 155 and 465, describe the archaeological studies of Hopkins and De Callatay showing that the number of shipwrecks at the end of the Roman Empire declined 90% from its peak.

[316] "Homage" was the contract executed between the lord and vassal in which the vassal promised to fight for the lord at his command, while the lord agreed to protect the vassal from external forces. "Fealty" (from the Latin *fidelitas*) denotes the oath of fidelity sworn by a vassal to his feudal lord.

they eventually succeeded in changing the natural law that governed contracts and property.

The first merchants could not rely on any enforcement of their rights, because they had none. They were fugitives, outlaws, strangers in a world where any stranger had been considered a menace for the previous 500 years or more.

As strangers, merchants were not only feared and reviled, but they also had Roman law against them: Table VIII of the ancient Roman *Lex XII Tabularum* provided that "*Furtivam (Rem) Lex XII Tabularum Usucapi Prohibet*", which can be translated, "Nobody can ever become the proprietor of stolen goods."

So in the 11th century, whenever a merchant sold an item in a market, he was exposed to terrible risks. In the worst case, he could be accused of being a thief, which, for a foreigner, was tantamount to being executed. In the best-case scenario, he could be forced to return payment to the buyer.

But they faced even more obstacles. There were no shared measures for time, weight, liquids. Every marketplace had its own rules for measurement, which were commonly inscribed on the facade of the local church.[317] A loaf of bread had to be of the local size and shape, and wine had to be placed in flasks bearing a local mark signalling the right amount, and so on.

The merchants of the 11th century faced quite a hostile environment for doing their business. They could rely only on themselves for protection and justice. They had to figure out how to earn the trust of their customers and protect themselves from fabricated accusations.[318]

In very early times, it probably helped to be feared as much as robbers themselves: Buying the merchant's "stolen" goods was a way for the people living within feudal society to establish good relations with the people living outside of the fiefdom. Mutual fear was the first step towards mutual respect. But trade, in order to flourish, needs trust rather than fear.

So the merchants had to invent a mechanism that could protect them, and at the same time, foster trust in them.[319] What they did was simply genius!

First, they created an obligation for the merchant to keep books and registers; all their commercial activities had to be duly recorded. These books had to be updated daily, and any failure to do so was punished harshly, even by death. These books were named "journals", precisely because of the obligation to record information before they adjourned for the day. Journals were supported by additional documents, like ledgers, in which each monetary transaction or credit had to be recorded.

To protect themselves, the merchants had to neatly record the name of the vendor, the date of the purchase and the amount paid. Normally, the vendors to the merchant were other merchants, artisans or farmers. The purchase of used

---

[317] The same was true in China, but only in Europe did the merchants of the 11th century and after play a decisive role in standardizing measures and providing a legal framework to support cross-border economic relations: ACEMOGLU, D., ROBINSON, J.A., *Why Nations Fail: The Origins of Power, Prosperity and Poverty*, 226.

[318] PIRENNE, H., *Mohammed and Charlemagne*, p. 96.

[319] GALGANO, F., *Lex mercatoria*, 34.

goods was considered suspicious (not unlike buying a used bicycle at a flea market today) and required additional precautions.

The journal and the ledger made the occasional purchase of goods of dubious provenance a risky endeavour – possible, but so risky that it required proper preparation and thorough organisation and execution.[320]

The early merchants were rovers. They established their temporary markets outside of the walls of the feudal estates and marked their arrival with loud music and games, not unlike a traveling circus of the last century. They created unauthorized new markets that competed with officially licensed markets by means of aggressive pricing and a wider selection of products – no different from today's traveling markets and fairs (and on-line marketplaces).

If you consider their starting point, the merchants of the Middle Ages had it a lot worse than today's start-ups. They were poorly positioned, like an ex-convict's co-op shop. These outside-the-wall merchants were feared and mistrusted by law enforcement agencies. On top of that, the merchants of the Middle Ages faced the surviving Roman law (*ius commune*) encouraging opportunistic claims against them. They had absolutely no chance of winning their case if it was tried in a court of the fief.

So they had to create an alternative dispute resolution system that was more trustworthy than the feudal judges. And so they did. The merchants' tribunals were swift, just and incorruptible. They never sided with the merchant for fellowship. They had the task of building trust in the merchants, and there was no room for favouritism.[321]

Some may wonder how they succeeded, considering that they were mistrusted, foreign outlaws. But if we look closely at the issue, we will realize that:

a) It is quite common for segregated communities to create their own rules and enforcement systems (inmates, segregated minorities, the military, etc.), and they are very strict with these rules.

b) This is exactly what online merchants and service providers have done today: eBay enforces its own rules in the marketplace that it provides; Amazon regulates and supervises the fairness of trade between third parties and Amazon users; Facebook closely monitors activities on its social network to avoid (at least in theory) offensive behaviour; Google polices its websites for fraudulent or incorrect information and blacklists posters who place it there.

So originally, there was no legal obligation to turn to the merchants' tribunals for cases involving merchants. But, as present-day online merchants do, there was a "*conventio ad excludendum*": If a merchant was called before the tribunal and did not appear in the court, he was excluded from the marketplace. Soon, this *conventio ad excludendum* was also extended to the customers: If you wanted one day to be accepted as a merchant or an artisan, you could never refuse the jurisdiction of the merchants' courts. Soon, the itinerant merchants

---

[320] GALGANO, F., *Lex mercatoria*, 43.
[321] GALGANO F., *Lex mercatoria*, 47.

were almost as rich as the feudal lords, and nobody was so foolish as to refuse the jurisdiction of a merchant's tribunal.[322]

If we look at today's new business models and new ways to enforce commercial transactions, we see a phenomenon that, in its essence, began 1,000 years ago. Still, we haven't explained how one can change the natural law, which is unchangeable.

Well ... you pretend not to change it, but you do it all the same. Let's see how: The *ius commune* and the *lex mercatoria* (law merchant) are both bodies of case law, governed by the principle of *stare decisis*. *Stare decisis* is the doctrine of the case law system that requires a court to follow a previous decision (precedent), either of that court or of a higher court in the jurisdiction, whenever the decision involves issues and key facts similar to those involved in the previous decision. Determining whether a case is on point and finding cases on point are important for the following two reasons:

a) The determination must be made before the case may be applied as a precedent and be relied upon by the court in its determination of how the issue will be decided.

b) Finding cases that are on point will guide the attorney as to how the issue in the client's case may be decided, and help the attorney decide what course of action to take.

Precedent is an earlier court decision on an issue that governs or guides a subsequent court in its determination of an identical or similar issue based on identical or similar key facts. There are two main types of precedents:

a) *Mandatory precedent* is precedent from a higher court in a jurisdiction. If a court opinion is on point, that is, if it is a precedent, the doctrine of *stare decisis* mandates that the lower courts in the jurisdiction follow it.

b) *Persuasive precedent* is precedent that a court may look to for guidance when reaching a decision, but the court is not bound to follow the precedent.

In order to allow a legal system based on *stare decisis* to evolve, it is necessary to provide a different definition of the facts, so that old decisions are not automatically applied to facts that may be deemed "new".

That is precisely what the merchants did.[323]

By creating a thorough system of documentation for their economic transactions, they were able to say that a merchant was a different kind of person – one in whom good faith could be presumed – because they had to produce so much documentation about their sales and purchases. The line of reasoning was more or less as follows: If a person has sold a stolen good and cannot document his previous purchase, then the old Roman rule (that nobody can ever become a proprietor of stolen goods) justly applies. But if a merchant is bound to painstakingly keep his books and record all of his transactions, and someone buys an item that the merchant guarantees is his own, then the situation is different, because of the bookkeeping. One could trust the merchant, because he must document all his acquisitions and sales, and the buyer is entitled to

---

[322] GALGANO F., *Lex mercatoria*, 49.
[323] GALGANO, F., *Lex mercatoria*, 41.

check the records. In principle, this is exactly what an e-commerce site does today: It generates reliable records of the transactions.

In Roman law, the reason why you could never become the proprietor of stolen goods was that it did not allow for *usucapio*[324] (adverse possession) by someone in bad faith. The fact that someone had purchased stolen goods led to a presumption that the transaction was in bad faith, and contrary proof was not allowed. The merchant's reasoning was that, because a merchant had to record all of his purchases, the presumption that he (and his customer) are acting in bad faith cannot be upheld in principle; so they must be allowed to prove their good faith.

The existence of the journal and of the ledgers and the strict controls on the merchants (imposed by the board of their trade) became socially accepted and served to increase trust in the merchants. The presumption of bad faith (of vendor and purchaser of stolen goods) became relative, and it became possible to prove the good faith of a merchant's customer – if the goods were recorded in the journal and the payments on the ledger and the recording were accurate. Even if the goods were stolen, there was proof of the good faith of the merchant and also of the buyer. Over time, trust in the honesty of merchants grew to the point that a presumption of good faith of the merchant's customer was established, even if he didn't look into the merchant's books. This presumption ultimately became absolute, so that proof to the contrary was inadmissible.[325]

This evolution occurred without anyone ever intending to change a rule as ancient as law. It simply intended to make the point that a professional buyer and seller (a merchant), keeping proper records of all his transactions and of those with whom he carried on business, earned a higher degree of trust than someone without a journal or a ledger and who had no way to demonstrate the origin and nature of his purchases.

The principle that stolen goods cannot be purchased was never overturned. But an exception was established for anyone obligated to keep a journal and a ledger, and to keep them correctly.

5.2.1. The Main Rules of the Law Merchant

Beyond the introduction of bookkeeping, the convention *"ad excludendum"* and the legal protection of purchases made from a merchant, there were other ancient rules that were twisted in order to adapt Roman law to the needs of trade:

- The principle of *favour debitoris* was turned into *favor creditoris* … if the creditor was a merchant.
- In order to avoid tricks at the expense of the clients of the *"societas mercatorum"* (the unlimited partnership of that time), a presumption was established that the partner acting on behalf of the partnership was duly authorized. This turned upside down the Roman rule that the partners were allowed to prove

---

[324] Wikipedia, *Usucapio*.
[325] GALGANO, F., *Lex mercatoria*, 91 and 99.

that they did not authorize a deal, with the consequence that it was binding only for the acting partner.

- The liability of the partners of a partnership was strengthened: Under the Law Merchant, all partners had equal and unlimited responsibility for the obligations of the partnership, irrespective of who was acting on its behalf. Even undisclosed partners were liable.[326]

- Bankruptcy rules were stiffened, so that the illiquidity of the partnership had, as a consequence, the bankruptcy of all partners.[327]

- Unless otherwise specified, the partnership was for life; only the death of a partner opened an opportunity to exit the partnership.

- The assets of the partnership were shielded from the personal creditors of the merchant, so they had no recourse to them.

If we consider all of these changes to the rules of Roman private law, we may recognize the following legal strategy:

a) Increase protections for the merchant's clients.

b) Avoid letting the merchant skirt his responsibilities.

c) Enable the capitalisation of a partnership, protecting its assets not only from the personal creditors of the merchant, but also from the merchant himself.

The Roman law protected property (and still does, through principles that are still in force). The Law Merchant was designed to protect business and trade.[328] If you look to the policies of eBay,[329] Amazon,[330] YOOX,[331] Facebook,[332] or any other large online merchant, you will recognize the same legal strategy: increase the trustworthiness of the (online) merchant. Like the merchants of the 11th century, online merchants had to overcome a (credible) prejudice: that they were untrustworthy, unreliable outlaws. It is more than a coincidence that Uber's and Airbnb's success stories are closely linked to their decisions to expand insurance protections to their customers and providers, beyond the minimums required by statutory law.

A merchant who sells a new type of goods or proposes a new kind of service needs to overcome the prejudice against the new, against the unknown. To overcome the reasonable prejudice against the insecurity of the web, today's online merchants have resorted to precisely the same strategy of the merchants of 1,000 years ago:

1) extended documentation and tracking for all transactions

2) enhanced service and protection for their customers

3) domestic (policing and) jurisdiction.

---

[326] GALGANO, F., *Lex mercatoria*, 50.

[327] GALGANO, F., *Lex mercatoria*, 55.

[328] GALGANO, F., *Lex mercatoria*, 59.

[329] Look at http://pages.ebay.com/help/policies/overview.html and you will read, "Our policies are designed to create a safe and fair environment for all eBay members. Learning what's allowed can help you avoid unintentionally breaking the rules and helps everyone in working with reliable, trustworthy members."

[330] https://www.amazon.com/gp/help/customer/display.html?nodeId=14309551.

[331] http://www.yoox.com/cms/legal/saleterms.asp.

[332] https://www.facebook.com/terms.

As you would expect, there is also a significant difference between today's merchants and the merchants of 1,000 years ago. The merchants of the Middle Ages clearly wanted to establish a legal environment that suited their trade – a trade in which an entire class of merchants participated, not just one! But today's merchants tend to see each of themselves as a special exception to the current rules governing trade (and human relations) – be it Facebook or Google, with respect to personal data, or eBay, Amazon or PayPal, with respect to their transactions. This may be because, like Google and Facebook, they all strive to become the de-facto standard (if not the de-facto monopolist) of their trade.

In any case, a strategy to become a permanent exception (or the unique owner of an entire trade) is quite different from a strategy to craft a legal environment in which every kind of trade may thrive.[333] This represents a great difference, in that the law of the digital economy may never be properly established, because each variety of digital trade is lobbying for different exceptions to the statutory law in force.

At international gatherings (such as workshops and conferences on eID and digital authentication or on cloud computing) and in European standardisation initiatives (such as the ETSI Cloud Standards Coordination),[334] Google has behaved as if it were a state in itself (or the sole legitimate representative of the digital community worldwide). Its representatives complain that sovereign states are creating "fictitious" borders within the digital world, of which they instinctively consider themselves the only legitimate guardians and representatives. Apple hasn't even bothered to participate: an attitude that is characteristic of the information technology de-facto monopolists, including (before Apple) Microsoft, and, earlier, IBM and AT&T.

In fact, 20 years ago, Microsoft adopted the same attitude towards the birth of the European Electronic Signature. The company seemed almost surprised that the European Union felt the need to regulate certification authorities

---

[333] In fact, the constant effort of the de-facto digital monopolists to be exempted from liability and other rules (in particular competition rules) has recently caused backlash in Europe and the U.S.

In Europe the EU Commission has drafted two proposals for European regulations (laws), that will regulate liability in detail: (EU Commission COM 825/2020) https://eur-lex.europa.eu/legal-content/EN/TXT/PDF/?uri=COM:2020:842:FIN&from=en and the competition rules (EU Commission COM 842/2020) for digital intermediaries https://eur-lex.europa.eu/legal-content/EN/TXT/?uri=CELEX:52020PC0825.

In the U.S., similar legislation is being considered, and several antitrust claims have been filed against the biggest "digital merchants":

THE ECONOMIST, *American trustbusters take on Google*.

THE ECONOMIST, *A formidable alliance takes on Facebook*.

It seems (thus far) that today's digital entrepreneurs, despite utilising the techniques of the merchants of the Middle Ages, have been far less farsighted or capable of taking responsibility for the new economy they have created.

[334] The ETSI Cloud Standards Coordination (http://csc.etsi.org/phase2.html) was carried out in the framework of the EU Cloud Computing Strategy (https://ec.europa.eu/digital-single-market/en/european-cloud-computing-strategy).

such as RSA and Verisign. Not much afterwards, a series of certificates issued improperly created mayhem, which still endures today[335].

As a consequence of such chaos, the European Union decided in 2014 to create new legislation favouring digital providers that voluntarily submit themselves to national security supervision and commit themselves to prompt security breach notifications. In this way, all stakeholders learn in real time that their service or infrastructure has been compromised.[336]

5.2.2. From the Unlimited Responsibility of the Merchant, to the Enterprise with No Personal Responsibility for the Entrepreneur

By the beginning of the 17th century, some merchant partnerships were so richly capitalized that the recourse of putting a lien on the personal assets of the merchant lacked the same economic relevance that it possessed five centuries earlier. It was reasonable to suppose that creditors had sufficient protection based on the assets of the company.

But the rule of unlimited liability would probably never have been changed if there hadn't been the need[337] and the opportunity to colonize new worlds: the East Indies and the Americas.

Colonisation was such a risky and expensive endeavour that not even kings (or nations) could support it without the contributions of private capital.

Average life expectancy at the beginning of the 17th century was around 50 years, and one came of age at 21. To make a quick profit from the establishment of a colony in Malaysia or Nicaragua wasn't a realistic expectation. It was more likely that the eventual profits would be paid out to the heirs of the original investor. Even though there were few liquid markets in the 17th century, not many would have invested in a venture whose profits would be paid out only to the next generation. Moreover, who would risk taking on personal liability in a venture where part of the "business model" involved enslaving people and killing any opponents?

That was why the colonial nations of the 17th century had to create a legal environment that was supportive of colonialism. For this, it was necessary to:

a) exclude the personal liability of the investor in the colonial company (at that time, the East India Company)

b) allow the investor to sell his or her participation in the company at any time.

These two rules, typical of any traded limited liability company today, were radical changes to the rules of the law merchant in the 17th century.[338]

---

[335] Wikipedia „DigiNotar".

[336] EU Regulation 910/2014/EU on electronic identification and trust services for electronic transactions in the internal market (eIDAS Regulation), adopted 23 July 2014,.

[337] There was a need to find new sources of wealth because of the low productivity of labour. Throughout the 16th century, the economic policy of nations dealt with the need to support and expand economic growth and trade, not all that different from today … and, we may say, even more unsuccessfully than today, when technological innovation sometimes helps us out of the doldrums.

[338] BARROW, I., The East India Company, 1600–1858, 1, 41 and passim; GALGANO, F., Lex mercatoria, 82.

This time, the legal innovation didn't take place through jurisprudence and best practices. Instead, it was the national legislature (the King and Parliament) who issued an "*ortroi*" (an executive order of public law), which changed the rules of commercial law for reasons of "public interest" and "national security".

In order to find the funds to build ships, to arm armies and send them away from the homeland for many months at a time, it was necessary to gather immense sums that were beyond the financial strength of the king or the treasury.

The slave trade resumed, and many people were eventually forced to work for the East India Company, but the pay-outs were handsome. The result was that Great Britain and the Netherlands became the richest nations in history. The accumulation of wealth accelerated, and the capital needed to start the industrial revolution was assembled.[339]

But let's consider the implications of this "new legal environment".

First: The limited liability of the shareholder eliminates the risk of personal insolvency. The maximum possible loss is the money invested in the company. The decision to invest is assessed against the risk of losing the investment, not against the risk of losing everything! This was a major incentive for investing, compared with the rules of the *lex mercatoria*.

Second: To buy shares, not to be paid dividends, but in order to sell them eventually for profit, implies that the purchase is made for speculative reasons, not as a "strategic investment". The invention of the limited liability company and of stock speculation occurred in one stroke, on the same day. When people today complain about financial speculation, they are evidently unaware that financial instruments and speculation have gone hand in hand from the very beginning: Stocks, obligations and any other financial paper were designed for making a profit through speculation and trading.

As at the time of the rise of the class of merchants, the rise of the limited liability company was also facilitated by new rules of accounting and documentation. The approval of the balance sheet by the shareholders and their decision on the eventual distribution of dividends were the other significant legal innovations applied to the unlimited partnerships of the law merchant.[340]

In chapter 4, we saw that the rise of the West was closely linked to the *lex mercatoria* and the birth of the limited liability company, because it allowed the accumulation of wealth in enterprises, which was reinvested in a capital intensive (and rich) economy. The economic hegemony of the West that began in the 16th century cannot be explained just by colonialism and the slave trade. After all, the Muslim countries, Africa, India and China were also slave-based economies. But only in the West did the law merchant allow for the capitalisation of profits, which turbocharged its economic expansion.[341]

---

[339] FERGUSON, N., *Empire: How Britain Made the Modern World*, loc. 2821.
[340] GALGANO, F., *Lex mercatoria*, 86.
[341] KURAN, T., *The Long Divergence*, loc. 3583; FRIEDMAN, B.M., *The Moral Consequences of Economic Growth*. 52 ff.

5.3. Nations, the Power of Law and the Striving for Constitutions in the Age of Enlightenment: Department of Powers, Freedom, Democracy, Pluralism

The Federalist Papers[342] are undoubtedly the most important effort to explain how democracy should work.

They are a particularly credible source of information, because the U.S. Constitution[343] (approved 17 September 1787) is still in force and has been amended just 27 times.[344] And the United States of America (at least until recently) was a free, rich and stable nation. Despite its recent troubles, it is more so now than in the 19th century, at the time of slavery and the Civil War.

The U.S. Constitution is a masterpiece of enlightened thinking, working to solve the issues that made democracy unfashionable for about two millennia. The issues were brilliantly summarized by Alexander Hamilton and James Madison in Federalist No. 9. The optimism that political science could make democracy work was typical of the Age of Enlightenment.

But the papers were not titled the "Democratic Papers" or the "Republican Papers". When you read them, you will understand that there was a reason for that. A large federal nation of states offered a solution against the tyranny of the majority and against the excessive power of a few.

The political situation in the U.S. has changed recently: There is a level of polarisation[345] not seen for centuries, and trust in its democratic institutions has seemed to fade.[346] In *The Economist*'s briefing of 12 July 2018, we can read, *"The (U.S.) constitution was not designed for the two-party politics it unwittingly encouraged."*[347] I believe that digitalisation plays a role in this and will try to explain (at least) some of the mechanisms in chapter 8.

The aims and the values that *The Federalist Papers* express are, in my opinion, universal. In this dire present time, it is worth reading them again and taking inspiration from their candour and farsightedness, which go well beyond partisan politics.

5.3.1. The Federalist Papers No. 9 and No. 10: Federalism = Pluralism

Hamilton and Madison (writing under the pseudonym of "Publius") titled papers No. 9 and No. 10 "The Union as a Safeguard Against Domestic Faction and Insurrection".

---

[342] see HAMILTON, A., MADISON, J., JAY, J. (1788), *The Federalist Papers, a Collection of Essays Written in Favour of the New Constitution as Agreed upon by the Federal Convention.*

[343] US Congress, Amendments to the Constitution of the United States of America.

[344] GovInfo, "Content Details of the Constitution of the United states of America".

[345] THE ECONOMIST, *United States of Amoeba.*

[346] THE ECONOMIST, *The art of losing. Accepting a disappointing election result is a key part of democracy.*

[347] THE ECONOMIST, *The minority majority. America's electoral system gives the Republicans advantages over Democrats.*

Their words speak loud and clear:

To the People of the State of New York:

A firm Union will be of the utmost moment to the peace and liberty of the States, as a barrier against domestic faction and insurrection. It is impossible to read the history of the petty republics of Greece and Italy without feeling sensations of horror and disgust at the distractions with which they were continually agitated, and at the rapid succession of revolutions by which they were kept in a state of perpetual vibration between the extremes of tyranny and anarchy. If they exhibit occasional calms, these only serve as short-lived contrast to the furious storms that are to succeed. If now and then intervals of felicity open to view, we behold them with a mixture of regret, arising from the reflection that the pleasing scenes before us are soon to be overwhelmed by the tempestuous waves of sedition and party rage. If momentary rays of glory break forth from the gloom, while they dazzle us with a transient and fleeting brilliancy, they at the same time admonish us to lament that the vices of government should pervert the direction and tarnish the luster of those bright talents and exalted endowments for which the favored soils that produced them have been so justly celebrated.

From the disorders that disfigure the annals of those republics the advocates of despotism have drawn arguments, not only against the forms of republican government, but against the very principles of civil liberty. They have decried all free government as inconsistent with the order of society, and have indulged themselves in malicious exultation over its friends and partisans. Happily for mankind, stupendous fabrics reared on the basis of liberty, which have flourished for ages, have, in a few glorious instances, refuted their gloomy sophisms. And, I trust, America will be the broad and solid foundation of other edifices, not less magnificent, which will be equally permanent monuments of their errors. But it is not to be denied that the portraits they have sketched of republican government were too just copies of the originals from which they were taken. If it had been found impracticable to have devised models of a more perfect structure, the enlightened friends to liberty would have been obliged to abandon the cause of that species of government as indefensible.

The science of politics, however, like most other sciences, has received great improvement. The efficacy of various principles is now well understood, which were either not known at all, or imperfectly known to the ancients. The regular distribution of power into distinct departments; the introduction of legislative balances and checks; the institution of courts composed of judges holding their offices during good behaviour; the representation of the people in the legislature by deputies of their own election: these are wholly new discoveries, or have made their principal progress towards perfection in modern times. They are means, and powerful means, by which the excellences of republican government may be retained and its imperfections lessened or avoided".

In Federalist No. 10, Madison wrote:[348]

Among the numerous advantages promised by a well-constructed Union, none deserves to be more accurately developed than its tendency to break and control the violence of faction. The friend of popular governments never finds himself so much alarmed for their character and fate, as when he contemplates their propensity to this dangerous vice. He will not fail, therefore, to set a due value on any plan which,

---

[348] MADISON J., *The Federalist Papers:* No. 10.

without violating the principles to which he is attached, provides a proper cure for it. The instability, injustice, and confusion introduced into the public councils, have, in truth, been the mortal diseases under which popular governments have everywhere perished; as they continue to be the favourite and fruitful topics from which the adversaries to liberty derive their most specious declamations. The valuable improvements made by the American constitutions on the popular models, both ancient and modern, cannot certainly be too much admired; but it would be an unwarrantable partiality, to contend that they have as effectually obviated the danger on this side, as was wished and expected. Complaints are everywhere heard from our most considerate and virtuous citizens, equally the friends of public and private faith, and of public and personal liberty, that our governments are too unstable, that the public good is disregarded in the conflicts of rival parties, and that measures are too often decided, not according to the rules of justice and the rights of the minor party, but by the superior force of an interested and overbearing majority. However anxiously we may wish that these complaints had no foundation, the evidence, of known facts will not permit us to deny that they are in some degree true. It will be found, indeed, on a candid review of our situation, that some of the distresses under which we labour have been erroneously charged on the operation of our governments; but it will be found, at the same time, that other causes will not alone account for many of our heaviest misfortunes; and, particularly, for that prevailing and increasing distrust of public engagements, and alarm for private rights, which are echoed from one end of the continent to the other. These must be chiefly, if not wholly, effects of the unsteadiness and injustice with which a factious spirit has tainted our public administrations. By a faction, I understand a number of citizens, whether amounting to a majority or a minority of the whole, who are united and actuated by some common impulse of passion, or of interest, adverse to the rights of other citizens, or to the permanent and aggregate interests of the community.

There are two methods of curing the mischiefs of faction: the one, by removing its causes; the other, by controlling its effects.

There are again two methods of removing the causes of faction: the one, by destroying the liberty which is essential to its existence; the other, by giving to every citizen the same opinions, the same passions, and the same interests. It could never be more truly said than of the first remedy, that it was worse than the disease. Liberty is to faction what air is to fire, an aliment without which it instantly expires. But it could not be less folly to abolish liberty, which is essential to political life, because it nourishes faction, than it would be to wish the annihilation of air, which is essential to animal life, because it imparts to fire its destructive agency.

The second expedient is as impracticable as the first would be unwise. As long as the reason of man continues fallible, and he is at liberty to exercise it, different opinions will be formed. As long as the connection subsists between his reason and his self-love, his opinions and his passions will have a reciprocal influence on each other; and the former will be objects to which the latter will attach themselves. The diversity in the faculties of men, from which the rights of property originate, is not less an insuperable obstacle to a uniformity of interests. The protection of these faculties is the first object of government. From the protection of different and unequal faculties of acquiring property, the possession of different degrees and kinds of property immediately results; and from the influence of these on the sentiments and views of the respective proprietors, ensues a division of the society into different interests and parties.

The latent causes of faction are thus sown in the nature of man; and we see them everywhere brought into different degrees of activity, according to the different circumstances of civil society. A zeal for different opinions concerning religion, concerning government, and many other points, as well of speculation as of practice; an attachment to different leaders ambitiously contending for pre-eminence and power; or to persons of other descriptions whose fortunes have been interesting to the human passions, have, in turn, divided mankind into parties, inflamed them with mutual animosity, and rendered them much more disposed to vex and oppress each other than to co-operate for their common good. So strong is this propensity of mankind to fall into mutual animosities, that where no substantial occasion presents itself, the most frivolous and fanciful distinctions have been sufficient to kindle their unfriendly passions and excite their most violent conflicts.

But the most common and durable source of factions has been the various and unequal distribution of property Those who hold and those who are without property have ever formed distinct interests in society. Those who are creditors, and those who are debtors, fall under a like discrimination.

A landed interest, a manufacturing interest, a mercantile interest, a moneyed interest, with many lesser interests, grow up of necessity in civilized nations, and divide them into different classes, actuated by different sentiments and views. The regulation of these various and interfering interests forms the principal task of modern legislation, and involves the spirit of party and faction in the necessary and ordinary operations of the government.

No man is allowed to be a judge in his own cause, because his interest would certainly bias his judgment, and, not improbably, corrupt his integrity. With equal, nay with greater reason, a body of men are unfit to be both judges and parties at the same time; yet what are many of the most important acts of legislation, but so many judicial determinations, not indeed concerning the rights of single persons, but concerning the rights of large bodies of citizens? And what are the different classes of legislators but advocates and parties to the causes which they determine? Is a law proposed concerning private debts? It is a question to which the creditors are parties on one side and the debtors on the other. Justice ought to hold the balance between them. Yet the parties are, and must be, themselves the judges; and the most numerous party, or, in other words, the most powerful faction must be expected to prevail. Shall domestic manufactures be encouraged, and in what degree, by restrictions on foreign manufactures? Are questions which would be differently decided by the landed and the manufacturing classes, and probably by neither with a sole regard to justice and the public good. The apportionment of taxes on the various descriptions of property is an act which seems to require the most exact impartiality; yet there is, perhaps, no legislative act in which greater opportunity and temptation are given to a predominant party to trample on the rules of justice. Every shilling with which they overburden the inferior number, is a shilling saved to their own pockets.

It is in vain to say that enlightened statesmen will be able to adjust these clashing interests, and render them all subservient to the public good. Enlightened statesmen will not always be at the helm. Nor, in many cases, can such an adjustment be made at all without taking into view indirect and remote considerations, which will rarely prevail over the immediate interest which one party may find in disregarding the rights of another or the good of the whole.

The inference to which we are brought is, that the causes of faction cannot be removed, and that relief is only to be sought in the means of controlling its effects.

If a faction consists of less than a majority, relief is supplied by the republican principle, which enables the majority to defeat its sinister views by regular vote. It may clog the administration, it may convulse the society; but it will be unable to execute and mask its violence under the forms of the Constitution. When a majority is included in a faction, the form of popular government, on the other hand, enables it to sacrifice to its ruling passion or interest both the public good and the rights of other citizens. To secure the public good and private rights against the danger of such a faction, and at the same time to preserve the spirit and the form of popular government, is then the great object to which our inquiries are directed. Let me add that it is the great desideratum by which this form of government can be rescued from the opprobrium under which it has so long labored, and be recommended to the esteem and adoption of mankind.

By what means is this object attainable? Evidently by one of two only. Either the existence of the same passion or interest in a majority at the same time must be prevented, or the majority, having such coexistent passion or interest, must be rendered, by their number and local situation, unable to concert and carry into effect schemes of oppression. If the impulse and the opportunity be suffered to coincide, we well know that neither moral nor religious motives can be relied on as an adequate control. They are not found to be such on the injustice and violence of individuals, and lose their efficacy in proportion to the number combined together, that is, in proportion as their efficacy becomes needful. From this view of the subject it may be concluded that a pure democracy, by which I mean a society consisting of a small number of citizens, who assemble and administer the government in person, can admit of no cure for the mischiefs of faction. A common passion or interest will, in almost every case, be felt by a majority of the whole; a communication and concert result from the form of government itself; and there is nothing to check the inducements to sacrifice the weaker party or an obnoxious individual. Hence it is that such democracies have ever been spectacles of turbulence and contention; have ever been found incompatible with personal security or the rights of property; and have in general been as short in their lives as they have been violent in their deaths.

Theoretic politicians, who have patronized this species of government, have erroneously supposed that by reducing mankind to a perfect equality in their political rights, they would, at the same time, be perfectly equalized and assimilated in their possessions, their opinions, and their passions. A republic, by which I mean a government in which the scheme of representation takes place, opens a different prospect, and promises the cure for which we are seeking. Let us examine the points in which it varies from pure democracy, and we shall comprehend both the nature of the cure and the efficacy which it must derive from the Union.

The two great points of difference between a democracy and a republic are: first, the delegation of the government, in the latter, to a small number of citizens elected by the rest; secondly, the greater number of citizens, and greater sphere of country, over which the latter may be extended.

He comes to the following conclusion:

Hence, it clearly appears, that the same advantage which a republic has over a democracy, in controlling the effects of faction, is enjoyed by a large over a small republic, – is enjoyed by the Union over the States composing it. Does the advantage consist in the substitution of representatives whose enlightened views and virtuous sentiments render them superior to local prejudices and schemes of injustice? It will not be denied that the representation of the Union will be most likely to possess these requisite endowments. Does it consist in the greater security afforded by a greater variety of parties, against the event of any one party being able to outnumber and oppress the rest? In an equal degree does the increased variety of parties comprised within the Union, increase this security? Does it, in fine, consist in the greater obstacles opposed to the concert and accomplishment of the secret wishes of an unjust and interested majority? Here, again, the extent of the Union gives it the most palpable advantage.

The influence of factious leaders may kindle a flame within their particular States, but will be unable to spread a general conflagration through the other States. A religious sect may degenerate into a political faction in a part of the Confederacy; but the variety of sects dispersed over the entire face of it must secure the national councils against any danger from that source. A rage for paper money, for an abolition of debts, for an equal division of property, or for any other improper or wicked project, will be less apt to pervade the whole body of the Union than a particular member of it; in the same proportion as such a malady is more likely to taint a particular county or district, than an entire State.

In the extent and proper structure of the Union, therefore, we behold a republican remedy for the diseases most incident to republican government. And according to the degree of pleasure and pride we feel in being republicans, ought to be our zeal in cherishing the spirit and supporting the character of Federalists.

How is it possible that Alaska, Vermont and Wyoming having respectively 750,000, 620,000 and 580,000 inhabitants elect two senators each, the same as California, Texas or Florida, with respectively 39 million, 27 million and 20 million residents? Less than 2 million people are (over)represented in the U.S. Senate by six senators, and six senators (under)represent 86 million other U.S. citizens.

Reading Hamilton and Madison we understand that "democracy is not enough." Democracy in itself is inherently unstable and prone to degenerate into "ochlocracy" (tyranny of the majority) or "tyranny of aristocracy", as it was for Machiavelli in the 15th century.[349] Democracy without pluralism doesn't work properly; it is necessary to fragment the interests and protect also the particular interests of small minorities.[350]

This is because, whenever a stable majority encroaches on power, it becomes extremely difficult, if not impossible, to allow another majority to unseat the incumbent and rise to power.[351]

In reading *The Federalist Papers* we learn the true meaning of "federalism": a federation is not a loose collection of states, like ancient Greece or even the European Union; it is a strong, centralized organisation whose mission is to keep the constitutional balance between several federated states that have

---

[349] MACHIAVELLI N., *Discorsi sopra la prima deca di Tito Livio*, ch. 10, revives the theory of the cyclic evolution of political order, first theorized by the Greek historian Polybius in the 2nd century B.C.

[350] ZAKARIA, F., *The Future of Freedom*, loc. 1475; POPPER, K., *The Open Society and its Enemies*, 161 ff.

[351] Here we have plenty of examples: from Iran, to Russia and Singapore, and even, recently, the United States of America.

renounced some of their sovereignty in favour of the federal government. In this respect, all states are equal, so it is necessary to have an assembly of the states: like the U.S. Senate.

For us Europeans, this is not as obvious.

The Swiss Confederation has adopted the same model as the U.S., with the Ständerat (Council of States, i.e., the federal assembly) equally representing all cantons. Curiously, in Switzerland there are six half-cantons, which have one representative each, instead of two like the full cantons.

In Germany, the Bundesrat (the federal assembly of the Länder) has four tiers of Länders, which have weighted voting rights, from a minimum of three votes to a maximum of six votes for each Land. This approach to democracy in Europe still primarily values representation over fragmentation and control. Yet, if Europe produced and practiced the ugly ideologies and policies of fascism and communism between 1929 and 1989, there must be something wrong in the assumption that representation is more important than pluralism.[352]

5.3.2. The Federalist No. 78: Department of Powers and (the Weakness of) the Judiciary

Hamilton (again writing as "Publius") titled paper No. 78 "The Judiciary Department".[353] It explains the role of the judiciary as twofold:
a) to check that the executive power is exercised in compliance with the law
b) to keep the legislative power within the limits of the constitution:

Whoever attentively considers the different departments of power must perceive, that, in a government in which they are separated from each other, the judiciary, from the nature of its functions, will always be the least dangerous to the political rights of the Constitution; because it will be least in a capacity to annoy or injure them. The Executive not only dispenses the honors, but holds the sword of the community. The legislature not only commands the purse, but prescribes the rules by which the duties and rights of every citizen are to be regulated. The judiciary, on the contrary, has no influence over either the sword or the purse; no direction either of the strength or of the wealth of the society; and can take no active resolution whatever. It may truly be said to have neither force nor will, but merely judgment; and must ultimately depend upon the aid of the executive arm even for the efficacy of its judgments. This simple view of the matter suggests several important consequences. It proves incontestably, that the judiciary is beyond comparison the weakest of the three departments of power;[354] that it can never attack with success either of the other two; and that all possible care is

---

[352] Between 1848 and 1929, during the introduction of constitutions almost everywhere in Europe (except in the United Kingdom), the U.S. was still quite autocratic and authoritarian, until the introduction of suffrage around 1870 (1848 for France, 1869-1870-1871 for Spain, the German Empire and the U.S., 1912 for Italy). Wikipedia, "*Universal suffrage*".

[353] HAMILTON A., *The Federalist Papers*, No. 78.

[354] Montesquieu, speaking of them, says: "Of the three powers above mentioned, the judiciary is next to nothing", *The Spirit of Laws*, vol. I, page 186.

In fact, before there was any division of power, the judiciary was seen as part of the executive power. Still today, as we will see, it is a small and underfunded branch of government.

requisite to enable it to defend itself against their attacks. It equally proves, that though individual oppression may now and then proceed from the courts of justice, the general liberty of the people can never be endangered from that quarter ....

For I agree, that "there is no liberty, if the power of judging be not separated from the legislative and executive powers." And it proves, in the last place, that as liberty can have nothing to fear from the judiciary alone, but would have every thing to fear from its union with either of the other departments; that as all the effects of such a union must ensue from a dependence of the former on the latter, notwithstanding a nominal and apparent separation; that as, from the natural feebleness of the judiciary, it is in continual jeopardy of being overpowered, awed, or influenced by its co-ordinate branches; and that as nothing can contribute so much to its firmness and independence as permanency in office, this quality may therefore be justly regarded as an indispensable ingredient in its constitution, and, in a great measure, as the citadel of the public justice and the public security.

The complete independence of the courts of justice is peculiarly essential in a limited Constitution. By a limited Constitution, I understand one which contains certain specified exceptions to the legislative authority; such, for instance, as that it shall pass no bills of attainder, no ex-post-facto laws, and the like. Limitations of this kind can be preserved in practice no other way than through the medium of courts of justice, whose duty it must be to declare all acts contrary to the manifest tenor of the Constitution void. Without this, all the reservations of particular rights or privileges would amount to nothing.

In other words, the whole idea of contemporary constitutions, which provide hard guarantees against the excesses of the legislative and executive powers, is hollow, if there isn't an independent and effective judiciary.

On this the constitutional doctrines have agreed almost unanimously for 250 years.[355]

---

[355] There are, here and there, particularly in autocratic regimes, constitutional doctrines such as Carl Schmitt's writings on the failure of democratic process and virtues of dictatorship: *Die Diktatur* (1921), *Politische Theologie. Vier Kapitel zur Lehre von der Souveränität* (1921), *Die geistesgeschichtliche Lage des heutigen Parlamentarismus* (1925), *Der Begriff des Politischen* (1926-1932). Schmitt defines sovereignty as the power to decide when it is appropriate to overrule the rule of law: The supreme needs of policy are positioned above the rule of law and the executive power above the judicial and even legislative power. In fact, there is a *Diktatur der Werte* (dictatorship of values) that cannot be constrained within the procedural and bureaucratic limitations of the law; so, whenever necessary, an *Ausnahmezustand* (state of emergency) must be called and a dictator appointed for the safety of the nation. It is unnecessary to underline how active this line of thinking is in current politics, during the Covid-19 pandemic, and before that, in addressing the problem of immigration.

Even in one of the leading democracies, the United States, there is a line of thinking called the "Chevron Doctrine" (or "Chevron Deference") that seeks to restrain the function of the judiciary in interpreting the law, particularly with respect to "political interpretations" of the executive branch: Chevron U.S.A., Inc. v. Natural Resources Defense Council, Inc., 467 U.S. 837 (1984).

I adhere to the constitutional doctrines that do not accept any restraint on the judiciary's interpretation of the law: The judiciary is bound only by the constitution and the laws. Even the legislature cannot impose any specific interpretation of the law (retroactively). In fact the legislator has quite limited powers of interpreting the law. If it doesn't agree with the judicial interpretation, it can only change the law for the future.

Today less than 1% of the national budget is devoted to the judiciary;[356] meanwhile, the executive absorbs 98% of national spending. It is evident that the judiciary today is underfunded and unable to impose the checks and balances that are needed on the executive power in a free society[357]. What kind of justice can we expect if a judge is paid on average between €70 and €350 for each court ruling? How effective can the checks be on the executive power, if the judiciary receives barely 1% of the budget devoted to the executive?

Furthermore, a worrying trend toward restraining judiciary review is consolidating,[358] even in some democratic, pluralistic nations. In the U.K., the government is pushing for a review of administrative law extending the non-justiciability of administrative acts.[359]

On the contrary the European Union has a powerful and unassailable judicial power, split amongst the European Court of Justice and the European Court of Human Rights. The fact that these two European Courts are staffed by nationals of the 27 E.U. member states and are directly funded by the European Union (not by the single member states) puts the two courts in a position of absolute impartiality. Their jurisprudence is effective in compelling the executive powers of the member states to abide by European law. The jurisprudence of the European courts is so stringent that, for the U.K., it was one of the chief reasons for leaving the E.U.

5.3.3. Freedom Requires Democracy, Pluralism and an Effective Judiciary

The lesson we learn from reading *The Federalist Papers* is that a working (pluralistic, free) democracy needs (in the words of the U.S. Founding Fathers):
1) the regular distribution of power into distinct departments
2) the introduction of legislative checks and balances

---

[356] According to the Council of Europe *2020 CEPEJ European judicial systems Evaluation Report*, where one can read (p. 21) that the yearly cost of the judiciary per inhabitant in the 47 member states varies between €23.81 and €123.79 (the average is €71.56 or 0.33% of GDP, of which €14.00 are for public prosecution). The judge's pay for one case is between €70 and €350. The cost of a judicial procedure varies between €500 and €2500 per case.
In the United States the Justice Department 2018 budget is $28.8 billion, while the combined state expenditures in 2016 amounted to $92.5 billion, according to data from the US Bureau of Justice Statistics, https://www.bjs.gov/index.cfm?ty=pbdetail&iid=6728. This is a yearly expenditure of about $375 per inhabitant, or 0.59% of GDP.

[357] Nobody doubts that there is a correlation between the slow and unpredictable judiciary in Italy, and its status as the „sick man of Europe", stagnating since 20 years: THE ECONOMIST, *Mario Draghi gives Italy another chance. From banker to prime minister (Leader).*

[358] The cases of Hungary and Poland, which have significantly curtailed the independence of the judiciary, are well known: THE ECONOMIST, *Poland and Hungary enjoy a physics lesson courtesy of the EU"* (Charlemagne).

[359] We can read on the U.K. government website: "The Independent Review of Administrative Law (IRAL) was launched in July 2020 to consider options for reform to the process of Judicial Review." It has also published the terms of reference for the Independent Panel.
There is widespread skepticism about this initiative in the U.K.

3) the institution of courts composed of judges holding their offices during good behaviour and with sufficient guarantees to protect them against the excesses of the executive

4) the representation of the people in the legislature by deputies of their own election, and

5) a (republican) union of federated states where the diversity and uneven distribution of wealth, commerce, industry and even knowledge create a system of checks and balances that makes it impossible for any faction to prevail and/or suppress the other factions.

A republic of states (some of them industrial, others agricultural, some dependent on trade, others exploiting natural resources) must maintain a balance between the factions and avoid the tyranny of the majority.

But even the American Constitution has repeatedly shown its limits.

It cannot be forgotten that, in 1831, after the French Revolution of 1830 ("*Révolution de Juillet*" or "*Trois Glorieuses*"), Alexis de Tocqueville (a French judge) wrote *Démocratie en Amerique*.[360] He had been sent to America to study the American prisons, but his observations went far beyond studying the American penal system.

He wrote in his first tome: "*In my opinion the main evil of the present democratic institutions of the United States does not arise, as is often asserted in Europe, from their weakness, but from their overpowering strength; and I am not so much alarmed at the excessive liberty which reigns in that country as at the very inadequate securities which exist against tyranny.*"

De Tocqueville was appalled by the idea that the majority was not only able to write laws, but then also to break them.

And he was right to be appalled. Thirty years later, seven slave states (the Confederated States of America or the "Confederacy") seceded from the Union[361] in an extreme act of factionalism, motivated by the strong support for slavery in the South of the U.S.

This was fundamentally a failure of the republican federal model, theorized by the Founding Fathers. In fact:

- The seceding southern states were all slave states where the majority of citizens were in favour of slavery.

- Newly elected President Lincoln didn't win any of the southern states, so he represented only northern constituencies. The southerners did not feel represented by him, with his abolitionist views.

- Slavery was an issue where all the compromises that had been made from 1787 (Constitutional Conventional approving the Three-Fifths Compromise)[362] to 1807 (Act Prohibiting the Importation of Slaves) and through to 1861 eventually became contentious. The slave states in the South were expanding faster than the free states, so that northern states feared they might be irreversibly outnumbered by slave states.

---

[360] Free Kindle edition of Alexis de Tocqueville, *De la Démocratie en Amérique*.

[361] Wikipedia, "*Union (American Civil War)*".

[362] Article 1, section 9 of the U.S. Constitution.

Despite all the good efforts of the Founding Fathers, the federalist structure, with its checks and balances, did not prevent a bloody clash between opposing factions.

The Federalist Papers and American history teach us two important lessons:

1) that it is necessary to pay a high price in order to build strong roots for pluralism and democracy

2) that if an entire society is divided into two (main) antagonizing socioeconomic factions, eventually the federal, democratic institutions are insufficient to mediate.

Pluralism requires several centres of interest. If over time, they merge into two large camps, it becomes increasingly difficult to mediate a compromise – as is the case today, with the urban-rural partisan gap in the U.S.[363] or the open vs. closed divide in Europe.[364]

Democracy without pluralism does not work! Quite often, when we say "democracy", we mean "pluralism".[365]

This confusion has historical reasons. The socialists at the end of the 19th century believed that there was nothing wrong with the tyranny of the majority. In fact, with universal suffrage, they were positioned to receive the long-term support of a large majority of voters, who were proletarians and workers. The aim of socialists was to radically change society and the economy – a radical change that would not have been possible in a pluralistic society.[366]

So their theory of democracy focused on the powers of the majority, in particular of an absolute majority of the people. Their theory of democracy found in the so-called "qualified majority" the sole protection against tyranny. In other words, it was deemed sufficient (to avoid dictatorship) to require 51% (or eventually, even two-thirds) of the votes to make any change in the law, or even in the constitution. Precisely when the risk of overpowering any minorities became most grave (because an extremely large majority represents a single set of interests), the protection of minorities was voided.[367]

Nothing in *The Federalist Papers* hints that if you have 67% in favour, pluralism becomes irrelevant or damaging. It expressly states the opposite, as we have seen.

The concept that an overwhelming majority has a right to crush a minority is a consequence of socialist ideology that was aimed at radical social change. Pluralism would have prevented this from happening.

---

[363] THE ECONOMIST, *America's urban-rural partisan gap is widening. Without reforms to its winner-take-all system, this trend will continue to benefit Republicans.*

[364] THE ECONOMIST, *Globalisation and politics. Drawbridges up. The new divide in rich countries is not between left and right but between open and closed.* THE ECONOMIST, *Globalisation. Some thoughts on the open v closed divide.*

[365] ZAKARIA, F., *The Future of Freedom*, loc. 170.

[366] POPPER, K., *The Open Society and its Enemies*, 329 f., 338, where he highlights that the communists *"never realized the danger inherent in a policy of increasing the power of the state. Although they abandoned more or less unconsciously the doctrine of the impotence of politics, they retained the view that state power presents no important problem, and that it is bad only if it is in the hands of the bourgeoisie."*

[367] ZAKARIA, F., *The Future of Freedom*, loc. 1482.

This explains why so many communist dictatorships enthusiastically used the word "democratic" in referring to their governments. They were right to do so: A large majority of the population voted in favour of their policies as late as the 1980s.

They were democracies without pluralism. Minorities had no protection from the overwhelming power of the majority, so they had to flee. Socialist states experienced mass flight from their democracy, which was bent on protecting the average citizen, depriving all others of alternative opportunities.

The recent evolution of our open, pluralistic, democratic societies, particularly in the United States, show that the digitalisation of politics is having a polarizing effect and that there is an increasing intolerance of whoever is in the minority. In chapter 8 we will see that it is a consequence of faulty design: Digital technology is designed to increase engagement, not to moderate the political discourse. And it shows!

5.4. The Great Depression, the New Deal, and the Birth of Social Security

Before the Great Depression, economic theories were liberal. Classical economics asserts that markets function best without government interference.

The stress on laissez-faire capitalism was one of the main points of the classical school of economics, theorized by Adam Smith, David Ricardo, Thomas Malthus, and John Stuart Mill in the late 18th and early 19th centuries. Many of the fundamental concepts and principles of classical economics were set forth in Smith's *An Inquiry into the Nature and Causes of the Wealth of Nations*, published in 1776. As Smith saw it, the entire community benefits most when each of its members pursue their own self-interest. In a free enterprise system, individuals make a profit by producing goods that other people are willing to buy. By the same token, individuals spend money for goods that they want or need most. (People even speak of an "Invisible Hand" – in Smith's words – that directs the market towards full employment.) Market forces, free to act without obstacles, achieve more efficient resource allocation. The state must not intervene in the marketplace with economic policy measures, because they present an obstacle to the freedom of market forces and, therefore, do not allow the achievement of full employment and productive efficiency.

The role of the state was to defend its citizen from internal and external aggression, to implement foreign policy.

5.4.1. The Crash: Theoretical Underpinning of the Causes of the Recession

The 29th of October, 1929, was "Black Tuesday", the event that triggered the Great Depression, the worst recession in the history of the United States. Given the gravity and reach of the crisis, it's clear that the factors that led to the Great Depression had been latent for a long time.

In the 1920s, while European countries were suffering the effects of World War I, the U.S. economy was flourishing. There were major technological improvements (such as the introduction of mass production) and essential progress in communication (the number of telephones and radios doubled). Along with this, there was a boom in consumption (thanks to mass production and low taxes). Buying on credit was all the rage. People borrowed huge amounts of money, and creditors had no doubt they were going to be able to repay it. The members of the American middle class felt wealthy and were extremely optimistic. They had good reasons to be so confident: Unemployment had dropped from 12% to 3.2%, and inflation was below 1%; purchasing power was stable. The rise in stock values, coupled with low interest rates, meant good investment prospects were expected. This is why in 1927-28 – the years preceding the crash – speculation and overinvestment expanded significantly. About 1 million Americans started to play the stock market and owned stocks and shares – often bought with borrowed money. The unchecked speculation was indirectly supported by the government. In those years, the U.S. economy was characterized by largely unregulated markets. In other words, the Republican presidents in office from 1921 to 1933 opted for a laissez-faire policy, meaning that the government interfered in the economy as little as possible.

It was on 29 October 1929 that Wall Street crashed. On that day, thousands of shareholders were ruined, businesses collapsed and bankruptcies reached record levels. It was just the beginning of a severe depression that was destined to last over a decade. In fact, the gross national product (GNP) declined from $190.9 billion in 1928 to $141.5 billion in 1933, while unemployment increased from 4.2% in 1928 to more than 25% in 1933. At the same time, the stock market's value declined dramatically from 1929 to 1932.

The **arguments and theories concerning the events leading to the Great Depression are numerous and contrasting**. However, there are **some main points on which the experts agree**.[368]

First of all, they agree that the U.S. economy had various **hidden weaknesses** and was built on an extremely wobbly base. High industrial production and **low consumer purchasing power** had led to market saturation.[369] This was largely due to the **unequal distribution of wealth**, supported by Republican fiscal policy. In fact, while only 5% of the American population earned nearly one-third of the entire national income, more than **60% of American families** were not able to satisfy their bare necessities and lived **on the margins of society**. This led to a slowdown in consumer demand. Another problem that individuals faced was the **expansion of instalment plans** – usually with salaries serving as the guarantee. The wide concession of credit at low interest rates encouraged the speculation in the stock market.

The **banking system was another weak point** in the American economy.[370] It included many independent local banks – mostly small institutions operating in rural areas – not associated with the Federal Reserve Bank but required to

---

[368] Summarised by GALBRAITH J. K., *The Great Crash 1929*, 176 ff.
[369] On this point GALBRAITH J. K., *The Great Crash 1929*, 173 disagrees.
[370] GALBRAITH, J. K., *The Great Crash 1929*, 177.

provide their own liquidity, and thus extremely vulnerable in a crisis. During the recession, three waves of bank failures shook the economy, and about 5,000 banks declared bankruptcy.

Finally, **the U.S. was a net exporter and (at the same time) a net lender** for more than a decade after World War I. Fundamentally, it lent the money to buy its exports and blocked imports through high tariffs. Countries could not cover (indefinitely) their adverse trade balances with the United States in increasing payments of gold. They either had to increase their exports to the U.S. (which President Hoover prevented with higher tariffs) or default on their debt. This duly happened, creating additional disruption, which hit particularly hard at farming and the value of land.[371]

Along with this, the Great Depression brought a contraction in the corporate sectors: Manufacturing production declined, and U.S. businesses showed extremely weak overall performance. (The proportion of firms with positive net income declined from 61% in 1928 to 18% in 1932).[372] Many firms suffered financial distress and declared failure; insolvency was tragically common. In particular, small firms were less profitable and faced distress more often than large firms.[373] The impact of the illiquidity of the many small firms on the many small banks was devastating.

The classical economic vision was strongly brought into question after the crash of '29.

At the height of the Great Depression, John Maynard Keynes' influential and revolutionary economic theory[374] asserted that classical economics rested on a fundamental error: It assumed that just the balance between supply and

---

[371] GALBRAITH, J. K., *The Great Crash 1929*, 181.

[372] GALBRAITH, J. K., *The Great Crash 1929*, 176.

[373] Here some other readings on the Great Depression, the subsequent New Deal, and the similarities to the Great Recession, which I have tried to summarize in this chapter, with the goal of **clarifying the origins of the welfare state and the reasons why today's idea of justice includes (to a varying degree) also the expectation of some form of social security**: K. GALBRAITH J.K., *The Great Crash, 1929*; KRUGMAN P., *The Return of Depression Economics and the Crisis of 2008*. JONES M. A., *The Limits of Liberty*; MITCHELL B., *Depression Decade: From New Era Through New Deal, 1929-1941*; ROMER, C., *Great Depression*; CROWLEY P., CHEE-HEONG QUAH, *A Reconsideration of the Great Depression*; GRAHAM J., HAZARIKA S., NARASIMHAN K., *Corporate governance, debt and investment policy during the Great Depression*; SHACHMUROVE Y., *A historical overview of financial crisis in the United States*; GRAHAM J., HAZARIKA S., NARASIMHAN K., *Financial distress in the Great Depression*; KENWOOD A. G., LOUGHEED A. L., *Growth of the International Economy 1820-2000: an introductory test*; EICHENGREEN B., O'ROURKE K., *What do the new data tell us?*; PHELPS E. S., *The boom and the slump: a casual account of the 1990s/2000s and the 1920s/1930s*; CRESWICK C., *The Great Depression - parallels for today*; LUPAN M., *Great Depression vs. The current financial and economic crisis*; CHONG-YAH LIM, SNG HUI YING, *The Great Depression, the Great Recession and the Next Crisis*.

In chapter 4.3 we have seen that social expenditure (welfare + healthcare) in OECD countries is about 30% of public expenditure, in Europe and even in the US: now, even if it is hotly debated how much social protection a "just" society needs, all OECD states devote a significant part of their budget to social protection. So, even if one believes that it is too much (or unsustainable), empirically it cannot be denied that social security is a significant part of the national expenditure and is a founding legal principle in developed countries.

[374] KEYNES J.M., *The General Theory of Employment, Interest and Money*.

demand would ensure full employment, and regarded the dynamics of the free market as the driving force of an economy. On the contrary, in Keynes' view, the economy was chronically unstable and subject to fluctuations. Keynes saw the need for strong state intervention in the economy through public policies and measures (such as the deficit spending); this would stimulate aggregate demand, achieve full employment and increase purchasing power.[375]
The classical economic theory, on the contrary postulated that by keeping taxes low and not intervening to smooth the down-cycle, businesses were supposed to have more money to invest and consumers more money to spend. The market – according to President Calvin Coolidge (1923-1929), Hoover's predecessor – had to follow its natural course, free from government restrictions. Coolidge often said, "The business of America is business." This classical view is still defended by some scholars, who argue that Keynesianism made things worse and not better. President Franklin Roosevelt (1933-1945) who started and implemented the New Deal, was convinced of the contrary.[376]
The aim of this publication is to identify the major changes that must be acknowledged, in order to prepare ourselves to govern a digital economy and a digital society – not to resolve the debate on the reasons for and consequences of the Great Depression, the Great Recession and the Covid-19 pandemic.

---

[375] In this regard, Keynes wrote: "… *public works even of doubtful utility may pay for themselves over and over again at a time of severe unemployment, if only from the diminished cost of relief expenditure, provided that we can assume that a smaller proportion of income is saved when unemployment is greater; but they may become a more doubtful proposition as a state of full employment is approached. Furthermore, if our assumption is correct that the marginal propensity to consume falls off steadily as we approach full employment, it follows that it will become more and more troublesome to secure a further given increase of employment by further increasing investment. It should not be difficult to compile a chart of the marginal propensity to consume at each stage of a trade cycle from the statistics (if they were available) of aggregate income and aggregate investment at successive dates.*" KEYNES J.M., *The General Theory of Employment, Interest and Money*, book III, ch. 5, p. 96.
The Covid-19 pandemic has been mitigated with the most Keynesian politics seen in a century, with the object of containing Covid-19-related deaths and avoiding mass bankruptcies, in particular in sectors of the economy most affected by the consequences of the pandemic: "*The Financial Times is a paper for the elite. Founded in London in 1888, its inaugural issue **promised to be the friend of 'the honest financier, the bona fide investor, the respectable broker, the genuine director, [and] the legitimate speculator.'** Through world wars and depression, fascism and socialism, it has been a consistent advocate of capitalism. It supported the free-market reforms of Margaret Thatcher and Ronald Reagan that ushered in the economic era we live in today, as well as the broad expansion of free trade that has brought virtually every country on the planet into a single world economy. Core to its identity is the belief that most problems in the world can be solved by more open markets and greater liberalisation. So the FT's readers must have been startled on April 3, 2020, when they opened the newspaper to a lead editorial that broke with much of its orthodoxy. The short essay began by noting that the coronavirus pandemic would call on people to make collective sacrifices, and that '**to demand collective sacrifice you must offer a social contract that benefits everyone.**'*" ZAKARIA, F., *Ten Lessons for a Post-Pandemic World*, 54.
In 2020, OECD nations and a few other selected countries enacted the biggest fiscal stimulus of all time: OECD, *Tax Policy Reforms 2020: OECD and Selected Partner Economies*, 10, 11 ff.
[376] Until the Covid-19 pandemic, it was still considered controversial whether Keynesian policies really do solve the problem; still, in 2020, all of the world's governments enacted some form of Keynesian policy in support of the faltering economy.

The history of market crashes and economic crises teaches us the steep price of not understanding the signs of a structural change and the dire consequences of assessing a new situation using inadequate parameters.[377] In 1929 the credit bubble in property was mistaken for economic exuberance – an error that we repeated in the decade preceding the failure of Lehman Brothers in 2007.

Given the era, President Hoover and the Republican Party reacted in a manner that historians now consider "partially experimental". Nevertheless, Hoover basically tried to avoid providing direct federal aid and let the free market operate. That is why he passed into the annals of history as a passive president committed to a laissez-faire policy, insensitive to the severity of the situation and to the suffering of his fellow citizens.[378]

5.4.2. President Roosevelt and the New Deal: The Reform of Finance and Banking

In stunning contrast to the previous policies, President Roosevelt inaugurated a new era – the so-called "New Deal" – characterized by strong federal intervention in the economy and in social matters.

In his earliest public speeches, Roosevelt did not present a well-framed program. Roosevelt's inaugural address is known for its combination of optimism, consolation and resolve. He reassured the nation that the problems were only material and could be solved. It was then that the country heard his immortal phrase, "The only thing we have to fear is fear itself." Thanks to his "fireside chats" – radio messages to the nation – he succeeded in cheering up Americans and in making them believe that a bright future was possible. "This nation asks for action, and action now", he said.[379]

Between 1933 and 1935, the U.S. Congress approved and Roosevelt signed 15 innovative (and systemic) legislative acts, which created, for the first time in the U.S., a social safety net.

First, Roosevelt signed the Emergency Banking Act in 1933. In essence, it allowed for the reopening of banks that could prove they were liquid, so that people could again deposit their money in banks. Then, in June 1933, he established the Federal Deposit Insurance Corporation (FDIC), an institution guaranteeing bank deposits up to $250,000. In 1934, Roosevelt signed into law the Securities and Exchange Act to regulate stock markets and prevent over-speculation.

---

[377] Some real masterworks on the subject include: GALBRAITH, J.K., *The Great Crash 1929*; GALBRAITH, J.K., *A Short History of Financial Euphoria*; REINHART, C.M., ROGOFF K.S., *This Time Is Different: Eight Centuries of Financial Folly*; GRANT, J., *The Forgotten Depression: 1921, The Crash That Cured Itself*; RAJAN, R.G., *Fault Lines: How Hidden Fractures Still Threaten the World Economy*; TETT, G., *Fool's Gold: How Unrestrained Greed Corrupted a Dream, Shattered Global Markets and Unleashed a Catastrophe*.

[378] GALBRAITH, J.K., *The Great Crash 1929*, 140; JONES M. A., *The Limits of Liberty*, p. 65; MACKENZIE D., *Industrial employment and the policies of Herbert C. Hoover*; THORNTON M., *Hoover, Bush, and the Great Depression*.

[379] SCALES, R.P., *Radio and the Politics of Sound in Interwar France, 1921-1939*, 11, 151, reports how in Germany and Italy, Hitler and Mussolini used radio talk in a similar way to orient the public mood.

5.4.3. The Birth of Social Security

In 1929 Mussolini in Italy and in 1932 Hitler in Germany started huge Keynesian stimulus programs, building infrastructures, such as railroads, dams, motorways, harbours and other civil works[380].

In May 1933, the U.S. Federal Emergency Relief Act was approved, allocating $500 million to the states to operate relief programs. The same year, the Work Progress Administration was created to employ millions of jobless people to carry out public works, such as the construction of schools, parks, streets and other infrastructure.

In winter 1934, the US federal government established the Civilian Conservation Corps (CCC), a public organisation which hired young, unemployed people to work on environmental conservation programs.

In 1934, the Committee on Economic Security (CES) was established, with the primary task of studying the needs of people who were unable to work (i.e., disabled or elderly people). There was no federal aid for those categories; family members or local communities were expected to care for them. In January 1935, the CES presented a plan for a national system of social security.[381]

On 14 Aug. 1935, President Roosevelt signed the Social Security Act, which guaranteed an income for the unemployed and retirees. Social Security was initially created to reduce unemployment, but became a safety net for retirees and the disabled. Social Security was (and is) funded mostly through payroll taxes called the Federal Insurance Contributions Act tax (FICA).[382]

The Social Security Act provides general welfare, assistance, a public healthcare system, and an insurance program for various categories of citizens – such as the aged, handicapped and dependent persons, as well as mothers and children. In the following years, some major changes and amendments were made to the original 1935 act.[383]

The Roosevelt administration also provided assistance to citizens and supported the economic recovery through cooperative programs administered by various agencies of the federal government. The most successful were those related to farming, electrical utilities, and healthcare.[384]

---

[380] In the introduction of the German edition of Keynes' *General Theory* dated 7 September 1936, one can read: "*Nevertheless, the theory of output as a whole, which is what the following book purports to provide, is much more easily adapted to the conditions of a totalitarian state, than is the theory of production and distribution of a given output produced under the conditions of free competition and a large measure of laissez-faire*".

[381] PATEL, K.K., *The New Deal: A Global History*, 197 ff.

[382] PATEL, K.K., *The New Deal: A Global History*, 193; *The Week*, "*Today in history: The birth of Social Security*" (online).

[383] Social Security Administration, "*Social Security History: The Social Security Act of 1935*"; MITCHELL D. J. B., *Townsend and Roosevelt: lessons from the struggle for the elderly income support*; KING T. T., CECIL H. W., *The history of major changes to the social security system*.

[384] PATEL, K.K., *The New Deal: A Global History*, 217 ff.

In Europe, similar policies had been already enacted by Mussolini, Hitler[385] and, Francisco Franco.[386] Meanwhile, Great Britain pursued more conservative policies, partly because it was an empire with large colonies. At the end of World War II, the U.K. also introduced extensive welfare legislation, under the Labour government of Clement Attlee.

Scholars have different opinions on the effectiveness of Roosevelt's policies: Some consider them to have been decisive in helping America recover,[387] while others believe they were counterproductive and made the Great Depression worse.[388] In any case, those years (in Europe and the U.S.) were characterized by strong government intervention in all sectors of society to support the economy and social cohesion.[389]

In any case, despite the diverging opinions of economic scholars, after World War II, all industrialised nations had introduced social security as a central feature of government. Protecting the disabled, the jobless and other socially weak citizens is considered in all OECD countries as an important mission of the state; and on average, 20% of GDP is spent on welfare (excluding healthcare).[390]

5.5. Justice in the 21st Century[391]

There are weighty books on this subject, some of which are inspiring to read.[392] How to summarize their diverging reasoning on justice in just one chapter?

---

[385] PATEL, K.K., *The New Deal: A Global History*, reports how several aspects of the American New Deal were inspired by policies of Hitler and Mussolini: see pp. 86 ff, 109, quoting Roosevelt saying to HAROLD L. ICKES, *"What we were doing in this country were some of the things that were being done in Russia and even some things that were being done under Hitler in Germany. But we were doing them in an orderly way."* See also RAUCHWAY, E., *The Great Depression & the New Deal*, 105.

[386] Chronologically the expansionary policies in Italy, Germany and in the U.S. predate the publication of Keynes' *General Theory* and it is debated, if Roosevelt's Brain Trust was indeed aware of Keynes already in 1933: GARVY, G. *Keynes and the Economic Activists of Pre-Hitler Germany*, 391-405.

[387] PATEL K.K., *The New Deal: A Global History*, 75; RAUCHWAY, E., *The Great Depression & the New Deal*, 105.

The conservative Chicago School maintains that the Keynesian policies were excessive, and the banking reform would have sufficed: FRIEDMAN, M., SCHWARTZ, A.J., *A Monetary History of the United States, 1867-1960*, 1963.

[388] COLE, H.L., OHANIAN, L.E., *New Deal Policies and the Persistence of the Great Depression: A General Equilibrium Analysis* (paper 597, Federal Reserve Bank of Minneapolis), vol. 112, no. 4.

[389] Other readings on the subject: JONES M.A., *The Limits of Liberty*; ROOSEVELT, F. D., *Fireside Chats, 1933-1944*. GALGANO F., *Lex mercatoria*; FERGUSON T., *From normalcy to New Deal: Industrial structure, party competition, and American public policy in the Great Depression*; RICHMAN S., *New Deal Nemesis*; HAWLEY E. W., *The New Deal and the Problem of Monopoly: A Study in Economic Ambivalence*; *Encyclopedia Britannica*, "Work Progress Administration (WPA)"; KAUFMAN, B. E., *Wage theory, New Deal labor policy, and the Great Depression*.

[390] The 2018 OECD average social expenditure is 20% of GDP (varying from 31% in France to 7.5% in Mexico). See OECD, *OECD Social Expenditure Update 2019*.

[391] For the definition of social security as an essential part of the social contract, see SHAFIK, M., *What We Owe Each Other: A New Social Contract*, 188 ff.

[392] RAWLS J., *A Theory of Justice*; SEN A., *The Idea of Justice*; SANDEL, M., "Justice, Lecture 1".

The lessons titled "Justice", delivered at Harvard University by Professor Michael Sandel, come in handy![393]

My aim is not to influence the philosophical debate on justice. I will simply state which theory of justice has the greatest appeal to me and why, in order to provide a rational background for the legal issues posed by the digitalisation of our society.

According to Sandel,[394] there are **three approaches to justice**:

The first says that **justice means maximizing utility or welfare.** It is the greatest happiness for the greatest number. This is the utilitarian and materialistic (socialistic) approach to justice.

This approach has two defects:

a) It makes justice a matter of calculation, not principle.

b) It tries to translate all human good into a single uniform measure of value; it flattens values and takes no account of the qualitative differences among them.

The second says that **justice means respecting freedom of choice** – either the actual choices people make in a free market (the libertarian view) or the hypothetical choices people would make in an original position of equality (the liberal egalitarian view). This approach solves the first problem of the utilitarian-materialistic approach, in stating that justice is more than calculation and that there are some unalienable rights. But beyond singling out certain fundamental rights as worthy of respect, it accepts peoples' preferences as they are. According to these theories, the moral worth of the ends we pursue, the meaning and significance of the lives we lead, and the quality and character of the common life we share, all lie beyond the domain of justice.

The third says that **justice means cultivating virtue and reasoning about the common good**. This approach clearly resonates with Aristotle's moral theory, which has been subsumed by **Christian morality**. Its weakness lies in the fact that it is entirely dependent on the moral and legal qualities of aprioristically determined moral absolutes to guide us.

The first two approaches try to find something objective and universal to serve as the foundation of justice; the third depends on a (culturally) given morality.

I adhere to liberal egalitarian theory of justice[395] for the following reasons:

1) Humans started to follow rules and laws, putting means before ends, because it was more practical to agree on some rules, than to have to fight to the bitter end for food, shelter and reproduction. **Human rules and the aim to improve living standards have been linked together since the onset of human history.**

---

[393] SANDEL, M., "Justice, Lecture 1"; SANDEL, M., "Justice, Lecture 2"; Sandel, M., "Justice, Lecture 3"; SANDEL, M., "Justice, Lecture 4"; SANDEL, M., "Justice, Lecture 5"; SANDEL, M., "Justice, Lecture, 6"; SANDEL, M., "Justice, Lecture 7"; SANDEL, M., "Justice, Lecture 8"; SANDEL, M., "Justice, Lecture 9"; SANDEL, M., "Justice, Lecture 10"; SANDEL, M., "Justice, Lecture 11"; SANDEL, M., "Justice, Lecture 12"; SANDEL, M., "Justice, Lecture 13"; SANDEL, M., "Justice, Lecture 14"; SANDEL, M., "Justice, Lecture 15"; SANDEL, M., "Justice, Lecture 16"; SANDEL, M., "Justice, Lecture 17"; SANDEL, M., "Justice, Lecture 18"; SANDEL, M., "Justice, Lecture 19"; Sandel, M., "Justice, Lecture 20"; Sandel, M., "Justice, Lecture 21"; SANDEL, M., "Justice, Lecture 22"; SANDEL, M., "Justice, Lecture 23"; SANDEL, M., "Justice, Lecture 24".

[394] SANDEL, M., *Justice: What is the Right Thing to Do?*, 259.

[395] The theory's most influential thinker is John Rawls (JOHN RAWLS, *A Theory of Justice*).

If everybody were entitled to take or destroy what others obtained through hard work (crops, shelter, family, etc.), there would never have been any reason to improve the world: The strongest would have had it all, and the others would have been better off doing nothing, avoiding anything that could motivate others to attack them. This underlines one of the two axioms of a liberal egalitarian theory of justice, i.e. that "*social and economic inequalities are to be arranged so that they are both (a) reasonably expected to be to everyone's advantage, and (b) attached to positions and offices open to all.*"[396]

2) Humans spontaneously renounced full, unrestricted "sovereignty" over their lives and the lives of other humans, for purposes of self-preservation. This anthropological and historical fact underlines the other axiom of a liberal egalitarian theory of justice, i.e., that "*each person is to have an equal right to the most extensive basic liberty compatible with a similar liberty for others.*"[397] States went through a similar process in the quest for peaceful stability – the federation of Greek cities, democracy in Greece and Rome, and all federations and alliances, up through the United States of America and the European Union. As theorized by John Rawls,[398] I believe **that the aim to achieve (relative) stability is an absolute value,** shared by all humans. As history proves, it does not matter if this is the expression of a deeper human, ethical need or just utilitarianism.

3) There is absolute, positive value in solving conflicts peacefully, ensuring (relative) stability and wide consensual support for conflict resolution. So, ultimately, **justice is not about the value you protect, but how you protect** it. It is a process that would meet with the (unbiased) approval of the vast majority. John Rawls[399] describes it as a decision taken behind the "*veil of ignorance*". This means that the decision is taken by a plurality of people who don't have a vested interest and don't remember if they are rich or poor, young or old, male or female, black or white, local or foreign, etc.

Apparently, this definition of justice is subjective. Actually, it is not, because it is based on the two positive axioms stated above: **equal freedoms and a fair shot at well-being for everybody**. The two axioms necessarily exclude all tyrannical power and embrace only unbiased conflict resolution and enforcement of rules.[400]

In the words of John Rawls:

Justice is the first virtue of social institutions, as truth is of systems of thought. A theory however elegant and economical must be rejected or revised if it is untrue: likewise, laws and institutions no matter how efficient and well-arranged must be reformed or abolished if they are unjust. Each person possesses an inviolability founded on justice that even the welfare society as a whole cannot override. For this reason, justice denies that the loss of freedom for some is made right by a greater good shared by others. It does not allow that the sacrifices imposed on a few are outweighed by a

---

[396] RAWLS, J., *A Theory of Justice*, 60.
[397] RAWLS, J., *A Theory of Justice*, 60.
[398] RAWLS, J., *A Theory of Justice*, 453.
[399] RAWLS, J., *A Theory of Justice*, 136.
[400] RAWLS, J., *A Theory of Justice*, 124.

larger sum of advantages enjoyed by many. Therefore, in a just society the liberties of equal citizenship are not subject to political bargaining or to the calculus of social interest. The only thing that permits us to acquiesce in an erroneous theory is the lack of a better one; analogously, an injustice is tolerable only when it is necessary to avoid an even greater injustice. Being the first virtues of human activities, truth and justice are uncompromising.

4) According to this definition of justice, social security (in today's meaning of state-funded social welfare) **is a necessary part of a just legal system**[401], provided that:

1) **There is enough available for saving**: A subsistence economy must take care of present needs and can't also focus on future needs. Currently, all OECD states are so wealthy that their legal systems wouldn't be just if they didn't provide some form of social security.

2) **Social security is sustainable in four ways**:

a) There **must be, in practice, adequate means to keep the promise** of economic protection.

b) The **protection must be meaningful**, i.e., sufficient to effectively address some of the needs of the protected person.

c) The **resources needed for the protection must be affordable,** in the sense that social protection should not make present life miserable.

d) The **protection provided should not induce (too many) people to depend** on the welfare.[402]

Still, the Covid-19 pandemic has unleashed the biggest fiscal stimulus in human history, without any conservative or libertarian commentators making a fuss about it.[403] In the executive summary of a recent OECD study we can read as follows:[404]

Looking at the reforms adopted before the COVID-19 crisis, the report identifies the following trends:

• Personal income tax (PIT) reductions, targeted in particular at low and middle-income households, have continued. While this trend represents a broad continuation

---

[401] I totally agree with the points made by SHAFIK, M., *What We Owe Each Other: A New Social Contract*, 23 ff., 124 ff. and 153 ff., on why we need a new a new social contract, tuned to the needs of the post pandemic society.

[402] SHAFIK, M., *What We Owe Each Other: A New Social Contract*, 165 ff.

It is extremely rare for people to be able to move to another country and continue to accrue their pension contributions. In the Scandinavian countries, there is such a possibility, but it is the only example that I could find. The current strictly national system of social/pension contributions has as a consequence that no one with a couple of decades of accrued pension contributions can leave his or her country of origin, without a heavy economic loss.

One can read about the social and political issues of the German system of welfare, in particular, the human and social consequences of a system that induces dependency among the citizens it tries to protect, in KLOEPFER I., *Aufstand der Unterschicht. Was auf uns zukommt.*

On a sustainable welfare in the 21st century, see STIGLITZ, J.E., *The Welfare State in the Twenty-First Century*, in *The Welfare State Revisited (Initiative for Policy Dialogue at Columbia: Challenges in Development and Globalisation)*, eds. OCAMPO, J.A., STIGLITZ, J.E., loc. 707.

[403] ZAKARIA, F., *Ten Lessons for a Post-Pandemic World*, 54.

[404] OECD, *Tax Policy Reforms 2020: OECD and Selected Partner Economies*, 10, 11 ff.

of PIT reforms in recent years, an intensification of PIT rate cuts has been observed. PIT base narrowing measures, often targeted at families and low-income earners, have also been frequent. Regarding the taxation of household capital income, limited changes have been introduced, involving both tax increases and decreases. These measures have included changes to the taxation of rental income as well as expanded tax reliefs to support small savers.

• Changes to social security contributions (SSCs) have been limited both in number and in scope. Most of the reforms were aimed at lowering SSCs, but changes were generally modest. This confirms that the pace of reform in this area has slowed. Corporate income tax (CIT) rate cuts have continued in 2020. As was the case last year, the most significant CIT rate reductions have generally been introduced in countries with higher initial CIT rates, leading to further convergence in statutory CIT rates across countries. Many countries have also reinforced the generosity of their corporate tax incentives to stimulate investment, innovation and environmental sustainability.

• With regard to international taxation, efforts to protect CIT bases against corporate tax avoidance have continued with the adoption of significant reforms in line with the OECD/G20 Base Erosion and Profit Shifting (BEPS) project. The tax challenges arising from the digitalisation of the economy continue to represent a major concern for many countries. Efforts to achieve a consensus-based multilateral solution to address those challenges are ongoing, but a growing number of countries have announced or implemented interim measures to tax certain revenues from digital services in the meantime.

• The stabilisation of standard value-added tax (VAT) rates observed in recent years is continuing, while VAT base changes have involved a mix of base broadening and base narrowing measures. High standard VAT rates in many countries have limited the room for additional rate increases. Instead, many countries have concentrated their efforts on the fight against VAT fraud and on ensuring the effective taxation of cross-border online sales to raise additional revenues and strengthen the functioning of their VAT systems. On the other hand, an increasing number of countries have narrowed their VAT bases by expanding the scope of their reduced VAT rates, which suggests a slight departure from trends in previous years, where the predominant objective of VAT reforms was to raise additional revenues. A number of countries have also raised their excise taxes, in particular on tobacco products and sugar-sweetened beverages, in line with trends in previous years.

• Environmentally related tax reforms have continued at a slow pace in 2020. While the number of measures adopted increased compared to 2019, reforms were concentrated in a few countries and their scope remained generally limited. Most of the reforms were related to the taxation of energy use, but unlike in previous years, transport fuels were not the main focus. Instead, changes were made to carbon taxes and taxes on electricity consumption. Tax reforms in the transport sector, aside from energy use, were limited to adjustments to vehicle registration taxes and tax reductions for vehicles running on alternative fuels. There was an increase in reforms related to other environmental tax bases (e.g., plastic and waste), but their overall number remained limited.

• There has been an increased focus on property taxation compared to previous years. Previous editions of this report have generally shown limited changes to property taxes. This year marks a change, with an increasing number of reforms in this area. In

addition, while previous years saw a mix of tax increases and decreases, this year shows a clearer trend towards increases in property taxation.

The Special Feature on **"Tax and Fiscal Policy Responses to the COVID-19 Crisis"** *shows that countries have taken swift and significant policy action in response to the crisis. While the size of fiscal packages has varied across countries, most have been significant, and some countries have taken unprecedented action. The initial measures introduced by countries focused on keeping businesses and households afloat, mainly through liquidity support for businesses, job retention schemes, and income support to households. As the crisis has continued, many countries have expanded their initial response packages. Some countries have also decided to adjust some of their initial measures or to wind back or delay tax reforms that were due to come into force. The most recent measures and discussions suggest that the recovery phase will be supported by expansionary fiscal policy in many countries, including through measures to support investment and consumption and ongoing support for households and businesses.*

When welfare isn't really sustainable, it is a cruel, immoral fraud that will hit hardest when those relying on it are weaker, if not defenceless. I fear that many of the OECD social security systems fall foul of the requisite of sustainability, in particular with respect to pensions[405] (see chapter 4.3).

---

[405] GHILARDUCCI, T., *Innovations in Protecting the Old*, in *The Welfare State Revisited (Initiative for Policy Dialogue at Columbia: Challenges in Development and Globalisation)*, eds. OCAMPO, J.A., STIGLITZ, J.E., loc. 6432. SHAFIK, M., *What We Owe Each Other: A New Social Contract*, 119 ff., 188 ff.

6

The Immaterial Society
(The Wordless Society)

"La vie se dresse, à tous les instants,
contre la mort;
la pensée contre l'impensé et le livre
qui s'écrit contre le livre écrit".

Edmond Jabès *Le Petit livre*
de la subversion hors de soupçon (1982)

6. The Immaterial Society (the Wordless Society)

This chapter is devoted to properly defining how relevant the digital (i.e., online) dimension has become in our lives. We will not try to "prove" it, because it is a generally accepted assumption. Several publications have already addressed the issue. Taking a philosophical point of view is Luciano Floridi's *The Fourth Revolution: How the Infosphere is Reshaping Human Reality*.[406] And taking a political point of view is Micklethwait and Adrian Wooldridge's *The Fourth Revolution: The Global Race to Reinvent the State*. Micklethwait doesn't directly address digitalisation in his book, but broadly assumes that it is the current way of spreading "global" political ideas, as does Paul Nemitz's *Prinzip Mensch*.[407]

In this chapter we will pin down the technological innovations that have transformed our society, separating them from developments that are still unproven or clearly just hype (chapter 7).

6.1. The Birth of Ubiquitous Computing (Y2K)

There is a clear difference in the impact of digitalisation, before and after ubiquitous connectivity. In 2000, Wi-Fi, Asymmetric Digital Subscriber Lines (ADSL) and Universal Mobile Telecommunications Systems (UMTS) were in their beginning phases. Omnipresent computer interconnection was the exception, but within a few years it became the norm.

In about six years (1998-2004), the speed of Internet connections (fixed or 3G) increased a hundredfold. From a user experience point of view, it was a radical change in the way we use the Internet: before ADSL and UMTS, the Internet was about emailing and downloading small files. But at an average speed of 4 Mbit/second, it has become a fully interactive "online" experience, with instant delivery of multimedia content and the possibility of interconnecting millions of users at the same time on the same application (gaming, Facebook, etc.).

Before 2000, computers were interconnected only through local area networks (LANs), of which the first commercial application was seen in December 1977, at Chase Manhattan Bank in New York. It wasn't until 2000 that Internet connection speeds were dramatically increased through ADSL for fixed land lines and UMTS for mobile networks. After that, it became normal to download at a speed of 8 Mbit/second (through ADSL) and 384 kbit/second (through UMTS). This was a great leap forward from the previous maximum download speed of 56 kbit/second. The Internet, as well as YouTube, Facebook, Pinterest and Tumblr, as we know them today, would not be viable with lower upload/download speeds. Even Twitter, which in theory does not require broadband,

---

[406] FLORIDI, L., *The 4th revolution: How the infosphere is reshaping human reality.*

[407] WOOLDRIDGE A., MICKLETHWAIT J., *The Fourth Revolution*, 178, 210, 281. NEMITZ, P., *Prinzip Mensch: Macht, Freiheit und Demokratie im Zeitalter der künstlichen Intelligenz.*

is popular because of its ability to post images and links, which require broadband.[408]

When Y2K heralded the new millennium, there were less than 400 million Internet users and about 500 million mobile subscribers. Today, we have 4 billion Internet users (or 50% of the world's population) and 7.2 billion mobile subscribers (almost as many subscriptions as people in the world), with 17% of the world population living in areas with no mobile coverage.[409]

We have made tremendous progress. Prior to 1999, computer Internet connections were no faster than 56.6 kbit/second for downloading and 36.6 for uploading (ITU-T [International Telegraph Union - Telecommunication Standardisation Sector] recommendations V.90 and V.92). ISDN (Integrated Services for Digital Network) offered download and upload speeds of just 128 kbit/second for each duplex connection (1988 CCITT [from the French Comité Consultatif International Téléphonique et Télégraphique] red book, then an ITU-T recommendation, now a European norm, ETSI (European Telecommunications Standards Institute EN 300 485).[410]

For mobile devices, ubiquitous connectivity became possible in 2000, with UMTS and then HSDPA (High-Speed Downlink Packet Access). UMTS supports maximum theoretical data transfer rates of 42 Mbit/second when HSPA+ is implemented in the network. Users in deployed networks can expect transfer rates of up to 384 kbit/second for Release '99 (R99) handsets (the original UMTS release), and 7.2 Mbit/second for HSDPA handsets in the downlink connection. These speeds are significantly faster than the 9.6 kbit/second of a single GSM (Global System for Mobile) error-corrected circuit-switched data channel (or multiple 9.6 kbit/second channels in HSCSD or 14.4 kbit/second for CDMA [code division multiple access] One channels).

Since 2006, UMTS networks in many countries have been upgrading to HSDPA (sometimes known as 3.5G). Currently, HSDPA enables downlink transfer speeds of up to 21 Mbit/second. Work is also progressing to improve the uplink transfer speed with High-Speed Uplink Packet Access (HSUPA). In the longer term, the 3GPP Long Term Evolution (LTE) project plans to move UMTS to 4G speeds of 100 Mbit/second for downloads and 50 Mbit/second for uploads, using a next-generation air interface technology based upon

---

[408] Ubiquitous connectivity, with upload/download speeds that allows the use of computers and mobile devices, has been a reality since 2000, when the Internet had about 400 million users and most of them were accessing it at a speed between 14.4 kbit/s and 56 kbit/s. Ubiquitous connectivity, as we know and use it today, started in 1999-2000 with the ADSL broadband connection: the ITU G.992.1 standard, with download speeds of up to 8 Mbit/s and upload speeds up to 1 Mbit/s. See International Telecommunications Union, "ADSL Transceivers".

The distinction between "before" and "after" ubiquitous computing and the date of 2000 are arbitrary; but for the purpose of this publication, it does not matter if it is more accurate to date ubiquitous computing back to 1996 (a very unlikely date, because Wi-Fi, UMTS and ADSL were not yet developed) or 2005. The year 2000 sounds momentous anyway, and therefore I will use it.

[409] International Telecommunications Union, "Statistics"; International Telecommunications Union, "Facts and Figures: The World in 2020".

[410] ETSI, "Integrated Services Digital Network".

orthogonal frequency-division multiplexing.[411] In 2019 the deployment of 5G began. 5G networks are predicted to have more than 1.7 billion subscribers worldwide by 2025, according to the GSM Association. The main advantage of the new networks is that they will offer greater bandwidth, giving higher download speeds, eventually up to 10 Gbit/second. Due to the increased bandwidth, it is expected the networks will not exclusively serve cell phones, like existing cellular networks, but will also be used as general Internet service providers for laptops and desktop computers, competing with existing ISPs such as cable Internet. It will also enable new applications in the Internet of Things (IoT) and machine-to-machine interactions. 4G cell phones are not able to use the new networks, which require 5G-enabled wireless devices.

LANs were popular for the purpose of sharing, generally in an office setting, the scarce resources of that time: large storage devices and printers. The Ethernet LAN is today a standard managed by the Institute of Electrical and Electronics Engineers: IEEE 802.3.[412]

The evolution of LANs has made them ubiquitous, not only in the office, but also at home with Wi-Fi, aka the IEEE 802.11 standard.[413]

Before ubiquitous computing, the only digital sharing was local, through LANs. We shared printers and other peripherals; content was produced locally and printed or sent out to recipients who were pre-defined by legal agreements, firewalls or marketing strategies.

Now, with ubiquitous computing, there is about four times more traffic incoming than outgoing for any given LAN,[414] and we share internal and external resources seamlessly.

The output of local working communities (using LANs that are now wireless) has been permanently enriched by content available online, and the speed of collaboration for any content available online has dramatically increased and is increasing still!

Ubiquitous computing has helped to transform us from wilful producers of information for pre-defined recipients, into serendipitous information consumers, whose consumption of information automatically (and mostly unintentionally) generates other information that has economic and social value. This other information, which sprouted from the original search for information, is then shared.

We broadcast our own consumption and generation of information, live and in real time.

Today, being is not enough for existing. You are also expected to provide some sort of account of yourself.

[411] Wikipedia, "UTMS"; ETSI, "Satellite UMTS/IMT-2000"; ETSI, "Universal Mobile Telecommunications System"; Wikipedia, "Internet access"; *Computerworld*, "The LAN turns 30 but will it reach 40?."

[412] http://standards.ieee.org/about/get/802/802.3.html; https://standards.ieee.org/search-results.html?q=802.3.

[413] http://standards.ieee.org/about/get/802/802.11.html.

[414] This is why telecom operators have designed download speeds to be about four times as fast as upload speeds in their networks.

Ubiquitous computing has unleashed three interconnected technological megatrends that are defining information technology at the beginning of the 21st century: cloud computing (see chapter 7.2), big data (see chapter 7.3), and artificial intelligence (see chapter 7.3).

6.2. Digitalisation of documents: What Has Changed and What Has Not

The function of documents and signatures has remained unchanged, if compared to their inherent nature, their ontology, over the last 2,000 years, even after digitalisation. What has changed is their significance and evidential value, as we will see in this chapter and in chapter 7.4, as a consequence of their complex technical features. As we have seen in chapter 3.3. and will discuss in depth in chapter 8.2, the problem is that, in the digital domain, we cannot differentiate between true documents on the one hand and inscriptions and recordings on the other.

There are three ontological (i.e., unavoidable) differences affecting how we interact with information managed by computers vs. how we interact with analogue (i.e., paper-based) documents. The first two differences are immanent, even with standalone computers, whereas the third is a consequence of computer networking on closed local area networks.

The digitalisation of information has changed the following three fundamental aspects of how information is generated, accessed and processed:

Change #1 (ontological): **Digital data, information and documents are not perceivable by humans without the use of some tools** (computer displays, speakers or printers). The relationship between a person and the information has become technologically mediated.

Change #2 (ontological): **The creation of documents and information has become much more complex and sophisticated**. Data crunching and word processors made it possible for a single user (since the start of personal computing) to create documents of great complexity, whereas before digitalisation, entire teams of dedicated people were needed in order to create a similar record.

Computers interconnected on a LAN have introduced a third ontological change in the way documentation is generated and shared: With standalone personal computers or mainframes, data was located in the same room as the hardware. With early LANs, the information was located in the mainframe of the LAN, normally in the same building. Later on, when the cost of geographic networks became affordable (i.e., the cost of data transmission was independent of the distance to be covered by the network, which was, again, around the year 2000), it was located somewhere in the same region. From that moment on, it became possible to distribute data over a set of different locations.

Change #3 (ontological): Even with LANs, **the physical location of the machine keeping the data became irrelevant,** as long as the information technology system keeping such data would admit only the person entitled to access the information.

These are the essential ontological changes that have affected digital documents (and digital registrations and digital inscriptions).

According to many, there was also a fourth change:

Change #4: Many (if not all) users of an information technology system have unrestricted access to the same digital data, without other users being aware of it. On the contrary, a paper document can be accessed only by those who can access the room or drawer where the paper is archived.

In my opinion, there is no "Change #4"; there is only a "**Bad Design #1**". The digital home of digital data has no doors and no locks; everyone has access to the system and is entitled to change the data (i.e., recordings, inscriptions, and documents).

Information technology systems that manage digital data can easily be redesigned from scratch in a way that would guarantee that:

a) access is monitored and regulated

b) access (when permitted) is monitored and traced

c) change is restricted

d) change (when permitted) is traced.

There is no inherent lifespan for any given document. A train ticket is relevant and useful for the duration of the trip. But if we want to deduct the cost of that trip from our taxes, then the ticket becomes relevant for as long as the tax authority is entitled to verify it. And if an audit requires the retention of the document for a longer time than its fiscal relevance, then, from an auditing standpoint, there is a third life for this ticket.

If we need to provide information for a timespan that falls within the combined duration of the language and of the medium used, then a static "document" (i.e., registration, inscription or document) can fulfil the task. Here, the meaning of "static" and "modifiable" are relative to the purpose of the "document" (i.e., document, inscription or recording).

Legislation may define the minimum formal requirements of legal documents. Depending on their use and relevance, there are requirements for how to write down legislation (parchment is required by some constitutions); for a contract in written form (all civil law systems provide such a definition); and for a handwritten will (most civil law systems provide a definition for a holographic testament). The strongest requirements are for a limited set of contracts:

1. For some of them, it is necessary to have not only a document, but also witnesses attesting to the origin and the authenticity of the document, with an interesting mix of written and oral documentation: e.g., marriage.

2. For others, it is necessary for them to be filed and archived by a competent authority (registrar of companies or secretary of state): e.g., limited liability companies or real property transactions.

Nevertheless, no legislation defines the validity of documents, in light of their inherent modifiability. What counts is that, in the few cases where a specific form of contract is required by law, the form of the document be compliant with such law.[415] So it should be for digital documents.[416]

---

[415] Irti, N., *Formalismo e attività giuridica*, 4.

[416] Sounds pretty obvious: but in the community of "experts" of digital documents and signatures, there are some that believe that technical flaws of the digital document (or signature) has the consequence of making them legally invalid.

There is a fourth true, fundamental change associated with digitalisation. **Change #4: Documents are no longer the only source of information; recordings have become the main means of sharing information in a digital society**. Before information technology, only humans were able to generate documents, and they were able to create them only intentionally. The possibility of someone writing a letter or a contract unintentionally was imaginable, but only in theory. On the other hand, in the analogue world, only machines could generate recordings: photographs, audio recordings, video recordings, photocopies were all machine-generated and easily recognisable as such.

So before the age of computers, whenever one saw a written document, one could safely suppose that someone had intentionally created it. This endowed any written document with the inherent status of being the intentional expression of someone's intention. Even if the document represents a lie or falsely simulates an intention, one could safely presume that the will to deceive was intentional.

And even when a written document was a forgery, one could assume without error that the forger created it intentionally. Before the age of computers, there were no automated writers (or printing machines) that could activate themselves to produce a forged document.

In the digital world, the assumptions that were true for analogue documents are no longer true.

Any written text can now be machine-generated, i.e., without anybody's intention or even consciousness. But this change is so recent, that we still tend to trust something written, assuming that it is the representation of some intentional activity. Hackers and marketing experts exploit the fallacy of these beliefs. Populists and extremists also use this fallacy to influence people, presenting manipulated recordings as factual, documented truth. A webpage or a blog are as easy to set up as a pulpit at the Hyde Park Speakers' Corner.[417] But nobody can doubt that the influence of blogs and webpages is incomparably greater than that exercised by the speakers at Hyde Park.

What has not changed with digitalisation?
The social function of a document has not changed.

It is practical to point out that digital documents are not inherently static, like paper-based documents. This implies that they may not be real documents.

Now the truth is that all documents become unreadable after 800 years or so, either because the markings on the page fade away or because the page itself decays.

So what is "static"? A written sheet of paper left in the rain becomes unreadable after few minutes. It used to be possible to forge passports and even banknotes. Think about how easy it can be to forge a contract written in ink on a standard sheet of white paper (known in Europe as DIN A4). If you keep an archive of chronologically organized papers in a building with walls made of mud, with no doors, locks, heating, ventilation or maintenance, the documents will mould, stick together and become useless after just a few years (or even

---

[417] Wikipedia, *Speakers Corner*.

149

one bad winter or rainy season). So the concept of a "static document" is relative and poorly defined – because it is commonplace, just a casual idea.

A "static" piece of paper implies a lot of organisation and technology, which are commonplace today in affluent parts of the world; we simply take it for granted. But if we lived in an igloo in the Arctic or a hut in the Amazon, or in ancient Rome, the need for such organisation and technology would be more evident.

Conversely, digital files can be protected by default and by design, i.e.:
- of the hardware used to store and manage such files
- or of the computer operating system
- or of the access management software
- or with a combination of the above-mentioned technologies.

So the only novelty involving digital documents is that humans are able to perceive them only with tools (computers) that carry out logical operations on them (not analogue tools, like magnifying glasses, microscopes or symmetric code-decryption devices). Indeed, digital documents are more complex than written papers.

The function of the signature has not changed. Handwritten signatures cannot be affixed to any digital document (i.e., registration, inscription or document) in order to validate it. But this is hardly new! Humanity is back to square one: A digital document may be marked with an elaborate sign that has no biometric connection to the author of the document (i.e., an electronic signature), just as was customary from the second century B.C. to the mid-17th century A.D. – a time when scribes drafted and signed documents on behalf of the author(s) … a time before graphology had been accepted as a (disputed) pseudoscience.[418]

For about two millennia, signatures were routinely affixed (in a mediated way) by slaves or employees of the signer. This is no more or less common in the present day, when we add our name at the end of an email, typing them on a keyboard. As with the handwritten signatures appended by scribes on behalf of the signer, the validation of digital registrations, inscriptions and documents has become a highly complex process, in which **social constructs and technology ensure the authenticity** and authenticate the origin of the digital data.

Such social constructs date back to Ancient Rome and the forum, where it was compulsory to close agreements with a wax seal in order to ensure their validity and effect.

In the Middle Ages, the forum was replaced by the notary's office.

Today, equivalent social constructs are provided by contract law, legal compliance and accountancy rules.

Technology in Ancient Rome was represented by sealed documents that were conserved by the parties to the agreement (very similarly to a digital document with an electronic signature!).

---

[418] Graphology was invented by the Abbé Michon, who became interested in handwriting analysis in 1830. He published his findings shortly after founding the Société Graphologique in 1871.

In the Middle Ages, the technology evolved to be handled by professional organisations known as archives (with encryption and decryption facilities), run by the notaries and clerks of the government.

Today, the technologies include enterprise resource planning (ERP) documents and public key infrastructure (PKI) management systems.

From a global, historical perspective, our reliance on verifying a handwritten signature using a graphologist has been in place for less than 150 years, out of two millennia. This is why the presence of witnesses has remained customary in private negotiations and is still mandatory (in many legal systems) for important notarized contracts.

To put this in perspective, the biometric, handwritten signature on paper achieved social acceptance for about as long as the tailcoat with a white bowtie!

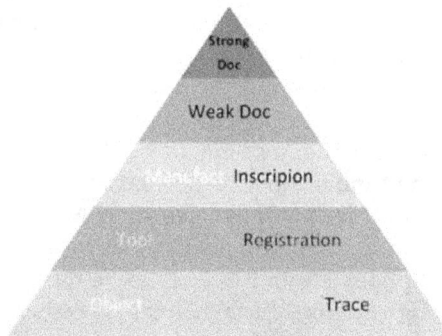

What are (digital) documents in the end? Memories!

Ontological philosophers have posed a nice paradox about the real relevance of written documents. Let's imagine that a woman meets with her son at a lawyer's office in order to execute the gift of a valuable painting to him. And let's imagine that her mind is unable to retain any memory of the transaction, so she goes on assuming that the painting belongs to her. She reports the missing painting to the authorities, and the police eventually find the painting at the home of her son. If, at this point, the donor is confronted with the written documentation of the gift, without having any memory of signing it, she will conclude that such a document is a forgery. Even if she recollects that she actually wanted to give away the painting, still she will be shocked to see that her son assumes he is the rightful owner, since she has no memory of signing the document. If the lawyer and those who witnessed the document testify that she actually signed it, she will be increasingly frustrated, but not convinced, as long as she cannot recall the event of meeting in the lawyer's office and signing the agreement.

This is the situation when just one of the involved parties has no memory of the generation of a document. Now what would happen if the human mind were unable to retain any memory of signing a document (like a dream that we are unable to recall)? What if nobody could recollect anything about what happened in the lawyer's office? Well, then documents would be utterly useless! They would simply not prove anything!

So if we look at either analogue or digital documents, we have to be mindful of something that is not apparent, but is still essential in the definition of a document: i.e., that it is an object created intentionally by a human being and is therefore something that ontologically leaves a specific record in the brain of the persons involved in the generation or execution of the document. Without that recollection of the generation of the document in the brain of the author (and the relying parties), no document can exist. (Or if it existed, as in the example of the gifted painting, it would be a useless document – which is almost a contradiction in terms.)

In fact, any so-called "document" generated without intention and without consciousness, is a registration. Think of a video camera inadvertently switched on and left running until the battery dies. In such a case, it might never even be discovered that there is a registration. In the documental pyramid, the registration is more than a trace because it has been generated by a tool, designed for that purpose. But it is less than an inscription, because it is not meant to be shared in any way: it is just a registration.

One fine example of an inscription is the operation of a security camera pointed at the entrance of a bank. A registration of this kind is meant to be accessed by the police in the event of a crime, or by the system administrator, in order to store it until the time it must be deleted for data protection reasons. Most likely, no one will ever look at the registration. Nonetheless, since it is designed to be accessed by more than one person, it is more than a registration; it is an inscription. Inscriptions are more likely to be transformed into documents at some point, through an intentional use that goes beyond their generation.

Material documents written or carved on a surface have several properties:[419]

1) They have the ontological property that they can be immediately perceived by the author (and the relying parties).

2) They have the ontological property that they are visible to humans without the use of any device (microscopes, sensors, etc.), which was true at least until the invention of the telegraph and radio.

3) Moreover, paper-based documents (again, ontologically) can be handled or exchanged without the need for any tools. (They are not liquid or gaseous, too hot or too cold, too big, too little, too heavy or too light to suit their purpose.)

4) Paper-based documents exist in the same dimension (i.e., the physical or analogue dimension) as the author and the relying parties themselves.

5) Before recording technologies were developed, there was no way to generate documents unintentionally!

For all the above-mentioned properties, the generation and validation or signature of a paper-based document is (almost) always a physical and immediate experience on the part of the author (and the other relying parties).

Things have become more complicated lately, due to technological evolution. First, in the 16th century, the invention of the printing press allowed for the reproduction of text and images. Since then, to reproduce information we have

---

[419] Analogue documents are not represented (or readable) in binary code, but rely on a sequential series of signs. Until the invention of the phonogram and the photograph, all sequential signs were directly or indirectly manmade and handmade.

used machines that record and reproduce images and sounds using various analogue media. These are, in chronological order:
- 19th century: celluloid for photographed and filmed images
- 19th century: shellac records for sound
- 20th century: magnetic tape for images and sound
- 20th century: cyclostyle and photocopier for reproduced text and images.

Before these technologies were developed, there was no way to generate documents unintentionally. But when it comes to "digital documents", we arrive at a situation where almost all the properties of paper documents and other analogue documents are turned on their heads:

1) Digital documents cannot be perceived without using complex tools (i.e., computers).

2) Digital documents are so complex that they cannot be understood without a "translator" (i.e., software that presents the contents of a file). So we can no longer tell the difference between a document and an automatic recording.

3) Digital documents can be accessed even when the geographic location of the files we want to access is unknown.

4) The tools for "creating" and the tools for "reading" digital documents are often identical. An analogy in the analogue world would arise if one could not tell the difference between a book and a typewriter or between a written document and the act of writing.

All this raises a fundamental question: If written documents were so complex when they were first adopted to document human life, would they ever have been chosen in the first place?

When you look at the picture below representing the complexity of digitally signing a legal document today, do you feel that a digitally signed file can really be the equivalent of a hand-signed document? It should be obvious that the answers to these questions are negative.

In trying to make digital and analogue documents equivalent, we take it for granted that the generation of a digital document also produces some memories of its generation and its content. But the contrary is true: Most "digital documents" can be created (and eventually even signed) without the "author" or the "signer" having any perception of their being created or signed. Therefore, the "author" and even the relying parties may not have any recollection of the generation or execution of the "digital document". This demonstrates that the semiotic function of digital documents is ontologically different from the semiotic function of analogue documents – unless IT can recreate the same existential experience that we used to have when signing paper documents.[420]

Digital documents are (semiotically) more efficient at providing facts. Analogue documents are more efficient at accurately representing a legally relevant intention.[421]

The technical verifiability of digital documents (at the current stage of technological and social evolution) is considered too cumbersome, so it has been superseded by some automatic digital recordings (generated unilaterally by just one of the relying parties). Think of any e-commerce transaction.

Before the digital revolution, you didn't need a written document to buy something in a shop. But if you bought it via correspondence, then some kind of written contract was necessary. When remote shopping went digital, the whole idea of using a contract to prove a purchase was disrupted. Instead of using intentional, bilateral documentation, the economy shifted to using unilaterally generated recordings and inscriptions, in order to make the purchasing experience more like being in a store.

It was a wonderful idea, and usually it worked fine.

Many lawyers and pundits have tried to work out in what way e-commerce produces any contract-like documentation. The outcome of their efforts has been unconvincing. A contract is something intentional, and a written contract even more so.

So e-commerce purchases must instead be understood as non-written, binding transactions, where the emails and clicks simply serve as a registration of what took place. In the best-case scenario, they are inscriptions, but not strong documents.[422]

This is actually nothing new. If you go back to chapter 3.8, you will read that for about two millennia there has been a distinction between "*Charta*" and "*Notitia*", the latter being a text generated by someone not involved in the transaction and which recorded the transaction, unlike the document that substantiated the mutual exchange of the contractual will.

So e-commerce today is based on some kind of "digital *notitiae*" (with no documents, just recordings!), generated by a server run by the online merchant, which produces some sort of audit trial of the transaction, like the scriveners did when they drafted a notitia in the 11th century. The papers written by these scriveners, having the substantial function of a recording/inscription, were formally documents, because they were generated to intentionally represent the actions and declarations of other people in the style of a witness. In contrast, the recordings and emails generated by the merchant's server today are the unintentional, automated activities of a machine.

Because digital documents are so complex, only the service of a trusted third party can ensure the same level of certainty and direct experience that we had with paper documents for millennia. For 1,500 years, people have relied on

---

[420] GENGHINI, R., *La Forma Notarile Digitale*, 26.
[421] GENGHINI, R., *La Forma Notarile Digitale*, 29.
[422] See chapter 3.3.

notaries to sign agreements for precisely this reason. The generation, reading, signing and archiving of a parchment was far beyond the technical capabilities of the relying parties; so they resorted to a service, provided by a trusted third party.

Today, the successful spread of e-commerce should be welcomed as a great improvement in the accessibility of goods and services. But we must be mindful that it is not based on an entirely new way of documenting legal transactions – because the "witnessing" of legal transactions is as old as contracts. What we have are non-written legal transactions, with some digital recordings relating to them. No more, no less. But this new way of documenting legal agreements has been working rather well, so far even better than paper contracts, with only one significant downside (increasingly exploited by fraudsters): the identities used by merchant and customer aren't proper digital identities, related to the physical person and to the legal entity of the merchant, but identification tools that are opaque and proprietary to the merchant itself (or its IT provider). This weakens significantly the evidential value of the digital recordings of the e-commerce transaction, creates opportunities for phishing attacks (or other scams) and increases dramatically the informative asymmetries.

For other kinds of legal transactions that are more socially important (or simply riskier), like incorporating a company, marrying, or writing one's final will, we need proper legal documentation and full, undisputable proof of the free will of the parties involved.

For this purpose, the only tested solution that works is to use a qualified, trusted third party to handle the complexity of digital documentation, leaving the parties free to concentrate on the negotiation of the content of the agreement. That gives all involved parties a level playing field and equal, transparent, non-discriminatory access to the legal documentation over time, ensuring that such legal transactions are preserved in the long term, with full protection against forgery and (unlawful) deletion. They can be executed digitally and at a distance – only provided that the trusted third party and the relying parties have access to technology that is properly designed.[423] Such technologies and the assistance of a trusted third party are needed also because, as we have seen in chapter 3.3, even intentionally generated digital documents are full of invisible automatically generated recordings. The trusted third party has the responsibility that such automated recordings do not alter the meaning (and legal relevance) of the digital document.

Today's digital documents are made of written words and other unwritten signs!

---

[423] GENGHINI, R., *La Forma Notarile Digitale*, 27, 30, 35, 64, 98.

7 Digital Common Sense (...and Digital Hype)

*"Governments of the industrial world,
you weary giants of flesh and steel, I come
from cyberspace, the new home of mind.
On behalf of the future, I ask you of the
past to leave us alone. You are not
welcome among us. You have no
sovereignty where we gather.
"We have no elected government, nor
are we likely to have one, so I address
you with no greater authority than that
with which liberty itself always speaks. I
declare the global social space we are building
to be naturally independent of the tyrannies
you seek to impose on us. You have no moral
right to rule us nor do you possess any
methods of enforcement we have true
reason to fear."*

John Perry Barlow
8 February 1996, World Economic Forum
Davos, Switzerland
https://vimeo.com/111576518

7. Digital Common Sense (... and Digital Hype)

7.1. Open source

As a supporter of open source,[424] I don't share the idea that "open" is good, enlightened and generous, or that "closed" is bad, short-sighted and greedy. It is impossible to "open" all R&D projects. This is not for reasons related to their economic exploitation, but for the reason of not interfering with proper scientific methodology. (Consider blind and double-blind experiments.)[425]

Methodology is imperative, but at some point, in any given project, the discussion of the methodology has to be brought to an end. If you open a project to any interested researcher, the issue of (diverging) methodologies will re-emerge cyclically, not always producing any real scientific improvement. What many projects need is the "vertical deepening" of research, which requires a uniquely homogenous approach.

From a purely scientific perspective, "stabilized knowledge" is of greater social use with open intellectual property rights (IPRs) and some kind of "free" or "open" but regulated form of sharing (like the Creative Commons[426] or GNU[427] or FRAND[428] licensing agreements). "Knowledge in the making" requires a carefully chosen environment to grow and flourish. Such environments only sometimes work better if they are open environments.

The definitions of "stabilized knowledge" and "knowledge in the making" are quite vague, so let's build on them with some general rules. The point is that the statement, "Shared knowledge is better, truer, deeper," is not universally true. It is an ideological and deontological statement, not a matter of fact.

Everybody is aware of the abuses of patent trolls,[429] and we all know that the monopoly provided by patents on innovations can actually stifle innovation and impede scientific research. Yet we also understand that, if an industry invests billions in research to produce an innovation, it would be unfair for others to have a free ride and reap the benefits without having made any investment or contribution to the innovation.

The question of "open" vs. "closed" is not the right question. If we could engage in the debate about shared knowledge, free from prejudice and without reciprocal accusations of bad faith, it would become possible to revise the current rules – which are clearly inadequate for a post-industrial, knowledge-based society. But this would require the warring factions to agree that compromise is the way to improve the current state of affairs.

---

[424] Lawrence Lessig, in his *Free Culture*, makes a powerful analogy for openness against "locked down knowledge". LESSIG L., *Free Culture*.

[425] Wikipedia, *Blind experiment*.

[426] http://creativecommons.org.

[427] https://gnu.org/home.en.html.

[428] Wikipedia, *FRAND*.

[429] See the Wikipedia definition for it Wikipedia, *Patent troll*.

The fundamental attitude among the supporters of openness is that if an author shares his knowledge with everybody, without charging for it but nonetheless reserving all further rights for himself, this is not considered "free", under the Creative Commons licensing structure. The CC Attribution-NoDerivatives 4.0 International license and the CC Attribution-Noncommercial-ShareAlike 4.0 International license are not Free Culture licenses.

To be "open", it is not sufficient to "share your work with others"; you have to renounce (at least partially) your exclusive ownership. It is required that you no longer consider your creation "yours" anymore.

Why? This is like saying that if I invite you to my home for dinner, I am not sharing. Under CC rules, we instead need to do the digital equivalent of going on a hunting trip together; and not only do we need to go hunting and catch the game together, we must then cook and eat it together while we're out on the range. Nothing belongs to me, nothing belongs to my fellow hunters. It's a little like being a prehistoric forager (see chapter 2.5).

This mindset is antiquated. It was clearly useful in the time of the hunter-gatherers, but it does not fit into a post-industrial, knowledge-based society. It is a rule that rather hints to the possibility that we live in some sort of digital prehistory!

Open knowledge and private knowledge are not mutually exclusive, unless one succeeds in making them so. We will have to live with the outdated laws regulating IPRs for as long as the two camps choose to act in a mutually exclusive way.

It is a completely different matter that the camp of the "IPR wielders" showed alarming signs of greediness and intolerance when they (successfully) lobbied for the extension of copyright and other monopolistic protections to last up to a century. This is unacceptable and deprives human society of essential ingredients for cultural and scientific development. We lose not only the best Mickey Mouse stories ever (i.e., those that are still unwritten), but also access to knowledge that has already been monetized for decades![430]

In Italy, we have a much beloved cartoon called "La Linea" ("Lineman"), which can no longer be developed or produced because of unresolved IPR issues.[431] The same holds true for early Van Halen videos.

A monopoly on knowledge and culture can kill a project or idea. But it doesn't have to. We are still looking for the proper solution, and digitalisation does not make it any easier.

One landmark case in the history of digital openness is the Wikipedia case.

For the last two decades, the Wikipedia project has been generating the same discussions that have gone on for centuries about how to write an encyclopaedia.

The still unanswered question is, who decides who is competent on what subject? And ultimately, what is the meaning of "competent"? Donald J. Trump may be the person who knows best what President Trump did and did not do (or say), but he (and his affiliates) are surely ineligible to write the Wikipedia entry

---

[430] If you compare the riotous, crazy, incorrect Mickey Mouse of yore to the law-abiding, logical, educated, middle-class citizen of today's cartoons (or to the never-changing representations of Beckett's *Waiting for Godot*), you see the damage that a monopoly does to culture, art, and knowledge, when protracted for too long a period. It sterilizes innovation into oblivion.

[431] Osvaldo Cavandoli, "La Linea".

about the presidency of Donald J. Trump. So the most "competent" person to write on a subject, from the perspective of an encyclopaedia, is not the most knowledgeable person, but the person whom you can most trust to be objective. The issue suddenly brings censorship to mind and all the cases involving school-books and newspapers where governments and national associations of scholars have meddled with the facts. They use the argument that a certain account of history (reality, politics, philosophy, ethics, aesthetics, etc.) is not adequately objective or does not comply with "scientific methodology", whatever that may be.

Yet knowledge is not a question that can be resolved "democratically". Brilliant thinkers like Galileo, Descartes and Einstein presented explanations of reality that were unsettling for most people, and even for the scientific community, but were eventually proved to be true. This shows that peer review is necessary, but it is not sufficient.

Wikipedia is a wonderful thing. (I regularly donate to the Wikipedia Foundation, as everyone who reads it should.) But Wikipedia is not the ultimate source of knowledge in the 21st century – not only because of the recurring inaccuracies of the information published, but also because it is a "text without a known author".

Peer-generated content is surely one of the most striking innovations made possible by digitalisation, but hardly replaces all other forms of content generation. There will still be books, radio and TV broadcasts, movies, newspapers, blogs, chats, software and hardware, generated by one or more authors collaborating in a structured way that is not peer-to-peer and is not "open", in the current (still ideologically tainted) sense.

(There will be more to say on openness in the last chapter of this book.)

7.2. Cloud Computing: Anything New?

Is cloud computing really something new?

"I think there is a world market for maybe five computers," stated Thomas Watson, president of IBM in 1943. This is renowned as one of the worst predictions of all time, but as cloud computing succeeds, Watson's prediction seems to be proving more accurate.

So we have to ask ourselves, can it be true that the real new thing in computing is the centralisation of computational power and applications, as predicted 70 years ago?

Let's start with the definition of "cloud computing", as provided by the US National Institute for Standards and Technology (NIST):[432]

Cloud computing is a model for enabling ubiquitous, convenient, on-demand network access to a shared pool of configurable computing resources (e.g., networks, servers, storage, applications, and services) that can be rapidly provisioned and released with

---

[432] The definition provided by NIST is globally accepted; see NIST, "Cloud Computing Program". It is referenced in Europe by the European Telecommunication Standards Organisation in its cloud standards (see ETSI, "CLOUD: Initial analysis of standardisation requirements for Cloud services") and in its Cloud Standards Coordination initiative (see ETSI, "Cloud Standards Coordination: Final Report"), in which I have been actively involved as one of the ETSI TB Chairmen.

minimal management effort or service provider interaction. This cloud model is composed of five essential characteristics, three service models, and four deployment models.

Essential Characteristics:

*- **On-demand self-service** - A consumer can unilaterally provision computing capabilities, such as server time and network storage, as needed automatically without requiring human interaction with each service provider.*

*- **Broad network access** - Capabilities are available over the network and accessed through standard mechanisms that promote use by heterogeneous thin or thick client platforms (e.g., mobile phones, tablets, laptops, and workstations).*

*- **Resource pooling** - The provider's computing resources are pooled to serve multiple consumers using a multi-tenant model, with different physical and virtual resources dynamically assigned and reassigned according to consumer demand. There is a sense of location independence in that the customer generally has no control or knowledge over the exact location of the provided resources but may be able to specify location at a higher level of abstraction (e.g., country, state, or datacenter). Examples of resources include storage, processing, memory, and network bandwidth.*

*- **Rapid elasticity**. Capabilities can be elastically provisioned and released, in some cases automatically, to scale rapidly outward and inward commensurate with demand. To the consumer, the capabilities available for provisioning often appear to be unlimited and can be appropriated in any quantity at any time.*

*- **Measured service** - Cloud systems automatically control and optimize resource use by leveraging a metering capability at some level of abstraction appropriate to the type of service (e.g., storage, processing, bandwidth, and active user accounts). Resource usage can be monitored, controlled, and reported, providing transparency for both the provider and consumer of the utilized service.*

Its Service Models are threefold.

*- **Software as a Service (SaaS)** - The capability provided to the consumer is to use the provider's applications running on a cloud infrastructure. The applications are accessible from various client devices through either a thin client interface, such as a web browser (e.g., web-based email), or a program interface. The consumer does not manage or control the underlying cloud infrastructure including network, servers, operating systems, storage, or even individual application capabilities, with the possible exception of limited user-specific application configuration settings.*

*- **Platform as a Service (PaaS)** - The capability provided to the consumer is to deploy onto the cloud infrastructure consumer-created or acquired applications created using programming.*

*- **Infrastructure as a Service (IaaS)** - The capability provided to the consumer is to provision processing, storage, networks, and other fundamental computing resources where the consumer is able to deploy and run arbitrary software, which can include operating systems and applications. The consumer does not manage or control the underlying cloud infrastructure but has control over operating systems, storage, and deployed applications; and possibly limited control of select networking components (e.g., host firewalls).*

It can be deployed as:

*a) **Private cloud** - The cloud infrastructure is provisioned for exclusive use by a single organisation comprising multiple consumers (e.g., business units). It may be owned, managed, and operated by the organisation, a third party, or some combination of them, and it may exist on or off premises.*

b) **Community cloud** - *The cloud infrastructure is provisioned for exclusive use by a specific community of consumers from organisations that have shared concerns (e.g., mission, security requirements, policy, and compliance considerations). It may be owned, managed and operated by one or more of the organisations in the community, a third party, or some combination of them, and it may exist on or off premises.*

c) **Public cloud** - *The cloud infrastructure is provisioned for open use by the general public. It may be owned, managed, and operated by a business, academic, or government organisation, or some combination of them. It exists on the premises of the cloud provider.*

d) **Hybrid cloud** - *The cloud infrastructure is a composition of two or more distinct cloud infrastructures (private, community, or public) that remain unique entities, but are bound together by standardized or proprietary technology that enables data and application portability (e.g., cloud bursting for load balancing between clouds).*[433]

Cloud computing is highly complex and comes with plenty of technical and legal issues, which must be addressed. A concerted effort to identify the issues and find proper technical solutions has been made in Europe by ETSI, through the Cloud Standards Coordination initiative, which began in 2014.[434] It has had a tangible influence on the European Cloud Computing Strategy.[435]

The hype about cloud computing has created the impression that there is a need for something new and bold to address so much innovation. A year of joint effort by cloud providers, users, and other stakeholders made the following findings:[436]

1. There is no such thing as a jungle of conflicting standards; some gaps are evident, but the endeavour to close them is realistically manageable.

2. There are legal issues, in particular for data protection and the portability of data and services. All of them can be resolved through proper service level agreements (SLAs), although it is evident that not all cloud users have the knowledge or the contractual power to negotiate SLAs that fit their needs.

3. Technically, many things in the cloud are neither new nor innovative; a great part of the innovation lies in the way the service is provided, i.e., in its business model rather than in its technical configuration; new business models are closely related to new types of contracts and liability.

Cloud computing is, in the end, just a new form of outsourcing. The Wikipedia definition of outsourcing is as follows:

In business, outsourcing involves the contracting out of a business process to another. The term "outsourcing" dates back to at least 1981. Outsourcing sometimes involves

---

[433] NIST, "The NIST Definition of Cloud Computing"; European Commission, "Shaping Europe's Digital Future: European Cloud Strategy 2012".

[434] ETSI, "Cloud Standards Coordination: Final Report".

[435] The European Cloud Computing Strategy (ECCS) is an initiative established by the European Commission to promote the adoption of cloud computing services. The strategy is based on three key points: the development of EU-wide voluntary certification schemes, the development of model contract terms to cover issues not addressed by the Common European Sales Law, and the creation of the European Cloud Partnership to drive innovation and growth from the public sector.

[436] ETSI, "Cloud Standards Coordination", http://csc.etsi.org/.

transferring employees and assets from one firm to another, but not always. Outsourcing is also the practice of handing over control of public services to for-profit corporations.[437] *Business process outsourcing (BPO) is a subset of outsourcing that involves the contracting of the operations and responsibilities of a specific business process to a third-party service provider. Originally, this was associated with manufacturing firms such as Coca Cola, which outsourced large segments of its supply chain.*[438]

The "new" aspect of cloud computing is that, for the first time, the management and processing of data have been outsourced.

But is it *really* an innovation, or is it more of an adaptation?

Humans have been innovating, compartmentalizing and specializing for at least 20,000 years.[439] There is nothing new in specialisation.

Actually, specialisation is more of an adaptive reaction to an environmental challenge, rather than an expression of human creativity. So cloud computing seems to be the latest (but not the last) step of human specialisation in the field of collecting, managing and processing digital information.

Not a game changer.

It may be easier to sell cloud services if they're branded as "creative", "new" and highly "innovative", rather than telling the prospective customer, "The sad truth is that in-house data processing has become too complex and expensive for you." There's nothing wrong with a good sales pitch. But please, don't think it is the new frontier in information technology. It is just business as usual, but with a new level of legal and technical complexity, inextricably tied to issues of data protection, security and transparency.

7.3. Big Data and Artificial Intelligence

What is **big data** really? Does quantity produce a shift in quality?

Second Life, Web 2.0, Web 3.0 … a lot of hype. Will it deliver?

There is a saying, "A map as detailed as the territory it describes is useless." Unless it is a digital, interactive "augmented reality" map … that is, a map telling you in real time where the hidden dangers lie, as well as the safest way to your destination, according to weather simulations (if there are no real-time feeds from sensors present in the territory, etc.). With such maps, we could possibly wear digital viewers that provide us with metadata on any landscape we look upon. Even if we are in a place for the first time, we would know as much about the territory as the most experienced local guide.

But the question is, what is the source of the metadata? Is it a computerized mathematical model? A statistical analysis? Information provided by the local association of guides? A mashup of all of that? And who has checked the authenticity of the sources? (Is there any "strong authentication" of the sources?) And who has checked the reliability of the metadata provided?

---

[437] Wikipedia, "*Outsourcing*".
[438] Wikipedia, "*Business process outsourcing*".
[439] See chapter 2.5.

It is of paramount importance to know, without question, the degree of accuracy and reliability of the data used for the analysis.[440]

Big data doesn't help us change the paradigms by which we decide what's relevant and what's not.

I belong to the big data sceptics: There is more information, more computational power; and some can access (sometimes illegally)[441] huge amounts of unstructured data. This is all true, but still, the use and value of big data depend on the methodology and the assumptions according to which we build on it.

So if I am not wrong, it will not be a game changer in itself. I think it is an accelerator, but even the most sophisticated AI today does not understand the data it is processing.[442]

In the end, if we have access to all digital data related to a company, a person or an object, how can we tell "the signal from the noise"?

We might select the information that we unconsciously "like" and discard the rest. If this selection process is sound, we could improve our understanding of reality. If it is biased, we could be badly misled. Nate Silver, in his book *The Signal and the Noise,* provides plenty of evidence of this. The book must be read by anyone who believes that our reality has changed and that we just "don't get it." In particular, it is thrilling how Silver shows that the same data-set can lead to a variety of interpretations, depending on the initial assumptions. On topics

---

[440] Silver N., *The Signal and the Noise: Why So Many Predictions Fail, But Some Don't*, 7, 12 and passim. Silver is also skeptical about the impact of big data. He writes, "*The instinctual shortcut that we take when we have 'too much information' is to engage with it selectively, picking out parts that we like and ignoring the remainder, making allies with those who have made the same choices and enemies of the rest. We face danger whenever information growth outpaces our understanding of how to process it.*" His book is emphatically pro-science and pro-technology, but in it, Silver argues that the views on big data "*are badly mistaken. The numbers have no way of speaking for themselves. We speak for them. We imbue them with meaning. Big Data will produce progress – eventually. How quickly it does, and whether we regress in the meantime, will depend on us.*" It reminds me of the storytelling experiment presented by Gottschall J. (see chapter 1.5.1), where we experience how we instinctively project meaning on whatever we observe, clouding the facts behind our projections.

Silver N., *The Signal and the Noise: Why So Many Predictions Fail, But Some Don't*, 9, 74-85.

[441] The most important questions about big data are legal: How is such data collected and accessed? How is it properly anonymized? Who can access it, why and under what supervision? In Europe, two legal proposals from the EU Commission address these issues, at least partially, providing (along with the GDPR and the eIDAS Regulation) the first comprehensive legislative framework for a digital society:

1) The Digital Services Act, EU Commission COM 825/2020, as of 15 December 2020, defines rules of quality and transparency for information society services, in particular for digital intermediaries, platforms and search engine algorithms (oddly called a "recommender system"), https://eur-lex.europa.eu/legal-content/EN/TXT/PDF/?uri=COM:2020:842:FIN&from=en.

2) The Digital Markets Act, EU Commission COM 842/2020, as of 15 December 2020, defines the obligations of the gatekeepers (such as operating systems, platforms, search engines, content aggregators and social media) and the rules for transparent competition that gatekeepers must comply with, to enable fair competition among themselves and for their users, https://eur-lex.europa.eu/legal-content/EN/TXT/?uri=CELEX:52020PC0825.

[442] The Economist, *Artificial intelligence. A new AI language model generates poetry and prose. GPT-3 can be eerily human-like for better and for worse.*

such as U.S. Senate elections,[443] professional baseball[444] and global warming,[445] his predictions have been about 95% accurate over several decades, beating all of the competition. This tends to the conclusion that the selection criteria for information matter more than the sheer amount of it. Nonetheless, Silver was wrong in forecasting the 2016 U.S. presidential election. Polling institutes failed to see that their "representative sample" wasn't representative anymore, and accuracy still eludes them, as we saw in the 2020 U.S. presidential election. This argument leads us directly to the issue of **artificial intelligence (AI)**.

It is beyond dispute that AI has been able to provide extremely useful and unpredictable insights in several cases, ranging from data analytics in genetics, medicine,[446] physics, astronomy, pharmacology and meteorology. Also, when applied to social sciences (including finance and macroeconomics), AI has proved quite useful at spotting behavioural patterns and megatrends that would have gone otherwise unnoticed. At the same time, it has proved itself extremely prone to the fallibility of biased assumptions. One must be aware of the fact that **AI often produces self-fulfilling (and self-reinforcing) prophecies**, which can quickly stretch any given system to the limits of sustainability. All this has led to a debate about how to make AI "ethically sustainable".

To me, this seems an odd discussion, like discussing on how to "think ethically".[447] I mean ... ethics is about behaviour, not about thought! And since the time of ancient Greek philosophy, we have believed that rationality is inherently good, as a driver of knowledge and science. How can a rationally computing AI "think" unethically? And what would the "ethical cleansing" of AI look like? Won't it look precisely like the Church (or the scientific establishment) dealing with Galileo Galilei or Albert Einstein, whose ideas were deemed "unsustainable"?

I think it is correct to point out that the core problem of AI is its use. This is an agency problem, with a legal and functional solution. Whoever uses AI has the responsibility to control AI.[448]

It is beyond dispute that AI is a new technology (perhaps covering a wide range of new methodologies) that will deeply impact science and society in the coming decades, starting from the present. And clearly the combination of big data and AI is already having some surprising and useful, but also unsettling outcomes. It also poses some difficult ethical and legal issues that need to be addressed.[449]

In chapter 8, I will try to provide some Lego blocks that can start to address the challenges posed by AI, without repeating the errors that governments, the

---

[443] SILVER, N., *The Signal and the Noise: Why So Many Predictions Fail, But Some Don't*, 57 -70.

[444] SILVER, N., *The Signal and the Noise: Why So Many Predictions Fail, But Some Don't*, 63 and ff.

[445] SILVER, N., *The Signal and the Noise: Why So Many Predictions Fail, But Some Don't*, 371 and ff.

[446] TOPOL, E.J., *Deep medicine: How artificial intelligence can make healthcare human again.*

[447] BOSTROM, N., *Superintelligence: Paths, dangers, strategies*, loc. 5322, is also skeptical that ethics can address the issues posed by AI; in fact, faulty ethical principles would have disastrous consequences, nly amplified by A.I. I don't know.

[448] BOSTROM N., *Superintelligence: Paths, dangers, strategies*, loc. 3319.

[449] What are the guiding ethical principles for its usage? What are the necessary functional and legal rules?

Church and the scientific community have made in dealing with disruptive discoveries, and which Umberto Eco so brilliantly characterized as a timeless problem in his masterwork *The Name of the Rose*. The main Lego blocks are proper definitions of digital identity (and legal subjectivity) in a digital society, as well as definitions of legal rights and obligations and digital accountability.[450]

In chapter 8, I will suggest considering AI from a legal standpoint similar to the jurisprudence of ancient Rome (or the Confederate States of America) with respect to slaves – who were treated as legal objects capable of (limited) self-determination. In evaluating the slave's legal accountability (and ultimately the accountability of its master), it was essential to establish whether the slave was executing the instructions of its master or acting wilfully. This brings four subjects into consideration, for resolving legal cases: an AI, its owner or user, its constructor and its programmer.

AI is a complex and extremely intriguing subject; it may well be the object of my next research project. From the perspective of this work, AI illustrates that there is an aspect of our digital society that is currently poorly served by established legal rules and requires a rethinking of the conceptual categories that we use to understand it.[451]

AI cannot be a problem as long as it just "thinks". The problems begin when AI is allowed to act, as is already[452] the case with robots.[453]

---

[450] I agree unconditionally with Nick Bostrom's analysis. Precisely because the core problem posed by AI is an agency problem, I accept his call to take a stand (BOSTROM, N., *Superintelligence: Paths, dangers, strategies*, loc. 6580), and in chapter 8.5 I offer some very preliminary proposals to address the problems that AI poses. If it makes autonomous decisions that impact people, it requires proper definition as a legal subject, and definitions of its relations with its owners, users, producers and programmers. Clearly, an inhuman machine, more intelligent than us, making decisions for us, is a ticking time bomb, with a potential for disaster that has become apparent in today's social media: The dysfunction seems to lack any identity or cause; it is like a force of nature. But in reality, it is a programmed, autonomous, deciding entity, owned and maintained by the companies that run the social platforms (or their subcontractors).

[451] BOSTROM, N., *Superintelligence: Paths, dangers, strategies*, loc. 6476. DAVIS, M. E., *Reboot: Getting to artificial intelligence we can trust* (2019), presents a rosy picture of the future with AI, but not much effort has been put into answering the hard questions posed by Bostrom.

[452] The British Home Office has been using a "black box algorithm" to streamline the settled status applications of EU citizens residing in the U.K. There have been complaints by lawyers and a warning issued in a 2017 report by the chief inspector of borders and immigration that there was "a risk that the screening tool becomes a de facto decision-making tool." Diane Abbott, Labour's shadow home secretary, said any indication that algorithms are being used in assessing visa applications without being open to scrutiny was "deeply worrying. Every system is only as good as the inputs used to create it", she said. "If there is bias, or they incorporate the prejudices prevalent in society, then those outputs will be similarly tainted." Reported by the *Financial Times* on 9 June 2019. In Italy the Consiglio di Stato (the supreme court for administrative law) has ruled that when algorithms are used by any public administration, their rules must be disclosed and are inherently part of the administrative act whose legitimacy is being assessed. There is no presumption that algorithms are objective, rational or impartial (Consiglio di Stato, sentenza n. 8472/2019).

[453] Boston Dynamic's robots make use of AI: https://www.youtube.com/watch?v=fn3KWM1kuAw

7.4. Static Digital Documents: Electronically Signed Files

Why does information technology consider static documents as the true documents that it should imitate? Why use a PDF-A to sign digital documents? Why are digital books static and not interactive? Why do computers try to imitate paper?

In chapter 3.3, we discussed the ontological definition of a document and cleared up some confusion among documents, recordings and other kinds of inscriptions.

During the early drafting of the European legislation on electronic signatures, it became clear that everybody assumed they knew the (obvious!) definitions for a document and a signature. In fact, nobody had a scientific definition at hand.[454]

The concept of a document assumes (if not expressly required by legislation) that it is made with non-ephemeral signs on a non-modifiable support: signs (letters) made with ink on paper are its paradigm. So legislation has mandated that digital documents deploy security and functional properties that are natural for paper-based documents, but which are utterly unnatural for digital documents (see chapter 6.2).

The law has focused on the formal properties of a digital signature without considering the process of generating a digital agreement. This is a mistake because, on paper, there is a clear (phenomenological) distinction between the act of writing and the written document; meanwhile in IT, this distinction is blurred, because the act of writing and the document itself are both "inside" the same tool. Without full control of the IT system, it is impossible to distinguish generation from representation.[455] For this reason, if I have sole control of a computer, I can see a document on it or listen to it. If I don't control the IT system, I am just watching the outcome of a dynamic computational activity.[456] The point is that the same digital data has different evidential value, depending on how the documents (inscritpions, recordings) were generated and how they are accessed.

One could suppose that the law on digital documents and signatures is attempting to repeat the feat of the merchants of the Middle Ages, who established written contracts as the principal and most trustworthy form of legal documentation. For contracts on paper, the conclusion of the *ius commune* (common law) and of the *lex mercatoria* (the law merchant) was to view the negotiations as less relevant than the final, formal document. This was a formalistic choice, especially in light of the fact that the use of written contracts was established when 90% of the population was illiterate. As we have seen in chapter 3, in an illiterate society, the oral contract (in the same oral format as the negotiations) is considered more trustworthy than a written contract, which was viewed as the replica of an oral agreement. With the expansion of literacy, the written document became more accepted as the original representation of

---

[454] Maurizio Ferraris' book *Documentalità* was published 10 years later.
[455] GENGHINI, R., *La Forma Notarile Digitale*, 13, 18, 21, 22.
[456] GENGHINI, R., *La Forma Notarile Digitale*, 17, 101, 133.

the agreement, and the spoken words (used in negotiation and in closing the agreement) became progressively less relevant than the written words.

We would be wrong to think that legislation that confers indiscriminate legal value on signed digital files will unleash a new type of legal documentation, without taking into consideration the process of generation and the evidential value of the signed documents.[457]

In fact, the formalism of the merchants of the Middle Ages was part of a cunning strategy to formalize all aspects of their business processes, with the object of making them more trustworthy and socially accepted. As we have seen in chapter 5, the formalism of written documents was part of a trust-building system.

Lawmakers who aim to make digital documents trusted in today's society and economy, must accept that the digital signature is just one of the two pillars needed for this purpose. The second pillar (also used by the merchants in the Middle Ages) is the formalisation of business processes and documentation procedures in a manner that enables independent, trustworthy, transparent legal documentation. To use a digital signature as an undisputable representation of will, it is necessary to have:

1) a transparent procedure

2) a safe, impartial and transparent signing environment

3) a safe, impartial and transparent environment for reading and verification.

I have repeated this mantra in every possible legislative context, and sometimes I have been accused of asking for the impossible. Yet what I am asking is not to require a given form for every kind of legal declaration; that would be the end of contractual freedom and commercial innovation. What we need is to establish a more open, peer-reviewed process for publishing and sharing legal declarations and documents – of the sort that has been brilliantly implemented by Bitcoin, which *The Economist* has labelled "the Trust Machine".[458] Alternatively, we could resort to an "old-fashioned" trusted third party, providing qualified digital trust services under the terms of the eIDAS Regulation.

Before widespread literacy, digitalisation and the Internet, negotiations were usually conducted verbally rather than in written form. So the concept of the contract as the original statement of an agreement is ultimately a legal fiction. We are so accustomed to this presupposition, that we see it as "real". We must be mindful that in the digital world, it is empirically more accurate to consider the written document as a representation of something that has already happened. It is a *"notitia"*, not a *"charta"* or *"instrumentum"* (see chapter 3.4.4). The digitalisation of legal agreements has more in common with the *negotia*, which were closed in the Forum Romanum,[459] than with written contracts.

Most of the legally relevant interactions that occur in the digital environment rely on a keyboard, not one's voice. Such interactions leave a trail of traces that

---

[457] In fact, in Europe, signed digital documents are almost only used when mandated.

[458] THE ECONOMIST, *The Promise of the Blockchain*.

[459] Wikipedia, *"Roman Forum"*.

precede and follow the formal agreement. Thus, some have come to the conclusion that in the digital world, treating the written document as the original statement of the agreement is not, at last, a legal fiction anymore!

This is wrong. The trail of digital traces of an online negotiation cannot be considered a document (or multiple documents) because they are a series of passive registrations (sometimes inscriptions. For the differences, see chapters 3.2 and 6.2.). How meaningful can it be to intentionally sign a series of digital registrations that are generated automatically (i.e., without any intention)? The answer to this question is twofold:

1) Much less meaningful than a handwritten, signed paper. A signed trail of data is almost useless as a legal fiction – not only because it wasn't created intentionally, but because most of the time, there is no such thing as a document.

2) Much more meaningful than a contract. This is because (if untampered with) the digital traces truly represent, not only the object of the agreement (without any formal document), but also the process of actually crafting the agreement and its subsequent execution. (See the end of chapter 3.3 and the example of the minutes from a board meeting.)[460]

A digital recording of online activity, if properly generated and preserved, is at the same time both more and less than a paper document. Actually, it is something different. It can be considered as proof of something only if its origin and method of production is known and verifiable. Digital data is less formalistic, but more substantial. Less static and more updatable. Its greater evidential value lies precisely in its automatic generation, which happens simultaneously with the crafting of the agreement. If correctly understood as **recordings without any intention,** and *not* as documents, even if they are a weaker form of documentation, they still provide enough information to prove the existence and the content of a legal agreement.

In contrast, even if we sign a digital document that we have personally generated using a word processor, and then transformed into a "static format" fit for signing under the law, we have still generated a signed document with a reduced evidential value.

In fact, a digital signature does not allow the signer to see what is being signed. The file displayed on the monitor is a copy of the file that is on the hard disk. The file that is hashed for signing is an additional copy of the same file. Moreover, the computer that we use for signing has many layers of software that are needed for the simple task of displaying a file and signing it. The document and the program reside in an environment with several hundred additional programs (most of them hidden) running on the computer being used for signing, which is connected to the Internet, where billions of additional programs are running.

---

[460] European Legislation already recognizes the significance of digital trials. Article 6 section 5 of EU Directive 2011/83/EU on Consumer Protection, explicitly considers the digital audit trial of a digital transaction as part of the contractual agreement between a professional vendor and a consumer. European Commission, *Consumer protection.*

The cartoon above, is a greatly simplified representation of this complexity. The complexity of the signature process and the impossibility of seeing files with the naked eye (without complex tools like computers) breaks the link between the information represented in the document and its author(s). So the legal fiction that it is the original representation of the agreement no longer holds. In fact, it becomes preposterous.[461]

Replicating the straitjacket of paper-based evidence in the digital environment is the wrong formalistic approach. The signed paper became the legal original of an agreement thanks to the involvement of a trusted third party – the scribe, and later the notary (see chapters 3.4.3 and 3.4.4). There is no such thing as a trusted, online third party for digital transactions today, with a few notable exceptions:

• the qualified trust service providers of the eIDAS Regulation
• some online notarization services provided by some European chambers of commerce:[462] According to EU Directive 2017/1132, as amended by EU Directive 2019/1151, beginning on 1st of August 2021, all member states shall allow the online incorporation of limited liability companies.
• special legislation for the Covid-19 pandemic, which, in most European states, allows notaries to act as trusted third parties at a distance[463]
• And debatably, once the Digital Services Act and the Digital Market Act take effect in Europe, gatekeepers, digital intermediaries, platforms and search

---

[461] GENGHINI R., *La Forma Notarile Digitale*, 19.
[462] In France, the Chambre de Commerce et de l'Industrie (https://www.cci.fr/web/accomplir-ses-formalites/immatriculation) is the first European institution to act as an online trusted third party, for the incorporation of a S.à r.l. (limited liability company).
[463] With the notable exception of Germany.

engine algorithms (as therein defined) shall be considered third parties bound to openness, impartiality and scrutiny very much like a trusted third party (with fiduciary duties).

Unless there is an online equivalent to the notary, digital documentation is (and will be) ordinarily generated by the party that is economically or legally stronger. Whenever an unwritten, unrecorded digital consent is considered formally insufficient to prove a legal transaction, we are bound to sign digitally some digital recording produced automatically by our counterparty (as in renting a car or sending a parcel). We still need to learn to understand the real evidential value of this new type of documentation. It is completely new, more thorough, more complex and thus more difficult to interpret and understand. In trying to understand it, we must be mindful that it represents the recordings of our contractual counterparty, and is therefore only very loosely linked to our intention. (It is a *notitia*, not a *charta*, as seen in this chapter and chapter 3.3.)

In the last 20 years, a lot of effort has gone into creating digital files that are inherently dynamic and modifiable, yet more static and more secure than paper. It was not wasted time. It is useful to have cryptographic protections for digital documents and recordings. It is very useful to know who has signed them. It was also useful to enable e-books, so that we can have static books in digital form.

But the real challenge is to figure out how to generate dynamic data that is also trustworthy. Trustworthy dynamic data is needed not only for smart (digital) contracts and for better securitisation of financial transactions, but also to enable civil discussion of politics online. We will discuss how to do this in chapter 8.2.2.3.

7.5. Who needs a (single) digital identity?

In the analogue world, we have just one body. In a person's body, several personalities live at once, (usually) in harmony: father or mother, husband or wife, citizen, worker, friend, customer, etc.

We are free to decide when to be what, and this is the most fundamental freedom guaranteed by our liberal, democratic constitutions: our freedom of expression. In the digital world today, for each of these expressions of ourselves, we maintain one or more digital identities.

Why are governments trying to reduce this freedom of expression, providing us with one "true" digital identity? The reasoning is this: "If we can trace whoever did something wrong, then we will be able to enforce the law on the Internet." The same reasoning could also apply in the streets of our cities, but we don't wear electronic bracelets or serial numbers on our chests in order to be identifiable. Only convicts are required to be identifiable at all times. So why is something that is unacceptable (even unconstitutional) in the physical world deemed acceptable in the digital world? Why is it that the police cannot order us to leave a pair of our house keys at the police station, but it seems appropriate for them to ask for a backdoor for encrypted messages or mobile devices?[464]

---

[464] THE ECONOMIST, *Internet Security: When Back Doors Backfire*; LICHTBLAU E., BENNER K., *Apple fights order to unlock San Bernardino gunman's iPhone*, in *The New York Times*, 17 Feb. 2016.

Perhaps it is because the digital world is perceived as intangible ... and therefore metaphysical. Law enforcement agencies may really believe that policing the Internet affects just a minor aspect of our social lives – so it makes sense to renounce civil liberties for security's sake.

In my eyes, this belief is utterly unsupportable, if one considers that the majority of our social lives now happens online, from politics to relationships, from shopping to health care.

As we have seen in chapter 6, the digital dimension has become the operational centrepiece of our lives, to the point that the U.S. Supreme Court has started to recognize that the digital dimension is part of our "*habeas corpus*", at least to the extent it is embodied in our mobile phones[465]

Any undue limitation on our constitutional rights in the digital world will trickle down to an undue limitation on all of our constitutional rights. A limitation of expression online will become a limitation of expression pervading all aspects of our lives.

Today, we are (or at least we feel) freer in our online lives, because we can choose who to be and how to look. In reality, social media sites, search engines and governments want to be able to know every bit of what we do, with almost no limitations. So the diversity of our online selves is being converged – a convergence that we cannot control and which will make it impossible to start a new life in the way that was possible even just 30 years ago.

To find a good balance between freedom and law enforcement in the digital environment is an urgent challenge.

The current approach is similar to what happened in Europe between 1920 and 1939. At that time there was pervasive fear of a communist revolution. The majority of the population, influenced by the mass media (newspapers and radio) became convinced that security was more important than freedom. This conviction, through democratic processes, brought the despots Benito Mussolini and Adolf Hitler to power, and World War II was the consequence.

Today people seem once again increasingly inclined to value security more than freedom, even in the United States of America. In the land of the free, built on immigration, a policy of mass deportation of illegal aliens has been implemented, starting in 2017. In the land of the free, nobody seems to remember that this was the very same policy that persuaded Germans to elect Hitler as Reichskanzler and which triggered Apartheid in South Africa.

The mass deportation of the Jews under the Third Reich would have been all but impossible without the "*Judenausweis*" (an identity card issued to Jews) and the general obligation to carry a piece of identification at all times. Personal identities managed by the police are the infrastructure needed for mass control and mass deportation.

We read in chapter 5.3 the words of the Founding Fathers – words of wisdom and inclusion for a nation that has been made great by its immigrants. Pope

---

[465] United States Supreme Court, Court ruling in Riley v. U.S.

Francis has said, "A person who thinks only about building walls, wherever they may be, and not building bridges, is not Christian."[466]
In the digital world, business and security policy rely increasingly on systems of (fire)walls and exclusion, and only a few "specialists" seem to have noticed the social and legal implications of this command-and-control approach. In the digital world, building impenetrable (and invisible) digital fences places a limitation on our freedom, because it puts us in digital silos that are not of our choosing – just like asking companies to implement some form of content censorship.[467] For some, it seems a price worth paying for security and some material benefits.
In chapter 1, we hypothesized that slaves were not originally labelled as slaves. Today, without even realizing it, we have become a sort of digital slaves, used as objects more than dealt with as subjects. We know that it didn't bother the majority of Italians and Germans when their democracies were dismantled by Mussolini and Hitler – because they valued security, order, and a strong state more than they valued liberty.
What do we value now? Are we swapping freedom for a free ride?
In chapter 8.1.4 we will define what a (digital) identity is.
History tells us that, whenever all our rights depend on a single piece of identification, we will not achieve the enforcement of our rights. On the contrary, to mandate a single digital identity restricts our fundamental rights and doesn't support the effective policing of the Internet.
In chapters 8.1.4 and 8.3, we will discuss the technical properties of trustworthy digital identities, and in chapters 8.5.1 (and following), the importance of trustworthy digital identities for the natural law of a digital society.

---

[466] YARDLEY J., *Pope Francis Suggests Donald Trump Is 'Not Christian'*, in *The New York Times*, 18 Feb. 2016.
[467] THE ECONOMIST, *Who controls the conversation. How to deal with free speech on social media. It is too important to be determined by a handful of tech executives.*
Even the EU Commission, with its "Proposal for a Regulation on a Single Market For Digital Services (Digital Services Act) and amending Directive 2000/31/EC", COM(2020) 825, 15 December 2020, is considering the use of intermediary service providers to monitor and act against illegal content (articles 7 and 8 of the proposal).
See also Judgments of the European Court of Justice:
Joined Cases C-92/09 and C-93/09: Judgment of the Court (Grand Chamber) of 9 November 2010 (reference for a preliminary ruling from the Verwaltungsgericht Wiesbaden — Germany) — Volker und Markus Schecke GbR (C-92/09), Hartmut Eifert (C-93/09) v Land Hess ECLI:EU:C:2010:662. (Grand Chamber), 13 May 2014. Google Spain SL and Google Inc. v Agencia Española de Protección de Datos (AEPD) and Mario Costeja González. ECLI:EU:C:2014:317.

8

Digital New Deal

*"In the beginning was the Word,
and the Word was with God,
and the Word was God"*

John 1:1 (King James Version)

8. Digital New Deal

In this chapter we will ask the hard questions that may determine the future of our digital society.

We have seen how deep digitalisation has redefined what is "natural" and "normal": this means that the "natural law" of a digital society may need new "universal principles" that are accepted in all legal and economic systems, like "property" or "contract" or "labour" are. These principles shall have the same fundamental value as "life, liberty and property" or "life, liberty and the pursuit of happiness" or "fair equality of opportunity"[468], which took about two millennia in the pre-digital world to be defined and agreed upon.

Life and property are mostly defined by nature, and therefore it is no wonder that they have been part of natural law since the origin of human history. But the "fair equality of opportunity" is a relatively recent representation of the enlightened ideal that happiness is the ultimate goal of life and hence something that cannot be denied by a just society.[469]

Fair equality of opportunity isn't something you find in nature: nature is unforgivingly selective. The fair equality of opportunity has become a goal of human society since its main function expanded from ensuring our survival to ensuring our wellbeing.

So, the quest for a natural law of a digital society must find - in both the ultimate function of human (digital) society and the ontological rules of technology - the principles to ensure that some form of (just) social order can be kept. If the fundamental principles of a (just) human society and the fundamental rules of technology clash, we must ask ourselves which principle/rule must or can be upheld. This is by no means an easy task![470]

Our society is built on words and kept together by human communication. The communication channels between humans have dramatically expanded and created a new virtual reality that is blurring our social institutions, without providing (thus far) a viable alternative.

If we do not follow some path toward a (Digital) New Deal, the alternative becomes quite unpalatable. We may become a dystopic society, where democracy becomes void of any moral significance, where fear, intolerance, exclusion and tyranny prevail and guide the laws, in particular the laws that govern the digital world. This vision is familiar to most science fiction writers, many of whom have explored one or more failures to answer the hard questions. The

---

[468] See chapters 2.2 and 2.2.

For the quote "life, liberty and property", see Wikipedia, Declaration and Resolves of the First Continental Congress, also known as Declaration of Colonial Rights.

For the quote "life, liberty and the pursuit of happiness", see the US Congress, Declaration of Independence: A Transcription. See chapter 5.3.

For "fair equality of opportunity" see chapter 5.3 and John Rawls, A Theory of Justice, 83.

[469] As theorized by John Locke. For bibliographic references see Wikipedia, Liberty and the Pursuit of Happiness. An essential reading on the topic: SHAFIK, M., *What We Owe Each Other: A New Social Contract*.

[470] Fundamental read on this topic: LESSIG L., *Code and other laws of the cyberspace*.

signs that we are heading towards a dystopic future are manifold. They have been addressed in the previous chapters of this publication:

1. Our definitions of what is "human" are bound to be disrupted by technological innovation. Artificial intelligence, genetic engineering and robotics will challenge our current definitions and prove them insufficient to guide us morally and legally. Would we still be eating cows if they could speak and read, understand Immanuel Kant and enjoy poetry? Would genetically improved humans be so ... inhuman to the rest of us? Again, yes, it is very likely, because their genetic enhancement would lead to an ontological misalignment between their needs and ours, their aims and ours. We all can see that the moral foundation of our society is in tatters. Currently we are failing to mount an adequate response to a rather mild pandemic, nor are we even meeting the needs of millions of people fleeing violence, war and abject poverty. And these people are human, like us; but building walls to protect "us" against "them" is a politically winning message in Australia, Great Britain, Italy, Hungary and even the United States, a nation built on immigrants and immigration!

2. Genetic engineering has become a reality: CRISPR-Cas9 technology[471] promises to make it possible to edit genetic information quickly and cheaply. This could correct terrible genetic defects that blight human life. It also heralds the distant prospect of parents custom-ordering their children. Other ways to edit DNA exist, but CRISPR holds the promise of doing so with unprecedented simplicity, speed and precision. How will genetically superior humans deal with genetically inferior humans? Will it end the way it ended between Homo sapiens and Neanderthals: with the extinction of the less developed species?

3. Artificial intelligence (AI) is dawning[472]. Firms such as Google, Facebook, Amazon and Baidu have gotten into an AI arms race, poaching researchers, setting up laboratories and buying start-ups. A breakthrough is not nigh, but most pundits agree that it would be irreversible once machines become able to think and self-determinate[473]. There is dystopic science fiction galore on the subject, from Isaac Asimov's *AI* to classic movies (e.g., 1951's *The Day Earth Stand Still*)[474] to more recent movies, *The Terminator, The Signal, Her, Ex Machina* and *The Machine*, just to name the most famous. But even if AI does not take over the human order and rule the world, a question still lingers: What will humans do in their working lives, if machines are smarter and stronger?

4. Nonverbal communication between the human brain and machines has become a reality. Cyborgs are just a decade away in the future. Will nonverbal communication surpass verbal communication? Will the future "human elite" will be wordless but able to communicate with machines (and other species?)

---

[471] THE ECONOMIST, *Editing Humanity*.

[472] THE ECONOMIST, *The Dawn of Artificial Intelligence*; THE ECONOMIST, *Rise of the Machines*.

[473] As one can read in the open letter edited by the Future of Life Institute, signed among others by Elon Musk, Nick Bostrom, Steve Wozniak: Future of Life Institute, *An Open Letter*.
Cambridge University, Centre for Studies on Existential Risk and Oxford University, FHI, Future of Humanity Institute, study extensively the possible impacts of artificial intelligence on human society.

[474] IMDb, The Day the Earth Stood Still.

using the electric impulses of the brain? How will human society look when words are overtaken by wordless communication? Will humans still be story-telling animals?

5. Language and its consequences: Semiology, as a science, is confined to the erudite discussions of semiologists and linguists. In the last 20 years, suddenly more than six billion people have started to communicate by typing on key-boards (mostly on mobile devices). Previously, less than half a billion of us used "written" words to communicate. The circulation of printed books arose in the 15th century, in the midst of a long period of extreme political instability, with several lasting wars and epidemics. Printed books, at their origin, were acces-sible only to a tiny fraction of rich and educated people, because they were extremely expensive. At the beginning of the 20th century, radio and cinema made it possible to broadcast to the vast majority of the population. In the fol-lowing 70 years, two world wars and the Cold War ensued. Today, the digital revolution - in just 20 years - has reached even the poorest and least educated people across the world. The **understanding of social reality** in relation to the use of human language became quite fashionable after Ludwig Wittgenstein's *Tractatus Logico-Philosophicus* was published. But the vast majority of people still believed that language was a neutral tool that improved human communi-cation. They didn't realize that humans started to speak because they wanted to change nature and reality. Our world, our society, are built on words and with words. A radical change in the way we communicate cannot be neutral with respect to our society and our rules.

6. People can access the **Internet everywhere** in the world and read or view whatever has been posted or published online. 3G is available even in the most underdeveloped or totalitarian countries (even North Korea). Law enforcers have sought to address these kinds of changes in two shocking ways:

a) requiring harsh limitations on constitutional rights,

b) proposing some sort of censorship of content.

These approaches didn't work in either fascist Italy or communist Russia. They didn't even work 500 years ago (in absolutist times), when the Church tried to curb the innovation of the printing press.

Will it work this time? It is a safe bet to doubt it.

7. Documents are not what they used to be. We can no longer tell the dif-ference between a digital document or a digital recording and automatically generated information. We instinctively trust written text as authoritative, but today, very little authoritative digital information is available. The **complexity of documents** has increased enormously, and so has the difficulty of interpret-ing them correctly.

8. Law and society have reached such a level of conceptual abstraction that most people can no longer understand them. Consequently, people tend to credit oversimplified explanations of reality and hope that naive solutions will work, only to become bitterly disappointed in the process. The most egregious symptom of this disappointment is that large segments of American, Asian and European society are now prepared to behave inhumanly to "aliens" in dire need.

9. The welfare state is virtually bankrupt. The number of people depend-ing on others is going to increase dramatically in the coming years for three reasons: a) the extension of life expectancy; b) the inversion of the demographic pyramid; c) the financial consequences of the Covid-19 pandemic. Welfare is stuck between broken promises and bankruptcy. Neither of these options will benefit democracy or trust in institutions. When people realize that their life savings have dwindled to a fraction of what they have paid in, don't expect them to accept it graciously.

10. Democracy is taken for granted by most people as a natural condition of mankind. Few remember how difficult the case was for democracy only a few decades ago. (Look back on the 20th century and recall the eras of fascism and communism). Nobody remembers the discussions of the 18th century on how to make democracy stable. The founding fathers of democracy proposed the safeguards presented in chapter 5. These safeguards are a) fragmenting the state's power in order to avoid the tyranny of the majority and the tyranny of the oligarchy; b) entrusting with voting rights only people who have a stake in society, in order to avoid social opportunism and expropriation; c) a strong independant judiciary.

11. Increasingly, **in politics and society, the end seems to justify the means**: Only two generations ago, every person took upon themselves the burden and the responsibility of carrying a tiny fraction of our human society. We saw ourselves as teammates, not as passengers. Today, society is objectified: It is made not of people, but of institutions. The failure of society is seen as a failure of rules and institutions, not as a collective failure of many/most people, including ourselves. We have become so apt at working with abstractions, that we see ourselves "here" and society "there". But "here" and "there" are abstractions, metaphors residing in our mind. In fact, we are inextricably part of the society in which we live, and we absolve ourselves of responsibility for it, at our peril. "*Them*" has become a dangerous abstraction in the digital society.

12. The environment in which we live is **strained, polluted and getting warmer**. For this reason, the current models of agriculture (GM crops, pesticides, etc.), industry (wasting energy and polluting), and economic growth should be reconsidered if we want to protect the natural equilibrium.

The list above indicates that, in many respects, mankind cannot just go on doing business as usual.

On the other hand, we have seen in the previous chapters that humans over the millennia have overcome no less daunting challenges: We survived ice ages and overhunting; we changed our metabolism to become omnivorous; we learned to improve nature to our benefit; we created tools, language, laws, rights.

From a millennial perspective, mankind has arrived at an evolutionary juncture that requires us to reconsider our rules and values, if we hope to achieve a peaceful and sustainable future. But in order to do so, we will probably need to challenge the meaning of some words, like "identity", "person", "right", "law", just to name some of the most relevant.

The readjustment will be so all-encompassing that the transition won't be easy and may not be peaceful. Still, we may have some useful tools for success:

1. Today, human society and laws are built on the moral axiom that we have an equal right to freedom and to a fair shot at a better future.

2. Digitalisation has dramatically increased the amount of information available and has made the cost of duplicating and sharing that information virtually non-existent. Any improvement may go viral and spread fast.

3. Philosophers, politicians, sociologists and economists are studying the impact of digitalisation and are well aware of the new challenges, in particular for civil liberties, data protection and the proper functioning of democracy.[475] There is a sincere desire to reap the benefits and keep the risks under control.

4. All economists (and many politicians) are aware of the challenge posed by the inversion of the demographic pyramid and of the need for the structural reform of welfare, which is otherwise bound to go bankrupt.

So, in this chapter, I will try to present some new conceptual categories and ideas that may help to shape a just, democratic and pluralistic digital society: The Digital New Deal.

8.1. Homo Digitalis: I, Myself and My Identity

As we have seen, "human" is not defined (just) by its genetic code (which has only minor differences from that of a bonobo or a chimpanzee). What makes us unique is our ability to communicate with other humans using a symbolic language suited to storytelling and creating an intangible but "objective" reality (social reality) based on conventions of significant language and concepts (social objects)[476]. Thus, **"human" is mostly defined by the context in which it lives**, and such context is the human society. This makes the definition of

---

[475] See the Digital New Deal Initiative of the German Marshall Fund: https://www.gmfus.org/press-releases/german-marshall-fund-launches-digital-new-deal-initiative-create-Internet-supports.

[476] See chapter 1.5 and 2.3. A fundamental reading for the mirror-like relation between me and my computer is Turkle, S., *The Second Self.*

human a recursive definition: We define human society, and human society defines us. Empirically this may be acceptable, but from an ontological perspective it appears to be a contradiction of terms.

Technological innovation has made it urgent to re-evaluate the definition of what is a human being (a digital persona) for the law, for three main reasons:

1. **We now participate and interact no matter where we are**, so that the physical person and its presence in a given geographical location are not necessarily linked.

2. There are several **technologies that will allow us to enhance the human body and mind**.

3. We can (and not just in theory) **create a being in a laboratory** that shares our genetic code but is completely engineered.

The digital "context" is 100% virtual and engineered, and thus different from the natural context, where everything is physical and most of it not designed by us. **My physical persona is ontologically unique and a natural phenomenon, but my digital persona must be designed and engineered in order to exist; and if its design is faulty, I will be a faulty person too**. So, it is of the utmost importance that the technical implementations of a digital identity don't miss anything of what makes me human. A free human being.

Thus, in this chapter and its subsections we look for a proper definition of what is human, for the purpose of devising what technologies are needed for us to be free individuals in a digital society.

8.1.1. I and my digital trail

In an open digital society characterized by ubiquitous computing, is the digital trail that we produce an object (like a publication or a piece of art)? Or is it part of our persona (like our dreams, or whatever we say or do in private)? Is it "us"?

There are **two engrained legal fictions to disagree with**:

1. **The law considers our digital trail as being in a different place from where we are**; thus, accessing it is not an infringement on our personal freedom, but a data protection issue.[477] But the existential and phenomenological truth is

---

[477] EU legislation requires express consent for planting cookies in the browsers and memorize and store our digital trail: Article 4(11) of the GDPR. The current best practices according to the EUROPEAN DATA PROTECTION BOARD, are published online as *Guidelines 05/2020 on consent under Regulation 2016/679 Version 1.1* Adopted on 4 May 2020.

In 2020 California has adopted an approach very similar to the GDPR, with an amendment to the 2003 California Online Privacy Protection Act (CalOPPA), that requires operators of commercial websites and online services to create a Privacy Policy that discloses how they collect personal information. In general, in the U.S. no consent is needed for accessing our digital trail, except for children. In this case §§ 6501-6509 of N. 15 U.S. Code Chapter 91, *Children's Online Privacy Protection Act* (COPPA) forbids to collect and store the digital trail of minors without "verifiable parental consent for the collection, use, or disclosure of personal information from children".

In the rest of the world there are some laws (Brazil, Canada) that replicate the GDPR's approach, with less stringent requirements. In a nutshell: outside of the EU our digital trail is just free data, up for grabs.

completely different:[478] Recording what we do when we surf the Internet and recording all our activities on our computers and devices is tantamount to putting a video camera in our homes. It is not just a data protection issue; it is a deep, painful, permanent infringement on our personal freedom.

2. **The law considers our digital trail as a wilful document**.[479] Law and jurisprudence even imply that if you don't hide your trail, you consent to its use by whoever is able to find and record it. So, we get much less protection, and our digital trail is prone to be exploited commercially or for any other (hopefully lawful) purpose.

These two legal fictions are almost universally accepted. They are the consequence of a terrible misunderstanding of the underlying facts.

If the law were to consider our digital trail as part of our persona, it would not be possible to use it without our consent. Furthermore, in some cases even our consent would not suffice, because our personal freedom is not disposable: We cannot consent to be kept captive for an indefinite time. Nor we can irrevocably consent to have our entire life recorded "live".[480]

The problem is that, **if we accept social and legal conventions, sometimes it becomes impossible to recognize any (other/better) reality beyond them.**

Here is an example: slavery. Supporters of slavery in the United States fought the Civil War to defend their right to keep slaves. They accepted as a matter of fact that:

1. Slaves were not subjects, but objects of rights.
2. Blacks were anthropologically inferior to Whites.

Once you are deeply convinced of these two axioms, everything else is consequential, even cruelty.

Slaves served a social function for millennia. But finally, human society became able to function without them. Still, the axioms and the legal principles that were established for millennia were difficult do overcome, as we noted in chapter 4.1., they shaped many peoples' perception of reality, in which slaves had an established economic and social function.

Exactly the same can be said of our axioms about our digital trail: At the time when computers were only a small part of our (business) life, some factual truths became axioms. Such axioms (in particular that our digital trail is an object other than our persona and not co-located with us) are simply untrue in a world where we are connected 24/7 with devices that allow ubiquitous

---

[478] There are several sites that allow you to check how your data are tracked/stolen by any accessed website: see for an instance The Markup, or The Washington Post Privacy Check Backlight.
For an informative dramatisation, watch, on Netflix, "*The Social Dilemma*".

[479] The legal fiction is that we create the digital trail and that we leave it to be collected (like garbage) by anyone interested. The (digital) truth is that our digital trail is generated automatically by several IT systems (not by us) and that it is made intentionally accessible by others, not by us.

[480] Currently the issue is dealt with, by jurisprudence, considering the actors in a reality show, as employees or freelance workers involved in the show's production. All such relations are valid only for a limited period of time. For a short but impressive depiction of legal releases for reality TV shows, see HOPKINS K. E., *Unique Legal Considerations in Reality Television*.

computing, even when we are in our bed or even lying in the bathtub (I'm guessing I am not alone here!).

If we look deeper into the facts, we see how wrong (and outdated) such axioms have become:

a) We have seen that **recordings and inscriptions are ontologically different from documents**, because they are not created with the intention of sharing them with anybody (see chapter 3.3). To treat an inscription or a recording as a document is a (misleading) legal fiction: They were not generated wilfully, and they do not represent any intention by the person to authorize the permanent logging and recording of their digital trail. The legal fiction that there is an (implicit) intention (to leave a trace) in our digital trail is false and deeply troubling, because it allows unilateral exploitation of our persona. It is even less liberal that the medieval "homage" and "fealty", in which the vassal submitted himself to the lord; at least this offered some form of voluntary submission and a quid pro quo.

b) **The digital trail is equivalent to someone following us with a videorecorder**, capturing everything we do: shopping at the mall, making love, chatting with friends, voting. In the analogue world this would be stalking and be punished by the law. In the digital world it is accepted as customary. The legal fiction is that there is a free consent. We have seen that this is a preposterous fable. In the digital world, snooping must be forbidden as it is in the physical world; it is not legal to unilaterally record whatever we do and use the ensuing information without restraint.

c) **This all-encompassing recording of our digital trail makes it virtually impossible to choose who we are**. There are entities and repositories of information that can link all our different identities together into one. So, there is only one true us ... and it is not us; it is that repository of digital trails that ultimately decides our social, political relevance and our economic value. The fundamental question is: are we truly free if we face an entity that knows us better than we know ourselves? I strongly doubt it - particularly if the business model of such an entity (Facebook, Google, Amazon, Apple, Microsoft, etc.) is to resell better-refined knowledge of us to whoever can afford to pay for it: carmakers, insurance companies, employers, marketers, even political candidates(!).

d) **The choice of who we are and to what community we belong becomes another fiction**. In fact, there is an entity able to reconstruct our persona better than we can and thereby nudge us into any community it considers fit for us. There, we cannot even (meaningfully) determine what information is shared by whom and with whom or for how long.

The Covid-19 pandemic has shown how true the four statements above are for the vast majority of people worldwide: Even the threat of a pandemic was not enough to convince barely more than 10% of the holders of smart devices to opt in and use the apps that were designed to protect their health (but which may ultimately have a negative impact on their personal freedom). Until recently, the adversaries of true privacy, as a fundamental right of freedom, used the argument that people don't care, they don't share the concerns of privacy activists. Well, the dismal fate of the Covid-19 tracking apps in the free world speaks volumes about how clearly everybody understands that the current use of technology represents a severe threat to our personal freedom. At least this is one positive takeaway from the disruptions of 2020!

In the US, the First Amendment has protected free speech for more than 200 years, as a pillar of freedom and democracy. To consider our digital trail as an object instead as a part of our persona voids our right of self-determination and of free speech: We cannot change our past opinions, we cannot restart from scratch. The true "us" is a cumulative entity, beyond our control, where nothing is ever lost or deleted.

In the digital world we travel as fugitives, with all our belongings following us, laid bare at the whim of whoever is interested in and can pay for them.

For these reasons, in a digital world the digital "us" ontologically includes: 1) **all the digital devices that we usually carry with us**, which have become de facto extensions of our ability to see, listen, speak and memorize. This part of our persona includes not only the mobile phone, as decided by the US Supreme Court, but also our portable personal computers, for exactly the same reasons. 2) **all digital trails that do not originate in a wilful decision to document what we do**, as it happens when we shop online. What we are debating here isn't data protection. It is a definition of what is a person in the digital dimension.

Data protection begins when data is intentionally generated or intentionally recorded. When digital data does not consist of wilfully generated documents, it lacks even the implicit intention of sharing such information. So, **accessing our personal devices (and their digital trails) is an infringement to our personal freedom**: It is equivalent to someone setting up a video camera in our home and recording whatever we do, or opening our briefcase and copying our letters, telephone bills and credit card records. Today, Google (the world leader in user experience!) asks, several times a day, anyone who uses anonymisation tools for browsing to consent to data snooping; by default, it sets the answer to "yes"[481] and forces us to reply (and confirm) again and again, that we don't want it. We are living with a crowd of paparazzi on our doorsteps, who knock every day, or several times a day, to ask if we are willing to let them install their cameras in our homes. See below the screen shots of Google asking us incessantly for permission to snoop into our browsing, with all answers set to "yes": it's a picture of our lost freedom.

---

[481] Which is a clear infringement to European data protection law, as decided by the European Court of Justice in the Judgement 1 October 2019 (Grand Chamber), Bundesverband der Verbraucherzentralen und Verbraucherverbände - Verbraucherzentrale Bundesverband eV vs. Planet49 GmbH, were one reads:

"54. In particular, Article 7(a) of Directive 95/46 provides that the data subject's consent may make such processing lawful provided that the data subject has given his or her consent 'unambiguously'. Only active behaviour on the part of the data subject with a view to giving his or her consent may fulfil that requirement.
55. In that regard, it would appear impossible in practice to ascertain objectively whether a website user had actually given his or her consent to the processing of his or her personal data by not deselecting a pre-ticked checkbox nor, in any event, whether that consent had been informed. It is not inconceivable that a user would not have read the information accompanying the preselected checkbox, or even would not have noticed that checkbox, before continuing with his or her activity on the website visited".

YouTube a Google company   English ∨   Sign in

Before you continue

Google uses cookies and other data to deliver, maintain and improve our services and
ads. If you agree, we'll personalise the content and ads that you see, based on your
activity on Google services like Search, Maps and YouTube. We also have partners that
measure how our services are used. Click 'See more' to review your options, or visit
g.co/privacytools at any time.

SEE MORE   I AGREE

There are many privacy controls that you can use, even when you're signed out, to
achieve the Google experience that you want. You can review these controls below and
in 'Other options', or visit g.co/privacytools at any time.

Edit Search Settings
Control whether or not search results are affected by search activity in this browser.

Edit Ad Settings
Adjust the types of ad you see from Google

Edit YouTube Settings
Control whether or not your YouTube experience is affected by YouTube search and
watch activity in this browser

Learn how Google uses data to improve your experience   ∨

Tip: If you sign in to your Google Account before agreeing, we'll remember your choice
across all of your signed in devices and browsers.

Other options   I agree

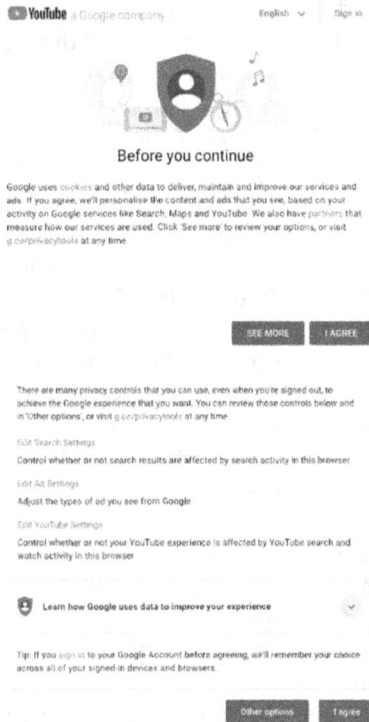

This is actually even worse than being followed by paparazzi. And so must
the law consider it. The current wrong legal assumptions are voiding our open
and liberal societies, providing too much and too precise data that can be used
by the state and by politicians to manipulate public opinion.

Whatever information about us is taken without our explicit consent is a breach
into our lives, into our (digital) homes.

Some will object instinctively that this definition of "home" and "persona" is
too extensive, even preposterous. Let's look into it, keeping in mind how we
use information technology in our daily lives. We can understand the consequences of ubiquitous computing in at least two ways:

a) We can consider **ubiquitous computing as an expansion of the "public
space"**, so that if we use a computer or mobile phone (even at home), in practice we are opening the door to anybody able to read our digital trail.
or

b) We can consider **ubiquitous computing as an expansion of our personal
freedom** and of our ability to be omnipresent, without losing our fundamental rights. In this case nobody has the right to sneak into our private lives just
because we cannot lock the digital door. In fact, we have purchased these technologies to empower us, not to deprive ourselves of our fundamental rights.

If ubiquitous computing has expanded the public space right into our homes,
beds and bathrooms, then we must realize that all the advertising about the
(mobile) Internet is misleading, because it seduces us to carry around one or
more electronic bracelets that enable complete control of our lives. Normally

the office of fair trade (or an antitrust authority) would prohibit such misleading advertising. Or it would impose, as with cigarette packages, to superimpose some label telling to the user "Beware, this device is snooping on you!"

Therefore, only the issue of how Facebook uses my posts or Google uses the information published on my blog should be handled as an issue of data protection. I believe that the profiles created using cookies and other tracking tools represent a limitation of our fundamental right to *habeas corpus* in a fair and just digital society: they are not just a collection of digital scraps about us. They are a constant presence of recording devices in our homes, in our bedrooms, in our bathrooms, in our cars... 24/7.

I am fully aware that this redefinition of current assumptions disrupts existing business models. But slavery (based on false assumptions about what is a person) also worked very well (for the slaveholders) and was therefore difficult to abolish. Since the time of the Lord Mansions ruling, the main argument in favour of slavery was that its abolition would cause economic disruption. This argument doesn't prove that slavery (or the systematic infringement of our digital persona) are good things.

So today, **Homo digitalis is interactive** - sending and receiving while participating - **just as, 2500 years ago**, we lived in an oral society. But there are several quite **important differences**:

- We can (at least apparently) quite **freely choose the community** to which we pledge our alliance.
- We can (at least apparently) quite **freely choose our identity** (with respect to the community of choice).
- The **communication is more complex**, yet does not require a physical presence.
- The **communication uses written words** more than spoken words.
- The **social communication is essentially mediated** by some (technological) tools and cannot be perceived without them. Without computers or smartphones, we are cut out, exiled, blind, deaf and dumb.

So, we can draw **some preliminary conclusions** on what is a digital identity.

The good news is that **we have many more options** and the ability to extend our reach immensely, as long as we can afford the underlying technology.

The bad news is that **we have completely lost control of our digital trail**: We live our (digital) lives followed each step of the way by automata that record and analyse everything we do, even when we do nothing.

We will discuss the digital identity and related privacy issues in chapter 8.1.4. We will discuss the social role of humans within digital communities in chapter 8.4.2.

8.1.2. I and my enhanced self[482]

The second issue involves the technological/digital enhancement of ourselves. Today's investment in human-enriching technologies is limited to computers

---

[482] Article 3, section 2, letters b) and d) of the Charter of Fundamental Rights of the European Union, prohibits *eugenic practices, in particular those aiming at the selection of persons* and *the*

and smartphones, and it seems that the majority of humanity can afford them. We have seen how important these technologies are, during the lockdown in 2020: Families who could not afford Internet access and computers were literally cut off from social and economic life. There will be more of that in the future.

The challenge here is that an incredible array of technological innovations will enable further improvements to our bodily functions, but apparently not all of them will be so cheaply available, potentially resulting in a **de facto split in social castes.**

Presently, we are a clumsy and primitive version of Homo digitalis, still fiddling with a bunch of unwieldy devices that we must drag along, and which we can only activate through physical motion (fingertips) or voice. It is only a matter of time before Homo digitalis is wearing such devices or will have them implanted and controlled by thought or even by impulses of the neural system.

Already, we are close to becoming cyborgs because we already interact with our (social) reality through electronic or mechanical devices, not with our body or voice. Most of the "facts" we react to and interact with are digital and presented to us by some digital device we covet. In 2015, the US Supreme Court[483] ruled that our mobile phones are more intimate and personal than any other device, so they should be considered as (almost) part of our persona.

Only a century ago, humans perceived all their (social) reality through their senses. Today, **the most important parts of our social interactions are carried out on digital platforms**, and we need sophisticated tools to do this. Without information technology, we miss most opportunities for social interaction. Metaphorically, without technology we have become deaf and dumb, if not blind.

Information technology has enabled billions of people, who were previously unknown beyond their own neighbourhoods, to tell their stories to a potentially unlimited audience. **Homo digitalis has become much more of a storytelling animal than ever before**. At the same time, his ability to see and be seen, to speak and be heard, is essentially dependent on some pieces of hardware and software.

This means that if we still want humanity to offer a fair chance to all, there is a need to grant a fair opportunity of accessing these technologies to all.

As for genetic engineering, the access to superior technological enhancements, reserved just to some privileged few, will mean that we have **a two-tier humanity, not unlike the era when Homo sapiens and Neanderthals coexisted**. Think science fiction: We would have situations not unlike *Gattaca*[484], *Planet of Apes*[485], *Blade Runner*[486] or *The Island*[487], just to mention a few dystopic

---

reproductive cloning of human beings. Eugenetic practices aimed at improving the genetic code aren't expressly considered.

[483] United States Supreme Court, court ruling in Riley v. US.

[484] IMDb, Gattaca.

[485] IMDb, Planet of the Apes (2001).

[486] IMDb, Blade Runner (1982).

[487] IMDb, The Island.

science fiction movies. Scientists and philosophers are debating the moral implications of human enhancement, and there is still little agreement on its moral foundations[488]. The main problem is to define the border that separates allowed and forbidden human enhancements. A smartphone and high-speed Internet are okay, but should we forbid cyber-implantations? And if so, why? Would a genetic cure for a disease be allowed, but not genetic enhancement? If so, where lies the morality in having to wait for a dangerous disease, if it can be avoided beforehand? And so on.

As a lawyer, I cannot wait for the (final?) outcome of such a complex (at times, impossible) moral debate. If practical problems arise, the law must address them.

Experience tells us that if there are some people who are much more powerful than others, and the rule of law eventually does not fully apply to them, then they will be feared - because they may easily abuse their "superpowers", as we saw in the Middle Ages and the Age of Imperialism.

Experience also tells us that if there are some people who are inherently much weaker than others, they are tendentially marginalized by the majority, as we see in our daily lives at school or the workplace.

So whatever the moral foundations of human enhancement will be, we can confidently say that the most sought-after improvements will be in health, in strength and endurance, and in intelligence. The more achievable they become, the greater will be the legal challenges involved in keeping our society peaceful, open and free.

Today it is access to ubiquitous computing that marks the key difference between fully developed and underdeveloped countries. In the near future, the individual pursuit of happiness will depend on **equality of access to technological enhancements to the human body**.

Technology will increasingly define not just what we have, but also who we are, in the sense that it will have a direct influence on what we know, what we can do, how healthy we are and, ultimately, how we think.

The social mobility that characterizes the open, free societies of the OECD is threatened by technological innovation: If only a few will have access to new human enhancement technologies, it will likely result in the reestablishment of a closed caste society. Whenever such societies have existed, the separation of the elite from the underdogs was the consequence of an effective restriction of access to wealth and/or education.

What are the legal rules that will guarantee a level playing field, without curtailing (too much) individual freedom? Legal history tells us that law is more successful at creating opportunities than at restricting them.

Law is pragmatic and tries to settle for the best possible balance of interests. This implies that, yes, it can be skewed in favour of the strongest, wealthiest or best educated; but it can also effectively reduce inequality[489]. The legal

---

[488] Savulescu Bostrom, *Human Enhancement*, p. 1 ff.

[489] The grade of inequality is measured by the so-called "Gini" coefficient, see Wikipedia, *Gini coefficient*. A Gini coefficient of zero expresses perfect equality, where all values are the same (for

model of reference is the welfare state, which provides universal schooling and access to university and healthcare, in order to allow people born into underprivileged families to have a fair shot at improving their social condition.

So **in a world with human enhancement technologies**, the state should:

a) **Provide legal and economic incentives supporting anybody who seeks to acquire lawful human enhancement technologies**, either (if affordable) in the same way it provides universal healthcare or schooling, or (if universal access is economically unsustainable) in the same way it supports young entrepreneurs, with loans and tax incentives.

b) **Drastically discourage the utilisation of human enhancement technologies that are forbidden**. This part is trickier, because legislation restricting the use of alcohol or drugs has never been truly effective. After little less than a century of drug prohibitions, today's use of drugs is much more widespread, and we live in a world experiencing a drug abuse pandemic. We know how difficult it is to devise a working definition of a forbidden substance. For human enhancement technologies, it will be the same: We will have a shifting border, where technological innovation stays constantly ahead of legal rules.

8.1.3. I and my genetically engineered self

The third issue involves the possibility of engineered humans. Will they be considered human or nonhuman? Will they be subjects or objects of rights?

The answer to these questions clearly depends on the previous two questions discussed in this chapter:

- What is a human persona?

- How much can we "enhance" ourselves before we cease to be human (or acceptable to a human society)?

Legally speaking, **the answer to these questions will depend on how effective legislation is at achieving a fair equality of opportunity for technological enhancement**.

As a lawyer, I tend to discredit only human behaviour that disrupts peaceful and orderly social coexistence.

Many of our human inventions didn't really improve human life (or when they did, they had very nasty side effects). Think of gunpowder, slavery, cookies … somewhat useful, somewhat nasty. The law never has succeeded in forbidding innovations. They happen anyway, no matter what their ultimate impact on society.

Some issues call out for strong moral foundations. We cannot successfully eradicate cannibalism, paedophilia, slavery or racial, social and sexual discrimination without support from widely held moral attitudes.

So we must act fast to address the moral part of the dilemma: **We need human morals that work in a digital society.**

---

example, everyone has the same income). A Gini coefficient of 1 (or 100%) expresses maximal inequality among values (e.g., for a large group of people, if only one person has all the income and all others have none, the Gini coefficient will be very nearly one).

When Jesus preached that we are all equal in front of God, it was not a phenomenological truth. Society was based on castes, and slaves were not even considered as subjects, but as objects. The adoption of Christian values has shaped Europe (with ups and downs) for at least two millennia and radically changed our social structure and values.

We are possibly heading toward a society where **human castes will not be a consequence of laws, but of technological innovation**: The differences between one caste and another will arise from factual differences in abilities and disabilities. It will be a matter of fact. How can or should the law deal with it?

While we seek to define a moral compass for the engineering of human life, what can the law do in the meantime? Should the law consider engineered creatures as animals/objects/slaves? Should it recognize them as human beings? There is no easy answer.

It is tempting to set a threshold of genetic identity. (Let's say that to be human, the DNA of an engineered creature - let's call it an "android" - must be 99.9% identical to human DNA). But we clearly understand that, as a consequence, there would be an incentive to engineer androids that have all "useful" human capabilities (like intelligence, strength, resilience, etc.) and also self-consciousness and self-determination, but would be legally treated as objects or animals. Thus they would be mere objects of rights, not subjects of rights. Like slaves. Any other possible measurable criteria for distinguishing "real humans" from "androids" would be fallible and prone to misuse.

What about using non-measurable criteria to distinguish humans and non-humans? Like (the potential for) self-consciousness, the (potential) ability to feel emotions, (the potential for) self-determination, the (potential) ability to speak, or (the potential) for autonomous thinking?

These are more ambitious, but also more subjective, criteria, that would lead us to consider as human the poetry-reding, self-conscious, speaking cow or an artificial intelligence that passes the Turing test.

So it seems the law will **need to combine measurable and non-measurable criteria to define what is a human being**. Morphology, conception/birth and DNA are currently the guiding criteria. Nothing that doesn't look like a human and have the human genome can be considered as a legal subject, no matter how self-conscious, self-determined, intelligent or articulate it is. So far, so good. But it is just a matter of time, and these criteria will be tested to their limits.

What is worrying for a lawyer is a scenario where a human being has been so enhanced/modified (or genetically engineered) that his or her interests and needs are totally different from those of other humans. This is not limited to the unlikely case of a human with X-Men powers, but could apply to humans who are extremely resilient to fatigue, heat or cold, or who are emotionally different from the rest of us or a combination of extremely intelligent and frail at the same time.[490]

When between different types of humans, there is a total misalignment of capabilities, disaster ensues. Whenever literate humans have encountered humans

---

[490] How would a society function with millions of Wittgensteins and Turings - fragile geniuses?

living in the oral tradition, the latter have been exterminated (in America, Africa and Oceania). Neanderthals and Homo sapiens were also unable to coexist for very long.[491]

Human enhancement and genetic engineering will possibly extend the range of human abilities with new strengths, but will also very likely introduce new (unwanted) weaknesses, making it very difficult, if not impossible, for the law to arbitrate (at least using the same principles and rules that apply today).

In my opinion, the methodology of John Rawls in *A Theory of Justice* (i.e., the discussion behind the veil of ignorance) could provide the process through which we update some fundamental principles, such as freedom, equal opportunity, solidarity and the pursuit of happiness.

The best moment for this ethical/philosophical discussion could be right now, before a specific set of diverging interests spoils it. We don't know if androids will be strong but stupid, or intelligent but weak. Now our discussion could take place behind the veil of ignorance, at least in theory.

From a legal perspective, on the other hand, I don't think that legislators or lawyers today can successfully attempt to redefine in abstract the founding principles of the current natural law that would regulate hypothetical androids, robots or AI. For lawyers, it is probably necessary to know the specific characteristics of enhanced humans, their different needs and their impact on the lives of others.

I would like to point out that **jurisprudence has dealt for centuries with the question of thinking and speaking "things"**: This is the jurisprudence addressing the legal consequences of a slave's actions.

For lawyers, the first historically tested option is to put AI, androids and robots all in the established (ancient Roman) category of *instrumenta vocalis*, the Roman legalese for slaves: speaking/thinking objects.

The second historically tested option, established between 1601 (the Dutch East India Company) and 1807 (the Napoleonic code de commerce) is the legal theory of a "legal person", i.e., a physical or fictive entity that the law treats as if it were a person, with its own rights and obligations. Androids, robots and AI would be legal entities, controlled by someone else.

---

[491] HARARI Y. N. *Sapiens a Brief History of mankind*, 15, asks what would have happened if Neanderthals and Denisovans would not have been extinct: *"Tolerance is not a Sapiens trademark. In modern times, a small difference in skin colour, dialect or religion has been enough to prompt one group of Sapiens to set about exterminating another group. Would ancient Sapiens have been more tolerant towards an entirely different human species? It may well be that when Sapiens encountered Neanderthals, the result was the first and most significant ethnic-cleansing campaign in history. Whichever way it happened, the Neanderthals (and the other human species) pose one of history's great what ifs. Imagine how things might have turned out had the Neanderthals or Denisovans survived alongside Homo sapiens. What kind of cultures, societies and political structures would have emerged in a world where several different human species coexisted? How, for example, would religious faiths have unfolded? Would the book of Genesis have declared that Neanderthals descend from Adam and Eve, would Jesus have died for the sins of the Denisovans, and would the Qur'an have reserved seats in heaven for all righteous humans, whatever their species? Would Neanderthals have been able to serve in the Roman legions, or in the sprawling bureaucracy of imperial China? Would the American Declaration of Independence hold as a self-evident truth that all members of the genus Homo are created equal? Would Karl Marx have urged workers of all species to unite?".*

The third tested option is the legislation and jurisprudence addressing the wellbeing of animals.

Maybe it is possible to combine the three criteria, or to create a new legal category for AI, androids and robots.

Popular culture is obsessed with the possibility that androids may possibly be "superior" to us in many, if not all aspects of life. But the greatest danger lies in the legal possibility of a new slavery. Because such entities are not human, they can be owned, exploited and thrown away. **History tells us that there is strong interest in "disposable humans"**. It took two millennia to root out this economic practice.

In my own way of looking at the Internet, digital slavery has already been reintroduced, and the sanctity and richness of our private lives has been (legally) transformed into tradable, disposable data.

Consider the moral and legal implications of human androids that are self-conscious, emotional and capable of self-determination, but with major structural flaws, such as sterility, dementia or immune deficiencies. Would it be morally and legally acceptable to engineer throwaway (or even single use) androids? This is the Blade Runner question posed by Philip K. Dick in "Do Androids Dream of Electric Sheep?".[492] It will need a legal answer, one way or another.

Legal history provides us some tools. The binary contraposition human/non-human, believer/unbeliever was prone to violent abuse over the millennia. This time we may try to choose a **nonbinary approach to what is human**.[493] We could have between subjects (following categories "a" and "b") and objects (category "g") at least other four intermediate categories of (legal) subjects:

a. Human being with all (civil) rights and obligations and the full freedom to act;

b. Human being under tutelage (human clones, minors and, until the 18th century, women) with all (civil) rights and obligations, but a limited freedom to act autonomously;

c. Living being under tutelage (androids and, until the 18th century slaves), with selected rights and obligations, and a limited freedom to act autonomously;

d. Intelligent (self-determining) legal entity with all rights of non-living beings (Robots and A.I.) with a limited set of rights and obligations (proper of non-living subjects), and a limited freedom to act autonomously: their actions are attributed to their owner/programmer according to a set of given legal rules;[494]

e. Technologic legal entity (Websites, computers, smart devices), not self-determining objects but with own rights: all their actions must be attributed to their owner;

---

[492] Philip K. Dick, 1968, "Do Androids Dream of Electric Sheep?", New York, Doubleday.

[493] The following categories "c", "d", "e", and "f" (androids, robots, A.I., computers smart devices and other legal entities), would be objects, that can be owned/leased, to which the law recognises subjectivity, and thus some autonomous rights and obligations as a legal entity.

[494] This is currently the mainstream of legal thinking:

f. Legal entity (Companies, Associations, Public Administrations): they aren't objects, but established legal fictions; not self-determining but with own rights. All their actions must be attributed to their owner;

g. Mere objects that are owned/leased, with no rights/obligations.

8.1.4. Digital identities vs. digital profiles (and the true meaning of digital privacy)

My physical persona is unique, as a matter of fact: I have just one body. **My digital persona is NOT unique**. It is more like the clothes that I wear. They may be changed at will. They influence my appearance, but they are not uniquely or inherently linked to my body. Digital identities and personal information are much more closely linked in the digital world than our bodies are to the clothes that we wear, to our homes or our furniture.

In a word, physically I am one, but my (moral, existential) digital self is inherently free to be more than one.

The freedom to choose and to shape our identity is an essential part of individual freedom of speech.[495]

The freedom to say what we think, without the freedom to choose who we are, is pointless. To force us to be one and indivisible in the digital world is equivalent to letting others (the state, corporations) heavily influence our decisions on who we are and who we want to be. This is even more true if you consider that we cannot control our digital trail, as we have seen in chapter 8.1.1. The unification (by others) of our various identities into one identity forces us to make decisions that we should never have to make. We don't want to be bound forever to everything we once did. Ultimately, we want to be free not to be compelled to know who we really are!

The idea of bestowing a single identity on a citizen is based on the same reasoning that lay behind providing all Jews with a *Judenausweis* and then compelling them to use it. The authorities of the Third Reich knew they were forcing a bad

---

[495] A right that was recognized in Greece and Rome as early as the 5th century BC, and formally enshrined in several democratic constitutions, starting with the Bill of Rights (1689) and article 11 of the Declaration of the Rights of Man and of the Citizen (1789), adopted during the French Revolution. Moreover, it is recognized in all international legislation on human rights: the Universal Declaration of Human Rights, adopted by the United Nations in 1948; the International Covenant on Civil and Political Rights (ICCPR), a multilateral treaty adopted by the United Nations General Assembly on 16 December 1966; the European Convention on Human Rights (ECHR) (formally the Convention for the Protection of Human Rights and Fundamental Freedoms), an international treaty to protect human rights and fundamental freedoms in Europe, drafted in 1950 by the then newly formed Council of Europe; the Charter of Fundamental Rights of the European Union (latest version on OJ C 326, 26.10.2012, p. 391–407), that is referenced by article 6 of the Treaty of the European Union (latest version on OJ C 202 7.6.2016, p. 13); the American Convention on Human Rights, also known as the Pact of San José, an international human rights instrument adopted by many countries in the Western Hemisphere in San José, Costa Rica, on 22 November 1969; the African Charter on Human and Peoples' Rights (also known as the Banjul Charter), an international human rights instrument intended to promote and protect human rights and basic freedoms on the African continent.

deal on the Jews. A census, an enumeration was necessary to make sure that nobody escaped their notice.

In making us detectable at all times online, the state weakens our freedom and our ability to be what we want to be. The pursuit of happiness will be (is already) compromised for whoever goes digital. There are better alternatives, and it is important that they are implemented as soon as possible. We should be mindful of the fact that the founding fathers of our democracies could challenge tyrants because they were able to hide behind pseudonyms, to travel undetected and to meet without leaving any trace. Many of them were revolutionaries, if not terrorists. This is all but impossible now. All fugitives are caught at some point[496] and/or are hit by a drone.[497] The only effective revolutionary seems to be the lone wolf; everyone else can be tracked down. But a lone wolf cannot be a revolutionary; he is just a terrorist with no prospect of success. It seems likely that in a totalitarian digital state (like a digital Third Reich) there will be no forceful opposition, because no one can hide. One of the reasons the Second Amendment upholds the right to bear arms is precisely that "*non-resistance against arbitrary power, and oppression, is absurd, slavish, and destructive of the good and happiness of mankind,*" as stated in Article 10 of the New Hampshire State Constitution ("Right of Revolution").[498]

In chapter 4.3 we considered how many aspects of the present social contract the state will be forced to renegotiate with its citizens[499]. In fact, it is very likely that we will have to accept a far worse deal than promised in recent decades. A "new deal" will be necessary and unavoidable, but the negotiation will be hard. We, the citizens, today don't have a good bargaining position, and we will probably regret the deal we will be induced to accept. The outcome of this renegotiation of the social contract will largely depend on what kind of cultural and legal idea of (digital) identity is presumed.

---

[496] Murphy H., Tim Arango T., *Joseph DeAngelo Pleads Guilty in Golden State Killer Cases*.

[497] Drones are another example of how new technologies change the rules. As former US President Jimmy Carter has remarked: "*We don't know how many hundreds of innocent civilians have been killed in these attacks .... This would have been unthinkable in previous times*", New York Times, June 24, 2012. With respect to drones I am curious if, since 2011, the military has implemented the security features recommended by The Economist in 2011. These security features were intended to monitor, record and trace the audit trail on how a drone has been used in combat. My curiosity relates to whether the state, which advocates monitoring and tracking what we do in our (mostly pacific) private lives, is prepared to do the same with its soldiers when dealing with other people's lives. I fear this isn't the case. If not, the state is (again) using a double standard, as when there were aristocrats and commoners, subject to different legal systems. This symptom does not bode well for democracy and individual freedoms.

[498] [Art.] 10. [Right of Revolution.] "*Government being instituted for the common benefit, protection, and security, of the whole community, and not for the private interest or emolument of any one man, family, or class of men; therefore, whenever the ends of government are perverted, and public liberty manifestly endangered, and all other means of redress are ineffectual, the people may, and of right ought to reform the old, or establish a new government. The doctrine of nonresistance against arbitrary power, and oppression, is absurd, slavish, and destructive of the good and happiness of mankind*".

[499] For a deeply engaging description of a possible new social contract, see Shafik, M., *What We Owe Each Other: A New Social Contract*, 188 ff.

One way to provide people with a digital identity would be a digital version of the system used for police officers and military personnel. They would have to wear a uniform (eventually one of their choice) and display a unique serial number. This has been such an effective way to identify people that the concept was expanded and used to identify individuals in prisons and concentration camps. Are there other, more humane ways to have one (or more) digital identities in the digital world? Or are we doomed to be catalogued and marked like cars or inmates?

The answer is yes, there are technical solutions that balance privacy and security,[500] but they have yet to be used beyond scientific trials. Most people seem to prefer simplicity and a "free ride". Nonetheless, the failure to disseminate Covid-19 tracking apps across the populations of free, liberal democracies sends a strong signal that awareness is arising on the subject.

Today, all digital identities are externally imposed, either through formal legal structures (like those provided by EU Regulation 910/2014/UE, which sets the current rules for electronic identification and trust services for electronic transactions in international markets) or imposed by informal identity providers, like Apple, Google, Microsoft, Facebook, etc. In theory, information technology should empower us to expand ourselves; in practice it allows others to collect snippets of our lives and recompose them into some sort of futuristic jigsaw puzzle that they use commercially (and even politically), selling it (or imposing it by law) as "us".

If today, we have multiple identities, it is because different information providers take interest in different aspects of our (digital) lives. It has even become customary for them to swap (among themselves) pieces of the jigsaw puzzle they have assembled (like seeking to identify us through our Facebook, Google+ or LinkedIn profiles) - a practice that we should absolutely avoid!

What should strike us as odd about the current state of the affairs is that it is reminiscent of the origins of slavery.[501]

Several millennia ago, humans needed to cooperate to produce crops reliably. Lacking the social structures and linguistic skills to regulate labour, they ended up treating people as part of the estate of the landowner. It was allowed by law to use the physical strength of other humans without paying any compensation (see chapter 5). The practice of slavery worked so well that it was ultimately abolished only about a century ago (see chapter 4.1).

As it was with the establishment of slavery, **today we lack the linguistic, cultural and legal skills to find proper regulation for the use of personal information in a digital environment**. The consequence is that we allow the utilisation of personal information about individuals - without compensation. We act as digital slaves. We don't understand that our digital trail isn't some sort of digital rubbish, but is an essential part of our identity and our personal freedom. And we are forced to be part of communities whose business interests differ from our own.

---

[500] abc4trust, Official Website, and David Chaum, List of Publications.
[501] See chapter 2.4.

As in the beginning of agricultural civilisation, when crops were produced with unpaid human labour, so it is in this early stage of the information society, where unpaid personal information is used to produce digital services.

Have we become digital-information-slaves?

Let's make a comparison: It was never a crime to use the body of a slave for any lawful purpose. Today, they have enslaved our personal information (the registration of some aspects of our minds, our souls and our daily lives) for more or less any lawful pursuit.

The current solution is so primitive that it cannot last forever. But it is deeply engrained in our economic and social order, so it will be extremely difficult to root it out without any viable alternative.

On the other hand, we have seen how the current state of affairs is damaging the social fabric of our society, which was built on trust and cooperation: the Covid-19 apps have been roundly rejected by people for fear of their impact on privacy and personal freedom[502]. Maybe this is the first uprising of the digital slaves!

Only if and when someone proposes shared values and working rules on how to commercially or politically exploit information about individuals (in a verifiable and transparent way) will there be a chance to upend the digital-information slavery practiced today and allow something more equitable to prevail. We can only hope this will not take three millennia to happen or require as many wars as the global abolition of slavery required. If we recognise that, under the current technical and legal rules, we are not prepared to band together to fight a common enemy (such as Covid-19), then it should be clear to us that the current situation is weakening our social fabric.

What will a **more equitable solution for digital identities** and the use of personal information look like? Let's take an educated guess:

1) We will **appear and disappear in the digital environment, as we do today in a shop or an office**. We will be able to do so at will, without prior screening or security checks at the entrance, yet there still will be no doubt about the fact that we are real human beings (and not bots or apps), even if our names and other personal details are unknown. The technology to do this is already established and stable. What we are missing is the proper business model and rules to shift from the current state of affairs to something more just and balanced. We are in the same old situation of presenting the concept of paid labour to a slave-keeper. It's not a big deal technically. Only a few years ago, all telephone calls where anonymous.

2) We will **choose what information to reveal about ourselves**, without any external constriction. We may be wooed into selling some information or exchanging it for other benefits. Information revelation will be tiered: the greater the benefit, the more we disclose about ourselves. The blockchains

---

[502] The Economist, *Don't rely on contact-tracing apps*; The Economist, *Countries are using apps and data networks to keep tabs on the pandemic*; The Economist, *Tracking and tracing Covid-19*; The Economist, *Some countries want central databases for contact-tracing apps*; The Economist, *Privacy in a pandemic*.

used in systems like bitcoin (together with group signatures and anonymous credentials as devised by David Chaum)[503] can deliver this limited and controlled availability of information, specifically handing it out for an approved purpose. The GDPR clearly states that privacy by default requires precisely such technological features.

3) Profiling (and stealing personal information) will cease, not only because it will be forbidden (as it already is, at least in theory), but because it will be either economically unattractive or morally loathed (as is the case today with child labour, prostitution and slavery), or both. It is hard to guess what will bring about the revolution. It may be the spreading of bots that will make online marketing (as we know it today) unviable. Or increased public awareness may lead people to ask their governments for the abolition of digital-information slavery. Perhaps new technologies (and related business models) will disrupt today's digital incumbents and the existing business models.

How do we get there, starting from here and now?

The first thing is to **define properly what a (digital) identity is**. This is difficult, because today we mix up (digital) identities and (digital) profiles. Half a millennium ago, anyone who confounded identity and profile would have been a laughing stock, as we can read in the tale of Manetto the woodcarver, as told by Filippo Brunelleschi. (The text of the original *Italiano volgare*, i.e., Florentine dialect, version can be found in annex I to this book). *La Novella del Grasso Legnaiuolo* ("**The Story of the Fat Woodcarver**") recounts the famous joke plotted by Brunelleschi, one of the greatest artists of the Renaissance, in 1409, during the plague in Florence, to humiliate the craftsman Manetto Ammanatini, called *Il Grasso*. It is considered one of the masterpieces of the *novella alla spicciolata*, popular in the Florentine Renaissance.

The story struck me because it explains how important it is for us to know that we are the only source and origin of our own identities. It can be summarized as follows:

Brunelleschi and his group of friends were disappointed that Manetto, despite his lower status in the guild, often failed to attend their dinner parties. Unsure whether this was due to avarice or pride, the group decided to teach him a lesson, playing a complicated prank intended to confuse him as to who he really was.

So, one evening Brunelleschi met Manetto and put in his mind that his mother, an attractive 40-year-old widow, was having an affair with a monk. He accompanied him to a farmhouse owned by Manetto, where his mother and the monk were supposedly meeting. In fact, the farmhouse was conveniently empty that evening, and some of Brunelleschi's friends had sneaked in, imitating the voices of his mother and Manetto and staging a loud argument between mother and son about the immoral alleged relationship with the monk. Manetto knocked on the door, as his keys had been stolen by Brunelleschi. Yet he could not help but notice that from inside the house came the voice of his mother and that he

---

[503] Wikipedia, "David Chaum"; David Chaum, "Security without identification"; David Chaum, Eugene van Heyst, "Group signatures".

himself seemed to be replying to her, arguing about matters that, in theory, only he and his mother could know about.

Just then, some other friends of Brunelleschi arrived and greeted poor Manetto as if he were a certain Matteo Mannini, a good-for-nothing who scrounged off his relatives. Others arrived, including some officers from the guild, seeking to imprison Matteo for running up debts. They proceeded to arrest Manetto as Matteo. Some days later, others claiming to be Matteo's brothers appeared before the magistrates of the guild and offered to pay his debts, providing that he gives up his degenerate lifestyle, which was breaking their mother's heart. Manetto, eager to get out of prison, promised his self-styled brothers that he would turn over a new leaf. He still believed that he was Manetto, but was hoping to find a chance to prove it.

So Brunelleschi's partners in pranking sent a monk from out of town to talk to him, convincing the monk that Manetto had lost his mind and thought he was Manetto rather than Matteo. The monk, acting, unlike the others, in perfect good faith, finally managed to convince Manetto that he was actually Matteo.

To make sure he was convinced, the following night Brunelleschi and his friends brought a coffin to Manetto's workshop. In the morning, they came to tell Manetto that Manetto had died and described how they prepared the body for the coffin. Poor Manetto attended his own funeral (as Matteo), where he meets his (real) mother not recognizing him and mourning her son's death.

After the funeral Manetto (now Matteo) went to an inn where a nobleman, Filippo Spano, was recruiting artisans and artists to work at the court of Hungary. He offered his services as a cabinetmaker and left Florence, where he no longer knew who he was. "And Giovan Pesce, our Florentine merchant and a trustworthy man who lived in Signa di Schiavonia, found him in 1446 in Buda di Schiavonia, about whom he had heard this tale, saying that the prank had made him rich".

This is what can happen to those who think of themselves whatever other people tell them they are.

One wonders: in today's world of social networking, how often are we subtly influenced to see ourselves as others see us? Probably more often than we realize. While in Manetto's time it was obvious that everyone had their own unique identity, today we can easily be led to confuse an identity and a profile. Let's start from the beginning, with a short **historical background**.

Identity, before the advent of parish registers (c. 15th century) and population registers (c. 19th century), was not attributed to people by a document or an office, but by their bloodline, if they had one. Since Roman times, the *pater familias* was the only individual who had the status and authority to act on behalf of all his family members (including extended family), but at the same time he was identified by this status.

Identity, indeed, was not for everyone. It was owned by patricians and the "*aequites*" (wealthy people or such influential figures as generals and magistrates). But most citizens (the "plebs"), including free men and freedmen, were eventually defined by the "*gens*", the clan they came from, not by a family or bloodline. Only those whose bloodline could be traced, through birth right and adoption and through an estate (*"domus"* or *"villa"*) belonging to their *familia*, possessed not just legal capacity but also a real identity. Those who lived in a *domus* or *villa* belonging to others or in an *insula* (apartment building), despite being *"cives romani"* (citizens of Rome) and thus having full legal capacity, still didn't have a real identity as we understand it today. Their identity was defined by the context of belonging, not by their family history. Their legal capacity was therefore more theoretical than a matter of fact. In Roman law, transactions were oral and required witnesses. The Roman patricians and *aequites* had (as part of their *familia*) all the witnesses they needed for their legal transactions. The plebeians, on the contrary, had to find reliable witnesses to execute their transactions. That was quite troublesome, because an unreliable witness (who couldn't remember, or wouldn't appear in court, or wouldn't be considered trustworthy by a judge) could jeopardize any agreement, otherwise valid and binding.

Roman law dealing with primogeniture, adoption and investiture of the *pater familias* must also be seen through the perspective of the need to ensure/certify the identity of the head of the family and his heritage, beyond any possible doubt or conflict.

Identity in ancient Rome and the Middle Ages was, therefore, a privilege (a true status symbol) accessible to those who had a suitable framework with which to identify themselves: a family (bloodline), an estate and a stable place of origin or residence.

Still in the French revolutionary constitution, the definition of a citizen with the right to vote was as follows: *"Pour être 'citoyen actif', il faut avoir au moins 25 ans, résider dans la ville ou le canton depuis au moins une année, être inscrit au rôle de la garde nationale dans la municipalité du domicile, avoir prêté le serment civique et acquitté le paiement d'une contribution directe égale à trois jours de travail"*.

"The Constituent Assembly created a tiered system of political rights based on tax thresholds. It excluded the poor and gave only the less poor the right to appoint a minority of well-off voters. 'Passive citizens' could not vote. Women, people who had been accused of a criminal act, people who were bankrupt or insolvent, and domestic servants, of which there were a great number at that time, were considered dependents and excluded from the right to vote"[504].

The "citoyens actifs" in 1790 were estimated at about 4 million, out of a population of 28 million. The Marxist interpretation of these rules stressed that the right to vote was withheld from the poor, who were the majority of the population. A different, less ideological, interpretation is that the right to vote was only granted to identifiable citizens, in other words, those with their own identity. Having served in the national guard was not a particularly elitist requirement[505]; however, it excluded many citizens who were

---

[504] Centre Historique des Archives Nationales, *Les citoyens actifs*.

[505] Also in ancient Rome, one became *aequites* by merit, not birth. One had to be able to afford a horse for military service. In the late republic, it was common to grant to particularly courageous soldiers a horse and the means to keep it.

malnourished and unhealthy. Despite the revolution, in France servants and their families, as in ancient Rome, were considered second-class citizens, because they weren't "traceable". They were, simply put, "nobodies out of nowhere"!

So, in the 18ᵗʰ century, you were ultimately a someone (with an identity) if you were able to establish your own estate, where you lived with your family. Today you are a someone if you obtain an ID (social security number) from the state in which you live.

In today's digital society, we experience first-hand the awful consequences that the social network has on the political discourse. In fact, even unidentified individuals and those who do not belong to our political community (state, region or national federation) can play a full part in the political discourse. The threat due to which many people were excluded from political rights in the past two centuries has materialized at last: the political discourse is influenced (often steered) by those who have "nothing to lose", because they are not identifiable or traceable. In fact, most fake news is an invention of "fake" (not existing) persons.

But back to the history of identification: The build-up, since the 15ᵗʰ century, of objective ways to provide people with a proper identity was of great importance for extending access to wealth and proper legal guarantees. On the other hand, registers and offices responsible for registering and certifying our identities are also the expression of a policy aiming to exert greater control over the population.

At the beginning of the 20ᵗʰ century, population registrars were ubiquitous and already able to trace people's ancestry back for generations. This had made obsolete (and thus discriminatory) the determination of active citizenship based on wealth, which was progressively repealed. Certainly, the social and political upheavals of the First World War were decisive in extending to women the right to vote (suffrage) and in abrogating the right to vote based on census. However, one cannot help but notice that the general obligation to register births and deaths at the population registrars (between 1860 and 1880) in Europe created an effective and extensive system of identification, or profiling, of all citizens and that the extension of political rights to all coincided with the implementation of an infrastructure for managing the identity of all citizens. The size and scope of this infrastructure were absolutely unprecedented in the history of mankind.

Population registrars were extremely effective at making draft avoidance all but impossible. On the other hand, all citizens benefited from having their own identity granted by the state, reducing the gap between those who had an identity of their own and those who instead (servants, tenant farmers, etc.) had a second-rate identity, derived from others. We have expanded access to political participation, at the price of greater control by the state over our lives. History books normally tell only the first part of the story.

History shows that there were two key factors in the birth of the middle class: first, having a demonstrable identity and second, having access to certain property titles.[506] This explains the mass identification programs that have been recently carried out by developing countries such as India and Egypt.

It is precisely the **success of this immense machinery for identifying and profiling citizens that has led to a change in the concept of personal identity**. Originally, having an identity was a sign of someone's achievement of full civil and legal rights - of having managed to build an identity so tangible and real that it could be passed on to the offspring. But with the implementation of universal civil registers and civil status records, identity became a condition imposed by the state on the citizen, to give him full access to his rights.

Our identity, as it exists at the population registrars, does not differ much from our profile on a social network. They are both databases in which each of us has a record and data that belongs to our personal sphere is gathered. Their purpose and function are different, not their structure or the way they work.

One of the effects of the ubiquity of computerisation is that today there is no longer any significant difference between the security and technical reliability of public and private registers or databases. Some public information systems have, by law, a special probative value, but if a computer expert were asked to analyse a database, it would be difficult to deduce from its technical properties whether it belongs to a public administration or to private entities.

On the contrary, in the world of paper, only the state had an adequately vast and complex organisation to create reliable registers, such as those of the population registrars (trusted by the public). In Italy in the 1940s,[507] the law provided that the local prefect[508] had to number and stamp every page of the birth registers before they were utilized; the registers were kept in double original, according to the "four eyes" security principle,[509] and their maintenance was subject to control by the state attorney, the governor and the mayor's secretariat. In short, no private organisation could maintain a comparable level of professionalism or power and such an elaborately ramified structure, able to provide so much documental security. Today a computerized population registrar is largely a "law-compliant" system for storing birth certificates with specially structured metadata. Its difference from any other legitimate private archive is negligible, from both a phenomenological and technical point of view.

Nevertheless, the prevailing opinion is that our "true" identity, both phenomenologically and technically, is nothing other than our administrative profile in the population registrar database, based on which identity cards and passports are issued.

This hides a **dangerous misunderstanding**, which in a digital society has terrible consequences. It is the misunderstanding into which Manetto fell in the story: He accepted that his identity was determined by others. To a Florentine

---

[506] Acemoglu D., Simon Johnson S., Robinson J. A., "*Institutions as a Fundamental Cause of Long-Run Growth*".

[507] Italian Royal Decree 09.07.1939 n. 1238.

[508] Art. 20 of Italian Royal Decree. 09.07.1939 n. 1238.

[509] Art. 17 of Italian Royal Decree 09.07.1939 n. 1238.

of the 15th century, this was absurd, since Manetto belonged to the 10% of the population with their own identity; it derived from his family's bloodline, his estate (first house, second house, farmhouse, workshop) and from his belonging to the guild of the woodcarvers. There was no other way to assess one's personal identity.

From the moment we accept that a record in a public database corresponds to our identity and that our rights descend from it, we have instantly weakened most of our (digital) constitutional rights, since their only point of origin is not part of us, but is a digital record held in computer archives not managed or controlled by us. Therefore, instead of holders of rights, we become licensees of these rights.

As long as our rights could only be exercised "offline", by going somewhere in person, it was obvious that the mistake of regarding our administrative profile (mostly recorded on paper) as our true identity had little consequence, because our physical presence (in flesh and blood) was required anyway in order to exercise our rights and fulfil our obligations. Through our physical presence we can "keep" our identity in our own hands (but only as long as the state is democratic, pluralistic, and respectful of our freedom). Identification and freedom are closely linked, as the debate on voters registration and identification in the US clearly demonstrates.[510]

However, now that the physical presence is no longer required and even public registrars are no longer physically managed by a plurality of physical persons, the administrative identity has a completely different quality from the old paper-based identity: It has lost all its connections to the physical domain, because it isn't linked anymore to my physical persona, neither is it physically linked to my town's administration and its functionaries. It is just a record in the cloud. So today, my "true (administrative) identity" is held elsewhere - for example in the Internet domain of my municipality, by definition inaccessible, or in a different accessible domain, regulated by different rules and purposes. And it has lost any tangible connection to my persona.

With such a detached (digital) identity, I operate ontologically *in absentia*: I cannot be in the same place where my "true identity" is. Never before have humans acted *in absentia* without a legal representative empowered in the forms of law. Today most digital transactions occur without our being present or represented by a representative of our choice.

The only way today to be "present" in a digital transaction is in the sense that it requires, or is proven by, the presence of a unique personal digital identifier, such as the European eIDAS Qualified Electronic Signature (according to the Regulation 910/2014/EU).[511]

---

[510] THE ECONOMIST, *Automatic voter registration. Left Turn*, THE ECONOMIST *Voter suppression. At risk of losing Texas, Republicans scheme to limit Democratic votes*, demonstrate that in US politics voters' identification has deep implications, both on the fairness of the elections and on the free expression of the constitutional right to actively participate to the political process.
Identity isn't just a means to an end; it is an essential part of our freedom.
[511] European Commission, eIDAS Observatory: Regulation N°910/2014.

I "exist" in a computer domain if three conditions are met:

a) **my "unique identifier"** (IP Address, hash, eID, digital signature, etc.) **is used in that domain** for the allocation of the transactions;

b) such **"unique identifier" is truly (verifiably) related to me**;

c) and it is **under my exclusive control**.[512]

It is telling that the eIDAS Regulation, in chapter II, does not require electronic identification to have a way to meet these same strong conditions! In fact, it assumes that electronic identifications are "issued" by EU member states. So, while a signature is under the sole control of the signer, an identity may be under the sole control of the state. So much for constitutional rights and digital citizenship in the digital environment!

If we want to uphold our inalienable rights in the digital environment and achieve, at the same time, proper technical security, **it is necessary that "digital presence and participation" aren't just a conceptual artifice or a legal fiction**. Presence and participation in the digital dimension are determined by procedures such as a login, creation of an audit trail of interactions, a signature of the trail (or of a document), etc. We have a real digital presence, phenomenologically verifiable, only if the data of the digital presence can be traced back to an information technology system that is truly under our exclusive control and if it is verifiable that our information technology system has actually activated and executed such transactions.

Before the Internet, a legal transaction *in absentia* (i.e., without my attending it in person and without the intervention of my proxyholder) was void, because for it to have an effect on me, I had to recognize and ratify it. Today, it is common practice to enter into agreements remotely, where something (computer, mobile phone, tablet) uses my name, my identity, but I (or rather my digital identity) have never been present in the domain in which the transaction is executed. Normally we can only find some sort of temporary, one-time allocation point for the transaction, indirectly linked to me. My personal identity is stated, but is not phenomenologically present in the transaction.

I still wonder why the fiction of presence through a PC is universally accepted, in the absence of any empirical foundation.

Well, part of the answer is based on the fact that we confuse identity with profile, since we consider our administrative profile to be our only "true" identity. A profile is never with us; it's not even "us". It's a page of a numbered and stamped DIN-A3 paper document, which is a record of a public administration database. Indeed, we have gotten used to thinking that our "true" identity is someone else's creation, and not inherently or ontologically with us - which is precisely the mistake that Manetto made, to his detriment.

At a psychological-sociological level, our mistake of perspective with respect to our identity is understandable, because part of the process of growing up and adapting to society consists of learning to recognize and accept what others think of us and the role that is attributed to us (that we choose) in society. We

---

[512] Such requirements are recognized by the eIDAS Regulation in chapter III, for advanced electronic signatures, Art. 26.

learn, in short, that it is not only what we think and tell others about ourselves that counts, but that we must be able to verify it, enrich it, filter it through the feedback that comes from others, in particular and especially from social institutions (family, school, the military, the workplace, etc.).[513]

Therefore, if the law suggests that our true identity is stored and represented by a common identity document, which becomes part of the social rite of verifying that I am really me ... then it is not surprising if, in the end, identity and personal administrative profile have become synonymous.

The risks are obvious, but we have ignored them, as we live in an open democratic society in which (in the last 30 to 75 years) the fundamental rights of the person have not been called into question. But the Internet is different, and we are seeing a dramatic shift of tone in open and closed networks. Censorship is no longer an evil; indeed, it is apparently the only tool at hand for trying to police social networks. It is an ancient tool, used over the millennia every time there was a need to support a certain account of reality. When Umberto Eco's *The Name of the Rose*[514] came out in 1980, we probably considered the issue archaic and (sort of) primitive; now 40 years later, the exact same issue of avoiding the dissemination of "false knowledge" is at the very centre of our political and constitutional discussion. It seems that we are living in the dark ages of information technology! I must admit: 40 years ago, I would never have imagined that we would be embroiled in the same discussions and that the majority of democratic and pluralistic governments worldwide would embrace the views of Jorge of Burgos (the blind monk), Malachia of Hildesheim and his assistant Berengar of Arundel, the monastery's librarians. Reading the novel 40 years ago, it seemed to me that Jorge, Malachia and Berengar were the epitomes of a dark and parochial view of knowledge. Today they represent (for many, not for me) the most appealing option at hand to deal with trolls and fake news.

Anyone who, before the fall of the Iron Curtain, met with a delegation from Russia or other Eastern European countries knows that the surrender of identity documents by citizens of the communist bloc was an essential part of the mechanics of controlling people. In order to exercise one's rights, physical presence wasn't sufficient; one had also to have proof of the existence of one's administrative profile and proof that the administrative profile really referred to oneself. In short, when the only "true" and acceptable identity is the one over which the state has monopoly control, all the rights we are supposed to possess become purely theoretical, because they are subordinate to the existence of the only acceptable proof that I am myself. The proof of my identity is inherently elusive when the means of identification are the monopolistic preserve of the entity, the state, against which I am supposed to assert my fundamental rights.

---

[513] In the prank played on Manetto, the magistrates of the guild who pretend to see Matteo instead of Manetto play an important role.

[514] ECO, UMBERTO, *The Name of the Rose*, first English translation of *Il nome della rosa*, Collana Letteraria, Bompiani, 1980, ISBN 88-452-0705-6.

This is why, in the digital world and also in any physical legal system, my identity must not be reduced to the existence of my own administrative profile. At the current stage of technological and social evolution, it must finally be recognized that there is only one true identity, and it is precisely the one which is incorporated and genuinely substantiated in my persona. **Any legal fiction of identity** (such as those currently accepted for online transactions) **represents a serious threat to our freedom and to legal certainty**.

There is a fallacy in talking of **"self-sovereign" identity**[515]. It assumes that there is a **"sovereign identity"** managed by the state. I would prefer to speak of a **"national administrative profile"** when discussing the identity managed by the state and of a genuine **"personal identity"** when discussing what today is known as "self-sovereign" identity. This isn't just a question of proper naming conventions for the definition of digital identity. It is about making it evident that, **to assert our constitutional rights, we cannot rely on something that is owned and managed by the very entity against which we may be seeking to assert these rights**. This is akin to having to register at the local police station and get an electronic bracelet before attending a public gathering such as a strike or demonstration. Such a system has never been seen before now, and we may guess what the consequences might have been if such an obligation were enforced (as is now true in the digital environment) prior to the French Revolution or the American War of Independence!

Today we are not free when we are active on open networks and social networks, where identity is attributed to us and managed by others, who also manage the domains themselves, without any possibility for us to influence them. We have even less say than Manetto, who decided in the end to run away from Florence and create a new identity and a new life. For Manetto, escape was easy, at a time when no passport was required, just a letter granting him free passage (signed in Manetto's case by the nobleman Filippo Spano). We cannot escape from the Internet; nor can we escape from the state if it should lose our identity, or if we should somehow lose it ourselves, like Manetto. **In today's digital environment, with electronic monitoring, facial recognition and state-owned identities, we are more controlled and less free than even the slaves of yore.**

According to Roman law, slaves were vocal instruments (*instrumenta vocalia*), lacking not only the capacity to act legally, but also bare of any personal identity, much like servants, who were similarly identified by the estate to which they belonged. Any person who received his identity from the same entity that controlled him was not a free man, according to the law of that time. This is also true today. If, in the digital environment, we don't possess a true digital identity as defined above (true, real and controlled by us), it is impossible for us to be truly free or self-determined, because we cannot enforce our rights. In

---

[515] The best known example of self-sovereign identity is found in the Blockcerts.
"Self-sovereign" is weak and misleading, because it accepts that the state has a legal control on my identity. Which I strongly dispute.

this way, our condition resembles that of serfs, who in theory have the same rights as their masters, but lack any real access to them.

We can conclude that identity over the centuries represented a laborious statement of who we are, achievable only by a minority of privileged individuals. Once our institutions made it possible for everyone to have access to an identity, the concepts of identity and administrative profile overlapped and became confused. But the confusion had no practical consequences, because it was ontologically impossible to identify anyone without their being on the spot.

However, the history of totalitarian regimes at the end of the 19th and in the first half of the 20th centuries have demonstrated that the imposition of a single, state-controlled identity as a prerequisite for access to rights can pave the way to serious forms of repression, even including genocide.[516]

We must therefore conclude that in order to perform its function, identity cannot simply be a profile or a legal fiction. A digital identity must exist as a real fact in an IT-based transaction and must therefore be connected to us in a unique and secure way. The digital identity must also be used personally by us, without any alternatives or fictions that lack a clear legal basis, such as, for example, a power of attorneys.

A proper definition of digital identity as a secure and transparent digital tool under our sole control, technically capable of ensuring our digital presence in an online transaction, **comes with four corollaries:**

1) We must note that, in the world of digital transactions, we currently operate on the basis of a series of fictions and presumptions that expose us to all the risks and legal consequences that derive from having actually participated in such transactions, even if many of the fundamental protections to which we could and should aspire (confidentiality, prohibition of profiling) are denied to us because **we are "*sans papiers*", not represented by a "true" identity but by a presumptive and ephemeral one** - only valid within the domain of the transaction, i.e., generated and self-certified by our transaction's counterpart. These fictions and presumptions need to be reviewed in the light of Roman case law on transactions between *pater familias* and *"propinquos"*[517] or *"famuli"*[518] and in the light of the fundamental rights of a person, which cannot be weakened merely on the basis of established practices in e-commerce.

It is false to say that we have spontaneously renounced our rights. We have been coerced, on pain of being excluded from many legal transactions and social interactions. Blackmail works, as we all know: "*If you want to be part of Instagram, Facebook, Amazon, Apple, etc., you must allow us to collect data on what*

---

[516] The experience of Ethiopia in recent years is significant here. Over the past few decades it has been decided that identity documents should record a person's ethnicity and the tribe to which they belong. This has resulted in identity documents becoming instrumental to interethnic feuds and ethnic cleansing. See Foreign Policy, 15 January 2019, "*Don't let Ethiopia become the next Yugoslavia*"; THE ECONOMIST, *How to save Ethiopia's democratic revolution*.

[517] Relatives in Rome were loosely defined in Latin: *propinquos* (those close by) or *familiars*. Like serfs, they were defined by belonging to a *familia*.

[518] Serfs and slaves of the Roman *familia*, identified and defined by belonging to a *familia*.

you do, so that we can generate a profile that will enable us to recognize you. If you don't agree, you are out." At this point, it has become necessary to claim the right to be identified by our true identity (and not by a surrogate one managed by others) and our right not to say anything about ourselves (just as, in any physical store, we would refuse to be profiled). This same right must be exercised immediately online. The excuse that profiling is necessary to enable proper identification is a fig leaf that no one believes anymore and on which legal reasoning can no longer be based. **Certain identifiers (SEID, IMEI, serial numbers, etc.) and the computer systems via which we operate on networks (smartphones, tablets, PCs)** should be recognized as **legal entities controlled by us,** for the same reason that associations, foundations and companies have been recognized as legal entities - in order to enable transparently regulated mechanisms that can translate human interactions and legitimate related expectations into legal effects.

2) The eIDAS Regulation describes an electronic personal identity (in chapter II) and website authentication (in chapter III) as elements phenomenologically required in a trustworthy digital transaction. Today, however, the practical application of the eIDAS Regulation is influenced by the superficial idea that one's only "true" identity is a profile generated and managed by a registry office and civil status records. It doesn't matter if the identity provider is the government or a private entity; in the end, what is being managed is a profile provided by the government. It is necessary for eIDAS to allow Qualified Trust Service Providers to promote tools for the **self-generation and self-management of identity** (such as **blockchain** or smartphones). These could be called **"freedom devices",** because they would present an image and idea of us to the network that we have chosen freely, rather than a profile that the domain manager has imposed on us as a requirement of entry, exposing us to generalized and total profiling. The law is beginning to move in this direction: In two cases, the US Supreme Court has decided that **smartphones are protected by *habeas corpus*[519],** as if they were part of ourselves. We can only hope that freedom devices will eventually function as our legal digital identities (see chapter 8.6).

3) No data without income[520]: If data collection and digital profiling were allowed only with our consent and only for the purposes we have authorized, we would retain control over such digital data and be able to ensure that

---

[519] United States Supreme Court, ruling in Riley v. US.

[520] A significant number of data protection advocates see data monetisation as being in conflict with privacy as a fundamental human right. Their reasons are clearly presented on the webpage of Verbraucherzentrale Bundesverband (in German). See https://www.vzbv.de/pressemitteilung/meine-daten-gehoeren-dir. The Verbraucherzentrale Bundesverband analysis considers current technologies and the current legal framework. I agree that today the disadvantages of data monetisation are greater than the advantages, without a technically secure qualified electronic identity, supervised as a Qualified Trust Service according to the eIDAS Regulation (see chapter 8.1.4) and without enhanced net neutrality (see chapter 8.3). But I also believe that without achieving the goals set forth in chapters 8.5 and 8.6, personal freedom and data protection are a lost cause.

it is deleted once the permitted use has been exhausted. For decades, cryptographic solutions have existed that can guarantee this, including algorithms from David Chaum[521] and now also blockchain. These solutions have never been viable, not only for lack of a proper business model, but also because the proper legal categories were lacking.

The missing (legal) category is **"no data without income"**. The existence of our personal data on a database, if not specifically authorized, must generate an obligation of remuneration that does not admit evidence to the contrary. As in labour law, if someone regularly serves customers at a restaurant, the law doesn't permit the restaurant owner to argue that the person didn't have an employment contract. Labour law looks at the simple fact that there has been a performance of work to the benefit of an enterprise. Likewise, one should only look at the fact that certain data was collected by a certain business. The data that we generate may be an indirect and unintentional by-product of our activity on open networks. Decades ago, this lack of intentional effort was used to argue that there was no need to pay softball players or black artists who played in jazz clubs. Here too, case law finally determined that it is not the subjective motive that counts, but only the objective use that an enterprise makes of human activity, even when the activity is subjectively recreational. Incredibly, with regard to our activities on open and social digital networks, jurisprudence has regressed about 100 years, aided by the fact that it is not ourselves (or our true digital identities) that produce the data, but a "user" vaguely identified within a third-party domain by a username and password that are only loosely connected to us.

4) Finally, we need a profound **cultural change**: While we would be horrified to discover that a building manager or telecom provider had illegally installed cameras and microphones in our home to record everything in our private lives, we are indifferent when the managers of social media and search engines know even more about us than if they had cameras in our homes. Lawyers tend to rationalize the different criminal and civil treatment of these two situations, restricting our domicile just to the four walls of our home and pretending that our computers and mobile phones are instead in a publicly accessible place. So "planting" cookies or other codes in our computers to simplify our profiling isn't a breach of our domicile, but the legitimate use of a private public space.[522] This is existentially false and serves only to legitimize an invasion of the private sphere. It is not legitimate and should never have been allowed to happen. Cookies and profiling are what they are (exactly how we perceive them): an intolerable interference in our lives and in our personal freedom.

---

[521] Chaum, D., *Security Without Identification*, Chaum, D., 2020. *Untraceable Electronic Mail, Return Addresses, and Digital Pseudonyms.*

[522] Imagine what would happen if the law stated that our homes are private public spaces, open to any intruder. It is no wonder that computer security is still just a distant utopia.

8.2. Digital language. The complexity of digital communication and its consequences

In chapter 8.1 we saw that a proper definition of (digital) identity and a more accurate distinction between our civil rights and data protection issues are two pillars of a just (natural) law in a digital society. The third pillar is a proper understanding of digital signs and the use of human language in a digital society. It will be addressed in this chapter.

Images, sounds, text, icons, voices ... we communicate digitally using a broad set of signs. Most of them are not physical and none of them has a precise location.[523] Even a voice is more like an echo.

Fundamentally, there are many messages and much information that cannot be linked to any particular source or author. This new phenomenon has led to the rise of "memes"[524] and "trending messages".

With respect to human communication and language, one of the most pressing challenges is to design technology in a way that will allow us to differentiate between information generated automatically and information generated intentionally by humans (see chapter 8.2.1). Furthermore, technology should enable us to differentiate between information generated by a known legal entity or physical person, and information generated and broadcasted by an undisclosed or unverifiable originator (see also chapter 8.2.2).

There is no need to be biased against automatically generated content. In some cases, it is more reliable than human-generated content (e.g., weather forecasts or webcam feeds). What is unacceptable and dangerous is that today we cannot know who or what originated the content we are looking at. In the physical world, would we accept not knowing if a shopkeeper is a human or a cyborg, which may be recording all our movements and profiling us? We would be right to complain about such a practice. So we must develop open standards that enable us to tell the difference between recordings and documents, between people and software-generated bots.

We have to work on two **technical aspects of online content** - one related to communicating subjects, and the other related to the communicated information:

1) We need **voluntary and transparent identification and authentication rules** for humans and for servers. In particular, we need to know (if and) how the origin of information has been ascertained[525] (see chapters 8.1.1 and 8.5.1).

---

[523] It is hard to resist wondering what Ludwig Wittgenstein would have said about such an extended semiotics of language. In fact, the distinction between "saying" and "showing" lies at the heart of the *Tractatus philosophicus*. RAY MONK, *Ludwig Wittgenstein: the duty of genius*, 92. In Wittgenstein's time, human language consisted of words and grammar, not links and dynamic content.

[524] "We need a name for the new replicator, a noun that conveys the idea of a unit of cultural transmission, or a unit of imitation. 'Mimeme' comes from a suitable Greek root, but I want a monosyllable that sounds a bit like 'gene'. I hope my classicist friends will forgive me if I abbreviate mimeme to meme. If it is any consolation, it could alternatively be thought of as being related to 'memory', or to the French word même. It should be pronounced to rhyme with 'cream'." DAWKINS, R., *The Selfish Gene*, 11, and 368.

[525] It must be acknowledged that the European Union has regulated these aspects with the eIDAS Regulation, in particular with current articles 6, 7, 8, 9, 10, 11, 12 and 45.

2) We need to know the **technical properties of the information** conveyed to us by the communication protocols (see chapters 8.2.2 and 8.5).

To distinguish memes from documents, we also need **new semiology**:

a) We need new symbols and tools that make it easy for us to know **what kind of entity we are communicating with** (human, server, hybrid, etc.).

b) We need new symbols that make it easy to **know when our communication with others is protected** (how and by whom) and when it is not.

c) We need new symbols and tools that allow us to see **in what capacity we are communicating online** (or under what identity).

d) We need new symbols that clarify whether the **content presented to us is static or dynamic**.

e) We need new symbols that clarify **whether the content presented to us is the same as that presented to everybody else or is assembled according to some profile of us**.

f) We need new symbols that **define the environment in which content is generated and shared** ... and so on.

Under the current situation, we simply don't have such information at all.[526] So some are considering the terrible idea of somehow curbing liberty of expression in order to allow only "truthful", "correct" or "transparent" information and communications.[527]

Information technology must not be used as an excuse to reintroduce the notion that someone or something is entitled to tell us what we can or cannot say or hear. Any limitation of our freedom of speech is a limitation of our inalienable rights, upheld for more than two and a half centuries by most constitutions and in half a dozen international treaties executed by nearly every existing state. Information technology can and must expand on our rights of self-expression and self-determination, not curtail them. This is particularly clear because the arguments used today in favor of digital censorship (such as content management) are exactly the same as those used over the centuries by all censors: i.e., censorship is needed to avoid the spread of fake news!

We currently lack new documental formats specifically designed for digital interactions. Consider the Synoptical Table of Oral Written and Digital Formats (page 212): For several million years, human communication lacked formal language and relied on just body language and sounds. Since humans became capable of speech,[528] we developed a series of formats and rituals to share information orally. Only some of them have an equivalent on paper or in the analogue or digital domains.

If we consider written language, there have been several different formats for writing, which have depended on their use and the technology available.

---

[526] The browser community has declared the issue of Extended Validation moot, because there is no interest on the user side. Well, user had no interest in a facebook or pinterest, also. But eventually they did.

[527] THE ECONOMIST, *Who controls the conversation. How to deal with free speech on social media. It is too important to be determined by a handful of tech executives.*

[528] About a hundred thousand years ago, according to my preferred explanation. See chapters 1.4 and 1.5.

We had the tablet, the inscription, the scroll, the letter. Later formats evolved, and we invented the book (or codex) and the journal. Each format had its preferred use and was thought of as a way to configure the presentation of information.

In the 20th century, globally accepted new formats were created for the presentation of information in new media:

1. Radio produced the radio show.
2. The gramophone and tape recorder led to records and albums.
3. Cinema resulted in movies and theatres.
4. For television, TV shows and sets were developed.
5. VHS, DVD and such led to videotapes and discs.

What are the native formats of digital online communications? The tweet? The post? The blog? The SMS?

In my understanding **there are only a handful of native digital formats today**. Most existing digital formats are based on the simple transposition into digital of things that existed before.

I consider the following to be native digital communication formats:
- peer-to-peer content sharing;
- collective online gaming;
- wiki;
- blockchains;
- social networks.

The email, which is still among the most used digital communication formats, isn't a native digital format, because it a digital transposition the paper-based letter.

The native digital formats currently in use are either extremely generic or too specific. All of them are proprietary or semi-proprietary (except emails, which are based on open standards set by the Internet Engineering Task Force, or IETF).[529] None of the existing native digital formats has the semiotic properties that we listed above ("a" to "f").

For a working hypothesis on the use of native digital formats to share information, see chapters 8.2.2 and 8.5.

In the following chapter 8.2.1 (and its subsections) we will define the digital document and its technical properties, its structural (8.2.1.1) and functional (8.2.2.2) differences from paper documents.

In chapter 8.2.2 we will review the technical (functional and legal) properties of trustworthy digital documents.

Following to the findings of chapters 8.2.1 and 8.2.2 in chapter 8.2.3 we will discuss the evidential value of digitally signed files.

In chapter 8.2.4 we will draw some conclusions about digital documents, what they are, what they should be.

---

[529] The open syntax of the email is currently set by IETF RFC 5322.

ORAL (year)	PAPER/ANALOGIC (year)	DIGITAL (year)
Fight (10.000.000 BC)		
Apprenticeship for tools, fire etc. (3.000.000 BC)		Flight simulator ? (*)
Music – Singing (40.000 -200.000 BC)	CD? ... (*)	CD? (*)
Music – Dancing (40.000 -200.000 BC)	Video Tape ? (*)	DVD Blu Ray ? (*)
Conversation with words (20.000 -200.000 BC)	Telephone (1871 Sound Telegraph)	VOIP (2004)
Tale (40.000 BC)	Radio Show (1920) (*)	Web Streaming (1995) (*) YouTube (2005) (*) Web Streaming (*)
Speech (40.000 BC)	Public Radio Broadcasting (1919)(*)	Web Streaming ? (*)
Feast, Celebration, Public rite (40.000 BC)		
Public games (5000 BC)	TV Broadcast ... (*)	Hackatons? Online Gaming ? (*)
	Tablet (3000BC)	Digital File (1950) portability issues
	Scroll (2400BC)	Digital File (1950) portability issues
Strike, Street protest (1500 BC)		
Council, Assembly, etc. (800 BC)		Videoconferencing ? (*) portable...
	Postal Voting (1872)	Electronic Voting (2001)
	Letter (600 BC)	Email (1960-1970) SMS (1993)
School lesson (600 BC)		VLE (1999) Virtual Learning Environments (*)
	Public Inscriptions (600 BC)	HTML Page (1991) Blog (1995)
Theatre (600 BC)	Cinema (1900) (*) TV Broadcasting (1940) ... (*)	CD (1982) (*) portability issues Blu Ray (2003) ? (*) portability issues MPEG ? YouTube (2005) (*)
	Codex (100 BC)	Digital File (1950) portability issues HTML Page (1991), Blog (1995) eBook (1970) Project Gutemberg
	Book (400 AD)	Digital File (1950) portability issues HTML Page (1991), Blog (1995) eBook (1970) Project Gutemberg
	Printed Book, journals and other printings (Europe 1500 AD; China 100 AD)	Digital File (1950) portability issues HTML Page (1991), Blog (1995) eBook (1970) Project Gutemberg
		Social Media (1995) several proprietary and mostly not-portable formats

SYNOPTICAL TABLE OF ORAL WRITTEN AND DIGITAL FORMATS
(*) Missing the interactivity that is ontologically given in the oral format

In the table above, it becomes evident that digital communication isn't just "the same thing on bits and bytes". In fact, there are forms of human communication (e.g., a dialogue) that simply cannot happen on paper and which began to develop analogue equivalents only with the invention of the telephone. The same is true for public singing and dancing (which lack paper-based equivalents) and for collegial discussions, celebrations, rites, street protests and strikes (all of which lack paper-based equivalents and actually have no real equivalent in the digital environment).

The eIDAS Regulation aims to differentiate open and trustworthy protocols for the exchange of legally, socially and politically relevant information from any other protocol or technology. Its approach is sound. It creates a legal and technical infrastructure to identify some providers of electronic services as trustworthy (because they are supervised by national authorities) and to ensure they use trustworthy open technologies to deal with our digital information and communications.

European legislation addresses some of the consequences of the complexity of digital communication, but it doesn't address all of them.

In particular, legislation cannot reduce the yawning gap between those who master the complexity of digital communication and the rest of humanity. To reduce this gap, humanity needs to use technologies that are open and transparent and requires a globally agreed upon semiology for human-computer interfaces. A new semiology was created for the safety of automotive transportation: The signage system in use today is understood all over the world.

It evolved from the first prototypes designed by the Touring Club Italiano in 1895 (10 years after the first car was built, the Benz Patent Motorwagen). Between 1926 and 1949 the signage system was ultimately standardized and internationalized by several International Road Congresses, which defined the pictorial symbols used in Europe and many other places today. Today we recognize and understand (most of) the traffic signs and lights wherever we go.

The same is needed for the human-computer interface when we travel in cyberspace. When will we have it? Hopefully it won't take another 50 years, like the traffic signage system!

Currently we have mostly proprietary digital signage systems for human interfaces with computers. This is odd: The law considers our computers and smart devices "public spaces", where cookies can be planted and privacy rights are widely restricted; but when it comes to symbols and signage, we are visiting a proprietary space owned by the technology providers.

8.2.1. Digital documents

Is there an ontological difference between our present "live reporting of life" and written history (or journalism) the way it was done in the era of paper publications? If there is such a difference, how can it be defined?

We must assume there is no difference between what inspired Wolfgang Goethe when he wrote his travel diaries and what inspires any blogger, Twitterer or selfie-shooting traveller: It is the desire to document and share our experiences as storytelling (and story-listening) animals. To assume that Goethe was more legitimate because he was well educated and somehow different from the many selfie-wielding travellers is unacceptable:

- first, because freedom of speech is not subject to any limitation related to level of education;

- second, because you rarely know if someone is a madman or a genius, or both, like Vincent van Gogh!

The difference between romantic travel diaries and instant digital broadcasting is not in the intention/quality, but in their structure and function (see also chapter 6.2):

8.2.1.1. Structural differences between paper documents and digital documents:

8.2.1.1.1. Digital documents do not only "*say*", they also "*show*" what is communicated.

8.2.1.1.2. It is difficult to tell the difference between digital documents and recordings, originals and copies.

8.2.1.1.3. Digital documents aren't easily attributed. Paper documents are.

8.2.1.2. Functional differences between paper documents and digital documents.

8.2.1.2.1. The potential audiences that may be reached.

8.2.1.2.2. The speed of interaction between author and audience.

8.2.1.2.3. The complexity of the tools used.

Let's now consider in detail each of these differences in chapters 8.2.1.1 and 8.2.1.2.

Afterwards, in chapter 8.2.2, we will consider how the structural and functional differences between analogue and digital documents impact on legal (chapter 8.2.2.1) and social (chapter 8.2.2.2) documentation. Finally, we will describe the technical properties of trustworthy dynamic legal and social documents (chapter 8.2.2.3) and how to preserve them in the long term (chapter 8.2.2.4). In chapter 8.3, we draw some conclusions on the proper use of digital signatures and their evidential value.

8.2.1.1. Structural differences between paper documents and digital documents

The faulty technical design of digital documents, inscriptions and recordings and our cultural unpreparedness to deal with them have relevant structural and functional consequences.

8.2.1.1.1. Digital documents do not only "say", they also "show" what is communicated

Paper documents are mostly limited to describing their subject, while digital documents can show their subject in a dynamic and multimedia-based manner. Wittgenstein's difference between "saying" (or describing) and "showing" has become blurred in the digital domain. This isn't just a philosophical question; it has practical implications. For example, is a video-recorded real estate transaction digitally signed by the parties equivalent to a written digital document signed by the parties, and thus valid as a proof of sale? What exactly is "written" in digital semiotics? Should we understand it functionally or formally?[530]. This change of meaning of the term "written" is an unavoidable, indirect consequence of ubiquitous computing (see chapter 6.1). But, some confusion aside, it has many useful consequences, because with the semiotic expansion of "written" language, many more people have become able to share their thoughts.

If we found a leaflet on the street saying that there is proof that our prime minister is plotting a coup, we would not immediately consider it trustworthy. But if we read an identical post on Facebook or some other social network, we might react in a totally different manner. In this example, the problem isn't the expansion of the ability to share our thoughts with others; the problem is that we are incapable of distinguishing between a dubiously attributed post and a trustworthy, documented one. Once it is on social media, we tend to perceive it as a sort of peer-reviewed broadcast. This is a terrible and dangerous mistake - but not a reason to curtail our freedom of speech.

8.2.1.1.2. It is difficult to tell the difference between digital documents and recordings, originals and copies. On paper it was not.

Paper documents were mostly real documents and not inscriptions or recordings (as defined in chapter 3.3), and it was easy to tell the difference. Digital

---

[530] Actually, in civil law, signatures are considered part of the form, while in common law, they are seen primarily from a functional perspective. Mason S., *Electronic Signatures in Law*, locc. 3002, 3803.

documents are mostly recordings, but they look exactly the same as documents, and it is very difficult to tell the difference. In theory it's technically possible to distinguish between digital originals and copies, between digital documents and recordings. Still we are not used to do this, because we lack the culture (and sometimes also the technical infrastructure) to do so. This situation perfectly suits the business models of most of today's information technology behemoths.

Thankfully, Europe is moving in the right direction, creating open and transparent technical services and infrastructure (like the Connecting Europe Facility)[531] for recognizing, managing and exchanging some digital documents and data in a trustworthy way.

8.2.1.1.3. Digital documents aren't easily attributed. Paper documents are.

Socially relevant paper documents could (almost) always be safely attributed to one or more authors; socially relevant digital documents are very difficult to attribute. The attribution problem of digital documents and data now has a technical solution, but its wide deployment is progressing rather slowly. Here also, European legislation is rightly encouraging and supporting the exchange of trustworthy and secure documents and data by means of the eIDAS Regulation. But why is progress so slow, if we have the required technologies and the legal framework?

Because we have made two conceptual mistakes.

The **first fallacy** is that there is no real difference between recordings, inscriptions and documents. This misconception stems from the fact that, until 20 years ago, there were only written documents on paper, and almost no inscriptions or recordings. So we are used to considering any information presented to us as a document, even if it is not.

The **second fallacy** is that the meaning of a paper document does not depend on where it was generated or who generated it and bears responsibility for it. A private letter to a friend is a completely different document compared to a court decision, a newspaper or a contract. The same is even more true of digital documents and data. But unsigned digital data is generally difficult to attribute and is used in widely differing contexts.

When we used to read Goethe, there was a publisher who verified that the publication's author was in fact Goethe; there were editors and printers who handled the formal perfection of the content.

At the end of the last century, computers and software were developed to create documents, which were still printed and then used and stored on paper. The attribution problem was still solved by the paper version.

But now digital documents are generated and intended to stay digital. Today, when we see video recordings and photographs posted online, it may be all but impossible to know the author or context of generation, or even to verify that the content hasn't been manipulated. The birth of social networks has allowed hundreds of millions of people to publish unverified content, with

---

[531] https://ec.europa.eu/inea/en/connecting-europe-facility.

the formal perfection of glossy publications, but without any verification of the author's identity or information contained. Nonetheless, after 70 years of TV broadcasting, where only real documents were broadcast, within a well-defined context (e.g., fiction, movies, documentaries, news, political debate) and with easy-to-identify authors, we perceive similar social media broadcasts as "documents". This misperception is dangerous and produces evident damage to the fabric of our society.

There is widespread consensus that social media must evolve and become better at preserving and disseminating trustworthy content, without curtailing our liberty of expression. Not an easy task.

This ambitious goal is attainable with the use of open, verifiable solutions and/or some variety of peer review. The two together should serve as digital equivalents to the ancient roles of publisher, editor and printer.

We are speaking of inventing not only a new service and new business model to spread digital content, but also a new culture, language and ethics of social and political engagement. This may prove to be a challenge. But services that represent steps in the right direction are already appearing online, for example, to address the need to expedite and improve scientific peer review[532].

Look, for some examples, at the following websites:
- http://www.iannotate.com/
- https://www.omicsonline.org/scientific-journals.php
- http://home.frontiersin.org/
- http://episciences.org/
- http://arxiv.org/

Some of these are run by traditional publishers. Others seek to become a viable alternative to for-profit publishing. All of them rely on a trusted, third-party service to publish scientific information. But the traditional process of a publisher vetting all research on the basis of scientific merit has proven too slow, cumbersome and prone to error. Thus, some digital web services (and even leading scientific publications) have reverted to peer review to replace the use of scientific committees, while also publishing online preprints. Most of the scientific advances made in fighting the spread of Covid-19 have been published in preprints[533].

As can be seen, if digital documents can be safely attributed, the problem of publishing erroneous or fake information can be dealt with efficiently, even in an emergency situation, as well as in scientific publications[534].

The eIDAS Regulation addresses the issue of trusted digital services (described as "Electronic Trust Services") in Europe, but is limited in scope to signed documents or services that use signatures and seals or signature/seal certificates. It offers an important starting point, but more may be needed to address the

---

[532] THE ECONOMIST, *Changing nature*; THE ECONOMIST, *How science goes wrong*; THE ECONOMIST, *Trouble at the lab*.

[533] THE ECONOMIST, *Covid-19. Scientific research on the coronavirus is being released in a torrent. Will that change how science is published?*.

[534] The Lancet, editorial, *"COVID-19: a stress test for trust in science"*, vol. 396, issue 10254, 799, September 19, 2020, DOI:https://doi.org/10.1016/S0140-6736(20)31954-1.

issue of trustworthy digital identities and, consequently, trustworthy social media and digital documents without resorting to censorship and other limitations to free speech. The proposed EU legislation on digital services and digital markets[535] is a further step in this direction, but it should be better co-ordinated with GDPR and eIDAS Regulations, Directive (EU) 2015/1535 and Regulation (EU) 2019/1150;

8.2.1.2. Functional differences between paper documents and digital documents

8.2.1.2.1. The potential audience for digital documents: fake news

The insignificant cost of duplicating and sharing digital content makes it accessible virtually to everybody, even the poorest people on earth. Intellectual property rights are currently the most relevant limitation on the dissemination of digital content.

Still, retrievability is a major issue. The only way to overcome this issue is to publish content that somehow "screams" louder than the rest. So screaming, saying outrageous things, publishing controversial opinions, has become the way our present-day "Goethes" seek to be read, seen, found. It is clearly cheaper than what Goethe and the other European literary figures of the 18th century had to do: i.e., go to a printer and pay to print their manuscripts, then go to a bookshop and put their books up for sale, on commission.

The unstructured search for content has put a lot of responsibility (and power) in the hands of providers of online search engines. Their algorithms use our digital trails to present us with what we are likely to be searching for. On the one hand, we have been freed from the restrictions of a librarian's categorisation of subjects; on the other hand, we have almost completely delegated to a third party the choice of what is of interest to us.

This approach will need some rethinking in order to combine freedom of expression, peer-to-peer review of published content and the freedom to decide for ourselves what is of interest to us.

Recent events have sparked discussion on how to curb fake news and hate speech, without curtailing free speech. Everybody seems to take for granted that it is okay to accept as a starting point the implicit censorship of search engines, which "hide" content that is not "loud enough", meanwhile putting forward memes and "trending" content that are intended to create outrage and "intense online interactions". But it is precisely these search algorithms

---

[535] 1) The Digital Services Act, EU Commission COM 825/2020, as of 15 December 2020, defines rules of quality and transparency for information society services, in particular for digital intermediaries, platforms and search engine algorithms (oddly called a "recommender system"), https://eur-lex.europa.eu/legal-content/EN/TXT/PDF/?uri=COM:2020:842:FIN&from=en.
2) The Digital Markets Act, EU Commission COM 842/2020, as of 15 December 2020, defines the obligations of the gatekeepers (such as operating systems, platforms, search engines, content aggregators and social media) and the rules for transparent competition that gatekeepers must comply with, to enable fair competition among themselves and for their users, https://eur-lex.europa.eu/legal-content/EN/TXT/?uri=CELEX:52020PC0825.

that have made fake news, outrageous content and conspiracy theories seem relevant, where they might normally have been seen only by a few dozen readers. Today it is easier to find a paper peddling debunked anti-vax theories than scientific research or statistics that present vetted data on the costs and benefits of vaccination. What we need to deal with is not the consequence of too much freedom of expression or enhanced pluralism. We are confronting the self-serving business logic of algorithms and social networks that seek to keep people highly engaged in their "social" environments, for the purpose of gathering more information and selling more advertising.[536]

It strikes me that our liberal societies are suffering the consequences of the perverse bias of search engines, which use implicit censorship to peddle digital crap and hide more reliable sources of information. Society then asks the same entities that are poisoning liberal democracy to come to the rescue with still more of the same censorship. I am dumbstruck by the fact that pluralistic, democratic governments, instead of addressing the underlying structural problem (i.e., the conflicts of interest of companies running search engines for profit), are turning to those who have created the problem to solve it by means of authoritarian tools such as censorship and exile (i.e., the exclusion individuals from the digital community).

Liberal democracies are thus starting to use tools to police the Internet that until recently have only been wielded by totalitarian states against dissidents. This means that liberal democracies are calling on the same people who have stoked social unrest by promoting fake news and hiding substantiated information ... and putting a gun in their hands to open fire on our freedom if we don't behave properly. I don't think this approach is going to work.

The owners of social networks, browsers and search engines rely on business models that make them agents, entrusted with the economic interests and moral interests of others, without no oversight of how they manage these responsibilities. Lawyers know this is a recipe for disaster[537] and that the law must provide rules and procedures to balance different interests and rights, as has been done with antitrust rules, the governance of public companies and regulations for handling industrial waste and financial instruments.

In my opinion, fake news is not a question of better Internet policing, but the fallout of flawed business models that can be corrected with better technology and better liability and competition rules - of a sort that provide the right incentives for proper handling of the rights and interests of those who rely on social networks, browsers and search engines (see chapter 8.5). The European Union is moving in this direction with the Digital Services and Digital Merket acts.

---

[536] THE ECONOMIST, *Who controls the conversation. How to deal with free speech on social media. It is too important to be determined by a handful of tech executives.*

Very informative two Neflix docudramas that present the thesis of the Centre for Humane Technology: *The great Hack* and *The social dilemma*.

The addiction by design has been anthropologically studied in SCHÜLL DOW N., *Addiction by Design: Machine Gambling in Las Vegas*.

[537] In the form of consumer fraud, stealth pollution, insider trading, over the counter transaction fraud, Ponzi-schemes, and many other kinds of abuses of unregulated positions of arbitrage.

8.2.1.2.2. Speed of interaction using digital documents

Instant content generation and instant sharing have created a challenge-response effect of storytelling. As events are unfolding, their account is simultaneously generated and shared. The narrative shared live is able to change the course of the events themselves, as we have seen in the Arab Spring[538], the Brexit referendum[539] and the "Black Lives Matter" protests[540], along with many other situations such as the storming of the US Capitol. Increasingly the storytelling has become part of the unfolding events. What Paul Verhoeven foresaw in his 1997 *Starship Troopers*,[541] live filming of violent encounters, has become reality, and not only for elite combat troops.

We live in a world where we do not just tell the story of events, but also trigger events in order to tell a story[542].

The problem lies not in the speed of interaction. A slower Internet or a quarantine of news before it is published would not solve the problem, unless there were some global censorship service charged with reviewing the quarantined news.

Instead, we can try to solve the problem through both of the following approaches:

a) changing how information can be found, utilizing better (unbiased) and transparent algorithms that we, the users of search engines, will be entitled to influence via explicit consent and explicit requests;

b) providing tools that link published information to its source and make it clear when published information cannot be traced back to an author (see chapter 8.2.2.2).

8.2.1.2.3. The complexity of the tools used

Digital social media and **digital documents are extremely complex**. Some technical, functional features are necessary in order to make online interactions simple and straightforward for the users, even when they don't know exactly how a social platform functions. Digital documents are almost always embedded in some highly complex process.

Complexity has a conceptual and a technological aspect.

8.2.1.2.3.1. Conceptual (semiotic) complexity

There is inevitable **confusion between digital form, digital formats and digital procedures**. An example may explain what I mean: If I create a written, paper-based document, it is impossible to mix up the process of creation with the document itself. In fact, if someone sees me writing with a pen or a typing machine, he knows he is witnessing the generation of a paper document, and

---

[538] Youtube, Tunisian Election 2011.
[539] THE ECONOMIST, *Britain moves to rein in data-analytics*.
[540] YouTube, George Floyd, "I can't breathe".
[541] IMDb, *Starship Troopers*.
[542] YouTube, *"Trump stands in front of church holding bible after threatening military action against protesters"*.

not looking at the document itself. This clear distinction is missing for digital documents, where it is only sometimes easy to extricate the document from the generation process. When a static file, like a ".txt" file or an image file, is displayed on a computer, we may only rarely be sure of what we are seeing. Normally we don't know if what we see is machine-generated or human-generated content; we don't know if it is an ongoing process or a static image. And there is typically no way for the average on-line user to tell the difference. The efforts of some legislators on all continents to create trustworthy digital documents, based on the electronic signature, has further complicated the matter. In fact, **the format of the documents has become part of their form**, according to the law. For example, if I write a contract today with a pencil on a slip of paper, we have a written document. Used in a legal setting, nobody would dispute that it is a written document. One could merely argue whether its format is suited to the kind of agreement that it represents (like a contract written with lipstick on a mirror).

But if we use an electronic signature on a digital file, according to many commentators, we don't have a "legally binding signature" if it doesn't meet all the following conditions:

- It has a valid certificate.
- It has a valid document format.
- It has a valid signature.
- And for some, it must even have a valid verification of the signature and/or a timestamp and/or long-term preservation of the document and/or signature[543].

This is a flawed way of looking at legal digital documents for two main reasons.

1) It **re-establishes legal formalism**, which is the twin brother of injustice: You may see your rights denied, just because of a technical flaw in a digital document. This is why the *lex mercatoria*, since the Middle Ages, has banned legal formalism, limiting it to very few legal transactions.

2) It **mixes up form, format and process of generation**. If we use digital documents, according to these theories, there are many purely formal reasons (all related to the formal generation process) why a digital document may not be used in a legal trial.

To avoid these dangerous confusions, **we should keep in mind a clear idea of the meaning of digital form, digital format and digital process**.

Digital (or electronic) form is whatever is presented by means of a computer (which includes mobile phones and tablets). A printed book may be presented in digital form, as with Google books or Kindle.

Digital format is a specific technical solution for presenting content: .doc, .txt., .pdf, .jpg, .tiff are all digital formats. In social media and online gaming, the environment of the displayed information also becomes part of the format. There may be closed (or even secret) groups, different gaming environments, etc. The fact that the environment is part of the format is nothing new.[544] This

---

[543] Consiglio Nazionale del Notariato, Studio 1-2017/DI, *Il documento informatico nel tempo*, by Eugenio Stucchi, Michele Manente, Sabrina Chibbaro, 5 December 2017, approved by C.N.N. as of 22-23 February 2018, online at https://www.notariato.it/sites/default/files/1-2017-DI.pdf.

[544] And I prefer not to quote here Ludwig Wittgenstein's *Philosophical Investigations*.

has always been the norm for verbal communications: The same sentence uttered in a pub, in a conference room, at Hyde Park Corner or in a building occupied by squatters, may have completely different meanings.[545] And every capable speaker is fully aware (like his intelligent listeners) of the relevance and the meaning of the context.

Digital formats do a decent job whenever they are a reproduction of some variety of paper-based document. In fact, paper-based documents have always been intended to be understood without needing to be read in any specific environment.

But for interactions that cannot be formalized in documents, this isn't true at all. Digital formats fail miserably in their function.

In real life, if you perform the role of Hamlet on a tramway, it has a completely different meaning from performing it on the stage. Social networks and digital communication are caught somewhere between oral and written communication, and their hybrid nature has some very nasty side effects related to context. Information is disseminated across different contexts: A joke posted in a chat about jokes may be transformed into a statement in another forum; an impersonation may become testimony; a paint-shopped image posted in a forum on photographic postproduction may be presented somewhere else as a fact. No wonder that populism, radicalisation and slander are all spreading irresistibly.[546]

Digital processes are information technology solutions for generating, formatting and presenting digital content. For paper documents, the process of generating a document only very rarely affects the survival or validity of the document. This is an issue for election ballots, legislative processes, marriage licenses and very few other cases. In most cases, the existence of a document that is formally valid overrules any procedural flaws in its generation.

What is happening with digital documents (in particular, digitally signed documents) is that, according to some digital-security pundits, procedural flaws in their generation (or preservation) can have an impact on their legal validity. This would be a terrible mistake. It would catapult us about four centuries into the past, when formal errors could void the validity of an agreement or other legal act. The idea behind legal formalism is that, in a normal status of affairs, we should be able to make a living from our estate, without any need to negotiate contracts. Since the contract represents an extraordinary (and unnecessary) event, it must be constrained within a clear-cut form that defines its identity, meaning and effect. Contracts are thus considered marginal or exceptional in certain ancient societies and economies, e.g.:

- in a hunter-gatherer society, where each hunter keeps his own hunting tools;
- in a slave-based economy, where the ownership of slaves is considered sufficient to make a living;
- and in subsistence farming, as practiced during the Stone Age, the Bronze Age and the Middle Ages.

---

[545] Again, no need to quote Wittgenstein's *Philosophical Investigations*.

[546] THE ECONOMIST, *Who controls the conversation. How to deal with free speech on social media. It is too important to be determined by a handful of tech executives.*

Today we live in a society where only a few wealthy people make a living from their estates. Everybody else has to work. And working implies making contracts and executing them on a daily basis. Legal formalism would bring our society to a grinding halt.

Correctly, article 25 of the eIDAS Regulation on the legal effects of electronic signatures makes the following statement: "An electronic signature shall not be denied legal effect and admissibility as evidence in legal proceedings solely on the grounds that it is in an electronic form or that it does not meet the requirements for qualified electronic signatures".

Hopefully there will be no trade-off between the security of documents and the freedom of their form. What Benjamin Franklin said about freedom is true also for documents: "Those who would give up essential Liberty, to purchase a little temporary Safety, deserve neither Liberty nor Safety".

Digital security isn't a sufficient reason to reintroduce legal formalism. Only in extreme, clearly defined and limited cases may the law invalidate a digital transaction merely because it lacks the proper format (of file, signature or certificate) or wasn't generated according to a given procedure.

Consequently, even where formalism may be of use, its application should be kept to the minimum necessary to ensure that the digital legal document properly fulfils its function. For example, if a digital signature cannot be verified, because the public key does not match the signed hash, the signature must be deemed technically invalid because it isn't linked to the signed document. But if the verification process of the signed hash is positive, flaws in the file format or the signature format or the format of the X509 certificate should not be taken to mean that it is not a signed digital document, even where the law requires the formalism of written and signed documents. And this is precisely what article 25 of the eIDAS Regulation states!

8.2.1.2.3.2. Technical complexity

The most egregious examples of complexity are found in HTML5 pages and all "active, online content" (particularly as used by Facebook and other sophisticated online service providers). We receive the impression of looking at static text and images, but what we are actually seeing is closer to a broadcast (i.e., a personalized stream of text and images) than to a static publication printed on paper. Each viewer sees different posts, despite the appearance of the webpage. This misleading appearance can affect our interpretation of the information that we read, as it suggests the credibility of printed documents. In fact, we are looking at a new form of broadcast, without any editor or publisher, that has more in common with robocalls than to printed texts or radio broadcasts.

Paper documents (and any other analogue inscription, like microfilm) present static "pictures" of letters on a surface, arranged to create words and sentences. The essence of the technical complexity of digital documents lies in the fact that they aren't static impressions of letters or images or sounds; they provide a dynamic environment in which it is possible to rearrange content and interact with it, or even with its authors.

With digitalisation, documents have acquired endless new features that go beyond the simple dissemination of static images of printed letters.

8.2.2. Technical (functional and legal) properties of trustworthy digital documents

What conclusions can we draw from the analysis of the previous chapter (8.2.1 and its subsections)?

8.2.2.1. Legal documents: Legal formalism isn't the solution. Security, impartiality, technological transparency and openness are.

Legal formalism is the wrong way to solve the problem of complexity, because it would deny justice in many cases where the only legal flaw is purely formal in nature (i.e., improper format or procedure).
Legal formalism is creeping up on us. Today, if an electronic signature doesn't have a proper certificate, a proper hash and a proper cryptographic application, and if the signature creation device has not been certified, it may not be considered equivalent (at least in some European member states) to a handwritten signature. This is equivalent to requiring a handwritten signature on paper to be signed with indelible ink, on linen paper, with a pen that has been certified by an evaluation facility. The requirements for digital signatures are meant to protect the parties who rely on them; but the formalism that (according to some pundits) they reintroduce into the legal system will deny legal protection to people whose only fault has been to use the wrong signature creation application.
The right response to the need for legal protections is technological transparency and openness of processes and technologies - not formalism.
There should not be any mandatory formal requirement for an electronic signature or document in order for them to be equivalent to a handwritten signature or printed document. The only requirement should be that it relies on an open technology, whose procedures are verifiable ex post. A digital file signed with a qualified electronic signature offers one of the many possible solutions. A superior solution would be any form of acceptance of the document or transaction, witnessed by a trusted third party, that safely archives in an open and verifiable format the log of the transaction (as with blockchains) and the digital identity of the interacting parties. This solution has already been tested in Roman law (see chapter 3.4.3) and in the law merchant (see chapter 3.4.4). Many other legal procedures for closing and witnessing a legal agreement are possible. Still, legislation in the US, Europe and Asia has focused mainly on the digitally signed file as a tool for providing trustworthy legal documentation.
Luckily, there are companies that have developed innovative services that cover many other ways to validate digital documents and transactions. Sadly, only a few of them are actually using open and transparent technologies, and their business models often overly restrict the access of the relying parties to the legal documentation that has been generated.
The best hope at present is that distributed ledgers will become an open global standard, like HTML or SMIME, and the default solution for providing

trustworthy, long-term digital documentation. ETSI is, in fact, considering blockchains as one of the options for long-term preservation.

Digital legal documents should possess the following technical features:

A) to be based on **open and transparent technology**;

B) to be **accessible** to everybody;

C) to have **transparent rules for their generation** that cannot be manipulated;

D) to be **supported by some sort of social/legal infrastructure that supervises the generation process** in an effective manner, so that any form of manipulation may be detected;

E) **not to be monopolistic or imposed** by the state or by a party; they should be open, in the sense that people may use them or switch to other (better) solutions at their will.

Additionally, a digital legal document for a digital society needs two more features:

F) to be **available, without restrictions**, to the relying parties;

G) to be **fit for long-term preservation**.

Short-term (F) and long-term availability (G) are two essential features for trustworthy digital documents. Unrestricted short-term availability is necessary in order not to curtail the right of legal self-defence of the relying parties. If only one of the relying parties has access to the legal documentation (or to the technical logs of the transaction), this may create (and has in effect created) an unequal situation, where only one party is truly capable of effectively protecting its interests.

Our current designs for digital legal documentation are, to my understanding, much like the designs of cars in 1915, when cars looked a good deal like stagecoaches: Where once there were horses, they installed an engine, and where there was a coachman, they placed the driver.

Hamshaw Rolls Royce 40/50hp Silver Ghost Limousine1915

But cars aren't coaches without horses. And digital documents aren't really paper documents without paper.

Our linguistic and semantic skills will have to improve to suit the increased complexity of digital information and communication. There are layers of hidden complexity that we must learn to master (once they are shown to us) if we are to understand the true significance of digital communications and documents.

As with cars and coaches, **digital documents will have a different use than paper documents**, and **their relevance will depend more on proper design and proper use than on their inherent security**. Digitally signed documents are like the Hamshaw Rolls Royce Silver Ghost limousine of 1915 compared to today's cars: a splendid, elitist beginning, that bears very little resemblance to the real thing. **The real thing in documents will be an open, transparent, impartial and secure process for documenting a legal transaction, with signatures and real documents, as defined in chapter 3.3, as just a small part of the package**.

8.2.2.2. Social digital documents and data: how to make them trustworthy

Social interactions over the centuries have been mostly oral. Since the 16th century, they have also been based on written documents, like religious services or theatre. Dancing and singing are probably the most ancient forms of human oral communication, and there is no analogue or digital equivalent. Thus it is not so easy to fit socially relevant information into the straitjacket of documentation. (Native formats for communication are discussed in chapter 8.2) Socially relevant communication is inherently fluid.

So with respect to socially relevant communication, the cryptographic protection of data can only occasionally be applied (signatures, timestamps, etc.). That is why **trustworthy socially relevant communication depends on the transparency of the data generation process, more than on the cryptographic security of the outcome**. If social networks (or digital documents) aim to influence or organize political or social dynamics (like the social networks of political parties or labour unions), then **proprietary solutions are problematic**, for at least two major reasons:

1) They may create a kind of **technologically induced allegiance** to whoever runs the social network, shifting the political balance of power within the organisation[547].

2) They may be **used to unduly influence the political debate**, as happened during the 2016 Democratic primaries in the US.[548] The partisanship of the chairwoman of the Democratic National Committee was uncovered in emails published by Wikileaks. If these internal communications had been in a proprietary technology, the irregularities may have passed unnoticed.

---

[547] This happened in Italy with the Five Star Movement, or M5S, a popular, anti-establishment, populist political party. One of its key features is the Rousseau platform, an online space designed to enable direct democracy. Named after the 18th century thinker Jean-Jacques Rousseau, it banks on the idea that the traditional state is corrupt and the people's will should be directly polled and executed as a governing force. However, a critical analysis of its procedures could raise questions about the platform's true meaning. It peddles the illusion of autonomous choice and is prone to covert authoritarianism. The platform has become a powerful tool of both preventive and repressive social control. As an anti-modern public sphere, it presents inherent threats to democracy itself. See STOCKMAN C., SCALIA V., *Democracy on the Five Star Movement's Rousseau platform*, 603-617.

[548] MARTIN J., RAPPEPORT A., *Debbie Wasserman Schultz to Resign D.N.C. Post*. THE ECONOMIST, *The Sandernistas' Last Hurrah in Philadelphia*.

Digital documents broadcasted via proprietary platforms (and/or social media) are problematic for the same reasons. But it is possible to make socially relevant information shared on social media trustworthy: i.e., by tracing the generation and publication process.

One fundamental feature of printed publications has always been the role of publishers and editors. We should ask ourselves, do publishers and editors still serve a true social function, or have they become obsolete? Let's consider editors and publishers from a historical perspective. Before there were editors and publishers, there were printers. They were paid by an author to print a work and did not normally participate in the sales proceeds. But because printers were commonplace at a time when censorship was customary practice, they always kept records about the authors who asked them to print something, to report to the police if necessary[549]. Later, with the invention of copyright, printers also became publishers and editors. The business model changed and allowed them to take a share of the profits from the author. In doing so, their social relevance increased, because they didn't just find authors, but also started to select what was worth publishing.

Thus, the main function of editors and publishers, from early on, has been to identify and select the sources of published content, enabling readers to rely on the authenticity and trustworthiness of the works published.

In digital content, this social function of the publisher has somehow been lost. Socially relevant digital networks and media need something to replace the long-established functions of publishers and editors; but, because the cost of publishing information online is close to zero, social networks and search engines publish whatever they get, with almost no control or selection. And it shows!

Printed publications could become authoritative and trusted, because the selection and authentication mechanisms generally worked well. Digital social media needs something equivalent based on a new business model, where they accept also the responsibility of the publisher. Certifying content and authors in a paper-based world spawned a completely different business model than what we see in digital publications. A digital editor faces no risk of unsold stock and no logistical issues. On the contrary, the chances of making a profit are directly related to the quantity of published information. The digital editor has no incentive whatsoever to control the identity of the author or the content of the publications. If a digital editor cannot or will not exercise any control over his or her publications, it becomes necessary to provide the readers with the tools to do it. To enable the readers of socially relevant information to assess its relevance and trustworthiness, published information should have the **same five technical properties** outlined in the previous chapter for legal documents:

A) to be **based on open and transparent technology**;

B) to be **accessible** to everybody;

C) to have **transparent rules for their generation** that cannot be manipulated;

D) to be supported by some sort of **social/legal infrastructure that supervises the generation process** in an effective manner, so that any form of manipulation may be detected;

---

[549] EISENSTEIN E. L., *The Printing Press as an Agent of Change*, 690.

E) **not to be monopolistic or imposed** by the state or by a party; they should also be open in the sense that people may use them or switch to other (better) solutions at their will.

We are not advocating less freedom of self-expression on social media. We are saying that the formats and protocols of social media need to include some precise and recognizable functions.

It is far **more difficult to make socially relevant documents trustworthy** than legal documents because:

a) Legal documents circulate among a limited number of people, so their origin and authenticity are easier to verify.

b) Legal documents are normally static and not dynamic.

c) Their generation process normally involves some form of negotiation, which leaves behind useful information on the generation process.

d) Legal documents are normally archived and preserved in a formalized way.

It is almost impossible for a legally relevant document to come from nowhere, with no apparent author, or for it to be unknown who has approved it. This is exactly what happens with most of the socially relevant digital documents that are exchanged today.

So, for socially relevant digital documents, we need a trust taxonomy, based on three trust factors:

A) **how the author is identified** (or identifies itself)

B) whether the **document is static or dynamic**

C) **how the document is preserved**

If these trust factors are correctly implemented:

A) We will be able to tell who the author is. It may be:

    A.1) self-declared

    A.2) identified by a third party

    A.3) identified by a Qualified Trust Service Provider ("QTSP" as defined in the eIDAS Regulation) or equivalent trusted third party

B) We will know if the published content is:

    B.1) un-editable and unedited, as guaranteed …

        B.1.1) by the author(s) only

            B.1.1.1) self-declared

            B.1.1.2) identified by a third party

            B.1.1.3) identified by a QTSP (or equivalent)

        B.1.2) by any third party

        B.1.3) by a QTSP (or equivalent)

    B.2) modifiable, and in that case, whether the changes are guaranteed by …

        B.2.1) only the author(s)

            B.2.1.1) self-declared

                B.2.1.2) identified by a third party

                B.2.1.3) identified by a QTSP (or equivalent)

            B.2.2) by any third party

            B.2.3) by a QTSP (or equivalent)

These criteria would allow nine types of modifiable digital documents and nine types of un-editable digital documents, with increasing levels of trustworthiness, depending on the criteria used to identify the author and the technical properties of the digital format.

Unmodifiable Publication	Author Identity	Modifiable Publication
TTP		TTP
TP	TTP	TP
S		S
TTP		TTP
TP	TP	TP
S		S
TTP		TTP
TP	S	TP
S		S

S= Self declared
TP = Declared by a nondescript Third Party
TTP = Certified by a Trusted Third Party

Users would not need to understand technology; it would suffice that they understand the difference between self-declared qualities, qualities assessed by nondescript third party, and qualities certified by a (supervised) trusted third party.

Today, virtually all content published on social media and websites belong to the lowest level of trustworthiness. They look like written words, but have the documental consistency of words whispered and repeated in full darkness, in a pitch-black hallway. This may explain the tendency to engage in online flame wars, steeped in outcry and shouting, that exclude any possibility of constructive interaction between people.

After the generation and exchange of socially relevant digital information, it is important that such information does not disappear. So there is a need for one further trust factor:

C) We will **know if the origin and integrity of published content is guaranteed** (and thus how its preservation is guaranteed) …

C.1) only by technical means under the author's control (such as a self-managed webpage, blog or database);

C.2) by technical means under any third party's control (such as hosted archives, like Dropbox.com, or hosted websites);

C.3) by a QTSP (or equivalent) responsible for identifying the origin of data and its integrity.

8.2.2.3. Trustworthy digital dynamic documents

Paper was extremely successful in spreading information and enabling mass education. But education and knowledge require much more than rote learning.

Printed books have expanded the dissemination of information, but have resulted in a passive mindset for learners that any teacher will notice in the majority of their pupils. **Digital text is inherently editable, so one could create trustworthy digital publications where the text can evolve via the contributions of their readers**.

Truly interactive dynamic texts would allow for Socratic and dialectic learning, without losing any trustworthiness or relevance, if properly managed. (See the technical properties of socially relevant digital documents, outlined in the previous chapter).

Digital society needs trustworthy, dynamic environments where ideas can meet and discussion can readily unfold, without being confined to the position of obscure footnotes to the published text.

I have been working on such an environment and have built a prototype, tested with some of my students at the Università Cattolica di Milano in 2017. Textbooks, manuals, newspapers, political blogs and the like, should evolve in order to support full and proper interactions. Authoritative publications will be easily recognisable, because they will be open for discussion and will routinely integrate contributions by readers and even dissenters.

Today's online publications are as unilateral as paper publications, with the exception that readers may comment on them in a social network, as opposed to writing a letter to the editor. This is insufficient and must evolve to meet the needs of a digital society.

As radio and cinema helped totalitarianism in the 20th century, digital broadcasting is helping a new breed of narrow-minded politics that is robbing us of our freedoms and our values. An open, democratic, pluralistic society needs open, democratic, pluralistic digital documents, which incorporate different opinions and inspire debate and the evolution of consensus.

Paper-based knowledge was great for the Middle Ages and two previous millennia. Today we need more sophisticated documents for our highly complex, open, democratic societies. Such documents should be at the same time dynamic and verifiable, as outlined in the previous chapter.

The **digital newspaper** will not simply publish news, but will follow the unfolding of events together with its readers. The New York Times (and other major newspapers) are doing something like this (though still in a unilateral way) when covering relevant social and political events. In our vision, the news should be selected and published by journalists and subsequently shaped, updated and discussed by readers. **The journalists would no longer just be producers of content; their aim would be to steer and coordinate the interaction *within* their publication**. They would guide the discussion around a subject and publish the starting points of a public online interaction, without knowing where or how it might end. Newspapers (and online journals like the Huffington Post) today publish complete stories (updated, as possible). In a truly open digital society, (digital) newspapers will publish the first news and subsequently steer the public discussion on this news while updating the information. Only if digital newspapers accept this challenge will they be able to reclaim their social (and economic) relevance. Just broadcasting some information doesn't meet the bill. The news is a commodity, available for free everywhere online and at any bus or subway station. **I see the journalists of the future like orchestra conductors, more than authors and composers.**

Digital manuals and textbooks today simply publish knowledge to be learned. In a truly digital society, they would be open-ended works, where all readers can go back to update what they have learned, and even contribute to the updating of the publication. Teaching would become a natural and normal evolution of learning as it existed at the time of the School of Athens and the gymnasiums of the ancient classical world.

If we look at the (semantic) potential of **trustworthy dynamic digital documents**, we can fully see how today's digital documentation is failing its mission, at least so far.

Interactive digital communities could work on important endeavours, such as political projects, social projects, community projects, research & development, etc., based on sharing ideas, information and documents - also benefitting from the availability of trustworthy, dynamic digital documents.

The equation that "dynamic" equals "untrustworthy" is not an ontological truth. Proper technological design can achieve both. And **in the last two centuries there have been several trustworthy dynamic documents**: the cadastre, and the civil code, just to name the most famous. Or, at airports and train stations, the departure board!

8.2.2.4. Trustworthy digital documents that cannot be (unilaterally) erased

The current method of long-term preservation of digital information allows for easy deletion of every unwanted record. Yet there are socially relevant documents (laws, public decrees, etc.) that should be undeletable. Open, democratic societies have nothing to hide. So their archives of public information should be protected against undue manipulation. Here we have many technologically sound solutions available (like Merkle trees of hashes and blockchains) that have yet to be used by state and public organisations.

The current way to preserve digital public information is pointless. The archives are at the disposal of those who need to be kept under control by the very existence of such archives. The cases of Hillary Clinton's mail servers and Donald Trump's telephone transcripts are egregious examples of how things shouldn't be managed in an open, democratic society[550]. Yet the social awareness of the deep meaning of these arbitrary actions is still so low that both Clinton and Trump were more or less unscathed by having tampered with evidence and the truth.

A society that has no trustworthy memory of itself is bound to become a dystopic society. If a nation runs extermination camps, carries out genocide or drops the atomic bomb, it must not be allowed to erase the memory of it or of the identities of the actors and their victims. The Germans tried to leave

---

[550] The Economist, *Already indicted.*

undocumented their atrocious war crimes during World War II; many other totalitarian regimes have done the same. All these efforts were unable to delete all the traces, and we have been able to reconstruct (at least partially) the facts of extermination camps, gulags and killing fields.

But digital records are much easier for the system administrator (the state) to delete. If we allow this to happen, our societies will become something like a schizophrenic with bipolar disorder - Dr. Jekyll and Mr. Hyde nations. We have the technologies to avoid this, and we must implement them now!

8.2.3. Legal relevance of digital signatures

As we have seen in chapter 6.2, the WYSIWYS problem has no solution. So whoever digitally signs a document whose process of creation they didn't fully control, doesn't necessarily know what they have signed.

This isn't a new problem for signatures. As we have seen in chapter 3.4.4, in ancient Rome and the Middle Ages, few people were able to read and sign their name. Often the signatures weren't even performed by the contractual parties, and graphology was non-existent. Still, the evidential value of written documents grew from "*notitia*" to "*charta*".

Today a digital signature attached to a digital document provides a strong presumption that it was wilfully signed with full knowledge of its content. But proof to the contrary shall be always admissible, as it is with paper-based legal documents. It is a matter of fact that the great complexity of digital documents significantly affects the ability of the signer to be fully aware of their content, unless they are generated in a controlled environment.

Today in Europe, according to a certain reading of the eIDAS Regulation, it is necessary to meet many technical and formal requirements for a digital signature to be equivalent to a handwritten signature. In the paper world, this would be like requiring proof of what paper and what pen were used for signing. If a formalistic view of electronic signatures prevails (i.e., they exist, or are valid, only if they are technically perfect), there will be no adoption of digitally signed agreements.

The digital signature applied to documents, inscriptions and recordings may have varying evidential value, depending on the context and on the use[551]. In certain cases, a recording may have a stronger evidential value than a document (as in the recording of events); in others, the opposite may be true (as with declarations).

If we look at it without prejudice, we must admit that the formalism of written and signed contracts would never have been established if the relying parties could not verify the identities of their counterparts or the integrity of the document. In fact, the relevance of legal written documents has always depended on the professionalism of their authors and witnesses - scribes and notaries, who personally guaranteed the truthfulness of the documents written and archived by them.

---

[551] Do we have to quote Wittgenstein's *Philosophical Investigations* ?

We should probably learn from the history of paper-based documents and accept that we are now at the beginning of the age of digital documentation. So, as it was at the origin of written documentation, probably **the best way to secure digital documents and transactions are**:

a) to **use them only within a trusted service**, that keeps track of how the agreement was reached;

b) to **rely on professional trusted third parties** (instead of personally handling digital signatures and taking on the risk of formal and procedural mistakes).

The European eIDAS Regulation states that a Qualified Electronic Signature has the same value as a handwritten signature only in the limited sense that the outcomes of the two actions must be considered equivalent in every member state of the European Union. For this to be true, it is necessary:

1) to use a Qualified Signature Creation Device and create a digital signature to which a Qualified Signature Certificate is attached applying it to a digital document;

2) to apply with a pen a handwritten signature to a paper document.

The eIDAS Regulation cannot (and does not) make any statement on the evidential value of the legal documents signed with a Qualified Electronic Signature, because **such evidential value depends on applicable national law**.

Still, the eIDAS Regulation makes some very important statements (particularly for codified civil law systems, like those of France, Germany, Italy and Spain).

Before ubiquitous computing (see chapter 6.1), there were no grey zones between written and oral documentation, with maybe a few exceptions. Now we have an indefinite number of varying shades of documentation that are neither written nor oral nor both together.

The European eIDAS Regulation fully understands this and has left it to jurisprudence to assess if a digital document signed with a Qualified Electronic Signature truly represents the signer's will or if there was an error in declaration or other pathologies that affect the legal validity and effects of the signed document.

The fact is that, **without procedures, technologies, formats and a new semiotics that can master the complexity of digital language** (see chapter 8.2), **the link between our intention and digitally signed documents is weak**. We have a document that is impossible to forge, with an indisputable link to the signer, but its content (without proper generation procedures) is only vaguely linked to the true intentions of the signer.

Therefore, in the coming years, digital signatures will be mostly used by professionals or in formalized environments, such as banking and public administration. If the eIDAS Regulation continues to successfully regulate European trusted third parties who provide electronic trust services, then **possibly the generation of some socially relevant documents will also become a service provided by Qualified Trust Service Providers**.

We have a lot of work to do to master the complexity of digital language. Until that work is done, the digital signature will be an esoteric activity for initiates, as was the written signature in the Middle Ages.

For all these reasons **my forecast is, that the future of legal documentation will be (also) in the recording of a transaction as a fact, not as a wilful declaration of intent**. For this purpose, it will be essential to have...

a) a **trustworthy digital identity** for each and every party involved (i.e. website and clients);

b) a trustworthy **transparent and verifiable procedure** for building the (factual) agreement;

c) free **access for all parties to the recording** of the transaction.

8.2.4. Some conclusions on digital documents - what they are, what they should be

The analysis of chapters 8.2.1, 8.2.2 and 8.2.3 allows us to draw some important conclusions.

Today's **digital documents differ from paper documents** in the following ways:

1. difficult to distinguish from recordings and inscriptions
2. technically opaque, particularly when shared online
3. difficult or impossible to attribute properly to an author
4. inherently dynamic
5. functionally and technically complex
6. impossible to perceive without the use of a computer
7. As a consequence of characteristics 5 and 6 above, a signed digital document may have varying evidential value, depending on the information available about the generation of the document and its signing.

These properties of digital documents are closely linked to the social and legal issues that are being experienced by social networks and other platforms.

Our open free, pluralistic democracies also need another kind of digital document, characterized by the following technical attributes:

A. able to provide trustworthy information on its author, and on how his or her identity was verified

B. able to provide trustworthy information on the document's generation process

C. able to provide trustworthy information on the document's technical properties, in particular whether it is a static or dynamic document.

Finally, we should acknowledge that it isn't factually true that today's online information (blogs, posts, chats, etc.) possesses an author, but not a publisher. Section 230 of the U.S. Telecommunication Act, approved in 1996, predates "social network services",[552] and thus could not have considered them when it stated, "No provider or user of an interactive computer service shall be treated as the publisher or speaker of any information provided by another

---

[552] In Wikipedia, *Social networking system*, we read: *"Early social networking on the World Wide Web began in the form of generalized online communities such as Theglobe.com (1995), Geocities (1994) and Tripod.com (1995). Many of these early communities focused on bringing people together to interact with each other through chat rooms and encouraged users to share personal information and ideas via personal web pages by providing easy-to-use publishing tools and free or inexpensive web space."*

In 1996, Geocities (at the time it was acquired by Yahoo) had about 2 million users; Tripod.com had 6 million users, and Theglobe.com just a fraction of that – nothing on a par with today's online communities.

information content provider." In 1996, there was no ubiquitous computing, and interaction was limited to (largely) closed communities.

The important contributions of publishers are the reason why print publications have become trusted and authoritative over the centuries. Publishers carefully select the authors and content to be published. This important social function has never been considered censorship, even though it had a major influence on what we could read and learn about.

Social media have taught us that publishers still serve an important social function. If we look at the policies of online platforms and search engines, if we read the jurisprudence of the European Court of Justice, or if we assess the obligations of gatekeepers in the EU Digital Service Act, it becomes very clear that some of the obligations placed on gatekeepers are the same as those of a publisher or the owner of a clearing house (or exchange).

We should not consider these essential obligations as exceptions to people's general freedom to do business. Rather, they are the expression of obligations of trust in a business model that no longer treats people as mere objects (digital slaves producing data for digital factories) – but as real people, with their own identities and rights, participating in the online lives of digital communities.

As we have seen in chapter 8.1 and will see again in chapter 8.5, without proper digital identities (for websites, apps and people) that enable us to enforce our rights online, none of these obligations of gatekeepers can become individual rights. This is because they will need some authority (an EU-backed antitrust or privacy agency) to enact and defend them. Normally, the best way to protect fundamental freedoms in the legal system of an open, free and democratic society also involves allowing people to act individually on their own behalf.

We must decide if, for social media, our digital society will opt for the rules of digital publishing or instead for the rules of censorship – controlled by the very same companies that created the problem with their algorithms in the first place.

8.3. Open standards. Enhanced, verifiable net neutrality

Today, the most important part of our social interactions, are carried out on digital platforms, and we need sophisticated tools to participate. These tools complement our ears and eyes in perceiving reality and complement our mouth and hands in communicating with others.

This indisputable fact makes open standards and open technologies a necessity: We must be able to trust the devices that present an account of reality to us - no more or less than if we relied on surgically implanted electronic eyes and ears.

This does not mean that proprietary solutions should be forbidden or discriminated against. But we must find a socially acceptable way to make it evident that we are using technology that is neither open nor transparent. We need to be warned whenever the information presented to us is not verifiable.

At the time when information was circulated via books, newspapers and audio-visual footage from news agencies, such a warning was implicit but self-evident, because it was clear we were consuming a subjective account of reality, presented by a journalist or a board of editors. **Whatever we saw had**

passed through a formal process of assessment; so if it was false or misleading, someone was eventually responsible for it.

But **when we are exposed to "live" footage, directly from a place where an event is happening, sent by someone unknown and unverifiable, we should be warned, we should know**. In fact, the tool most used by fanatics to solicit support online is the broadcasting of unverified (or even manipulated) digital recordings of events that never happened, or didn't happen in the way they are presented to their audience.

The solution to this problem is not censorship. It is to create systems of peer-to-peer vetting of information and technologies that make it clear when the origin of the information has been identified and when not. The digital audience should know when they are being presented with information whose source cannot be verified.

To **prevent our digital society from becoming a dystopic nightmare**, we need open standards for:

1. the **identification of servers and websites**[553], linking them to some existing legal or physical person. This issue has been addressed in Europe by article 45 of the eIDAS Regulation.

2. the **identification of physical persons**, through profiles and/or digital identities. This has been partially addressed in Europe by chapter II of the eIDAS Regulation, but will hopefully be dealt with further in the near future under a new Digital Qualified Trust Service according to the eIDAS Regulation.

3. the **identification and protection of digital data and documents**, as partially addressed in Europe by chapter III of the eIDAS Regulation. What's missing is an open taxonomy that encompasses all kinds of data and documents, like the one proposed in chapter 8.2.2, which would define their evidential value and make it possible to differentiate between registrations, automatically generated content and real documents that have been intentionally created by one or more authors.

4. **a signage system that allows people to know if any security is provided**, what kind of security, and who is responsible for it. Again, in Europe, there is the Digital Trust Mark, provided by article 23 of the eIDAS Regulation, but it is just one trust mark. We will need many more.

5. an **enhanced conformity assessment scheme** for all kinds of trust services, completing the existing ETSI European Norms implementing the eIDAS Regulation[554].

6. a **supervisory scheme that ensures that providers do not cheat on their statements about security and privacy**. Today in Europe, the conformity assessment of providers that create, manage and store electronic signatures and electronic documents is required by article 3.18 of the eIDAS Regulation.

---

[553] ETSI TS 119 495 V1.3.1 (2019-03), Electronic Signatures and Infrastructures (ESI); Sector Specific Requirements; Qualified Certificate Profiles and TSP Policy Requirements under the payment services Directive (EU) 2015/2366.

[554] ETSI EN 319 403-1 V2.3.1 (2020-04), Electronic Signatures and Infrastructures (ESI); Trust Service Provider Conformity Assessment; Part 1: Requirements for conformity assessment bodies assessing Trust Service Providers.

The supervisory schemes are managed by the EU member states. As soon as possible, identification and identity management should also be treated as Qualified Trust Services under the regulation[555].

Nobody should be asked to trust documents generated or preserved on proprietary technology. This is for two reasons:

a) If such a technology were subject to the payment of royalties, then the documents would become unreadable to anyone unable or unwilling to pay the royalties.

b) Even if such a technology were free to all, but proprietary (i.e., with an unknown source code), we could not assess whether the information being presented to us has been tampered with.

It is also obvious that any "document" written in a proprietary format peculiar to a specific company or government is ultimately bound to become unreadable. We saw this happen with the first digital archives and floppy discs; today, they can no longer be used because they were hardwired to specific hardware and software solutions.

The law merchant (*Lex mercatoria*) has spread, and is still spreading, because innovative legal solutions are copyright-free and freely replicable and modifiable. Copyright-free ideas spread more quickly than protected ideas.

The Creative Commons approach to balancing copyright protection and openness is a powerful tool that simultaneously offers openness and accountability. Open standards of this kind are necessary in a digital society to make sure that the metaphorical "digital paper" on which information is presented to us is just as neutral and trustworthy as physical paper.

Net neutrality is the principle that Internet service providers (ISPs) must treat all Internet communications equally, and not discriminate or charge differently based on user, content, website, platform, application, type of equipment, source address, destination address, or method of communication[556].

---

[555] The Digital Services Act, EU Commission COM 825/2020, as of 15 December 2020, puts a series of obligations on the largest "Providers of Core Platform Services", denominated "Gatekeepers". Article 2.2 defines 'Core platform service' as follows:

(a) online intermediation services;

(b) online search engines;

(c) online social networking services;

(d) video-sharing platform services;

(e) number-independent interpersonal communication services;

(f) operating systems;

(g) cloud computing services;

(h) advertising services, including any advertising networks, advertising exchanges and any other advertising intermediation services, provided by a provider of any of the core platform services listed in points (a) to (g).

The six standards mentioned in the text seem to me essential tools for making the compliance to the obligations of the Digital Services Act transparent and verifiable. Without them compliance may be not only costly, but also difficult to assess.

[556] Wikipedia, "Net neutrality" (2020); Tim Wu, "Network Neutrality, Broadband Discrimination", Journal on Telecom and High Tech Law (2003).

Two decades later, we see that net neutrality isn't sufficient. **Enhanced net neutrality** means that the Internet must provide (through open standards and open technologies) immanent technical tools and signage to verifying the origin and integrity of published content. Such technical tools should be easily available. Their use should not be mandated, and there should not be any discrimination against content whose origin and integrity cannot be verified. Such content should be simply labelled as such: "origin unknown", "integrity unknown". The labelling should not result from some sort of censorship or "peer review of the truth" (which somehow makes me think of the Holy Inquisition). It should simply be an automatic consequence of two technical features of the published content:

1) The publishing URL has no Qualified Website Certificate[557].

2) The published content has no Qualified or Advanced Electronic Signature to protect its integrity[558].

Or other equivalent, open transparent, audited solutions. We are advocating here nothing that is particularly new: It is the same approach that has been used by legislators to regulate the production of components for cars, ships and airplanes, for the pharma industry, and consumer goods, and even services like hairdressing. For some reasons the IT services industry was exempted, until now.

8.4. Cultural change: a new approach to freedom in a digital society

8.4.1. Digital ubiquity: being together all over the place, but going nowhere

What is today's equivalent of boarding the Mayflower to begin a new life elsewhere? What options do people now have to escape a social contract they disagree with, when the state has full control over our movements by means of digital and biometric identification tools?

Today we cannot simply disappear and start a new life, as hundreds of millions of emigrants have done over the millennia (see chapter 8.4.1).

People who have been discriminated against, persecuted, ostracized since prehistory have had the option of leaving and starting new lives somewhere else. Information technology makes that all but impossible. Even if we manage to change our country of residence, assume a new identity and, finally, obtain

---

[557] ETSI TS 119 495 V1.3.1 (2019-03), Electronic Signatures and Infrastructures (ESI); Sector Specific Requirements; Qualified Certificate Profiles and TSP Policy Requirements under the payment services Directive (EU) 2015/2366.

[558] The reference here is to several European norms and technical standards that can be found online:

https://ec.europa.eu/digital-single-market/en/trust-services-and-eid

https://www.etsi.org/deliver/etsi_en/319400_319499/31940301/02.03.01_30/en_31940301v020301v.pdf.

new identification papers, then central databases, social security numbers and (last, but not least) the Internet are all there to track us back to what we were. **How do we balance the need to hold people responsible for their actions** (an essential feature of any legal system) **with the right to start a new life** (without having to drag along all the mistakes and issues of their past lives)? Today, technology makes us continuously traceable. To disappear is no longer an option. There are no more remote territories for freedom-seeking people to migrate to (besides the South Pole), as they could until after World War II.[559]

Historian Frederick Jackson Turner,[560] in presenting his Frontier Thesis in 1893, theorized that the frontier triggered a process that transformed Europeans into a new kind of people: the Americans, whose core values were equality, democracy and optimism, as well as individualism, self-reliance and even violence. Turner wrote: "*American democracy was born of no theorist's dream; it was not carried in the Susan Constant to Virginia, nor in the Mayflower to Plymouth. It came out of the American forest, and it gained new strength each time it touched a new frontier*".[561] According to this thesis, the American frontier was a key factor in shaping the American path to liberty; it released Americans from the European mindset, eroding ancient and dysfunctional customs. The frontier had no need for standing armies, established churches, aristocrats or nobles, nor for landed gentry who controlled most of the land and charged heavy rents. Frontier land was free for the taking. Turner's emphasis on the importance of the frontier in shaping American character has been interpreted in thousands of scholarly histories. By the time Turner died in 1932, 60% of the leading history departments in the US were teaching courses on frontier history along Turnerian lines.[562]

Even if we consider Turner's theories outdated because of their ideological content, it is a matter of fact that the frontier not only shaped American culture (as in literature and movies), but still today influences the nation's ongoing constitutional debate (as in the dispute over the right to keep and bear arms). Similarly, the "right" to go away, to rescind the social contract and choose to be oneself, is (at least historically) a major feature of the "Land of the Free".

It was not until 1920 that the first international conference on passports took place. During the mass migrations at the end of the 19th century and the beginning of the 20th, most people had no passport at all. **The normal condition was that, if we were free people, we were also free to move across borders.** Borders were made to keep out armies (and tax collectors) - not immigrants. Information technology is exposing the unnaturalness of these barriers and is helping to soften them.

National borders are necessary to establish the precise geographical extension of the sovereignty of a state, not to keep their citizens in captivity or to keep foreigners out.

---

[559] In 1912 the last US territory became a state. Alaska and Hawaii became states in 1959.

[560] TURNER F. J., *The Frontier in American History*.

[561] TURNER F. J., *The Frontier in American History*, 293.

[562] John Perry Barlow's *Declaration of Independence of the Cyberspace* may also be understood as an example of the influence of frontier thinking on the American mind.

The US is the only OECD nation that has had the same constitution for the past 250 years. It is a democracy that has inspired many other nations and their constitutions. Still, the opportunities to run away from a system whose values and practices we don't share anymore are dying out. Inadvertently we have slipped into a world where the Mayflower and the Susan Constant are no longer possible. The issues with Hispanic and Syrian immigration in the US and Europe point to an increasing and alarming expectation to "keep the others out". If that expectation is universally applied (as increasingly it is), it means that we will no longer be free to go wherever we choose.

What has truly sealed our borders is information technology - the ability to record, store and make data available anywhere - in particular when issuing new passports or verifying them at national borders.

We cannot escape the feeling that the emergency exits (and all other options) have been sealed off. Now that we are locked in, multiple unknown entities can access our digital trails. Next, will we have microchips implanted, instead of passports? The app without which we cannot leave home has become a reality already[563]. **This feeling of being caged is not making us better people; it makes us more intolerant, fearful and exacting**. What if true democracy and freedom are possible only if we are free to go away (at least as long as we are not convicted criminals)? If this assumption (made by many philosophers, starting with John Locke) is accurate, then we may discover that global digitalisation can become a force of evil, curtailing our freedom and caging us in.

At the same time, **global digitalisation has made most people familiar with cultures and opportunities from far away**. Once upon a time, even beyond physical distance, there were cultural barriers that made the idea of emigrating daunting. Today, would-be immigrants are in direct contact with fellow citizens who have already migrated. They have done their homework and even know why countries like Germany and Sweden may offer a better quality of life compared to other European nations.

From a **moral standpoint, barriers to migration are unacceptable**. The industrialized world has benefitted from exploiting its ex-colonies; it cannot now exclude their citizens from participating in the accumulated wealth, without once again becoming colonialists. Even if the policy of exclusion is practiced by a non-colonial state, it is morally arbitrary: It postulates a division of humanity into first-class and second-class humans.

From a **logical point of view, it is a contradiction in terms for an "open" society to be closed**. Digital globalisation has made it evident that the OECD's open societies are not so open after all.

Those who believed that it would be possible for cyberspace to be stateless and lawless were clearly mistaken. Wherever there is human activity (beyond mere subsistence), there is some form of law.

Nonetheless, **information technology is disrupting the traditional idea of state borders** in several ways:

---

[563] THE ECONOMIST, *Creating the coronopticon. Countries are using apps and data networks to keep tabs on the pandemic (and also, in the process, their citizens).*

1. It has **lowered the cultural barriers** faced by those who seek to move to another country.
2. It has **facilitated the planning and execution of emigration**, thanks to the possibility of connecting with friends and relatives already living in the destination country.
3. It has **exposed two hidden functions of national borders**, beyond national security:
a. to **exclude "others"** (foreigners) from the opportunities available within a nation;
b. to **prevent nationals from leaving** with their assets, businesses and savings.
4. **It may shift people's allegiance** away from the general state (and other traditional communities) **to virtual communities**, where the sharing of ideas and values is more intense, continuous and personal; these communities reach beyond political borders and have a stronger allegiance than the state itself, as it became indisputable with the storming of the US Capitol on the 6th of January 2021.

Before digital globalisation, we were largely stuck in the place where we were born for logistical and economic reasons. Now, natural and cultural barriers are no longer daunting enough to prevent people from moving to another place.

Information technology, coming two centuries after the first transatlantic steamers, has dramatically reduced the human cost of moving to another place. It has made it easier to get information on living conditions, find local contacts and organize the migration itself. It has also reduced the cost of traveling.

It is true that the Internet has made the cyberworld borderless. In doing so, it has weakened the arbitrary use of borders that was introduced during World War I, which was subsequently retained in order to restrict people's freedom of movement.

So today, most people (in most countries) can move freely in a borderless cyberworld, but controls on the physical borders of our nations have increased and will go on increasing - mostly thanks to information technology. There is a risk of transforming our liberal, pluralistic societies into walled communities.

Information technology has opened cyberspace and is helping to seal national borders. We can see how beautiful our neighbour's garden is, but it is becoming all but impossible to get to it.

Even if there is no scientific evidence to support the Frontier Thesis, today's mass emigration shows that people are seeking to abandon countries where living conditions are difficult or there is a lack of freedom. When rich nations find ways to make immigration impossible, their citizens lose most, if not all, of their freedom. They are signing a devil's pact, bartering freedom for security.

Digital globalisation has made it apparent that hardware and software incompatibility does not just happen. Technical incompatibilities are the consequence of design and strategic choices. The same is happening with political borders: Digital globalisation makes it evident that legal and political borders exist by design, in order to keep out the "others", particularly the less privileged.

Until recently, few objected to the immigration of wealthy and educated people. This is changing. Not only has it become much more difficult to obtain a green card for the United States, but it has become almost impossible - even in many developing countries.

The philosophical foundations of "Western" democracies[564] should require us to throw open the borders of our nations ... but also the firewalls of the digital world. The time is over when distance and cultural barriers kept people in their place. We have access to all the information we need to choose the best place for us to live. Any impediment is revealed for what it is: an arbitrary barrier to keep the "others" out.

Most developing countries have at one time been European or American colonies. If one tries to look at things from their perspective, it is obvious why many in the developing world are angry. Europe and the US built their industries and "open societies" while exploiting colonies and trading slaves. The agricultural revolution in the United Kingdom was financed with capital accumulated through the colonies. It was not until after World War II that most of the colonial holdings gained independence.

The period of time between 1750 and 1950 is when Europe and the US underwent democratic revolutions (the US in 1776, France in 1789), constitutional revolutions (1848 throughout Europe) and the establishment of universal suffrage (between 1910 and 1950). In 1750, absolute monarchs ruled most of the world. By 1950, in Europe and the US, democracy was the prevailing form of government. Today, most of the former colonial powers don't offer the people of their former colonies the benefit of citizenship and restrict their right to emigrate.

8.4.2. Social networks and the wearing of our social fabric

Digitalisation has provided a place where we can put our most intimate thoughts and feelings (our soul) and share them with our family and closest friends, and even transmit it to our heirs after the end of life. This works fairly well, as long as the communities are small and consist of people who also know each other outside of the virtual community.

Most of the **new possibilities offered by social media** are obvious:
- a **permanent connection** with friends and family;
- a **more informed way to approach friendships and dating**;[565]
- an immense **extension of what and how we can communicate**, using audio, video and links to third-party content.

Some other possibilities are less obvious:
- We are empowered to **influence the impressions that others have of us**. We have become stage directors, conductors and broadcasters of ourselves. A lot of complexity also comes with these advantages.
- We are now **empowered to take a dialectical approach to ourselves**. The Freudian "self" is no longer confined to the subconscious; we now have a place to let it emerge. What has been a privilege of elites (writing, recording, broadcasting) is now accessible to everyone.

---

[564] POPPER K., *The Open Society And Its Enemies*.
[565] THE ECONOMIST, *How the Internet Has Changed Dating*.

But **new challenges** also arise:
1) By putting our inner essence into images and writing, **we subject it to open interpretation and discussion**, even beyond those who know us in person. It is possible that, unexpectedly, that data will be thrown in our faces by someone we allowed to access it.
2) We are increasingly accustomed to **thinking of ourselves as "other" or "external" to the society in which we live**. This misrepresentation of reality, through the human interface of social media, supports the divisive rhetoric about "us" and "them". Social media emphasizes those "like me" aggregating around "me". Their structure and semiotics suggest a series of concentric circles at the centre of which stands myself or another single entity. "Social" is not primarily about "us"; nowhere in social media can you feel or see that "we" make up the society in which we live. The creation of a group named "Italy" or "United States of America" would be completely pointless. So in recent years, we have come to see **society** (as represented in social media) **as a living entity "other" and** (very far) **apart from us**. We are our pictures, our chats, our emails and the communities and groups in which we participate. **Human society and the state appear as just a distant background**, hidden by social media's user interface. The state is not "us" anymore; it is made up of "the others". This extreme, abstract dualism between us and the society in which we live is dangerous for four reasons:
2a) It promotes a false perception of reality, because **we are part of the society in which we live** and actually create it ourselves.
2b) It justifies **taking less responsibility for our fellow citizens** and showing more allegiance to "our" party or group or personal interest; politics everywhere provides numerous examples, ranging from divisive rhetoric to abuse of institutional rules.
2c) The **void** created by the semiotic disaggregation of the society in which we live is promptly **filled by other communities** to which we instinctively pledge our allegiance.
2d) Only a decade ago, the communities that represented our interests included **trade unions, parties and other associations that worked for decades to establish their representativity**. Today we have groups created on social media by unknown people, for unknown reasons, which are very prone to manipulation and misrepresentation, while pretending to represent us.
3) Social networks and similar technologies have empowered us to interact with dozens of other people - perhaps a hundred, at most. **When it comes to hundreds of thousands or millions, the interface of social media doesn't help**. The consequence is that we more readily assimilate with smaller communities with which we are more compatible; we reject (or are rejected by) communities that are less compatible with us; and meanwhile, the greater society has become a faceless abstraction. Thus, individuals are increasingly living in cultural, social and affective silos that isolate them from others with whom they don't share any community or specific interest. I wouldn't assume that this is human nature. It is more likely a consequence of technological design.
4) We still **lack a technology or process that can organize and structure the interactions of hundreds of thousands of people**, without manipulating them.

It took millennia to develop successful approaches to collective participation in political decision-making in large communities where most of the members don't know each other - what we call today the democratic process. A similar such process is urgently needed for digital participation in democracy. In social media, the current model of interaction is the broadcast of ideas from one to many, spreading in concentric circles. The new approaches proposed by political organisations that are now experimenting with digital direct participation in the democratic process unfortunately resemble autocratic, illiberal regimes: Security prevails over freedom, with content filtering and systematic pre-selection of those who are entitled to discuss and vote. This cannot be the right way to keep our society open and democratic.

5) Finally, the generation of digital content has **blurred the line that separates original content from the reuse and reinterpretation of others' content**. As our ideas mesh with the ideas of others, collective visions emerge that are almost impossible to attribute to any specific individual. It is even impossible to tell if the content was generated by software, if it emerged from some search engine's aggregation algorithm, or if it was created intentionally by a person. Most online content is not verifiable. It is nameless, and it is faceless (see chapter 8.2).

The largest social communities are aggregated by Twitter and Facebook, where one user may have tens of millions of followers. If we look at who built the communities on Twitter, their ephemerality becomes obvious.[566] If we analyse the largest fan pages on Facebook, things look exactly the same, just with different rankings.[567]

It is of the utmost importance that different technologies and processes bring the state and greater society back into the foreground of our digital social lives. These **technologies should place the focus on "political" ideas or facts, and not people.**[568]

One possible starting point may be e-learning technologies, which have always been content-centred. If, on the one hand, e-learning is generally a lesser experience than classroom learning, then on the other hand, properly designed processes could nonetheless tear down the physical and other barriers that exclude greater society from classroom learning. A good example of this is found in the experiments made by the Tate Modern in London, where selfies, social media and the activities of visitors in the museum have been used to make the museum experience available to people around the world who have never been there.[569]

---

[566] The Twitter Counter.

[567] http://fanpagelist.com/category/top_users/.

[568] A technology designed and perfected for gossip (such as tabloids or Facebook) may not be ideally suited for disseminating ideas, as should be expected in the democratic process. The impact of "tabloidisation" on democracy has been widely debated. An extended examination can be found here: C. SPARKS, J. TULLOCH, *Tabloid tales: global debates over media standards*, p. 294.

[569] THE ECONOMIST, *Home of the Brave*; THE ECONOMIST, *State of the Art*; HIGGINS C., *How Nicholas Serota's Tate changed Britain*.

Several projects are exploring this direction. Most recently, the Scholas Occur-rentes, a Papal foundation,[570] has sought to broaden the reach of classroom education through technological means, breaking it free from schools and uni-versities. Its theory is that **the natural evolution from being a student is to become a teacher**. By teaching, everyone can feel that they are an essential part of human society and that their knowledge is part of the greater knowl-edge needed to make human society function. A social obligation to work as a teacher for a year could become the information society's equivalent of compulsory military service in pre-industrial society. There was a time when defending its borders and independence were the preeminent tasks of a state. Today, the state has more complex obligations, the most challenging of which is to preserve social order and freedom at the same time. **The state must regain its central position in the social narrative, while enabling the transparent and open participation of its citizens**.

Technologies that enable us to participate digitally in society present com-plex challenges. Such technologies and processes **call for the same character-istics that are required for trustworthy digital documents** (see chapter 8.2.2), **and particularly, for digital dynamic documents** (see chapter 8.2.2.3):

A) to be **based on open and transparent technology**;

B) to be (at least potentially) **accessible to everybody**;

C) to have **transparent rules for attribution**, which cannot be manipulated in order to promote consensus or dissent;

D) to be **supported by appropriate social infrastructure** that supervises it in an effective manner, so that any form of manipulation would be detected;

E) **not to be monopolistic** or imposed by the state or a political party; they should be open in the sense that people can switch to other (better) solutions at will;

F) **to solve the problem of enabling hundreds of thousands of people to interact; a new semiology would likely need to be defined**.

This last characteristic presents the greatest challenge for our new technolo-gies. We have a long way to go before we get there.

To understand the importance of the issues caused by the fragmentation of society, try to imagine how concerned we would be if we could not confirm that all of the children attending school in a region were being taught the same things from the same syllabus. It would be unacceptable. The same would be true if everyone were receiving different versions of the same newspaper, without knowing it.

But we think this is normal and acceptable in social networks. Why? Because they are not ... "real"?

The current state of affairs is so intolerable that we can be tempted to ignore how technologies have weakened the fabric of open, democratic societies. Unrestricted broadcasting of undocumented, unproven accounts of reality (or rumours) is shattering social cohesion and trust, and empowering extremists and populists peddling simple solutions to complex problems. A growing

---

[570] MACI L., "L'hackathon del Papa, il racconto di chi c'è stato".

number of people are more loyal to some party or association to which they belong than to the state of which they are citizens. One of the preconditions for a working democratic society as devised by America's founding fathers (see chapter 5.3) is faltering for technological reasons: **Small, intermediated groups are building stronger allegiances than the greater state**.

This is a technologically induced problem. **We need to redesign our social media technologies. Legislation cannot solve the problem** by imposing bans, rules, restrictions or ultimately some form of censorship. We must be allowed to go on telling our stories and sharing our views, no matter how extreme or unfounded.

The strongest definition of what it is to be human is that we are "the story-telling animal" (see chapter 1.6). But we don't just sing and dance anymore, nor write books and love letters. We have evolved into a googling-tweeting-social-networking animal: Homo digitalis. We no longer just live, but document our lives as they are happening. We don't write in our journals after events have happened; we chronicle events as eyewitnesses. Therefore, the events themselves unfold differently now. There is an "observer effect" from the way we share the making of history. This is different from the passive experience of watching TV.

In the time of the oral tradition, things were not so different: Whole communities gathered to watch plays performed by mostly nonprofessional players. A real-life shepherd might act in the role of a king, and the richest merchant in town might have a minor role in the choir. In that era, **the social function of public displays of theatre, music and poetry was the same as social networks today**. Through storytelling, a common understanding of social values was built and disseminated. In the oral society, communal gatherings also served the function of strengthening the long-term preservation of knowledge, turn it into saga and lore.

Before digitalisation and ubiquitous computing, we began to rely on analogue machines to remember things - scrolls, books, magnetic tapes. These new tools led to the disappearance of communal displays of collective knowledge (and of some level of playfulness). We eventually ceased to gather in squares, courts or churches to share the account of our lives, build libraries ... and started to buy tickets to listen to professional storytellers and musicians. Or we bought books so that we could sit alone with a printed page and read an author that we didn't even know - someone we hoped might tell us who we were, where we were going or what had happened in the past. Seen from this perspective, it is possible to understand why we, as storytelling animals, all but stopped participating actively in public culture and education, even as our lives became richer, more industrialized and more urban. We were not needed by others to participate in the trustworthy recording of collective knowledge. **With the printing press, our own personal knowledge lost its social relevance**.

The 19th and 20th centuries must really have been very lonely times, since so many people had the luxury of sitting alone in front of books (and then radios, movie screens and TV sets) in silence, passively consuming an experience that used to be live, vibrant and emotionally engaging, something to be shared with others, while actively participating in it.

We consider the spread of social media a new phenomenon, but from a millennial perspective, it possibly represents the revival of popular, bottom-up culture, following a relatively short period (500 years) marked by the supremacy of top-down culture, with intellectuals in the role of superstars.

The fact that we have ceased to be passive readers and listeners and that we have resumed a role of active participation in creating a social account of the world should be good news ... but two problems are messing up an evolution that would otherwise be very welcome:

1) **We no longer have an oral mind** (see chapter 3.1). As Walter J. Ong has clearly demonstrated, once people become literate, they lose the oral mind forever. The literate man is focused on interpreting and better understanding what he reads. He is not formulaic or conservative - attitudes that contribute to social cohesion. The literate man is critical and creative. He actively affirms his interests. In the literate society of yore (20 years ago), each human society operated selection processes to determine who was qualified to broadcast via mass media (the press, books, radio, cinema, television). Today, society allows anybody to broadcast, no matter the level of qualification. In principle, the louder you shout, the more attention you get.

2) **Modern technology is better at broadcasting than at fostering true discussion.** A wiki is a powerful tool if the people co-creating the text share the same opinions and methodologies. But the process fails horribly if opinions diverge, as the split between "inclusionists" and "deletionists" within the Wikipedia community has shown. Dissent can't be handled by a technology designed to consolidate all contributions. In fact, to read about the epistemological problems that underlie the Wikipedia project, you need to rely on external sources. The topic is ignored by the "Wikipedia" entry in Wikipedia itself.[571]

Information technology has provided powerful tools to reinvent reality and broadcast new ideas (good and bad alike). But it has not provided the social glue to keep all these virtual accounts of reality together on the same page.

Having too many accounts of our social reality is splitting social cohesion apart. The information society provides tools to broadcast new ideas, but not to keep our social narrative together. The most extreme views, from ISIS to the wildest conspiracy theories, will appear plausible to some. Extreme views are spread very effectively by digital media; they bypass vetting, discussion and evaluation. The broadcasting of ideas was in itself dangerous enough, as 20th century totalitarianism clearly demonstrated. Now that anyone's "crazy uncle" can broadcast anything, we need to develop new technological protocols that can maintain openness while still making it possible to dispute what is broadcast.

For that purpose, we need not only to solve some tricky technological challenges, but also to redefine some semiotic formats that have been carried over unmodified from the era of paper-based documents (see chapter 8.2).

---

[571] THE ECONOMIST, *The battle for Wikipedia's soul*; THE ECONOMIST, *The Wiki Principle*; THE ECONOMIST, *The Free-knowledge Fundamentalist*.

8.4.3. A digital economy, but without digital slaves

The digital economy was first considered as a topic in itself in *The digital economy: Promise and peril in the age of networked intelligence,* a prescient book by Don Tapscott[572].

The term is now in such common use that several governments have published strategies to "support" or "enhance" the digital economy (sometimes also dubbed the "electronic economy" or "digital market").[573] National statistics bureaus take regular steps to measure the digital economy.[574]

I won't devote much time to discussing the boundaries of the digital economy, because they are changing fast. When Tapscott's book was written, Netscape was the only available browser, Google was still half a decade away, average connection speeds were 9600 bits per second (vs. 10.000.000 bits per second today, i.e., a thousand times faster; fiber optics are even 10.000 times faster), and mobile phones were analogue devices (TACS and ETACS in Europe)[575] and not digital. Not until 1995 was GSM, based on an ETSI technical standard (ETSI TS 151 010 Ver. 1)[576] commercially deployed in Europe.[577]

In his new book, *The Digital Economy Anniversary Edition: Rethinking Promise and Peril in the Age of Networked Intelligence,*[578] Tapscott acknowledges that he didn't consider mobile technology, and thus ubiquitous computing, in his 1994 publication, so he has now factored it in.

The focus of my work here is on the semiotic, semantic, social and legal changes that digitalisation is driving, in a quest for universally shared new values and rules for a digital society. So we will not delve into the details of digitalisation's impact on business models and corporate organisations and culture (a field covered by numerous publications).

The future impact of eugenics and artificial intelligence and their moral and legal challenges have been considered in chapters 1.1, 2.1, 8.1.1, 8.1.2 and 8.1.3. It is a vast topic, and we hope we have asked at least some of the relevant questions, with the aim of promoting an open and interactive debate on them.

The central question we want to address is: ***What is the digital economy to us, today?***

---

[572] Tapscott, D., *The digital economy: promise and peril in the age of networked intelligence.*

[573] US Department of Commerce, "*Digital Economy*"; European Commission, "*Shaping the Digital Single Market*".

[574] Mesenbourg T.L., *Measuring the Digital Economy*, the latest statistics published by the US Census are for the year 2014, US Census Bureau, E-Stat 2014 Report; in Europe, statistics and predictions are published by Eurostat: European Commission, *Monitoring the Digital Economy and Society 2016-2021*; and by the OECD, *Measuring the Digital Economy*.

[575] Wikipedia, "*Total access communication system*".

[576] ETSI, "*About us*"; the oldest version of the GSM standard currently available on the ETSI website is Ver. 4.

[577] Wikipedia, "*GSM history*".

[578] Tapscott D., *The Digital Economy*

It seems that many things have undeniably changed for everyone who has access to ubiquitous computing (see chapter 6.1). These represent stark changes from what the economy was less than 20 years ago.

The digital economy today provides us with the following **new features and services**:

- We have **ubiquitous and instant access to information and services**.
- People **consume information as much as they produce it** for commercial or professional use.
- The **purchase of goods is morphing into the purchase of services**.
- The **focus of services is shifting** from providing tools (or partial results) to delivering the final results.
- The **border between employment and freelance** work has been further **blurred**.
- **Serial and repetitive work is increasingly being replaced by IT** services or software, particularly machine learning.

As stated in chapter 8.1.4, today's most important source of wealth, i.e., information, is mostly collected like digital garbage, without any legally binding relationship between the producers of the data and those who horde it and transform it. This is an incredible anomaly, because the most advanced commercial companies in human history are building their business models on a pre-juridical, archaic, de facto relationship that has more in common with slavery than with contemporary contracts.

The social and economic damage caused by considering personal data a free commodity is immense, as we have seen. In the digital economy (as in the so-called "old economy") we will see two eras: before and after the abolition of (digital) slavery. Unless we will experience the abolition of freedom.

In my opinion, **the current digital economy lacks solid foundations** because:

a) It **exploits its main commodity for free**, bereft of any legal relationship between producer and utilizer. We the people are "protected", like subjects in colonies (or Native Americans in the territories), by the same entities that exploit us.

b) The market value and vast profits of several digital behemoths reflect this **unilateral exploitation of data**.

c) It is **hindering other possible business models**, which would remunerate the production of raw personal data and its (truly) authorized utilisation.

d) It **excludes from the profits 99.999999% of the subjects involved** in the generation, transformation and utilisation of such data, keeping them in a lawless area of legal irrelevance.

e) **The current top-down approach** to technology and data utilisation is **incompatible with an open, pluralistic, free society**. So, either these business models will change, or our society will become more autocratic and eventually illiberal, if not totalitarian.

Frankly speaking, we should be mindful that **we are living in the era of the digital hunter-gatherers, under a primitive form of economy**. We must hope that our free, liberal, democratic societies will be able to change the current technological and economic practices, or these savage practices will continue to change our society. And not for the best.

8.4.4. Digital freedom vs. security?

Those who would give up essential Liberty, to purchase a little temporary Safety, deserve neither Liberty nor Safety[579].

Do we have any better options to make open networks secure than tagging all people and machines in order to be able to trace their activities?[580]

Freedom is not a theory; it's a practice: We are free only if we can strive for our own self-fulfilment and if the law provides a favourable environment where everybody can try to achieve happiness.

As expressed by Amit Yoran, president of RSA, a computer and network security company, at the RSA information security conference in 2015 in San Francisco, *"We still live in the dark ages of information technology security, where the enforcement of law in the information society is modelled after the citadel: a small (fire) walled secure environment, with an 'outside world' that is insecure, even dangerous"*. This approach has failed miserably. The barbarians are not just at the gates, they are already inside the citadel, and there is no way we can dislodge them. Curiously, this is not very different from what happened in the 11th century. **The siege mentality is not capable of lasting or succeeding**. In the end, the social nature of humans prevails; a gated life is not what we strive for.

So **information technology security must change radically in order to succeed**; it must become as simple to follow as highway signs. There should be no "inside", with local security policies that are specific to a single network and unknown to the rest of the world (something like the rules of a fiefdom in the Middle Ages), running in tandem with an "outside", where life is crazy, like the world of *Mad Max*. The same rules, agreed upon by the digital community, must be applied globally, so that the lawless space is vastly reduced and data traffic is policed like the vehicle traffic on our streets.

What are the "natural rules" that would have to be accepted by the global digital community in order to nurture the cross-border flow of goods and services? **What lessons can be learnt from the history of the *Lex mercatoria*?** That a (digital) merchant should not base it's policies, business models and technologies on the purpose the become/remain a monopoly, with its exclusive rules. The merchants that created the *Lex mercatoria,* were looking at the greater picture and strived to build a legal system that was useful not only for the entire class of merchants, but also for their customers. They had to replace an economy based on serfdom and absolute power wielded unlaterally.

The biggest IT conglomerates of today (in particular Apple, Facebook, Google, Amazon, Microsoft) aptly named "Gatekeepers" by the EU Digital Services Act, seem only interested in improving their control over their community of customers, in the same way (and sometimes with the same tools) that have

---

[579] FERENSTEIN G., *"How the World Butchered Benjamin Franklin's Quote on Liberty vs. Security"*.

[580] ZUBOFF S., *The Age of Surveillance Capitalism*, loc. 107. NEMITZ P., *Prinzip Mensch: Macht, Freiheit und Demokratie im Zeitalter der künstlichen Intelligenz*, 20.

The blockchain smart (self enforcing) contracts are within this pattern of machine-control on human activity, where machine control is deemed more efficient/reliable than voluntary cooperation and fulfilment.

been used by feudal lords. But they are playing with fire: Their policies have create a new law, that is entirely incompatible with the rules of an open free and democratic society, that doesn't support serfdom. They have the tools to fully control us, because they know much more about us than ever before, including the content of our mail and even our whereabouts. Stalin, Hitler and Mussolini could only dream of having such a wealth of information and controls to wield against their people.

The monopolistic rules of the digital Gatekeepers are damaging the fabric of our society and are even becoming incapable of keep order in their fiefdoms.

So, something needs to change, technologically, legally or both. We must recreate the factual preconditions for freedom that were a given only a half century ago.

On the technical side, privacy advocates with the support of the European Commission have initiated several projects focusing on digital identity, identity management and associated technologies and have recently compiled them into the Attribute-based Credentials for Trust (ABC4Trust) Project.[581]

ABC4Trust believes that digitally signed pieces of personal information or other information used to authenticate or identify a user were not designed to respect the users' privacy in online transactions. Attribute-based credentials allow a holder to reveal just the minimal information required by the application, without giving away full identity information.[582]

The weakness of ABC4Trust lies in the fact that these technologies would disrupt the business of global giants like Google, Facebook and Apple, as well as credit card companies, that monetize the profiling of their users: These corporations are opposing all technologies that would enable more transparency and openness, such as website certificates, digital identities, qualified certificates and so forth, in order to protect their monopolies.

We have learnt in chapter 5.2.1 that the "gated community" was never a satisfactory solution, even in the Middle Ages! Eventually people escaped from the guarded security of the manor and ventured into dangerous and lawless territory, where in the previous 500 years robbers and invaders roamed free. They chose freedom instead of security.

What eventually enabled trade to flourish was not (just) the projection of the military power of the king beyond the gated fiefdoms; it was that the people who ventured forth had a plan and a business model that benefitted not only themselves, but many others as well (see chapter 5.2 and ff.).

The business model of mercantilist expansion, which began in the 11th century, was an alternative to the slave economy. Whoever made use of slave labour was never interested in capital investment or innovation. Slavery was (from a purely economic point of view) the ideal solution to the problem of labour productivity, and was therefore hard to eradicate. The economic and cultural gap between the Confederacy and the Union in the United States speaks volumes on the consequences of slave labour. The animal spirits of entrepreneurs are

---

[581] abc4trust, official website.
[582] abc4trust, official website.

easily dampened if the need to keep the slaves at bay outweighs the attractions of innovating or investing in capital goods.

If we look to the IT economy, it has evolved from a smattering of would-be monopolies (AT&T, IBM, Cisco, Microsoft, Google, Apple) into a scheme to profit from digital slaves (first the credit card companies, then DoubleClick, and now Google and Facebook, imitated by just about everybody else). The acquisition, consolidation and reselling of personal information is an essential element of its chain value.

We don't yet know what the digital equivalent of the American Civil War will be. But surely, such a conflict will be needed to end this undue appropriation of our lives by others. It has started to poison the morality not only of the great IT corporations, but even of sovereign states and of democracy itself.

Slavery is a contagious evil. The US Constitution contained an exclusion clause to preserve slavery in the states where the practice was allowed, and subsequent political wrangling served to maintain a balance between slave-holding and non-slave-holding states.

There is no need for any of us to be constantly traceable online, like inmates in a high-security prison (or like an actual user of Gatekeeper's online platform). There are better ways to combine freedom with security.[583]

We deserve to be treated as free people, not as inmates.

8.5. Digital New Deal: A Natural Law for a Digital Society

The four corollaries of a proper definition of digital identity (see chapter 8.1.4) lead us to the four pillars on which to base a natural law for a digital society.

In the digital environment, **the first precondition** necessary to uphold the fundamental rights that our liberal, pluralistic, democratic constitutions consider inalienable is the use of **open and transparent systems** - i.e., a digital environment with no hidden features and in which everyone is treated in the same way.[584] Let's call it "**enhanced net neutrality**" (see chapter 8.3.3).

The second precondition for upholding our fundamental rights in the digital environment is a **true digital identity** under our sole personal control (as discussed in chapter 8.1). To this end, it would make sense for digital identities to be treated as Qualified Trust Services, under the eIDAS Regulation, rather than as an expression of national sovereignty. Thus they should be moved from section II to section III of the eIDAS Regulation and subject to centralized European supervision, following the principles and rules posited in articles 20 to 24 of the current version of the Regulation.

Identity has been referred to as "the new oil".[585] Personally, I believe that our digital identity is much more important than oil, a mere commodity. We have seen (in particular in chapters 2.5, 2.6 and 8.1.4) that property (the estate) was

---

[583] CHAUM D., *Achieving Electronic Privacy*; CHAUM D., *Security Without Identification*.

[584] WU T., *Network Neutrality, Broadband Discrimination"*.

[585] THE ECONOMIST, *Fuel of the future, Data is giving rise to a new economy*; SZCZEPAŃSKI M., "*Is data the new oil?"*, by the European Parliamentary Research Service (EPRS), January 2020, PE 646.117, *Competition issues in the digital economy*.

used to define the personal identity and extent of freedom granted to an individual. **Property existed long before identity. Today, in the digital environment, the only self-established identities are those of the tech giants that provide us with digital profiles** (not digital identities!) that identify us online, and they are the only legal subjects that enjoy all freedoms online. Meanwhile, we the people can only rely on the profiles provided by them. They are the *"first estates"* of the digital world.

The third precondition for upholding our fundamental rights is provided in Europe by chapter III of the eIDAS Regulation: **trustworthy digital trust services.** Trust services ensure that:

a) Each citizen is entitled to a secure electronic identity.

b) A given set of data was created by a true/given electronic identity.

c) A given set of data is unchanged since its creation.

d) A given set of data can be communicated (or published) in a trustworthy and secure way (see chapter 8.2 and, in particular 8.2.4).

e) When we access a domain, we can identify its owner and who is responsible for it.

The fourth precondition for upholding the fundamental rights is provided in Europe by the General Data Protection Regulation (EU) 2016/679,[586] and it is **the fundamental right to maintain control over our personal data, so that profiling cannot happen without our knowledge and consent** (see chapter 8.2.1). On this topic, it must be said that a technically sound digital identity is a technical prerequisite to enforcing the GDPR in an effective and affordable way. Moreover, it would make it easy to implement the principle of no data without income (see chapter 8.1.4).

These four pillars would provide the supporting structure of a free digital society.

But what does freedom mean in a digital society, and what rules are necessary to make freedom work?

The most likely way to save our freedom in a digital society lies with the establishment of **proper legal principles**, not unlike those that guided the United States' struggle for freedom two and a half centuries ago. Theories of natural law, in particular, theories of the social contract, like those of Hobbes and Locke, inspired James Madison, John Jay and Alexander Hamilton in drafting the US Constitution.

But how can we have "natural rights" in a completely unnatural environment, like the one created by information technology? Does this mean that in the digital world we are caught between a rock and a hard place? That in the digital environment there is nothing left between anarchy and totalitarianism? I don't think so.

There are four possible ways to construe "natural" legal principles for a digital society:

1. We can seek "natural" legal founding principles in the technical features of information technology (see chapter 8.5.1).

---

[586] Euro Lex, General Data Protection Regulation.

2. We can implement the founding principles of our constitutions in information technology (see chapter 8.5.2), something that Lawrence Lessig has strongly advocated in his *Code and other laws of the cyberspace*.

3. We can try to solve the Matrix dilemma (see chapter **8.5.3**), i.e., the antinomy between a world that is more interconnected than ever, but with the most impenetrable borders ever. It is pointless to be free in the digital world when the law makes us traceable at all times and, ultimately, keeps us caged somewhere.[587]

4. We can capitalize on information technology to realize certain political goals toward which all our societies (at least formally) strive: freedom of information, the sanctity of our private lives and the protection of our savings (see chapter 8.5.4).

All this boils down to **13 fundamental "natural" rules** that in my opinion are essential if our digital societies are to remain free, open and just. They are as follows.

8.5.1. Finding "natural" legal founding principles in the technical features of information technology

Significant technical challenges are presented by seeking **to use the parameters of information technology to define some rules or founding principles that would be necessary to allowing online "life, freedom and the pursuit of happiness"**.[588] After all, information technology can be designed in any way we wish. It is bound only by very abstract functional rules, and almost all of them apply to the inner workings of software and hardware, not to any resulting functional design. In a digital environment, you can design immortal entities, borderless environments, objects with no geographical location and many other things not found in nature. Information technology subverts so many natural laws that it may be hard to find any "natural" a priori principles that could inspire digital rules or agreements.

Nonetheless, there are a few promising starting points:

Fundamental digital "natural" rule #1: our identity as a fundamental right. We need a proper technical definition of digital identity.[589] There is one phenomenological point of contact between the physical and the digital world, and that is the concept of identity. In information technology, every resource needs

---

[587] Currently the cage is large enough that most people never experience its borders. But it is changing and becoming smaller.

[588] Wikipedia, *"Life, liberty and the pursuit of happiness"*.

[589] As we have seen in chapter 8.1.3, a (digital) identity has several possible flavours, and is a non-binary concept, depending on whom or what is identified:

a. Human being with all rights
b. Human being under tutelage (minors)
c. Living being under tutelage (slaves, androids)
d. Intelligent (self determining) legal entity with all rights of non living beings (Robots A.I.)
e. Technologic legal entity (websites, computers, smart devices)
f. Legal entity (Companies, Associations, Public Administrations).

an "object identifier" (OID). A proper technical definition of digital identity and a proper legal definition of how it is related to a physical or legal subject are necessary for rights to flow seamlessly between the digital and physical domains. Therefore, we need to define two kinds of identities:

a) The **technical identity of the hosts** (servers, webservers, apps, payment gateways, etc.) and their legal relation to a physical or legal person. The law should ensure that when we interact with a website or an app's IP address, we can easily find out who is responsible for what happens on that URL or IP address. In Europe since 1968, every citizen can access a registrar of companies to see (either for free or for a fee of less than 20 euros) who owns a company and the location of that legal entity.[590]

b) The **technical identities of our personal devices** and their LDAP[591] "clients" (browsers, smart devices, apps, etc.) and their legal relation to a physical or legal person. Such technical identities are the hardware, such as mobile phones, tablets and computers, that define our digital persona. Whatever happens inside their firewalls represents an infringement on our *habeas corpus*. If the law recognized that our digital devices are part of our persona, the digital-slave economy would end swiftly, and anyone seeking to exploit our personal data would be required to ask for our consent. We have seen in chapter 8.1 how these devices have become part of our physical persona. Because they are **"controlled by us", but are not "us"**, the law, in order to avoid creating any legal fiction, would have to stipulate that each of our devices accessing the Internet (or any app or gated community) is a legal entity linked to us through the purchase agreement (or license/lease agreement). Today, these agreements are often verbal, or signed and thrown away, but they would become essential in defining my digital persona and should be executed in digital form and preserved for the long term. A device that protects our identity and is recognised as a legal entity controlled by us is a **"freedom device"**, because it transforms the current legal fiction of me "being there" in a (legal and) phenomenological fact, that is truly verifiable.

The possession/property of freedom devices are even more important than the purchase and lease agreements of our cars (or houses), because they define what we are and where we are in the digital domain. They are the digital birth certificates of our digital persona. We finally will be allowed to (digitally) exist also outside and beyond the archives and files of some public (or private) organisation that controls us.

---

[590] All the European directives on corporate law have now been organized into Directive (EU) 2017/1132 of the European Parliament and of the Council of 14 June 2017 relating to certain aspects of company law. Directive (EU) 2019/1151 of the European Parliament and of the Council of 20 June 2019 amending Directive (EU) 2017/1132 addresses the use of digital tools and processes in company law.

[591] The Internet Engineering Task Force's (IETF) Lightweight Directory Access Protocol (LDAP) describes the protocol elements, along with their semantics and encodings. LDAP provides access to distributed directory services that act in accordance with X.500 data and service models. These protocol elements are based on those described in the X.500 Directory Access Protocol (DAP). https://tools.ietf.org/html/rfc4511#page-4.

Fundamental digital "natural" rule #2: our digital home as a fundamental right.

We need a proper technical definition of my digital home. The relevance of this has been outlined in chapter 8.1.4: Today's legal scholars treat our computers as public open space. In order to avoid making our digital homes a pointless legal fiction, prone to abuse, the law should recognize that the agreements we enter into with telecoms and ISPs define our home addresses, in much the same way as our tenancy agreements. The IP address assigned to us to access the Internet via a physical connection to our home is our digital address (of which we may have more than one). Whatever happens inside the router's firewall on that IP address represents an infringement on our privacy; and if it reaches past our personal devices, it becomes a (criminal) infringement on our personal freedom. The license or lease agreements for our Internet connections and thereto-related firewalls are not simply IT service agreements, but also essential tools that define the perimeters of our digital homes. Such agreements should be executed in digital form and stored for the long term. They serve as our digital residency certificates.

Fundamental digital "natural" rule #3: proper signage.

We need proper signage to distinguish between open and proprietary technological environments and tools. Computers know exactly what kind of code they are running and exactly what domains they are accessing. But because of the lack of proper digital identities, they don't currently know *whose* code they are running and *whose* domain they are accessing. Because there is no clear working definition of where my private space ends and where the public space begins, it is all but impossible to know when we are in a private or public space or whether we are using proprietary or open software. Maybe the computer knows, but we don't. We occupy a digital world that by design lacks road signs or street names and where the borders between public and private spaces are intentionally blurred. There is no publicly available equivalent of Google Maps for the Internet. That kind of information is available only to a handful of companies worldwide. Deploying properly designed digital identities would serve to end this chaos, which only benefits the few companies that can steer us through the digital jungle. What we are asking for here is much less than a traffic code; we are only asking for basic signage on digital roads and digital identities.

Fundamental digital "natural" rule #4: conformity assessment.

Conformity assessment rules for Qualified Trust Services related to our digital identities, signatures, correspondence and archives. Today these are the only relevant legal rules in existence. In Europe, they are provided by the eIDAS Regulation. Digital tools are essential to our lives more than the security of cars, airplanes and homes. Their security and transparency needs to be assessed.

There may be additional "natural laws" for digital systems - such as the technical rules for "trusted computing" - but I believe the most important of these are those closely tied to the origins of natural law: the definition of a "private" space, points of reference for obligations and rights, and the common language that defines subjects and objects of legal relations. In applying the above-mentioned rules to a virtual world, there is a need for trusted third parties to assess the underlying technologies and processes. Such an assessment is possible only on the basis of non-proprietary technological solutions.

Additional relevant rules include a number of fundamental legal principles that enabled the abolition of slave labour and the recognition of our fundamental rights as human beings. They will be addressed in chapter 8.5.2.

8.5.2. Implementing the founding principles of our constitutions[592] in information technology

The second way forward is legally and socially more challenging: **to use information technology to protect (or recreate) the conditions that were essential to the establishment of free and democratic societies**. This approach confronts us with the task of finding a globally shared definition of freedom and inalienable human rights, such as those enshrined in contemporary democratic, pluralistic constitutions and in several international treaties on human rights (see chapter 8.1.4).

We must be mindful that in doing nothing to shape technology in a way that supports our freedoms, we are exposing ourselves to the risk that technology will shape our reality in a way that may be suitable to machines, but not necessarily for human self-fulfilment. Since the publication of Isaac Asimov's *I Robot*,[593] there has been awareness of the need for some a priori rules governing robotics and technology in general,[594] but we have yet to create standards equivalent to "life, freedom and the pursuit of happiness" in a digital world.

What follows are some legal principles that could govern information technology, in order to preserve our fundamental rights in the digital environment.

Fundamental digital "natural" rule #5: digital *habeas corpus*

5. We should **avoid general identification and recording policies and the obligation to be traceable.** These were the policies enacted by Eichmann under National Socialism that led to genocide. Whenever a (corporate) bureaucracy is furnished with such detailed information and vast powers to "keep order", abuse swiftly follows. Sadly, security agencies around the world today advocate precisely this kind of approach. It didn't work in the Middle Ages; it didn't work under Communism. Why would the refusal to recognize digital rights work any better when it is managed by the US National Security Agency ("NSA") or any other national or supranational agency of this kind? The loss of freedom has always led to an expansion of illegal activity because people follow the rules only if they can trust the system in which they live. Technology should ensure that any digital identity is definitely linked to someone, without compelling us to give up any personal information for that purpose.

Fundamental digital "natural" rule #6: digital assault.

---

[592] The close relation between source code and legal codes has been analyzed in depth by Lessig L., *Code and other laws of the cyberspace.*

[593] Asimov I., *I Robot*; Chaum D., *Security without Identification.*

[594] Wikipedia, *"Three Laws of Robotics".*

Our digital trail shall be considered part of our persona (see chapter 8.1.1) and not just as digital garbage, to be collected. Our digital trail isn't simply a data protection issue, it is a matter of integrity of our digital persona, that must be protected against assault.

Fundamental digital "natural" rule #7: digital trespassing

7. The law should not ask people to leave the back doors of their homes unlocked so that the police can pursue criminals wherever it is deemed necessary. If it is true that an important part of freedom is the right of self-defence (at least in a figurative sense) against the abuse of power by the state, then it is contradictory to pass laws that weaken cryptography for the benefit of state agencies (via back doors). In the United States, security agencies are trying to leave people (in particular aliens) digitally transparent and unprotected from the state; at the same time, the US Constitution ensures the right to own and carry arms for self-defence.

This weird approach to national security has created (at least from the American perspective) a two-tier world: In tier A, we have the American citizen, whose privacy and right of self-defence is constitutionally protected (at least in theory). In tier B, the rest of the world can be spied upon and has no right of self-defence on American soil. Even if the world may not be entirely segregated, the American approach to IT security comes dangerously close to it.

Fundamental digital "natural" rule #8: digital participation to the democratic process.

Participation in digital democratic processes (through caucuses, active voting, standing for election, etc.) should have proper technological means to ensure the full protection of citizen's political freedoms and democratic representation. This isn't just a technological challenge that could be overcome using complex cryptographic algorithms, like those of David Chaum.[595] It also requires a redefinition of the digital semiotics of "vote", "ballot" and "elected representative". The truth is that being an elected official doesn't mean one is limited to functioning as the mouthpiece of one's constituency. The instant availability today of opinion polls discourages too many elected representatives from making choices that appear not to be supported by their voters. Technology lets us know at any given moment what people think about some meme,[596] but it has proved itself incapable of promoting free and peaceful political discourse. Social networks never ask the right (political) questions and thus can never arrive at a (politically) viable answer. Search engine algorithms select eye-catching memes, because they are designed to increase our interactive engagement, not to build a constructive discourse.

8.5.3. The Matrix[597] rules

What is the point of being perfectly free in the digital environment, but not free in the physical world?

---

[595] David Chaum, homepage.
[596] DAWKINS, *The Selfish Gene (2nd ed.)*, 11.
[597] Wikipedia, *"Matrix"*.

And what is "free enough"? Just because I am not locked in a pod where I am induced into artificial sleep 24/7, am I free enough just because I am allowed to walk around my home without restrictions? Or do I need to be free to travel about in my city, region or nation? Or is true freedom the liberty to choose where to live (and where not to live)?

This is the "Matrix paradox" - a world where humans are confined in pods and used as energy sources, but are allowed to live a free life virtually.

I think we all agree that it's pointless to be free only in the virtual world. It also seems likely that a "perfectly free" digital world, located in a physical world with no freedom, might look very different from the Internet you would find in a truly free world.

The point that I am trying to make is that there is a correlation between the openness of the Internet and the openness of our societies, as discussed in chapter 8.4.1.

We may believe that open borders are good or bad for our societies. But the fact is that biometrics and information technology are capable of completely sealing off nations from each other. So if we are in favor of closed borders, we need to be aware that they indicate there is no escape for anyone. Technologically, we are already locked inside.

This is fundamentally why I am opposed to closed borders - because I don't want to be an inmate, a prisoner of the state I was born in. I don't want to live in a ghetto, even if it is one of the richest ghettos in the world. No matter how wealthy it may be, I fear that a ghetto inevitably becomes a brutal place[598] to live in. Barbed wire works both ways! http://www.economist.com/news/world-week/21678845-kals-cartoon

If one believes that closed societies are permanently exposed to the risk of becoming like North Korea, then the direct relationship between an open and free Internet and the character of an open society points to two legislative changes that need to be made to preserve our (supposedly) free and open societies.

Fundamental digital "natural" rule #9: the right to digital free movement.

A truly free society must allow its citizens to leave with all their belongings (and renounce citizenship) if they are unhappy with the social contract. The principle of free movement established in article 45 of the EU Treaty should set an example to follow globally. Sadly, today the contrary is true. If an entrepreneur lives in Europe or the US, they are taxed if they sell all their assets, making it all but impossible to leave. If a worker leaves his or her country, normally he or she will lose his or her accrued pension benefits. Thus, after two decades, leaving is no longer an option for a worker or an entrepreneur. Furthermore, Europe[599] and the US have tight restrictions on immigration. In peaceful times,

---

[598] This can be seen in a recent documentary from Italian television, produced with Il Corriere della Sera. The footage of rescue operations is real. In particular the sequence at 1h.24'.30" is upsetting: real people screaming, drowning, dying, in their quest to reach Italy to start a better life. See also YouTube, *La Scelta di Catia "Film Integrale"*. This cannot be just. It cannot be that the law has no solution for this. In looking at such images, I cannot feel that I am in the right and they are breaking the law.

[599] Some interesting data may be found in LUYTEN K., GONZÁLEZ DÍAZ S., CLAROS E., "*Legal migration to the EU*", by the European Parliamentary Research Service, The foremost reason for migration is

a truly free nation should have simple and clear rules for nationals to emigrate and for foreigners to immigrate.[600]

Information technology has been used to seal the exits and the entrances of nations. Instead, it could (and should) be used to allow every freedom-seeking citizen of the world to move freely with his or her assets to any country that presents them with an enticing social contract. Information technology makes it possible not only to transfer money from one country to another, but also to transfer accrued retirement payments.[601] It is odd that it is unlawful to transfer one's social security payments from one country to another. Maybe the law should recognize that our pension savings belong to us and should be treated fairly and reasonably.

Information technology today could enable every person with a social security account (ideally held by a central bank) to view the current value of their payments and the accrued pension entitlements. This was unthinkable only two decades ago. Providing citizens with these tools would probably end the dirtiest trick in today's politics: i.e., promising voters something that won't be paid out until after the current government is no longer in charge. If voters had access to their pension accounts, they could immediately see the impact of such promises on the monthly total of their pension savings and on their forecasted pension payments. Such tools would show citizens that pensions are not a gift, but something for which they work hard and pay dearly.[602]

Whenever we reject people fleeing from war or dictatorship, we ultimately support warmongers and dictators. Whenever we restrict the freedom of others to leave the country where they live, we allow their state to become more authoritarian. Whenever we accept that, due to technology, it has become impossible for any of us to rebuild our lives elsewhere, we have accepted a captive life.

Fundamental digital "natural" rule #10: (digital) citizenship.

If in a digital world it has become all but impossible to keep "others out", we should find ways to make migration sustainable for everybody. **The path for**

---

work (with social security) (1,010.000 of EU first permits), followed by reuniting families (830.000 permits); third is protection from violence or persecution (760.000 permits); fourth is study (535,000 first permits).

[600] The debate about when and how to allow immigration has gone on for centuries. There must be some form of border control, and nations must preserve some degree of social order. This volume will certainly not provide the final word on how to do this. I would nonetheless like to outline some rules that are customary in immigration forms and do not contradict the idea of an open and free society:
- Foreigners must speak the local language.
- Foreigners must not be convicted criminals in their country of origin.
- Foreigners must be able to sustain themselves for a certain period of time.
- Foreigners (who are not rentiers) must find a lawful occupation within a reasonable period of time.

[601] Funds could be moved from one central bank or national/private social security system to another.

[602] Social security contributions in the OECD are about 9% of GDP, https://data.oecd.org/socialexp/pension-spending.htm, and pension spending averages 8% of GDP, https://data.oecd.org/tax/social-security-contributions.htm.

foreigners to citizenship must be straightforward. After a certain number of years living in a country and paying taxes there, in a free society one should enjoy the benefits of becoming a citizen.

Global migrations have shown that violence, hunger and dictatorships have global impacts in the form of increasing the population of refugees and migrants. The boldest move we could make to contain the spread of illiberal and violent regimes, in my opinion, would be to create a **citizen of the world passport,** entitling every holder to move from any country to any other, even if the conditions of the 1951 UNCHR Refugee Convention don't apply. I believe that, if certain conditions are met, everybody should have the right to ask an international organisation (e.g., the United Nations) to issue them a citizen of the world passport, entitling them to free movement across the borders of all countries that are part of the United Nations.

What would the conditions be for issuing such a passport?

At the beginning of this chapter, certain requirements were outlined that are customary in immigration forms. One additional requirement should be that the applicants have a certain amount of savings (including their pension savings).[603]

---

[603] What would be the right amount of savings? Possible answers include: some multiple of per capita PPP GDP in the country of origin; some multiple of the average per capita PPP savings in the country of origin; a combined measure of both. Eventually a top-up could be implemented in cases where a migrant seeks to establish permanent residence in one of the world's wealthiest countries, e.g., a country with more than 200% or 300% of global per capita GDP, which in 2019 nominal figures equals US \$11,428.57, https://data.worldbank.org/indicator/NY.GDP.PCAP. CD, and within a range of US \$16,000 – US \$22,000 PPP, depending on the country, https://www. worldometers.info/gdp/gdp-per-capita/. It should be a challenging sum, but not impossible to achieve for many people in the country of origin. In seeking to choose a number that is selective within reason, I landed somewhere between US \$15,000 and US \$30.000 at current value.

Some of my students have criticized this idea, because it links freedom to wealth. I understand that it appears morally disputable. Yet the idea aims to solve practical legal questions related to two major practical goals:

a) making human rights truly enforceable for every person on earth;

b) allowing migration to be regulated somehow, balancing the social stability of richer nations with the aspirations of people in poorer nations.

Still, I believe that the "**citizen of the world passport**", even when linked to monetary assets, would be a great leap forward for mankind, for the following reasons:

1. The establishment of the legal category of "**free citizen of the world**" would be an **important achievement per se**.

2. The **legal category would be measurable and negotiable** at the United Nations, depending on economic and migratory trends.

3. It can be **linked to the digital identity** (using the blockchain, for example), making the concept of electronic identity something tangible and personal, rather than a legal abstraction.

4. It will **encourage people to save** something for old age, because a certain amount of pension savings would enhance personal freedom, making us truly free citizens of the world and rewarding self-reliance.

5. Paradoxically, the **poorest countries would have a competitive advantage**, because they are young and don't have large pension schemes requiring about 1% of GDP in monthly contributions, as in Europe and the US.

6. It would make it easy to recognize truly free and open societies, beyond any possible dispute. Free countries would be those that allow their citizens to go and free citizens of the world to move

A world citizenship passport offers us the last chance of retaining, in a digital world with digitally sealed borders, an outlet of opportunity that resembles the Mayflower or the Susan Constant - a last chance for an open and free world.

8.5.4. Legal rules for information technology to make it an enabler of human rights

Fundamental digital "natural" rule #11: open trustworthy documents.
Digital documents should be open, trustworthy and dynamic (see chapter 8.2.4). We have discussed this issue in chapters 7.4 and 8.2. In Europe, the eIDAS Regulation provides a large part of the rules that are needed. There is still a need for new semiotics (or signage), for Qualified Trust Services for identity management, and for implementing enhanced net neutrality, as discussed in chapter 8.3. But the browser community isn't supporting anymore Extended Validation[604] and passively accepts that nobody seems interested in freedom and security. As I wrote in chapter 2.5: there was a time when slaves were happy of their condition and didn't see any possible alternative. This book is a call on the digital Gatekeepers, to choose if to be slaveholders or merchants.
Fundamental digital "natural" rule #12: No data without income.
This principle has worked very well in stemming the exploitation of unpaid labour, as we have seen at the end of chapter 8.1.4. Today, no respectable vendor has goods in its inventory of which the origin cannot be traced. The same should apply for any company that catalogues our digital trails. As we have seen, this is only feasible if we have technically sound digital identities (see chapter 8.1.4) and enhanced net neutrality (see chapter 8.3).
Fundamental digital "natural" rule #13: digital protection of my savings.
Today's money is inherently digital. 90% of the existing "cash" is in some form digitalized. This means that my digital identity and my personal savings are ontologically fit to be digitally merged. So let's consider if it my make sense to **"merge" my digital identity and my pension savings:** In chapter 8.1.1 we discussed the importance of a true digital identity and its impact on our freedom. We have also seen that our digital identity should be incorporated into one or more devices (see chapter 8.5.1). We have also seen in chapter 4.3, that the demographic pyramid is capsizing and that no government knows how to keep the promise of a pension for those who are paying into state led pension schemes. Pensions are becoming the greatest Ponzi-scheme of all times, and the political incentive to address the issue is non-existent, because it is clearly a problem for... not this, but the next government! Merging our digital identity with our social security savings would enhance our freedom and protect us from being systematically defrauded of our savings (for illness and old age).[605]

---

in. Nations that don't allow people to leave are despotic. Nations that don't recognize the free citizens of the world would be apartheid nations, where not all humans are born equal.

[604] https://duo.com/decipher/chrome-and-firefox-removing-ev-certificate-indicators.

[605] Still, we should pay a significant fraction of our contributions to the general scheme, that has to provide for the generality and for socially/physically weak. Today my educated guess is that in the OECD the ratio is that about 65% of our lifetime's contributions are devoted to others. In

Information technology, in particular peer-to-peer systems such as the block-chain, make it possible to link monetary values to a cryptographic identity (no hardware needed). If my savings for retirement were protected by a simple smart contract, that makes the money available at retirement age (which I choose myself within a reasonable range), or in case of death makes it available for the benefit of my spouse/partner and offspring, and if all payments that I make were counted and accrued, we would have achieved something that has only recently become possible through technological progress.

If my digital identity could also represent the actual value of my pension savings, we would see some striking positive effects:

1. Any country today that lacks a general entitlement to pension benefits could start one, bringing tangible benefits to its citizens, i.e., the chance to become a free citizen of the world. With the funds being tied to my digital identity, they would be safe, impervious to embezzlement by legislators seeking funds for some petty political project that has nothing to do with my pension.[606]

2. It would teach us that our digital identity has real value, because it is technically linked to our savings and social protections for old age and death; additionally it would serve as the token to make our fundamental rights intangible. Our heirs would inherit not only assets (or debts) but also part of our digital identity, as the foundation of theirs.

3. Pensions would become real entitlements, and not alms.

I know that there is a gap of dozens of trillions between the current system and a digital identity that represents me and my social security savings. All Ponzi-schemes have a common feature: when you try to correct (stabilise) them, they implode, because the fraud becomes apparent.

Fortunately we live in extraordinary times, where social protection schemes have dared something that only one year ago (before the Covid-19 pandemic) would have deemed wrong and impossible. If we don't try now, we will do it when the social security will bankrupt.

A technically trustworthy, transparent and secure digital identity in a digital society, where 90% of the money is electronic, can actually make the impossible

---

Europe the accrued value of a lifetime's contributions is about 600.000 €, that is enough for paying an average pension for no less than 40 years. Almost nobody lives for 40 years after retirement. A pension (and social security) scheme for being just and sustainable, shouldn't re-direct more than 25-30% to others. As it is with taxes. If more than 30% of society is totally depending on others, there would be a sustainability problem.

[606] Paradoxically, the countries with the most generous pension schemes today would have the greatest problem with linking the accrued payments to the digital identities of their citizens; this is because pensions are more or less everywhere run as Ponzi schemes that will fail when there an inversion of the demographic pyramid occurs. See SCHWARZ A.M., *The Inverted Pyramid: Pension Systems Facing Demographic Challenges in Europe and Central Asia*.

See also the analysis of EUROSTAT: https://ec.europa.eu/eurostat/statistics-explained/pdfs cache/1271.pdf. In this case, late starters have a competitive advantage over OECD nations with established pension programs. They can leapfrog the Ponzi scheme pension systems of the 20th century and provide their citizens with true economic protection for old age, with the fringe benefit of becoming free citizens of the world.

become possible. Provided our liberal open societies really are prepared to allow us to be free again.

8.6. I have a dream[607]

Let us not wallow in the valley of despair, I say to you today, my friends.
And so even though we face the difficulties of today and tomorrow, I still have a dream.
It is a dream deeply rooted in everybody's dreams.
I have a dream that one day this world will rise up and live out the true meaning of its creed: "We hold these truths to be self-evident, that all men are created equal".
I have a dream that one day on the Internet, *the sons of former slaves and the sons of former slave owners will be able to sit down together at the table of brotherhood.*
I have a dream that one day even social media, *sweltering with the heat of injustice, sweltering with the heat of oppression, will be transformed into an oasis of freedom and justice.*
I have a dream that my four little children will one day live in a world where they will not be judged by the colour of their skin but by the content of their character.
I have a dream today!
I have a dream that we will all hold a **freedom device**,[608] a trusted tool that protects our identity and our entitlements and open the gates of the world to us, so that we can move freely with our savings.
I have a dream that nobody will be allowed to snoop in my personal life for personal gain, without my consent.
I have a dream that nobody will be able to filter and censor my access to the free flow of data or curtail my freedom to seek knowledge and truth.
I have a dream that nobody will be entitled to build business models, algorithms and policies on fear and exclusion.
I have a dream that our free and liberal societies will base their social fabric on freedom devices made available to everybody, everywhere.
I have a dream that one day our freedom will be founded not on exclusion, but on inclusion.
On that day we will all roam without any restriction on our physical and digital lives, in liberty and in pursuit of happiness.
I have a dream today!

Any contribution to this research is welcome, and each and every contributor will be credited.
Please write to me at rg@digitalnewdeal.eu

---

[607] https://www.youtube.com/watch?v=vP4iY1TtS3s.
[608] A trusted computing smartphone, running on open source operating system, able to connect to global mobile networks that are not subjected to state control, protective of our digital persona and our digital home.

ANNEX I

Fondo Palatino Manoscritto 51.
Wikipedia, Novella del Grasso Legnaiuolo.

Fu in Firenze nel 1410 certi giovani che dubitandosi di pistolenzia per alquanti che di ciò sé 'ammalarano, la qual pistolenzia seguì" l'anno seguente 1411; onde e detti giovani, per fuggire quegli pensieri, si radunavano quasi ogni sera a cena insieme, quando a casa d'uno e quando a casa de l'altro, con facendo insieme molte piacevolezze e giuochi. Infra gli altri v'era uno giovane che avea nome Mariotto, ma non era chiamato né tenuto se non per el Grasso legnaiuolo. Ora costui era semplice persona, ma bonissimo maestro de l'arte sua, e massime di tarsie; e per faccende, ovvero per avarizia, sé'era alquanto tolto da queste cene, e era stato parecchi d" che non v'era suto; onde la brigata ne incominciò a mormorare che 'l Grasso gli aveva cosi" abbandonati, e massime perch'era di bassa condizione a rispetto degli altri. Onde una sera infra l'altre, ragionando infra loro che 'l Grasso non gli degnava, disse uno di loro che aveva nome Filippo di ser Brunellesco: Per la mia fé, se voi volete aiutarmi, io gli farò un giuoco, che gli farò parere [d'essere] uno altro. Risposono tutti essere contenti. Ora costoro rimasano insieme d'accordo di quello volevano fare, come udirete. L'altro d", presso alla sera, Filippo se n'andò alla bottega del Grasso: la quale bottega era in sulla piazza di San Giovanni; e sopra la bottega avea la casa della sua abitazione, quantunque avesse l'entrata seperata dalla sua abitazione; [e 'n] casa era el Grasso e la madre, e non altri. Ora usava la madre del detto Grasso, alcuna volta quando voleva fare bucato, andare a farlo a una loro possessione che si chiamava in Polverosa, appresso alla città, dove avea una acconcia abitazione, oltre a quella del suo lavoratore; e costei in questi d" v'era andata. Ora stando Filippo a vedere lavorare el Grasso, disse Filippo al Grasso: -Vuo' tu darmi stasera cena? Rispose el Grasso: -No, perché mia madre non è nella terra. Disse Filippo: -Dove è? Disse el Grasso: -Egli è più d'un d" ch'ella andò in villa a fare il bucato, ed è dua d" che doveva tornare e non è tornata, di che molto me ne maraviglio. Allora Filippo cominciò a ghignare: -Io non me ne maraviglio già io. Disse il Grasso: -Perché non te ne maravigli tu? Disse Filippo: -Perché no. Allora il Grasso gli entrò sospetto, e disse: -Deh, dimmi perché. Rispose Filippo: -Io non tel voglio dire. Disse el Grasso di nuovo: -Perché non me lo vuo' tu dire? Disse Filippo: -Perché tu ti crucceresti. Disse el Grasso: -Non farò. Disse Filippo: -Se tu mi voi promettere di non ti crucciare, io tel dirò. Rispose el Grasso: -Non farò, per la mia f; [non] mi corruccerò di niente. E in questo parlare Filippo il tenne tanto in tempo, che pensò che le porte della città fussono serrate; poi gli disse: -Fratel mio, tu sai ch'io sono venuto più volte teco in villa e statovi un d" e dua per volta, quando v'è stata monna Giovanna tua madre; e sai che tu hai per vicino el prete, che è giovane fresco e bello, e fatti molte carezze; e ho veduto che fa uno buono occhio a monna Giovanna tua madre, e monna Giovanna a lui; sì che sé'ella vi soprastà, non te ne maravigliare. Allora el Grasso udendo quelle parole, che invero non credo ne fusse niente, perché essendo il prete giovane [ed ella] di circa a anni quaranta sana e fresca donna sanza marito e avendo l'agio e il tempo, nonn'è da credere; ma pure el Grasso ne prese grande maninconia, e disse: -Tu hai fatto male a penare tanto a dirmelo, perché se me lo avessi detto prima che fussono serrate le porte, sarei andato insino in villa e nascostomi in luogo, che quando el prete fusse intrato in casa, gli arei insegnato cantare una nuova messa. Ma io mi leverò domattina dall'aprire della porta e anderonne là, e se vel giungo, el concerò per modo non ne mangerebbono e cani. Disse Filippo: -Non ti dissi io che tu ti crucceresti? Disse el Grasso: -Come diavole! sono queste cose da non si crucciare? Disse Filippo: -Mai no, che non se [ne] vuole crucciare: lascia fare a chi fa -E' par sé" buono a te? disse el Grasso. -Tu mi faresti rinnegare la f, che quello schericato traditore faccia simil cosa a mia madre! E al corpo di Giuda, sé'io vel giungo, il concerò per modo che non ne mangerebbono e cani. Disse allora Filippo: -Tu se' una bestia. Come vuoi tu far male a chi vuol bene a te e alle tue cose? El Grasso disse: -Tu mi faresti dare l'anima al diavolo. Disse Filippo: -El pensiero lascio a te, poiché tu vuoi essere una pecora. Disse el Grasso: -Io non viddi mai il più strano omo di te! Rispose Filippo: -Se tu mi volessi credere, io ti direi il parere mio, che sarebbe il ben tuo; ma poi che tu [non] mi vuoi credere, io non tel voglio dire. -Per certo disse el Grasso -tu mel dirai, e ti prometto di fare quello che mi dirai. Allora Filippo disse: -Poi che tu [ti] vuoi attenere al mio consiglio, io tel dirò. Tu sai che queste sono cose rincrescano, e massime agli uomini che hanno alquanto d'intelletto: el prete è pure astuto, e tua madre invecchierà; fa vista di non vedere, lassagli fare tanto che esca loro gli occhi. El prete n'anderà pure col peggio, credimi: che vuoi tu maggior vendetta? -El Grasso cominciò a soffiare, e andava di su in giù per la bottega senza parlare niente. In questo andare, Filippo, sapea dove stava appiccata la chiave della casa in bottega, tolsela che 'l Grasso non se ne avvide, e poi disse al Grasso: -Serra la bottega, e andiamo alla Nunziata inanzi che sia più notte. E così andarano senza parlare niente l'uno a l'altro; e giunti in chiesa andarano a torre l'acqua benedetta, e come sapete ch'è usanza che ognuno va a 'nginochiarsi chi in uno luogo e chi in un altro, Filippo lasciò andare el Grasso inanzi, e lui diè volta indrieto con uno de' loro compagni, che l'aspettava; e andarono a casa del Grasso, e apersono l'uscio e entrarono dentro, e andarono suso e accesono in sala un gran fuoco, e lasciarano le finestre aperte, acciò che si vedesse il lume su per la piazza di San Giovanni. E avea Filippo lasciato uno delli suoi compagni in sulla detta piazza e dettogli: -Quando tu vedi che 'l Grasso viene, fischia forte, sé" ch'io t'oda. El Grasso poi ch'ebbe dette le sue divozioni a Nostra Donna, si levò ritto e guardò per Filippo, e non vedendo se ne venne verso casa. E quando giunse in sulla piazza, il compagno di Filippo fischiò; e Filippo, intese, cominciò a contraffare monna Giovanna madre del Grasso, e 'l compagno contraffacea il Grasso: e contendendo insieme, il Grasso guardò alle finestre e vidde sì gran lume, e disse in fra sé: -Forse che monna Giovanna sarà tornata, e andò verso l'uscio e sentì contendere che gli parea la madre con uno. Maravigliossi, e trovò che la chiave non v'era, e andò a l'uscio di casa e stava a udire. E quello che contraffacea il Grasso diceva a monna Giovanna: -Che vuol dire che voi siate tanto stata? Ella rispondea: -Ho fatto quello m'è piaciuto. Diceva quello che contraffaceva el Grasso: -Eh, quanto v'è piaciuto! Voi vi doveresti ben vergognare. Ella diceva: -Di che? Lui diceva: -Eh! 'l sapete ben voi. Ella diceva: -Che vuo' tu dire? -Vo' dire che voi faresti il meglio attendere ad altro e tenere altri modi, ché non si dice altro per questa terra se non de' modi che voi tenete in questa maladetta villa. Disse quello che contraffaceva monna Giovanna: -Dio ti dia il male anno e la mala pasqua, ribaldo che tu se'! Diceva quello che contraffaceva il Grasso: -Pure oggi venne da me uno buono cittadino, mio caro amico.... e qui li disse appunto quello che Filippo glie avea detto al Grasso proprio in bottega la sera. Maravigliandosi forte el Grasso diceva in fra sé: -Che diavolo è questo? Quella è monna Giovanna, e quello parla con lei, alle parole pare essere me. Monna Giovanna diceva al Grasso: -Grasso, tu se' impazzato o tu se' imbriaco, alle parole che tu di'. El Grasso non si arrischiava di picchiare l'uscio, e pure infine picchiò forte. Quello che contraffaceva el Grasso disse: -Chi è laggiù? Rispose el Grasso: -Sono io. Disse quel di dentro: -Che vuo' tu? Rispose el Grasso: -Apri. Disse colui: -Matteo, vatti con Dio per istasera, ch' i' ho altro che fare. Disse el Grasso: -Io sono il Grasso e non Matteo. Disse colui: -Qual Grasso? Rispose el Grasso: -El padrone di questa casa. Allora disse quel d'entro: -Tu mi darai ad intendere ch'io sia Calandrino, a dire che tu se' me. Io ti dico: Matteo, se tu hai troppo beuto, vattene a casa e dormi e non mi dar più affanno, ch'io ne [ho] troppo. Allora el Grasso picchiava, e stava come smarrito. E quello di dentro disse: -Per la mie f, se tu picchi più, io torrò uno bastone e verrò giù e darotti tante bastonate, che tutto ti romperò. E non restando el Grasso di picchiare, quello di dentro tolse un bastone e corse giù per la scala e aperse l'uscio; e 'l Grasso, ch'era vile, fuggì in sulla piazza, e vide colui che ha il suo cuoio indosso e la sua cappellina in capo, e sta come smarrito. Quello d'entro diceva: -Vien qua, poltrone! In quello passò dall'uscio quello che aveva fischiato, e disse a quello ch'era in su l'uscio: -Buona sera, Grasso: che romore è questo? Disse colui: -Egli è un pazzo d'un Matteo che mi picchia l'uscio e dice che vuol venire in casa a mio dispetto. Disse colui: -E' debba essere imbriaco. Grasso mio, vattene e lascialo ire in mala ora. Allora serrò l'uscio, e 'l Grasso che avea udito ogni cosa, [stava come] insensato e non sapea che si fare. In questo passò Piero Pecori, uno de' loro compagni, e il Grasso se gli f incontro e disse: -Chi sono io? -Disse Piero: -Se' una bestia; e andò via. In quello venne un altro lor compagno che avea nome ser Iacopo Mangiatroia: il Grasso se gli f incontro, e ser Iacopo disse: -Buona sera, Matteo. El Grasso rispose: -Che Matteo? Io sono el Grasso. Disse ser Iacopo: -Che Grasso? Io ti conosco che tu se' Matteo; e andò all'uscio della casa e chiamò forte: -O Grasso! El Grasso di dentro rispose: -Messere. -Apri l'uscio. Colui gli aperse, e ser Iacopo andò su. Ser Iacopo diceva: -Grasso, tu se' una bestia; tu ti fai sentire per tutta la piazza! E monna Giovanna diceva, e 'l Grasso rispondea. El Grasso stava in sulla piazza e udiva ogni cosa, e era mezzo morto. In questo venne uno messo degli ufiziali della Mercatantia con parecchi birretti. Innanzi venne uno giovane del fondaco degli Alessandri, e presono il Grasso e dissono: -Matteo, vien con noi. Disse el Grasso: -Io non sono Matteo, anzi sono il Grasso. Disse quel giovane: -Tu non dicesti così quando togliesti quel panno dal fondaco. Io t'ho fatto credenzia, e chiesi cento volte questi danari, e ha' ti fatto beffe di noi, e di' che se' il Grasso:

menatel via e vederemo chi sarà. E così lo menorono alla Mercatantia, e messollo in prigione. Erano e prigionieri informato di questo fatto, e quando entrò dentro, tutti dissono: -Ben venga Matteo. Che vuol dire questo che tu se' qua? Disse il Grasso: -Io n'uscirò domattina. E la mattina venne alla prigione uno loro compagno che aveva nome Filippo Rucellai: el Grasso era alla finestra, e Filippo fé vista di nollo conoscere e disse: -O compagno, deh, in servigio, chiamami il tale, che era in prigione. Colui l'ud" e venne oltre. Disse al Grasso: -Matteo, deh levati un poco di qui, ch io ho bisogno di parlare con costui di segreto. El Grasso si levò, e quando costoro ebbono parlato, volendosi Filippo partire, disse el Grasso: -O valente uomo, conoscete voi uno che ha nome il Grasso legnaiuolo, che ista in sulla piazza di Santo Giovanni? Rispo[se] Filippo: -Non conosco io? altro! Egli è grande mio amico, e pure iermattina fu io da lui a sollecitare uno colmo d'altare che mi fa. E era vero. Disse il Grasso: -Io vi priego che gli diciate che venghi insino qui ad uno suo amico che ha nome Matteo. Disse Filippo: -Volentieri; e andò via. Dipoi venne il giudice della Mercatantia con libro ove erano scritti il nome de' prigioni e disse: -Qual è Matteo? El Grasso rispose: -Eccomi. In sull'ora del disinare venne uno garzonetto che avea un fiasco di vino e uno canestro di pane e altre cose da mangiare, e domanda di Matteo; el Grasso rispose e venne a lui. Disse quel garzonetto: -Tenete questa vivanda [da]i vostri fratelli. Disse el Grasso: -Gran merc a loro; e d" loro per mia parte che io gli priego che venghino oggi insino qui a parlarmi. E colui rispose: -Volentieri; e partissi…. in sulle ventidua ore, e dipoi vennono due giovani e domandarono di Matteo. Disse uno de' prigioni: -E' dorme. -Chiamatelo, e ditegli che sono qui e fratelli che gli vogliono parlare. Allora quello prigione chiamò: -O Matteo, e' son qui e tuo' fratelli che ti vogliano parlare. El Grasso si levò cos" sonnacchioso per la malinconia e del disagio dello stare in prigione, che per avventura non era uso, e andò a loro; e giunto disse: -Siate i ben venuti. Rispose el maggiore: -El mi viene voglia di dire: tu sia el mal trovato, ch se' pur giunto dove sempre abbiamo dubitato. Matteo, tu sai quanto la vita tua è stata scellerata, d'andare dirieto a' ribaldi e al giuoco e a mille altre disonestà: per li modi tuoi facesti morire nostra madre inanzi al tempo. Ma come si sia, tu ci se' fratello e siamo d'un padre e d'una madre; la carne ci stringe: se tu ci vuoi promettere d'attendere a fare bene, noi te ne cavereno. Allora cominciò il Grasso a lagrimare e disse: -Frategli miei cari, del male ch'io ho già fatto, e d'essere stato cagione della morte di quella poveretta di nostra madre, me ne incresce insino all'anima, e promettovi, se mi cavate di qui, io attenderò a fare bene e non mi partirò da' vostri comandamenti. Risposono i fratelli: -Noi siamo contenti pagare questi debiti e cavarti di qui, ma guarda attenderci quello ci prometti, ch nollo attendendo, se ti vedessimo in sulle forche non ti ricompreremmo un danaio. Rispose il Grasso: -Sicuramente io ve lo atte[nde]rò. Or quelli fratelli si partirono. Eccoti tornare quello garzonetto per lo [canestro del] pane e per lo fiasco. Disse il Grasso: -Eccolo; e non arrecare più niente, perché credo venire stasera a cena a casa. In sull'avemaria eccoti venire e fratelli, e trassono el Grasso di prigione; e missollo in mezzo e menarollo in una casa rimpetto a Santo Giorgio, e missollo in una camera terrena dove era uno buono fuoco, e dissono: -Statti qui insino a ora di cena. El Grasso rimase solo, e' fratelli feron vista d'avere a fare per casa e uscirono fuori di casa e andarono alla chiesa di Santo Giorgio, dove il dì avevano parlato con uno cappellano forestieri che v'era venuto a stare di pochi d", e aveva[n]gli detto come avevano uno loro fratello, che aveva nome Matteo, e eragli entrato in capo una fantasia che gli è uno che si chiamava el Grasso legnaiuolo e non se gli potea cavare della testa, e pregorollo per Dio che volesse visitare e ingegnarsi di cavarlo di tal fantasia. Onde il prete avea loro risposto: -A vostra posta; e loro andarono per lui, e menarallo nella camera ove era el Grasso e disso[n]gli: -Matteo, tu sai quello che tu ci hai promesso, di volere attendere a fare bene per l'avvenire e pentirti di quello hai fatto per lo passato: e per tanto noi ti vogliamo pregare, acciò che Dio ti dia grazia acciò che tu ce lo possa attendere, che tu ti confessi; e però t'abbiamo menato questo venerabile padre, il quale lasceremo qui con teco. E detto questo uscirono di camera e lasciorono il prete con el Grasso. El prete si pose a sedere a lato al Grasso, e cominciollo a esaminare qual fusse stata la vita sua per lo passato. El Grasso cominciò a dire come era legnaiuolo e invero avea nome el Grasso, ma costoro volevano che fusse Matteo. El prete gli rispose: -Figliuol mio, cavati questa malinconia della testa e datti ad intendere d'essere Matteo como tu se', e lascia andare questo maladetto Grasso Disse el Grasso: -Di quali peccati volete voi mi confessi, di quegli di Matteo o di quegli del Grasso? Disse el prete: -Di quegli di Matteo. Rispose il Grasso: -Questa è una nuova cosa che io sia il Grasso e convengami confessare e peccati di Matteo. El prete diceva: -Tu hai voglia d'impazzare, ché ogni uomo dice certo che tu se' Matteo; e parmi, poi che tu non conosci te medesimo, una strana fantasia la tua a volere diventare un altro! El Grasso diceva: -Fatemi un servigio; poiché io sono Matteo, fatemi parlare al Grasso e sarò contento. Diceva il prete: -Questo non fa per te; lascia istare questo Grasso, e cavati questa fantasia del cervello. E infine tanto gli disse, che 'l Grasso promisse al prete di non si dare più ad intendere d'essere se non Matteo. Chiamò il prete e fratelli: -Matteo vostro è qui, farà per l'avvenire ciò che voi vorrete, e sé" sé'è avveduto dello errore suo e vuole essere Matteo e vostro fratello come egli è: e così ritificò el Grasso. Or fatto questo, el prete fece collazione con loro, e poi il prete si partì, e li detti gli feciono compagnia infino alla chiesa; e tornando a casa trovorono Filippo di ser Brunellesco, che diede loro una impolletta d'acqua addoppiata da fare dormire sei ore ferme. E andarossene e fratelli a casa a cena col Grasso, e nella cena dierono nel vino quella acqua alloppiata a bere al Grasso; e come ebbe beuta, cominciò el sonno a vincere el Grasso per modo che 'nanzi che avesse cenato sé'adormentò a tavola. E adormentato che fu, Filippo venne qui con parecchi compagni con una bara e missonvi dentro el Grasso, e sé lo portorono a casa sua e missollo nel letto spogliato e colla sua cappellina in capo: e tolso[n]gli le chiavi della scarsella e andorono aprire la bottega, e quanti ferri v'erano trasseno del manico e rimiso[n]gli al contrario, e simile alle seghe e alle pialle, per modo che ogni cosa stava a ritroso: e fatto questo serrorono la bottega e rimisono le chiavi 'ndella scarsella al Grasso,'e serrarono l'uscio dentro e con una scala uscirono per la finestra. El Grasso dormì presso a d", e dipoi si destò e guardando per la camera, che v'era la lucerna accesa, apparvegli pure dov'egli [era e ripensando ciò che gli] era advenuto el d" dinanzi, diceva in fra sé.... l'avemaria di Santa Liperata; e allora el Grasso si levò, e aperse la finestra di sala e vide la piazza di

San Giovanni. Allora disse: -Laudato sia Iddio, ch'io sono pure il Grasso e sono in casa mia! E andossene giù e aperse la bottega, e volendo cominciare a lavorare, trovò tutti i ferri messi a ritroso. E allora cominciò a 'mbizzarire in fra se medesimo dicendo: -Cred'i' che la fortuna m'abbia tolto a ciancia. E stando in questo venne lì alla bottega quelli dua giovani che avevano [detto] d'essere suoi fratelli, e come giunsono, el Grasso li riconobbe. Allora dissono: -Bon dì, maestro. El Grasso rispose: -Bon d" e buono anno. Dissono costoro: -Noi abbiamo uno nostro fratello che ha nome Matteo, e ègli entrato una pazzia nel capo che dice che ha nome il Grasso legnaiuolo, e iersera uscì di casa e non sappiamo dove si sia capitato: noi vi preghiamo, se vien qui, che gli caviate del capo che sia il Grasso e rimandatelo a casa, e sarenvi sempre ubligati. El Grasso si schifò, e gittò quelli ferri che racconciava per la bottega dicendo: -Andatevi con Dio, al nome del diavolo: che Grasso e che Matteo è questo? Per lo corpo di Dio, io mi vi leverò dinanzi. E serrò lo sportello della bottega e tolse il mantello, e andò verso l'abergo della Corona. E di rimpetto al detto albergo era la casa di messere Filippo Scolari, grande spano d'Ungheria, el quale, come sapete, era il maggior barone che avesse lo imperadore Sismondo; e in quel tempo era venuto in Firenze onorevolmente con più di trecento cavalli e molti signori e gentili uomini in compagnia. E nel tempo che stette in Firenze cercò di menar seco maestri di diversi arti con promettere loro grande provvisione; e in fra gli altri avea fatto richiedere questo Grasso, e lui avea risposto al tutto di non volere andare, ed erasi spiccato di questa pratica. Onde essendo lui in su questa bizzarria, vidde molti cavalli carichi di forzieri e di valigie, e udì uno che disse: -Che some son queste?, e uno famiglio rispose: -Sono dello Spano che va via stamane. Allora el Grasso si ricordò di quello che lo Spano l'avea richiesto e fatto da altri richiedere, e subito n'andò a casa lo Spano, e trovò che già era montato a cavallo; e andò da lui e, fattogli riverenzia, gli disse: -Signor mio, voi m'avete fatto richiedere se io voglio vevenire con voi in Ungheria, e io ho risposto di no. Al presente, in questo punto, se 'l vi piace, io verrò con la S. V.: fatemi dare uno ronzino. E sanza dire niente a persona andossene in Ungheria; dove la fortuna gli fu sì favorevole, che vi diventò gran ricco. E Giovan Pesce nostro fiorentino, mercatante e abitante in Signa di Schiavonia, uomo degno di fede, lo trovò nel 1446 a Buda di Schiavonia, di cui sentì ordinatamente questa novella, dicendo che le beffi l'avevano fatto ricco.

BIBLIOGRAPHY

References

1807. *Code Napoléon: Édition Originale Et Seule Officielle.* [online] Available at: Paris: Imp Imperiale. https://archive.org/details/bnf-bpt6k5406276n/page/n9/mode/2up [Accessed 31 October 2020].

abc4trust, 2020. *Official Website.* [online] Abc4trust.eu. Available at: <https://abc4trust.eu/> [Accessed 31 October 2020].

Acemoglu, D. and Robinson, J., 2012. *Why Nations Fail.* London: Profile.

Acemoglu, D., Johnson, S. and Robinson, J., 2005. chapter 6 *Institutions as a Fundamental Cause of Long-Run Growth. Handbook of Economic Growth,* [online] pp. 385-472. Available at: <https://economics.mit.edu/files/4469> [Accessed 29 October 2020].

Acemoglu, D. and Robinson, J., 2020. *The Narrow Corridor. How Nations Struggle for Liberty.* New York Penguin. Kindle Edition.

Adema, W. and Ladaique, M., 2009. *How Expensive is the Welfare State?. OECD Social, Employment and Migration Working Papers,* [online]. Available at: <https://www.oecd-ilibrary.org/social-issues-migration-health/how-expensive-is-the-welfare-state_220615515052> [Accessed 14 September 2020].

Adema, W., Fron, P. and Ladaique, M., 2011. *Is the European Welfare State Really More Expensive? Indicators on Social Spending, 1980-2012*; and a Manual to the OECD Social Expenditure Database (SOCX). *OECD Social, Employment and Migration Working Papers,* [online] 124(1). Available at: <https://read.oecd-ilibrary.org/social-issues-migration-health/is-the-european-welfare-state-really-more-expensive_5kg2d2d4pbf0-en#page1> [Accessed 14 September 2020].

Adler, G., 1866. *Wilhelm Von Humboldt'S Linguistical Studies.* 1st ed. New York: Wynkoop & Hallenbeck, pp. 1-47.

Allan, D., 2012. *Ecological Role Of Prehistoric Humans.* [online] Www-personal. umich.edu. Available at: <http://www-personal.umich.edu/~dallan/nre220/outline4.htm> [Accessed 4 September 2020].

Aspen, P., 2015. *Simon Rattle, Lightning Conductor.* [online] Ft.com. Available at: <https://www.ft.com/content/12c60b72-c292-11e4-a59c-00144feab7de#axzz4CPq8Q1hC> [Accessed 3 September 2020].

Asimov I., 1950, I Robot, New York Gnome Press.

Barber, E., 1999. *The Mummies Of Ürümchi.* New York: W.W. Norton & Co.

Barkow, J., Cosmides, L. and Tooby, J., 1992. *The Adapted Mind: Evolutionary Psychology And The Generation Of Culture.* New York: Oxford University Press.

Barras, C., 2016. *Mystery Invaders Conquered Europe At The End Of Last Ice Age.* [online] New Scientist. Available at: <https://www.newscientist.com/

article/2076477-mystery-invaders-conquered-europe-at-the-end-of-last-ice-age/> [Accessed 4 September 2020].

Barrow I., 2017, *The East India Company, 1600–1858*, Indianapolis, Hackett Publishing Company, Inc. Kindle Edition.

Barsky, R., 2011. *Zellig Harris: From American Linguistics To Socialist Zionism*. 1st ed. Cambridge: The MIT Press, pp. 45-180.

Baumann, G., 1986. *The Written Word: Literacy In Translation (Wolfson College Lectures 1985)*. Oxford, England: Clarendon Press, pp. 23-48.

BBC Bitesize, 2020. *America In The 1920S: Triumph Or Disaster?* [online] Downloads.bbc.co.uk. Available at: <http://downloads.bbc.co.uk/bitesize/gcse/audio/history/pdf/america_in_the_1920s_triumph_or_disaster.pdf> [Accessed 29 September 2020].

BBC Bitesize, 2020. *The Wall Street Crash And Depression*. [online] BBC Bitesize. Available at: <https://www.bbc.co.uk/bitesize/guides/ztxbsg8/revision/1> [Accessed 29 September 2020].

Bekoff, M. and Pierce, J., 2009. *Wild Justice*. Chicago: University of Chicago Press.

Bentham, J. and Harrison, R., 1988. *A Fragment on Government. Cambridge Texts in the History of Political Thought*, [online] Available at: <https://www.cambridge.org/core/books/bentham-a-fragment-on-government/FD26D81A692C949C624FDF6622F41774#fndtn-contents> [Accessed 29 November 2020].

Bieber, F. and Goshu, W., 2020. *Don'T Let Ethiopia Become The Next Yugoslavia*. [online] Foreign Policy. Available at: <https://foreignpolicy.com/2019/01/15/dont-let-ethiopia-become-the-next-yugoslavia-abiy-ahmed-balkans-milosevic-ethnic-conflict-federalism/> [Accessed 2 October 2020].

Biot, E., 1841. *Sull'abolizione Della Schiavitù Antica In Occidente*. Milano: Tipografia e Libreria Pirotta e Co.

Bloomfield, L., 1914. *An Introduction To The Study Of Language*. London: G. Bell and Sons LTD, pp. 1-290.

Bolus, M. and Conard, N., 2001. *The late Middle Palaeolithic and earliest Upper Palaeolithic in Central Europe and their relevance for the Out of Africa hypothesis* in *Quaternary International*, [online] 75(1), pp. 29-40. Available at: <https://www.sciencedirect.com/science/article/abs/pii/S1040618200000756> [Accessed 4 September 2020].

Bostrom, N. (2017). *Superintelligence: Paths, dangers, strategies*. Oxford, UK: Oxford University Press.

Boyd, B., 2010. *On The Origin Of Stories*. Cambridge, Mass.: Harvard University Press.

Brault, M., 2012. *Americans With Disabilities: 2010*. [online] Www2.census.gov. Available at: <https://www2.census.gov/library/publications/2012/demo/p70-131.pdf> [Accessed 14 September 2020].

Bronwyn F. 2003, Storytelling That Moves People in Harvard Business Review, 2003, 06 [online] https://hbr.org/2003/06/storytelling-that-moves-people [Accessed 14 September 2020].

Burns, J., 2005. *Happiness and Utility: Jeremy Bentham's Equation. Utilitas*, [online] 17(1), pp. 46-61. Available at: <https://www.utilitarianism.com/jeremy-bentham/greatest-happiness.pdf> [Accessed 14 September 2020].

Carreira, J., 2009. *Kant And The Creation Of Reality*. [online] Philosophy Is Not A Luxury. Available at: <https://philosophyisnotaluxury.com/2009/11/01/kant-and-the-creation-of-reality/> [Accessed 3 September 2020].

Carroll, J., 1964. *Language, Thought And Reality: Selected Writings Of Benjamin Lee Whorf*. Cambridge: The MIT Press.

Carusi, C., 2008. *Il Sale Nel Mondo Greco (VI A.C.-III D.C.)*. Bari: Edipuglia.

Castiello, U., Becchio, C., Zoia, S., Nelini, C., Sartori, L., Blason, L., D'Ottavio, G., Bulgheroni, M. and Gallese, V., 2010. Wired to Be Social: The Ontogeny of Human Interaction. *PLoS ONE*, [online] 5(10), p. e13199. Available at: <https://www.researchgate.net/publication/47430546_Wired_to_Be_Social_The_Ontogeny_of_Human_Interaction> [Accessed 3 September 2020].

Cavandoli, O., 2020. *La Linea 101*. [online] Youtube. Available at: <https://www.youtube.com/watch?v=6iw_rdx11V0> [Accessed 1 October 2020].

Centre for Biological Diversity, 2020. *Human Population Growth And Extinction*. [online] Biologicaldiversity.org. Available at: <https://www.biologicaldiversity.org/programs/population_and_sustainability/extinction/index.html> [Accessed 4 September 2020].

Centre Historique des Archives Nationales, 2020. *Le Citoyens Actifs*. [online] Histoire-image.org. Available at: <https://histoire-image.org/fr/etudes/citoyens-actifs> [Accessed 1 October 2020].

Chandler, D., 2020. *The Sapir-Whorf Hypothesis*. [online] Visual-memory.co.uk. Available at: <http://visual-memory.co.uk/daniel/Documents/short/whorf.html> [Accessed 9 September 2020].

Chaum D., 1982, *Blind Signatures for Untraceable Payments*, in , *Advances in Cryptology Proceedings of Crypto 82*, edited by D. Chaum, R.L. Rivest, & A.T. Sherman, Plenum, pp. 199-203, [online] Available at: <https://www.chaum.com/publications/Chaum-blind-signatures.PDF> [Accessed 2 October 2020]

Chaum, D., 2020. *Achieving Electronic Privacy*. [online] Chaum.com. Available at: <https://chaum.com/publications/ScientificAmerican-AEP.pdf> [Accessed 2 October 2020].

Chaum, D., 2020. *Homepage*. [online] Chaum.com. Available at: <https://www.chaum.com/> [Accessed 2 October 2020].

Chaum, D., 2020. *Untraceable Electronic Mail, Return Addresses, and Digital Pseudonyms* in *Communications of the ACM* edited by Rivest R., February 1981, Vol. 24, N. 2, 84-89. [online] Chaum.com. Available at: <https://www.chaum.com/publications/chaum-mix.pdf> [Accessed 1 October 2020].

Chaum, D., 2020. *List Of Publications*. [online] Chaum.com. Available at: <https://chaum.com/publications/publications.html> [Accessed 1 October 2020].

Chaum, D., 2020. *Security Without Identification*. [online] Chaum.com. Available at: <https://chaum.com/publications/Security_Wthout_Identification.html> [Accessed 2 October 2020].

Chaum, D., 2020. *Security Without Identification: Card Computers To Make Big Brother Obsolete*. [online] Git.gnunet.org. Available at: <https://git.gnunet.

org/bibliography.git/plain/docs/10.1.1.48.4680.pdf> [Accessed 1 October 2020].

Chaum D., Evertse J.H., 1986, *A Secure and Privacy-Protecting Protocol for Transmitting Personal Information Between Organizations*, in *Advances in Cryptology CRYPTO 1986*, edited by A.M. Odlyzko, Berlin, Springer-Verlag, pp. 118-167

Chaum, D., Hosp, B., Popoveniuc, S. and Vora, P., 2009. *Accessible Voter-Verifiability.* [online] Chaum.com. Available at: <https://chaum.com/publications/AccessibleVoterVerifiability.pdf> [Accessed 2 October 2020].

Chaum, D. van Heyst, E., 2020. *Group Signatures.* [online] Chaum.com. Available at: <https://www.chaum.com/publications/Group_Signatures.pdf> [Accessed 1 October 2020].

Chomsky, N., 1998. *Linguistic Contributions To The Study Of Mind, By Noam Chomsky (Excerpted From Language And Mind).* [online] Chomsky.info. Available at: <https://chomsky.info/mind01/> [Accessed 4 September 2020].

Chomsky, N., 2006. *Language And Mind.* Cambridge: Cambridge University Press, pp. 1-22.

Cole H. L., Ohanian L. E., 2001, *New Deal Policies and the Persistence of the Great Depression: A General Equilibrium Analysis (Paper 597 Federal Reserve Bank of Minneapolis)* in *Journal of Political Economy*, August 2004, Volume 112, Number 4. And [online] Available at: <https://www.minneapolisfed.org/research/working-papers/new-deal-policies-and-the-persistence-of-the-great-depression-a-general-equilibrium-analysis> [Accessed 10 September 2020].

Conseil constitutionnel, 1789. *Déclaration Des Droits De L'homme Et Du Citoyen De 1789.* [online] Conseil constitutionnel. Available at: <https://www.conseil-constitutionnel.fr/le-bloc-de-constitutionnalite/declaration-des-droits-de-l-homme-et-du-citoyen-de-1789> [Accessed 10 September 2020].

Consiglio di Stato, Sentenza 13 December 2019, n. 8742, [online] Available at: <https://images.go.wolterskluwer.com/Web/WoltersKluwer/%7Baee89464-6ad9-479d-ac0b-ce43a7f69612%7D_consiglio-di-stato-sentenza-8472-2019.pdf> [Accessed 10 September 2020].

Consiglio Nazionale del Notariato, *Studio 1-2017/DI, Il documento informatico nel tempo*, by EUGENIO STUCCHI, MICHELE MANENTE, SABRINA CHIBBARO, as of the 5th December 2017 approved by Consiglio Nazionale del Notariato as of the 22-23 February 2018, online at https://www.notariato.it/sites/default/files/1-2017-DI.pdf.

Corte Dei Conti, S., 2014. *Gli Organismi Partecipati Dagli Enti Territoriali.* [online] Eticapa.it. Available at: <http://www.eticapa.it/eticapa/wp-content/uploads/2014/07/delibera_15_2014-Corte-dei-conti.pdf> [Accessed 29 September 2020].

Council of Europe, 2020, CEPEJ European judicial systems Evaluation Report [online] Available at: https://rm.coe.int/rapport-evaluation-partie-1-francais/16809fc058 [Accessed 1 October 2020].

Creative Commons, 2020. *Liscenses.* [online] Creativecommons.org. Available at: <https://creativecommons.org/licenses/by-nc-nd/4.0/> [Accessed 1 October 2020].

Creswick, C., 2011. *The Great Depression - Parallels For Today*. [online] Issuu. Available at: <https://issuu.com/rbia/docs/mmaug25_web/17> [Accessed 30 September 2020].

Crowley, P. and Quah, C., 2020. A Reconsideration of the Great Depression. *South Asian Journal of Management*, [online] 16(3), pp. 7-23. Available at: <https://www.researchgate.net/publication/228291463_A_Reconsideration_of_the_Great_Depression> [Accessed 29 September 2020].

Curnoe, D., 2011. *Climate Change, Doomsday And The 'Inevitable' Extinction Of Humankind*. [online] The Conversation. Available at: <https://theconversation.com/climate-change-doomsday-and-the-inevitable-extinction-of-humankind-1656> [Accessed 4 September 2020].

D. Roosevelt, F., 1944. *8 Fireside Chats (F. Roosevelt) | The American Presidency Project*. [online] Presidency.ucsb.edu. Available at: <https://www.presidency.ucsb.edu/documents/presidential-documents-archive-guidebook/fireside-chats-f-roosevelt> [Accessed 30 September 2020].

Darwin, C., 1895. *On The Origin Of Species By Means Of Natural Selection, Or The Preservation Of Favoured Races In The Struggle For Life*. New York: D. Appleton and Company.

Dawkins, R. (1989), *The Selfish Gene* (2nd ed.), Oxford: Oxford University Press.

DeNavas-Walt, C. and Proctor, B., 2015. *Income And Poverty In The United States: 2014*. [online] Census.gov. Available at: <https://www.census.gov/content/dam/Census/library/publications/2015/demo/p60-252.pdf> [Accessed 14 September 2020].

Dennett, D., 1986. *Content And Consciousness*. 2nd ed. London: Routlege & Kegan Paul Books Ltd.

Der Tagesspiegel, 2009. *Sozialausgaben Steigen Um 33 Milliarden Euro*. [online] Tagesspiegel.de. Available at: <https://www.tagesspiegel.de/politik/sozialbericht-2009-sozialausgaben-steigen-um-33-milliarden-euro/1558648.html> [Accessed 14 September 2020].

Diamond J., (2013) *Guns, Germs, and Steel: Guns, Germs, and Steel: A Short History of Everybody for the Last 13,000 Years*, New York: Vintage.

Diamond Cora, (1975-1989), *Wittgenstein's Lectures on the Foundations of Mathematics Cambridge, 1939: from the notes of R. G. Bosanquet, Norman Malcolm, Rush Rhees, and Yorick Smythies*, Chicago, The University of Chicago Press.

Dick P.K. 1968, *Do Androids Dream of Electric Sheep?*, New York Doubleday.

Dipartimento bilancio, S., 2012. *Documentazione E Ricerche: Le Società A Partecipazione Pubblica*. [online] Documenti.camera.it. Available at: <http://documenti.camera.it/leg16/dossier/Testi/bi0506.htm> [Accessed 29 September 2020].

Droitromain.univ-grenoble-alpes.fr. 2020. *Corpus Iuris Civilis: Institutiones 4*. [online] Available at: <https://droitromain.univ-grenoble-alpes.fr/corpjurciv.htm> [Accessed 10 September 2020].

Dunbar, R., 2004. *Gossip in Evolutionary Perspective* in *Review of General Psychology*, [online] 8(2), pp. 100-110. Available at: <https://www.semanticscholar.org/paper/Gossip-in-Evolutionary-Perspective-Dunbar/dc988db35a1a3558de7e782ad5c2ef84f9c98487> [Accessed 3 September 2020].

Eco, U., 1983. *The Name Of The Rose*. London: Harcourt.

Eco, U., 2012. *The Name Of The Rose*. London: Vintage Books.

Eichengreen, B. and O'Rourke, K., 2010. *What Do The New Data Tell Us? A Tale Of Two Depressions*. [online] Voxeu.org. Available at: <https://voxeu.org/article/tale-two-depressions-what-do-new-data-tell-us-february-2010-update> [Accessed 30 September 2020].

Eisenstein, E., 1973. *The Printing Press As An Agent Of Change*. Cambridge: Cambridge University Press.

Emanuel, C., 2013. *Rome'S Fifth Century Grain Supply*. [online] Medieval History Geek. Available at: <https://medievalhistorygeek.wordpress.com/2013/06/23/romes-fifth-Century-grain-supply/> [Accessed 10 September 2020].

Encyclopedia Britannica, 2020. *East India Company: Definition, History, & Facts*. [online] Encyclopedia Britannica. Available at: <https://www.britannica.com/topic/East-India-Company> [Accessed 10 September 2020].

Escalas, J., 2007. *Self-Referencing and Persuasion: Narrative Transportation versus Analytical Elaboration* in *Journal of Consumer Research*, [online] 33(4), pp. 421-429. Available at: <https://www.jstor.org/stable/10.1086/510216?seq=1#metadata_info_tab_contents> [Accessed 3 September 2020].

ETSI, 2014. *Electronic Signatures And Infrastructures (ESI); Cryptographic Suites*. [online] Etsi.org. Available at: <http://www.etsi.org/deliver/etsi_ts/119300_119399/119312/01.01.01_60/ts_119312v010101p.pdf> [Accessed 10 September 2020].

ETSI, 2020. *About Us*. [online] ETSI.org. Available at: <https://www.etsi.org/newsroom/news/14-about/32-our-history> [Accessed 2 October 2020].

ETSI, 2020. *Cloud Standards Coordination: Final Report*. [online] Etsi.org. Available at: <https://www.etsi.org/images/files/Events/2013/2013_CSC_Delivery_WS/CSC-Final_report-013-CSC_Final_report_v1_0_PDF_format-.PDF> [Accessed 1 October 2020].

ETSI, 2020. *CLOUD; Initial Analysis Of Standardisation Requirements For Cloud Services*. [online] Etsi.org. Available at: <https://www.etsi.org/deliver/etsi_tr/102900_102999/102997/01.01.01_60/tr_102997v010101p.pdf> [Accessed 1 October 2020].

ETSI, 2020. *Integrated Services Digital Network (ISDN); Definition And Usage Of Cause And Location In Digital Subscriber Signalling System No. One (DSS1) And Signalling System No. 7 (SS7) ISDN User Part (ISUP)*. [online] Etsi.org. Available at: <https://www.etsi.org/deliver/etsi_en/300400_300499/300485/01.03.01_20/en_300485v010301c.pdf> [Accessed 1 October 2020].

ETSI, 2020. *Satellite UMTS/IMT-2000*. [online] ETSI. Available at: <https://www.etsi.org/technologies/satellite/satellite-umts-imt-2000> [Accessed 1 October 2020].

ETSI, 2020. *Universal Mobile Telecommunications System (UMTS); Selection Procedures For The Choice Of Radio Transmission Technologies Of The UMTS (UMTS 30.03 Version 3.2.0)*. [online] Etsi.org. Available at: <https://www.etsi.org/deliver/etsi_tr/101100_101199/101112/03.02.00_60/tr_101112v030200p.pdf> [Accessed 1 October 2020].

Euro Lex, 2020. *General Data Protection Regulation 32016R0679*. [online] Eur-lex. europa.eu. Available at: <https://eur-lex.europa.eu/legal-content/IT/TXT/?uri=CELEX%3A32016R0679> [Accessed 2 October 2020].

European Commission, 2015. *Communication From The Commission To The European Parliament, The Council, The European Economic And Social Committee And The Committee Of The Regions*. [online] Eur-lex.europa.eu. Available at: <https://eur-lex.europa.eu/legal-content/EN/TXT/PDF/?uri=CELEX:52015DC0429&from=EN> [Accessed 10 September 2020].

European Commission, 2015. *European Commission, Monitoring The Digital Economy And Society 2016-2021*. [online] Ec.europa.eu. Available at: <https://ec.europa.eu/eurostat/documents/341889/725524/Monitoring+the+Digital+Economy+%26+Society+2016-2021/7df02d85-698a-4a87-a6b1-7994df7fbeb7> [Accessed 2 October 2020].

European Commission, 2020. *Consumer Protection: Consumer Protection Policies, Strategies And Statistics*. [online] European Commission. Available at: <https://ec.europa.eu/info/policies/consumers/consumer-protection_en> [Accessed 1 October 2020].

European Commission, 2020. *Eidas Observatory: Regulation N°910/2014*. [online] FUTURIUM - European Commission. Available at: <https://ec.europa.eu/futurium/en/content/eidas-regulation-regulation-eu-ndeg9102014> [Accessed 2 October 2020].

European Commission, 2020. *Shaping Europe'S Digital Future: European Cloud Strategy 2012*. [online] European Commission. Available at: <https://ec.europa.eu/digital-single-market/en/european-cloud-computing-strategy> [Accessed 1 October 2020].

European Commission, 2020. *Shaping The Digital Single Market*. [online] European Commission. Available at: <https://ec.europa.eu/digital-single-market/en/policies/shaping-digital-single-market> [Accessed 2 October 2020].

European Court of Justice, Google Spain SL v. Agencia Española de Protección de Datos, Case C-131/12 (May 13, 2014), Harvard Law Review 128, no. 2 (2014): 735.

European Data Protection Board, 2020, *Guidelines 05/2020 on consent under Regulation 2016/679 Version 1.1* Adopted on 4 May 2020 [online] Available at: <https://edpb.europa.eu/sites/edpb/files/files/file1/edpb_guidelines_202005_consent_en.pdf> [Accessed 14 September 2020]

Eurostat, 2017. *Being Young In Europe Today - Demographic Trends - Statistics Explained*. [online] Ec.europa.eu. Available at: <https://ec.europa.eu/eurostat/statistics-explained/index.php/Being_young_in_Europe_today_-_demographic_trends> [Accessed 14 September 2020].

Eurostat, 2020, Old-age dependency ratio increasing in the EU, 13 july 2020, [online] Ec.europa.eu. Available at: <https://ec.europa.eu/eurostat/web/products-eurostat-news/-/DDN-20200713-1> [Accessed 14 September 2020].

Feci S., (2010), *La capacità di agire (Italia, secc. XII-XIX)*, in *Donne e Diritti*, [online] Available at: <http://www1.unipa.it/storichedeldiritto/Materiali/DOSSIER/FECI.html> [Accessed 10 September 2020].

Federal Reserve Bank of Chicago, 2020. *Understanding Derivatives: Markets And Infrastructure*. [online] Chicagofed.org. Available at: <https://www.chicagofed.org/publications/understanding-derivatives/index> [Accessed 10 September 2020].

Ferenstein, G., 2020. *How The World Butchered Benjamin Franklin0s Quote On Liberty Vs. Security*. [online] Techcrunch.com. Available at: <https://techcrunch.com/2014/02/14/how-the-world-butchered-benjamin-franklins-quote-on-liberty-vs-security/?guccounter=1> [Accessed 2 October 2020].

FERGUSON, N., 2004, *Empire. How Britain made the Modern World*, London, Penguin.

Ferguson, T., 1984. *From Normalcy to New Deal: industrial structure, party competition, and American public policy in the Great Depression* in *International Organisation*, [online] 38(1), pp.41-94. Available at: <https://www.cambridge.org/core/journals/international-organisation/article/from-normalcy-to-new-deal-industrial-structure-party-competition-and-american-public-policy-in-the-great-depression/910BEA2D7C0FDBE2BA4B08660C9438DB> [Accessed 30 September 2020].

Ferraris, M., 2009. *Documentalità: Perché È Importante Lasciare Tracce*. Bari: Laterza.

Ferraris, M., 2012. *Documentality: Why It Is Necessary To Leave Traces (Commonalities)*, translated by Richard Davies, New York, Fordham University Press.

FHI, 2020. *Future Of Humanity Institute*. [online] The Future of Humanity Institute. Available at: <https://www.fhi.ox.ac.uk/> [Accessed 1 October 2020].

Finnis, J., 1980. *Natural Law And Natural Rights*. 2nd ed. New York: Oxford University Press.

Flannery, K., Marcus, J., 2012. *The Creation Of Inequality: How Our Prehistoric Ancestors Set The Stage For Monarchy, Slavery, And Empire*. Cambridge: Harvard University Press.

Fought, J., 1999. *Leonard Bloomfield*. London: Routledge, pp. 3-198.

Friedman, B. M., 2005. *The Moral Consequences of Economic Growth*. New York, Knopf Doubleday Publishing Group. Kindle Edition.

Friedman M., Schwartz A. J., 1963, *A Monetary History of the United States, 1867–1960*, Princeton Oxford, Princeton University Press.

Friedrich, J., 1973. *Decifrazione Delle Scritture E Delle Lingue Scomparse*. Firenze: Sansoni.

Fryer, B., 2003. *Storytelling That Moves People*. [online] Harvard Business Review. Available at: <https://hbr.org/2003/06/storytelling-that-moves-people> [Accessed 3 September 2020].

Future of Life Institute, 2020. *An Open Letter: Research Priorities For Robust And Beneficial Artificial Intelligence*. [online] Future of Life Institute. Available at: <https://futureoflife.org/ai-open-letter/?cn-reloaded=1> [Accessed 1 October 2020].

Gabba E., Schiavone E., 1989-1997, *Storia di Roma*, Vol. IV, Torino, Giulio Einaudi editore.

Gabriel, R., 2002. *The Great Armies Of Antiquity*. Westport, Conn.: Praeger.

Galbraith, J. K., 1954, *The Great Crash 1929*. London: Hamish Hamilton. Kindle Edition 2012.

Galbraith, J. K., 1990, *A Short History of Financial Euphoria*. New York: Wittle Books. Kinde Edition.

Galgano, F., 2010. *Lex Mercatoria*. Bologna: Il Mulino.

Gallup, G., 1977. *Self recognition in primates: A comparative approach to the bidirectional properties of consciousness* in *American Psychologist*, [online] 32(5), pp. 329-338. Available at: <https://www.semanticscholar.org/paper/Self-recognition-in-primates%3A-A-comparative-to-the-Gallup/32d-2dd1fb12aaf89a1bfdfb115479ac0fe07ecc2> [Accessed 4 September 2020].

Garvy, G. *Keynes and the Economic Activists of Pre-Hitler Germany*. in *Journal of Political Economy* 83, no. 2 (1975): 391-405. [online] Available at http://www.jstor.org/stable/1830929. [Accessed 1 October 2020].

Genghini, R., 2020, *La Forma Notarile Digitale*, Padova, CEDAM Wolters Kluwer.

Genghini, R., 2020. *Digital Agreement: Traces, Recordings, Inscriptions And Documents*. [online] Digitalagreement.eu. Available at: <http://www.digitalagreement.eu/2012/12/10/traces-recordings-inscriptions-and-documents/> [Accessed 1 October 2020].

Gerrig, R. and Rapp, D., 2004. *Psychological Processes Underlying Literary Impact* in *Poetics Today*, [online] 25(2), pp. 265-281. Available at: <https://www.researchgate.net/publication/249879655_Psychological_Processes_Underlying_Literary_Impact> [Accessed 3 September 2020].

Ghilarducci T., 2018, *Innovations in Protecting the Old*, in *The Welfare State Revisited (Initiative for Policy Dialogue at Columbia: Challenges in Development and Globalisation)* edited by OCAMPO J. A. STIGLITZ J. E. New York. Columbia University Press. Kindle Edition.

Gottschall, J., 2012. *The Storytelling Animal: How Stories Make Us Human*. Boston: Mariner Books Houghton Mifflin Harcourt.

Gottschall, J., Wilson, D., Wilson, E. and Crews, F., 2005. *The Literary Animal: Evolution And The Nature Of Narrative*. Evanston: Northwestern University Press.

GovInfo, 2020. *Content Details Of The Constitution Of The United States Of America*. [online] Govinfo.gov. Available at: <https://www.govinfo.gov/app/details/GPO-CONAN-REV-2014> [Accessed 29 September 2020].

Graeber D., 2011, *Debt: the first 5000 years*, Brooklyn, NY, Melville House.

Graham, J., Hazarika, S. and Narasimhan, K., 2011. Corporate Governance, Debt, and Investment Policy During the Great Depression. *Management Science*, [online] 57(12), pp.2083-2100. Available at: <https://www.researchgate.net/publication/228319142_Corporate_Governance_Debt_and_Investment_Policy_During_the_Great_Depression> [Accessed 30 September 2020].

Graham, J., Hazarika, S. and Narasimhan, K., 2011. *Financial Distress in the Great Depression*. in *Financial Management*, [online] 40(4), pp. 821-844. Available at: <https://www.jstor.org/stable/23882748?seq=1#metadata_info_tab_contents> [Accessed 30 September 2020].

Grant J., 2014, The Forgotten Depression. 1921: The Crash That Curet Itself, New York, Simon & Schuster Kindle Edition.

Grant, M., 1986. *The World Of Rome*. London: Faber.

Gray, R., 2020. *The Body Parts Which Can Be Regrown In A Laboratory*. [online] The Telegraph. Available at: <https://www.telegraph.co.uk/news/science/science-news/10275996/The-body-parts-which-can-be-regrown-in-a-laboratory.html> [Accessed 3 September 2020].

Green, R., Krause, J., Briggs, A., Maricic, T., Stenzel, U., Kircher, M., Patterson, N., Li, H., Zhai, W., Fritz, M., Hansen, N., Durand, E., Malaspinas, A., Jensen, J., Marques-Bonet, T., Alkan, C., Prufer, K., Meyer, M., Burbano, H., Good, J., Schultz, R., Aximu-Petri, A., Butthof, A., Hober, B., Hoffner, B., Siegemund, M., Weihmann, A., Nusbaum, C., Lander, E., Russ, C., Novod, N., Affourtit, J., Egholm, M., Verna, C., Rudan, P., Brajkovic, D., Kucan, Z., Gusic, I., Doronichev, V., Golovanova, L., Lalueza-Fox, C., de la Rasilla, M., Fortea, J., Rosas, A., Schmitz, R., Johnson, P., Eichler, E., Falush, D., Birney, E., Mullikin, J., Slatkin, M., Nielsen, R., Kelso, J., Lachmann, M., Reich, D. and Paabo, S., 2010. *A Draft Sequence of the Neandertal Genome* in *Science*, [online] 328(5979), pp. 710-722. Available at: <https://science.sciencemag.org/content/328/5979/710> [Accessed 9 September 2020].

Gregorovius, F., 1972. *Storia Di Roma Nel Medioevo, VI*. Torino: Newton Compton Srl.

Gregory XIII, P., 1580. *Statuta Almae Urbis Romae*. Rome.

Hamilton, A., Madison, J. and Jay, J., 1788. *The Federalist Papers*. New York: J. and A. Mc Lean.

Hancock, J., 2012. *Plant Evolution And The Origin Of Crop Species*. 3rd ed. Wallingford: CABI.

Hansen M., Krasemann H., Rost M., Genghini R. (2003). *Datenschutzaspekte von Identitätsmanagementsystemen - Recht und Praxis in Europa,* in *Datenschutz und Datensicherheit*, 2003, 27(9).

Harari, Youval N., 2011. *Sapiens a Brief History of mankind,* London, Vintage.

Harris, W., 1989. *Ancient Literacy*. Cambridge: Harvard University Press.

Hastorf, C. and Johannessen, S., 1994. *Corn And Culture In The Prehistoric New World*. Boulder (Col.): Westview Press.

Havelock, E. and Plato, 1963. *Preface To Plato*. Cambridge: Basil Blackwell.

Havelock, E., 1978. *The Greek Concept Of Justice*. Cambridge: Harvard University Press.

Hawley, E., 1995. *The New Deal And The Problem Of Monopoly*. New York: Fordham Univ. Press.

Hendry, L., 2014. *First Britons*. [online] Nhm.ac.uk. Available at: <https://www.nhm.ac.uk/discover/first-britons.html> [Accessed 4 September 2020].

Heuman G. Burnard T., 2012, *The Routledge History of Slavery (Routledge Histories),* London, Routledge. Heward, E., 1979. *Lord Mansfield: A Biography Of William Murray, 1St Earl Of Mansfield, 1705-93, Lord Chief Justice For 32 Years*. Chichester: Barry Rose.

Higgins, C., 2020. *How Nicholas Serota'S Tate Changed Britain*. [online] the Guardian. Available at: <https://www.theguardian.com/artanddesign/2017/jun/22/how-nicholas-serota-tate-changed-britain> [Accessed 2 October 2020].

Hirsch, E., 1977. *The Philosophy Of Composition*. Chicago: University of Chicago Press.

History World, 2020. *Hunter Gatherers To Farmers*. [online] Historyworld.net. Available at: <http://www.historyworld.net/wrldhis/PlainTextHistories.asp?historyid=ab63> [Accessed 4 September 2020].

Hopkins, K., 2012. *Unique Legal Considerations in Reality Television* in *Pittsburgh Journal of Technology Law and Policy*, [online] 13. Available at: <https://www.researchgate.net/publication/274669844_Unique_Legal_Considerations_in_Reality_Television> [Accessed 1 October 2020].

Hsu, J., 2008. *The Secrets Of Storytelling: Why We Love A Good Yarn*. [online] Scientific American. Available at: <https://www.scientificamerican.com/article/the-secrets-of-storytelling/> [Accessed 3 September 2020].

Hubner, R., 1918. *A History Of Germanic Private Law*. Boston: Little Brown And Company.

IMDb, 2020. *Blade Runner (1982)*. [online] IMDb. Available at: <https://www.imdb.com/title/tt0083658/> [Accessed 1 October 2020].

IMDb, 2020. *Gattaca (1997)*. [online] IMDb. Available at: <https://www.imdb.com/title/tt0119177/> [Accessed 1 October 2020].

IMDb, 2020. *Planet Of The Apes (2001)*. [online] IMDb. Available at: <https://www.imdb.com/title/tt0133152/> [Accessed 1 October 2020].

IMDb, 2020. *Starship Troopers (1997)*. [online] IMDb. Available at: <https://www.imdb.com/title/tt0120201/> [Accessed 2 October 2020].

IMDb, 2020. *The Day That The Earth Stood Still (2008)*. [online] IMDb. Available at: <https://www.imdb.com/title/tt0970416/?ref_=fn_al_tt_1> [Accessed 1 October 2020].

IMDb, 2020. *The Day The Earth Stood Still (1951)*. [online] IMDb. Available at: <https://www.imdb.com/title/tt0043456/?ref_=fn_al_tt_2> [Accessed 1 October 2020].

IMDb, 2020. *The Island (2005)*. [online] IMDb. Available at: <https://www.imdb.com/title/tt0399201/> [Accessed 1 October 2020].

Industrial Development Organisation, International and Fertilizer Development Center, 1998. *The Fertilizer Manual*. 3rd ed. Dordrecht: Kluwer Academic Publishers with UNIDO and IFDC.

International Telecomunication Union, 2020. *(ADSL) Asymmetric Digital Subscriber Line Transceivers*. [online] Itu.int. Available at: <https://www.itu.int/rec/T-REC-G.992.1> [Accessed 1 October 2020].

International Telecommunications Union, 2020. *Facts And Figures: The World In 2013*. [online] Itu.int. Available at: <https://www.itu.int/en/ITU-D/Statistics/Documents/facts/ICTFactsFigures2013-e.pdf> [Accessed 1 October 2020].

International Telecommunications Union, 2020. *Statistics*. [online] Itu.int. Available at: <https://www.itu.int/en/ITU-D/Statistics/Pages/stat/default.aspx> [Accessed 1 October 2020].

Irti N., 1990, *Formalismo e attività giuridica*, in z. 1990, I, 4.

Jones, M., 1995. *The Limits Of Liberty: American History, 1607-1992*. Oxford: Oxford University Press.

Jordan, D., 2013. *The Neolithic (Essay 1)*. [online] Pages.ucsd.edu. Available at: <http://pages.ucsd.edu/~dkjordan/arch/neolithic/Neo1-AgRev.html> [Accessed 4 September 2020].

Jordan, D., 2017. *The Neolithic (Essay 2)*. [online] Pages.ucsd.edu. Available at: <http://pages.ucsd.edu/~dkjordan/arch/neolithic/Neo2-Beyond.html> [Accessed 4 September 2020].

Jordan, D., 2018. *The Neolithic (Essay 3)*. [online] Pages.ucsd.edu. Available at: <http://pages.ucsd.edu/~dkjordan/arch/neolithic/Neo3-LivRev.html> [Accessed 4 September 2020].

Justia, 2014. *Riley V. California, 573 U.S. 373 (2014)*. [online] Justia Law. Available at: <https://supreme.justia.com/cases/federal/us/573/373/> [Accessed 3 September 2020].

Kant, I., 1783. *Prolegomena To Any Future Metaphysics That Will Be Able To Present Itself As A Science*. [online] Oregonstate.edu. Available at: <http://web.mnstate.edu/gracyk/courses/phil%20306/kant_materials/prolegomena1.htm> [Accessed 3 September 2020].

Karl Marx Online Archive, 2013. *Alcuni Dati Sulla Fortuna Del 'Capitale' Di Marx*. [online] Marx-karl.com. Available at: <https://www.marx-karl.com/2013/12/alcuni-dati-sulla-fortuna-del-capitale-di-marx/> [Accessed 10 September 2020].

Katan, N. and Mintz, B., 1985. *Hieroglyphs: The Writing Of Ancient Egypt (Revised Edition)*. London: Published for the Trustees of the British Museum by British Museum Publications.

Katz, S., n.d. *Memory And Mind: An Introduction To Augustine's Epistemology*. [online] Faculty.georgetown.edu. Available at: <https://faculty.georgetown.edu/jod/augustine/sheri> [Accessed 3 September 2020].

Kaufman, B., 2012. Wage Theory, New Deal Labour Policy, and the Great Depression: Were Government and Unions to Blame?. *Industrial & Labour Relations Review*, [online] 65(3), pp. 501-532. Available at: <https://www.jstor.org/stable/24368882?seq=1#metadata_info_tab_contents> [Accessed 30 September 2020].

Keenan, J., 2014. *Law And Legal Practice In Egypt From Alexander To The Arab Conquest: A Selection Of Papyrological Sources In Translation, With Introductions And Commentary*. Cambridge: Cambridge University Press.

Kelsen, H. and Knight, M., 1934. *Pure Theory Of Law*. Vienna: Deuticke.

Kemmerer, D., 1948. MITCHELL, BROADUS. Depression Decade: From New Era Through New Deal, 1929-1941. "The Economic History of the United States". Vol. IX. Pp. xvii, 462. New York: Rinehart and Com pany, 1947. $4.00. *The ANNALS of the American Academy of Political and Social Science*, [online] 257(1), pp. 210-212. Available at: <https://journals.sagepub.com/doi/abs/10.1177/000271624825700134> [Accessed 29 September 2020].

Kenwood, A. and Lougheed, A., 1999. *The Growth Of The International Economy 1820-2000*. London: Routhledge.

Keynes J.M., 1936, *The General Theory of Employment, Interest and Money*, London, Palgrave Macmillan.

Keynes, J. M., 1926. *La Fine Del Laissez-Faire (1926)*. [online] Panarchy.org. Available at: <https://www.panarchy.org/keynes/lasciarfare.1926.html> [Accessed 30 September 2020].

King, T. and Cecil, H., 2006. *The History Of Major Changes To The Social Security System*. [online] Archives.cpajournal.com. Available at: <http://archives.cpajournal.com/2006/506/infocus/p15.htm> [Accessed 30 September 2020].

Kitchen, A., Miyamoto, M. and Mulligan, C., 2008. *A Three-Stage Colonisation Model for the Peopling of the Americas. PLoS ONE*, [online] 3(2), p. e1596. Available at: <https://journals.plos.org/plosone/article?id=10.1371/journal.pone.0001596#abstract0> [Accessed 4 September 2020].

Kloepfer I., 2008 *Aufstand der Unterschicht. Was auf uns zukommt* Hamburg Hoffmann und Campe Verlag.

Koch, C., Hawking, S., Low, P., Pepperberg, I., van Swinderen, B., Edelman, D., Boyden, E., Reiss, D., Pfaff, D., Remedios, R., Karten, H., Vollenweider, F., Tsuchiya, N., Boly, M. and Laureys, S., 2012. *The Cambridge Declaration Of Consciousness*. [online] Fcmconference.org. Available at: <http://fcmconference.org/img/CambridgeDeclarationOnConsciousness.pdf> [Accessed 3 September 2020].

Kohn, M., 1996. *IT's ALL IN THE MIND*. [online] The Independent. Available at: <http://www.independent.co.uk/arts-entertainment/its-all-in-the-mind-1357092.html> [Accessed 4 September 2020].

Königs, S., Immervoll, H. and Jenkins, S., 2015. *Are Recipients of Social Assistance 'Benefit Dependent'? in OECD Social, Employment and Migration Working Papers*, [online] 162(1). Available at: <https://www.oecd-ilibrary.org/social-issues-migration-health/are-recipients-of-social-assistance-benefit-dependent_5jxrcmgpc6mn-en> [Accessed 14 September 2020].

Krautkraemer, J., 2005. *Economics Of Natural Resource Scarcity: The State Of The Debate*. [online] Resources for the Future. Available at: <https://www.rff.org/publications/working-papers/economics-of-natural-resource-scarcity-the-state-of-the-debate/> [Accessed 4 September 2020].

Krugman, P., 2008. *The Return Of Depression Economics And The Crisis Of 2008*. London: Penguin.

Kuran, T., 2013. *The Long Divergence: How Islamic Law Held Back The Middle East*. Princeton: Princeton University Press.

Kurlansky, M., 2002. *Salt: A World History*. New York: Walker & Co.

Lange, D., 2020. *Migrant Farm Families*. [online] Historyplace.com. Available at: <http://www.historyplace.com/unitedstates/lange/> [Accessed 30 September 2020].

Landrock P., T. Pedersen T. *"WYSIWYS? -- What you see is what you sign?"*. *Information Security Technical Report*, Volume 3, Number 2, 1998, 55-61.

Lanzieri, G., 2011. *The Greying Of The Baby Boomers: A Century-Long View Of Ageing In European Populations*. [online] Ec.europa.eu. Available at: <https://ec.europa.eu/eurostat/documents/3433488/5578868/KS-SF-11-023-EN.PDF/882b8b1e-998b-454e-a574-bb15cc64b653> [Accessed 14 September 2020].

Leakey, R. and Lewin, R., 1979. *People Of The Lake*. New York: Avon Books.

Lee, P., 1996. *The Whorf Theory Complex: A Critical Reconstruction*. Philadelphia: John Benjamins Publishing, pp.89-96.

Lee, R. and Daly, R., 1999. *The Cambridge Encyclopedia Of Hunters And Gatherers*, Cambridge: Cambridge University Press.

Lessig L. 1999. *Code and other laws of the cyberspace*, New York Basic Books.

Lessig, L., 2004. *Free Culture*. New York: Penguin Press.

Lichtblau, E. and Benner, K., 2020. *Apple Fights Order To Unlock San Bernardino Gunman'S Iphone*. [online] Nytimes.com. Available at: <https://www.nytimes.com/2016/02/18/technology/apple-timothy-cook-fbi-san-bernardino.html> [Accessed 1 October 2020].

Lim, C. and Ying, S., 2011. *The Great Depression, the Great Recession and the Next Crisis* in *World Economics*, [online] Available at: <https://www.research-gate.net/publication/227641365_The_Great_Depression_the_Great_Recession_and_the_Next_Crisis> [Accessed 30 September 2020].

Lipton, P., 2009. *The Evolution of the Joint Stock Company to 1800: A Study of Insti-tutional Change*. *SSRN Electronic Journal*, [online] Available at: <https://www.researchgate.net/publication/228229288_The_Evolution_of_the_Joint_Stock_Company_to_1800_A_Study_of_Institutional_Change> [Accessed 10 September 2020].

Liquisearch, 2020. *Subjected - History - Middle Ages - Medieval Europe*. [online] Liquisearch.com. Available at: <http://www.liquisearch.com/subjected/history/middle_ages/medieval_europe> [Accessed 10 September 2020].

Lucy, J., 1992. *Language Diversity And Thought: A Reformulation Of The Linguistic Relativity Hypothesis*. Cambridge: Cambridge University Press, pp. 17-66.

Lupan, M., 2012. *Great Depression vs. The current financial and economic crisis* in *Faculty of Economics and Public Administration*, [online] 12(16), pp. 27-35. Available at: <https://www.academia.edu/4351228/GREAT_DEPRES-SION_vs_THE_CURRENT_FINANCIAL_AND_ECONOMIC_CRISIS_Ph_D_Mariana_LUPAN> [Accessed 30 September 2020].

Luria, A., 1976. *Cognitive Development: It's Cultural And Social Foundations*. Cambridge: Harvard University Press.

Luyten K., González Díaz C., Claros E., 2019, *Legal migration to the EU*, European Parliamentary Research Service EPRS, https://www.europarl.europa.eu/RegData/etudes/BRIE/2019/635559/EPRS_BRI(2019)635559_EN.pdf.

Macchiavelli, N., 1931. *Discorsi Sopra La Prima Deca Di Tito Livio*. Firenze.

Maci, L., 2020. *L'hackathon Del Papa, Il Racconto Di Chi C'è Stato*. [online] Econo-myup. Available at: <https://www.economyup.it/startup/l-hackathon-del-papa-il-racconto-di-chi-c-e-stato/> [Accessed 2 October 2020].

Mackenzie, D., 2010. *Industrial employment and the policies of Herbert C. Hoover* in *The Quarterly Journal of Austrian Economics*, [online] 13(3). Available at: <https://www.researchgate.net/publication/268052605_IndustrIal_EmploymEnt_and_thE_polIcIEs_of_hErbErt_c_hoovEr> [Accessed 30 September 2020].

Maddison, A., 2001. *The World Economy*. Paris: OECD Publications.

Maddison, A., 2003. *The World Economy: Volume 1: A Millennial Perspective And Volume 2: Historical Statistics*. Paris: OECD.

Maddison, A., 2020. *The West And The Rest In The World Economy: 1000-2030*. [online] Researchgate.net. Available at: <https://www.researchgate.net/

publication/23991697_The_West_and_the_Rest_in_the_World_Econo-my_1000a2030> [Accessed 10 September 2020].

Madison, J., 1787. *The Avalon Project: The Federalist Papers No. 10.* [online] Ava-lon.law.yale.edu. Available at: <https://avalon.law.yale.edu/18th_cen-tury/fed10.asp> [Accessed 9 November 2020].

Marcus, G., & Davis, E. (2019). *Reboot: Getting to artificial intelligence we can trust.* New York, NY: Pantheon Books.

Marshack, A., 1976. *Some implications of the paleolithic symbolic evidence for the ori-gin of language* in *Annals of the New York Academy of Sciences,* [online] 280(1 Origins and E), pp.289-311. Available at: <https://www.researchgate.net/publication/227592425_SOME_IMPLICATIONS_OF_THE_PAL-AEOLITHIC_SYMBOLIC_EVIDENCE_FOR_THE_ORIGIN_OF_LAN-GUAGE> [Accessed 4 September 2020].

Martin, J. and Rappeport, A., 2020. *Debbie Wasserman Schultz To Resign D.N.C. Post.* [online] Nytimes.com. Available at: <https://www.nytimes.com/2016/07/25/us/politics/debbie-wasserman-schultz-dnc-wikileaks-emails.html?_r=0> [Accessed 2 October 2020].

Marx, K., 2020. *Das Kapital: Kritik Der Politische Ökonomie.* [online] us.archive.org. Available at: <https://ia902708.us.archive.org/6/items/KarlMarx-DasKapitalpdf/KAPITAL1.pdf> [Accessed 10 September 2020].

Mason S., *Electronic Signatures in Law,* 2016, Institute of Advanced Legal Stud-ies for the SAS Humanities Digital Library, School of Advanced Study, University of London, Kindle Edition.

Matthews, S., 2011. *What is a "Competitive" Tax System?* in *OECD Taxation Work-ing Papers,* [online] 2(1). Available at: <https://read.oecd-ilibrary.org/taxation/what-is-a-competitive-tax-system_5kg3h0vmd4kj-en#page1> [Accessed 14 September 2020].

Mayer-Schoñberger, V., 2009. *Delete: The Virtue Of Forgetting In The Digital Age.* Princeton: Princeton University Press.

Mazzotti, F., 2009. *Nota Sull'analisi Della Spesa Sociale In Italia.* [online] Cliclav-oro.gov.it. Available at: <https://www.cliclavoro.gov.it/Moduli%20e%20Documenti/NotaspesasocialeinItalia.pdf> [Accessed 14 September 2020].

McGhee, G., 2011. *Convergent Evolution: Limited Forms Most Beautiful.* Cam-bridge: Massachusetts Institute of Technology Press.

McLuhan, M., 1962. *The Gutenberg Galaxy: The Making Of Typographic Man.* Toronto: University of Toronto Press.

Melani, M., 2008. *Dottrine Generali Di Storia Del Diritto Medievale.* Lulu.com.

Mellars, P., 2006. *Why did modern human populations disperse from Africa ca. 60.000 years ago? A new model.* In *Proceedings of the National Academy of Sciences,* [online] 103(25), pp. 9381-9386. Available at: <https://www.pnas.org/content/103/25/9381> [Accessed 4 September 2020].

Merzbach, U. and Boyer, C., 2011. *A History Of Mathematics.* 3rd ed. Hoboken: John Wiley & Sons Inc.

Mesenbourg, T., 2020. *Measuring The Digital Economy.* [online] Census.gov. Available at: <https://www.census.gov/content/dam/Census/library/working-papers/2001/econ/umdigital.pdf> [Accessed 2 October 2020].

Meyer Elizabeth A., 2004, *Legitimacy and law in the Roman world: tabulae in Roman belief and practice*. Cambridge: Cambridge University Press.

Michael, R., 2020. *Immanuel Kant*. [online] Plato.stanford.edu. Available at: <https://plato.stanford.edu/entries/kant/> [Accessed 3 September 2020].

Micklethwait, J. and Wooldridge, A., 2014. *The Fourth Revolution: The Global Race To Reinvent The State*. Penguin.

Miller, G. and Spoolman, S., 2012. *Environmental Science*. 14th ed. Belmont: CENGAGE Learning Custom Publishing.

Mitchell, D., 2001. *Townsend and Roosevelt: Lessons from the Struggle for Elderly Income Support*. In *Labour History*, [online] 42(3), pp. 255-276. Available at: <https://www.researchgate.net/publication/232823867_Townsend_and_Roosevelt_Lessons_from_the_Struggle_for_Elderly_Income_Support> [Accessed 29 September 2020].

Mithen, S., 1998. *Creativity In Human Evolution And Prehistory*. London: Routledge, pp.165-191.

Mithen, S.,2003, *After the Ice: a Global Human History 20.000BC-5,000BC*. London, Weidenfield & Nicholson.

Mithen, S., 2005. *The Singing Neanderthal*. Cambridge: Harvard University Press.

Mithen, S., 2006. *The Singing Neanderthals: The Origins Of Music, Language, Mind, And Body*. Cambridge, Mass.: Harvard University Press.

RAY MONK, *Ludwig Wittgenstein: the duty of genius*, London, Cape 1990.

Mugasha, A., 2003. *The Law Of Letters Of Credit And Bank Guarantees*. Sydney: Federation Press.

Murphy, H. and Arango, T., 2020. *Joseph Deangelo Pleads Guilty In Golden State Killer Cases*. [online] Nytimes.com. Available at: <https://www.nytimes.com/2020/06/29/us/golden-state-killer-joseph-deangelo.html> [Accessed 1 October 2020].

Nadelhaft, J., 1966. *The Somersett Case and Slavery: Myth, Reality, and Repercussions*. In *The Journal of Negro History*, [online] 51(3), pp. 193-208. Available at: <https://www.journals.uchicago.edu/doi/10.2307/2716061> [Accessed 10 September 2020].

Nader, L., 2009. *The Anthropological Study of Law1*. In *American Anthropologist*, [online] 67(6), pp. 3-32. Available at: <https://anthrosource.onlinelibrary.wiley.com/doi/pdf/10.1525/aa.1965.67.6.02a00920> [Accessed 14 September 2020].

National Geographic, 2020. *Global Human Journey*. [online] National Geographic Society. Available at: <https://www.nationalgeographic.org/media/global-human-journey/> [Accessed 4 September 2020].

Nevin, B., 2010. Noam and Zellig. *Chomskyan (R)evolutions*, [online] pp. 103-168. Available at: <https://benjamins.com/catalog/z.154.05nev> [Accessed 4 September 2020].

Nicolaj, G., 1994. *Il Documento Privato Italiano Nell'Alto Medioevo In Libri E Documenti D'italia: Dai Longobardi Alla Rinascita Delle Città, Atti Del Convegno Dell'associazione Italiana Dei Paleografi E Diplomatisti*. [online] Scrineum.it. Available at: <http://www.scrineum.it/scrineum/biblioteca/nicolaj-documentoprivato.pdf> [Accessed 10 September 2020].

NIST, 2020. *Cloud Computing Program.* [online] NIST. Available at: <https://www.nist.gov/programs-projects/nist-cloud-computing-program-nccp> [Accessed 1 October 2020].

NIST, 2020. *The NIST Definition Of Cloud Computing.* [online] NIST. Available at: <https://csrc.nist.gov/publications/detail/sp/800-145/final> [Accessed 1 October 2020].

OECD, 2008, *Taxation Working Papers No. 26. Tax Design for Inclusive Growth,* by Bert Brys.

Sarah Perret, Alastair Thomas, Pierce O'Reilly, [online] Available at: <https://dx.doi.org/10.1787/5jlv74ggk0g7-en> [Accessed 14 September 2020].

OECD, 2011, *Taxation Working Papers No. 2. What is a "Competitive" Tax System?,* by Stephen Mattews, [online] Available at: < https://dx.doi.org/10.1787/5kg3h0vmd4kj-en> [Accessed 14 September 2020].

OECD, 2014. *The crisis and its aftermath: A stress test for societies and for social policies.* In *Society at a Glance 2014,* [online] 1(1), pp. 15-75. Available at: <https://read.oecd-ilibrary.org/social-issues-migration-health/society-at-a-glance-2014/the-crisis-and-its-aftermath-a-stress-test-for-societies-and-for-social-policies_soc_glance-2014-5-en#page1> [Accessed 14 September 2020].

OECD, 2015. *Health At A Glance 2015.* Paris: OECD Publishing.

OECD, 2015. *Revenue Statistics 2015.* Paris: Organisation for Economic Cooperation & Development.

OECD, 2018, *Taxation Working Papers No. 38. Corporate Effective Tax Rates: Model Description and Results from 36 OECD and Non-OECD Countries,* by Tibor Hanappi, [online] Available at: <https://dx.doi.org/10.1787/a07f9958-en> [Accessed 14 September 2020].

OECD, 2019. *OECD Social Expenditure Update 2019.* [online] Available at: <http://www.oecd.org/social/expenditure.htm> [Accessed 2 October 2020].

OECD, 2020. *Measuring The Digital Economy.* [online] Ec.europa.eu. Available at: <https://ec.europa.eu/eurostat/documents/341889/725159/OECD+Manual+Measuring+the+Digital+Economy/6418c566-4074-4461-9186-9ad509bc4a4d> [Accessed 2 October 2020].

OECD (2020), *Tax Policy Reforms 2020: OECD and Selected Partner Economies,* OECD Publishing, Paris.

Olson, D., 1980. *On the Language and Authority of Textbooks.* In *Journal of Communication,* [online] 30(1), pp. 186-196. Available at: <https://www.researchgate.net/publication/228025636_On_the_Language_and_Authority_of_Textbooks> [Accessed 10 September 2020].

Ong, W., 1954. *Johannes Piscator: One Man Or A Ramist Dichotomy?.* Cambridge: Harvard Library Bulletin, pp. 151-162.

Ong, W., 2002. *Orality And Literacy: The Technologizing Of The Word.* London and New York: Routledge.

Parker Pearson, M. and Richards, C., 2004. *Architecture And Order: Approaches To Social Space.* New York: Routledge.

Parthasarathi P., 2011. *Why Europe Grew Rich and Asia Did Not: Global Economic Divergence, 1600–1850* New York, Cambridge University Press.

Parthasarathi, Prasannan. Why Europe Grew Rich and Asia Did Not. Cambridge University Press. Kindle Edition.

Patel K.K., 2016, *The New Deal. A Global History*, Oxford-Princeton. Princeton University Press.

Phelps, E., 2004. *The Boom and the Slump: a Causal Account of the 1990s/2000s and the 1920s/1930s*. In *The Journal of Policy Reform*, [online] 7(1), pp. 3-19. Available at: <https://www.researchgate.net/publication/24085185_The_Boom_and_the_Slump_a_Causal_Account_of_the_1990s2000s_and_the_1920s1930s> [Accessed 30 September 2020].

Philosophy Index, 2002. *Baruch Spinoza*. [online] Philosophy-index.com. Available at: <http://www.philosophy-index.com/spinoza/> [Accessed 3 September 2020].

Piketty T., 2014, *Capital in the Twenty-First Century*, Cambridge MA London UK, Harvard University Press. First published as *Le capital au XXI siècle*, Éditions du Seuil, 2013.

Piketty T., 2015, *The Economics of Inequality*, Cambridge MA London UK, Harvard University Press.

Piketty T., 2020, *Capital and Ideology*, Cambridge MA London UK, Harvard University Press.

Pinker, S. and Bloom, P., 1990. *Natural language and natural selection*. In *Behavioral and Brain Sciences*, [online] 13(4), pp. 707-727. Available at: <https://stevenpinker.com/files/pinker/files/pinker_bloom_1990.pdf> [Accessed 3 September 2020].

Pinker, S., 1994. *The Language Instinct*. New York: William Morrow and Company.

Pinker, S., 1997. *How The Mind Works*. New York: Norton.

Pinker, S., 2003. *Language as an Adaptation to the Cognitive Niche* *. In *Language Evolution*, [online] 1(1), pp. 16-37. Available at: <https://www.researchgate.net/publication/246646025_Language_as_an_Adaptation_to_the_Cognitive_Niche> [Accessed 9 September 2020].

Pirenne, H., 1954. *Mohammed & Charlemagne*. London: Dover Publications.

Plato, 2020. *Phaedrus By Plato*. [online] Classics.mit.edu. Available at: <http://classics.mit.edu/Plato/phaedrus.html> [Accessed 3 September 2020].

Plato, n.d. *Seventh Letter*. [online] Perseus.tufts.edu. Available at: <http://www.perseus.tufts.edu/hopper/text?doc=Perseus:text:1999.01.0164:letter=7> [Accessed 10 September 2020].

Pomeranz K., 2000, *The Great Divergence. China, Europe, and the making of the Modern World Economy*. Princeton Oxford. Princeton University Press.

Popper, K., 1945 (2011 Kindle Edition). *The Open Society And Its Enemies; P.* London: Routledge Classics.

Posner, R., 2020. *Und In Alle Ewigkeit: Kommunikation Über 10 000 Jahre: Wie Sagen Wir Unsern Kindeskindern Wo Der Atommüll Liegt?* [online] Semiotik. tu-berlin.de. Available at: <https://www.semiotik.tu-berlin.de/menue/zeitschrift_fuer_semiotik/zs-hefte/bd_6_hft_3> [Accessed 1 October 2020].

Pulsiano, P., 1993. *Medieval Scandinavia*. New York: Routledge.

Purpura, G., 1991. *Sulle Origini Della Notitia Dignitatum In: Atti Del X Convegno Internaz. Accad. Costantiniana Di Perugia, 8 Ottobre, 1991*. [online] Www1.

unipa.it. Available at: <http://www1.unipa.it/dipstdir/pub/purpura/notitia_dignitatum.htm> [Accessed 10 September 2020].

Rajan R. G., 2010, *Fault Lines. How Hidden Fractures Still Threaten the World Economy*, Princeton-Oxford, Princeton University Press, Kindle Edition 2011.

Rauchway E., 2008, *The Great Depression & the New Deal*, Oxford-New York, Oxford University Press.

Rawls, J., 1971. *A Theory Of Justice*. Cambridge: Belknap Press.

Reinhart C. M. Rogoff K. S., 2011. *This Time is Different. Eight centuries of Financvial Folly*. Princeton-Oxford, Princeton University Press. Kindle Edition.

Religious Tolerance, 2020. *Christian Support Of Slavery: 5Th To 17Th Century CE.* [online] Religioustolerance.org. Available at: <http://www.religioustolerance.org/chr_slav4.htm> [Accessed 10 September 2020].

Richards, M., 2002. *A brief review of the archaeological evidence for Palaeolithic and Neolithic subsistence*. In *European Journal of Clinical Nutrition*, [online] 56(12), pp. 1270-1278. Available at: <https://www.researchgate.net/publication/10980853_A_brief_review_of_the_archaeological_evidence_for_Palaeolithic_and_Neolithic_subsistence> [Accessed 4 September 2020].

Richards, M., 2020. *Neolithic Agricultural Revolution: Causes And Implications.* [online] Study.com. Available at: <https://study.com/academy/lesson/neolithic-agricultural-revolution-causes-and-implications.html> [Accessed 4 September 2020].

Richman, S., 1996. *New Deal Nemesis*. In *The Independent Review*, [online] 1(2). Available at: <https://www.independent.org/publications/tir/article.asp?id=473> [Accessed 30 September 2020].

Ricoeur P., 1987. *La Configurazione Nel Racconto Di Finzione*. Milano: Jaca Book.

Ricoeur P., 1986, *Time and Narrative*, Vol. 1, Chicago, The University of Chicago Press.

Ricoeur P., 1987, *Time and Narrative*, Vol. 2, Chicago, The University of Chicago Press.

Ricoeur P., 1988, *Time and Narrative*, Vol. 3, Chicago, The University of Chicago Press.

Rincon, P., 2011. *Blow For European Origins Theory*. [online] BBC News. Available at: <https://www.bbc.com/news/science-environment-14630012> [Accessed 4 September 2020].

Rincon, P., 2013. *Making Of Europe Unlocked By DNA*. [online] BBC News. Available at: <https://www.bbc.com/news/science-environment-22252099> [Accessed 4 September 2020].

Roberts, A., 2010. *The Incredible Human Journey*. London: Bloomsbury.

Romer, C., 2013. *Great Depression | Definition, History, Dates, Causes, Effects, & Facts*. [online] Encyclopedia Britannica. Available at: <https://www.britannica.com/event/Great-Depression> [Accessed 29 September 2020].

Salmon C., (2008), *Storytelling: La machine à fabriquer des histoires et à formater les esprits*, Paris: La Découverte.

Sandel, M., 2010. *Justice*. London: Penguin Books.

Sandel, M., 2020. *Justice*. [online] Justiceharvard.org. Available at: <http://justiceharvard.org/> [Accessed 30 September 2020].

Sandel, M., 2020. *Justice Lecture 19: The Good Citizen - Harvard Justice.* [online] Justiceharvard.org. Available at: <http://justiceharvard.org/lecture-19-the-good-citizen/> [Accessed 30 September 2020].

Sandel, M., 2020. *Justice Lecture 1: The Moral Side Of Murder - Harvard Justice.* [online] Justiceharvard.org. Available at: <http://justiceharvard.org/themoralsideofmurder/> [Accessed 30 September 2020].

Sandel, M., 2020. *Justice Lecture 2: The Case For Cannibalism.* [online] Justiceharvard.org. Available at: <http://justiceharvard.org/lecture-2-the-case-for-cannibalism/> [Accessed 30 September 2020].

Sandel, M., 2020. *Justice Lecture 3: Putting A Price Tag On Life.* [online] Justiceharvard.org. Available at: <http://justiceharvard.org/lecture-3-putting-a-price-tag-on-life/> [Accessed 30 September 2020].

Sandel, M., 2020. *Justice Lecture 4: How To Measure Pleasure.* [online] Justiceharvard.org. Available at: <http://justiceharvard.org/lecture-4-how-to-measure-pleasure/> [Accessed 30 September 2020].

Sandel, M., 2020. *Justice Lecture 5: Free To Choose.* [online] Justiceharvard.org. Available at: <http://justiceharvard.org/lecture-5-free-to-choose/> [Accessed 30 September 2020].

Sandel, M., 2020. *Justice Lecture 6: Who Owns Me?.* [online] Justiceharvard.org. Available at: <http://justiceharvard.org/lecture-6-who-owns-me/> [Accessed 30 September 2020].

Sandel, M., 2020. *Justice Lecture 7: This Land Is Your Land.* [online] Justiceharvard.org. Available at: <http://justiceharvard.org/lecture-7-this-land-is-your-land/> [Accessed 30 September 2020].

Sandel, M., 2020. *Justice Lecture 8: Consenting Adults.* [online] Justiceharvard.org. Available at: <http://justiceharvard.org/lecture-8-consenting-adults/> [Accessed 30 September 2020].

Sandel, M., 2020. *Justice Lecture 9: Hired Guns?.* [online] Justiceharvard.org. Available at: <http://justiceharvard.org/lecture-9-hired-guns/> [Accessed 30 September 2020].

Sandel, M., 2020. *Justice Lecture 10: For Sale: Motherhood.* [online] Justiceharvard.org. Available at: <http://justiceharvard.org/lecture-10-for-sale-motherhood/> [Accessed 30 September 2020].

Sandel, M., 2020. *Justice Lecture 11: Mind Your Motive.* [online] Justiceharvard.org. Available at: <http://justiceharvard.org/lecture-11-mind-your-motive/> [Accessed 30 September 2020].

Sandel, M., 2020. *Justice Lecture 12: The Supreme Principle Of Morality.* [online] Justiceharvard.org. Available at: <http://justiceharvard.org/lecture-12-the-supreme-principle-of-morality/> [Accessed 30 September 2020].

Sandel, M., 2020. *Justice Lecture 13: A Lesson In Lying.* [online] Justiceharvard.org. Available at: <http://justiceharvard.org/lecture-13-a-lesson-in-lying/> [Accessed 30 September 2020].

Sandel, M., 2020. *Justice Lecture 14: A Deal Is A Deal.* [online] Justiceharvard.org. Available at: <http://justiceharvard.org/lecture-14-a-deal-is-a-deal/> [Accessed 30 September 2020].

Sandel, M., 2020. *Justice Lecture 15: What'S A Fair Start?.* [online] Justiceharvard.org. Available at: <http://justiceharvard.org/lecture-15-whats-a-fair-start/> [Accessed 30 September 2020].

Sandel, M., 2020. *Justice Lecture 16: What Do We Deserve?*. [online] Justiceharvard.org. Available at: <http://justiceharvard.org/lecture-16-what-do-we-deserve/> [Accessed 30 September 2020].

Sandel, M., 2020. *Justice Lecture 17: Arguing Affirmative Action.* [online] Justiceharvard.org. Available at: <http://justiceharvard.org/lecture-17-arguing-affirmative-action/> [Accessed 30 September 2020].

Sandel, M., 2020. *Justice Lecture 18: What'S The Purpose?*. [online] Justiceharvard.org. Available at: <http://justiceharvard.org/lecture-18-whats-the-purpose/> [Accessed 30 September 2020].

Sandel, M., 2020. *Justice Lecture 20: Freedom VS. Fit.* [online] Justiceharvard.org. Available at: <http://justiceharvard.org/lecture-20-freedom-vs-fit/> [Accessed 30 September 2020].

Sandel, M., 2020. *Justice Lecture 21: The Claims Of Community.* [online] Justiceharvard.org. Available at: <http://justiceharvard.org/lecture-21-the-claims-of-community/> [Accessed 30 September 2020].

Sandel, M., 2020. *Justice Lecture 23: Debating Same Sex Marriage.* [online] Justiceharvard.org. Available at: <http://justiceharvard.org/lecture-23-debating-same-sex-marriage/> [Accessed 30 September 2020].

Sandel, M., 2020. *Justice Lecture 24: The Good Life.* [online] Justiceharvard.org. Available at: <http://justiceharvard.org/lecture-24-the-good-life/> [Accessed 30 September 2020].

Sandel, M., 2020. *Jutsice Lecture 22: Where Our Loyalty Lies.* [online] Justiceharvard.org. Available at: <http://justiceharvard.org/lecture-22-where-our-loyalty-lies/> [Accessed 30 September 2020].

Sanfilippo, c., 2002. *Istituzioni Di Diritto Romano.* 10th ed. Rubettino.

Santarpia, V., 2014. *Corte Dei Conti: Le Società Partecipate Costano 26 Miliardi All'Anno.* [online] Corriere della Sera. Available at: <https://www.corriere.it/economia/14_giugno_29/corte-conti-societa-partecipate-drenano-26-miliardi-all-anno-a17398ae-ffa0-11e3-ae4d-7c1f18234268.shtml> [Accessed 29 September 2020].

Savulescu, J. and Bostrom, N., 2011. *Human Enhancement.* Oxford: Oxford University Press.

Scales R. P., 2016, *Radio and the Politics of Sound in Interware France, 1921-1939.* Cambridge UK, Cambridge University Press. Kindle Edition.

Scheibelhofer K., "*Signing XML Documents and the Concept of What You See Is What You Sign*", Graz University of Technology, Austria, 2001.

Scheidel, W. and Friesen, S. J., 'The size of the economy and the distribution of income in the Roman Empire', in *Journal of Roman Studies*, 99 (2009), pp. 61–91.

Schmitt Carl, (1921), *Die Diktatur. Von den Anfängen des modernen Souveränitätsgedankens bis zum proletarischen Klassenkampf,* München Leipzig, Duncker & Humblot.

Schmitt Carl, (1922), *Politische Theologie. Vier Kapitel zur Lehre von der Souveränität,* München Leipzig, Duncker & Humblot.

Schmitt Carl, (1924), *Die geistesgeschichtliche Lage des heutigen Parlamentarismus,* München Leipzig, Duncker & Humblot.

Schmitt Carl, (1932) *Der Begriff des Politischen (Erweiterung des Aufsatzes von 1927),* München Leipzig, Duncker & Humblot.

Schüll Dow, N., 2012, *Addiction by Design: Machine Gambling in Las Vegas*. Princeton University Press.

Schwarz, A. M., *The Inverted Pyramid: Pension Systems Facing Demographic Challenges in Europe and Central Asia (Europe and Central Asia Reports)*, 2013, World Bank Publications; Illustrated Edition. [online] Available at: <https://www.worldbank.org/content/dam/Worldbank/Event/pensions/3.%20Schwarz_The%20Inverted%20Pyramid%203-04-2014.pdf.> [Accessed 9 September 2020]

https://www.worldbank.org/content/dam/Worldbank/Event/pensions/3.%20Schwarz_The%20Inverted%20Pyramid%203-04-2014.pdf.

Seager, W., 2007. A Brief History of the Philosophical Problem of Consciousness. *The Cambridge Handbook of Consciousness*, [online] 1(1), pp. 9-34. Available at: <https://www.cambridge.org/core/books/cambridge-handbook-of-consciousness/brief-history-of-the-philosophical-problem-of-consciousness/F095FDAB8783EE7B0E6BB6F9D9179569> [Accessed 9 September 2020].

Searle, J., 1996. *The Construction Of Social Reality*. London: Penguin Books.

Searle, J., 1998. *Mind, Language And Society: Philosophy In The Real World*. London: Basic Books.

Searle, J., 2007. *Freedom And Neurobiology*. New York: Columbia University Press.

Searle, J., 2007. *The construction of social reality*. New York, NY: Free Press.

Searle, J., 2010. *Making The Social World: The Structure Of Human Civilisation*. Oxford: Oxford University Press.

Sebeok, T. A., 2001. *Signs: An Introduction To Semiotics*. Toronto: University of Toronto Press.

Sebeok, T. A., 2001. *Global Semiotics*, Bloomington (USA): Indina University Press.

Sen, A., 2011. *The Idea Of Justice*. Cambridge: Belknap Press of Harvard University Press.

Shafik, M., 2021, *What We Owe Each Other: A New Social Contract*, London, Vintage.

Shachmurove, Y., 2011. A historical overview of financial crises in the United States. *Global Finance Journal*, [online] 22(3), pp. 217-231. Available at: <https://www.researchgate.net/publication/251637572_A_historical_overview_of_financial_crises_in_the_United_States> [Accessed 30 September 2020].

Silver, N., 2012. *The Signal And The Noise: Why So Many Predictions Fail, But Some Don't*. Turtleback Books.

Social Security Administration, 2020. *Social Security History: The Social Security Act Of 1935*. [online] Ssa.gov. Available at: <https://www.ssa.gov/history/35act.html> [Accessed 30 September 2020].

Sosnowski, R., 2005. *Origini Della Lingua Dell'economia In Italia*. Milano: Franco Angeli.

Sparks C. Tulloch J., *Tabloid tales: global debates over media standards*, University of Colorado at Boulder, Rowman Et Littlefield Publishers, Inc. 2000.

Spini, G., 1965. *Storia Dell'età Moderna, Volume I*. Torino: Giulio Einaudi editore.

Stiglitz J. E., 2018, *The Welfare State in the Twenty-First Century* in *The Welfare State Revisited (Initiative for Policy Dialogue at Columbia: Challenges in Development and Globalisation)* edited by OCAMPO J. A. STIGLITZ J. E. New York. Columbia University Press. Kindle Edition.

Stockman C., Scalia V. (2020), *Democracy on the Five Star Movement's Rousseau platform*, in European Politics and Society, 21:5, 603-617

Stuart, A., 2005. *The extinction of woolly mammoth (Mammuthus primigenius) and straight-tusked elephant (Palaeoloxodon antiquus) in Europe*. In *Quaternary International*, [online] 126(1), pp. 171-177. Available at: <https://www.researchgate.net/publication/222707214_The_extinction_of_woolly_mammoth_Mammuthus_primigenius_and_straight-tusked-elephant_Palaeoloxodon_antiquus_in_Europe> [Accessed 4 September 2020].

Sugiyama, M., 1996. *On the Origins of Narrative: Storyteller Bias as a Fitness-enhancing Strategy*. In *Human Nature*, [online] 7(4), pp. 403-425. Available at: <https://www.researchgate.net/publication/258349654_On_the_origins_of_narrative_Storyteller_bias_as_a_fitness-enhancing_strategy> [Accessed 3 September 2020].

Sugiyama, M., 2008. *Narrative as Social Mapping - Case Study: The Trickster Genre and the Free Rider Problem*. In *Ometeca*, [online] 12(1), pp. 24-42. Available at: <https://ometeca.org/journal/#Vol_12_(2008)> [Accessed 3 September 2020].

Sugiyama, M., 2011. *The Forager Oral Tradition and the Evolution of Prolonged Juvenility*. In *Frontiers in Psychology*, 2.

Sugiyama, M., 2012. *From theory to practice: Foundations of an evolutionary literary curriculum*. In *Style*, [online] 46(3), pp. 317-337. Available at: <https://www.researchgate.net/publication/259971260_From_Theory_to_Practice_Foundations_of_An_Evolutionary_Literary_Curriculum_The_Need_for_a_Prehistory_of_Literature> [Accessed 3 September 2020].

Swift, J., 1726. *Gulliver'S Travels Into Several Remote Nations Of The World*. London: Middle Temple-Gate.

Szado, E., 2011. *Defining Speculation: The First Step toward a Rational Dialogue*. In *The Journal of Alternative Investments*, [online] 14(1), pp. 75-82. Available at: <https://jai.pm-research.com/content/14/1/75.abstract> [Accessed 29 September 2020].

Tanzi, V. and Schuknecht, L., 2000. *Public Spending In The 20Th Century: A Global Perspective*. Cambridge: Cambridge University Press.

Tapscott, D., 2014. *The Digital Economy: Rethinking Promise And Peril In The Age Of Networked Intelligence*. New York: McGraw-Hill Education.

Tattersall, I., 2009. *Human origins: Out of Africa*. In *Proceedings of the National Academy of Sciences*, [online] 106(38), pp. 16018-16021. Available at: <https://www.pnas.org/content/106/38/16018> [Accessed 4 September 2020].

Tett, G., 2009. *Fool's Gold: How Unrestrained Greed Corrupted A Dream, Shattered Global Markets And Unleashed A Catastrophe*. London: Little, Brown.

The Economist a, 2015. *The Dawn Of Artificial Intelligence*. [online] The Economist. Available at: <https://www.economist.com/leaders/2015/05/09/the-dawn-of-artificial-intelligence?zid=291&ah=906e69ad01d2ee51960100b7fa502595> [Accessed 3 September 2020].

The Economist b, 2015. *Editing Humanity*. [online] The Economist. Available at: <https://www.economist.com/leaders/2015/08/22/editing-humanity> [Accessed 3 September 2020].

The Economist, 1999. *The Road To Riches*. [online] The Economist. Available at: <http://www.economist.com/node/346598> [Accessed 3 September 2020].

The Economist, 2006. *The Wiki Principle*. [online] The Economist. Available at: <https://www.economist.com/special-report/2006/04/22/the-wiki-principle> [Accessed 2 October 2020].

The Economist, 2009. *Old-Age Dependency Ratios*. [online] The Economist. Available at: <https://www.economist.com/economic-and-financial-indicators/2009/05/07/old-age-dependency-ratios> [Accessed 14 September 2020].

The Economist 30th July 2016, *Globalisation and politics. Drawbridges up. The new divide in rich countries is not between left and right but between open and closed.* [online] The Economist. Available at: https://www.economist.com/briefing/2016/07/30/drawbridges-up [Accessed 14 September 2020].

The Economist, March 16th 2018, *Globalisation. Some thoughts on the open v closed divide.* [online] The Economist. Available at: *https://www.economist.com/bagehots-notebook/2018/03/16/some-thoughts-on-the-open-v-closed-divide* [Accessed 14 September 2020].

The Economist, August 10 2020, *Artificial intelligence A new AI language model generates poetry and prose. GPT-3 can be eerily human-like-for better and for worse,* [online] The Economist. Available at: *https://www.economist.com/science-and-technology/2020/08/06/a-new-ai-language-model-generates-poetry-and-prose* [Accessed 14 September 2020].

The Economist, 2012. *The Road To Riches*. [online] The Economist. Available at: <http://www.economist.com/node/346598> [Accessed 3 September 2020].

The Economist, 2015. *The Promise Of The Blockchain: The Trust Machine*. [online] The Economist. Available at: <https://www.economist.com/leaders/2015/10/31/the-trust-machine> [Accessed 1 October 2020].

The Economist, November 21st 2015, *Automatic voter registration. Left Turn,* [online] The Economist. Available at: <https://www.economist.com/united-states/2015/11/19/left-turn> [Accessed 22 December 2020]

The Economist, 2018, *The minority majority. America's electoral system gives the Republicans advantages over Democrats.* [online] The Economist. Available at: <https://www.economist.com/briefing/2018/07/12/americas-electoral-system-gives-the-republicans-advantages-over-democrats> [Accessed 22 December 2020].

The Economist, 2020, *A formidable alliance takes on Facebook.* [online] The Economist. Available at: <https://www.economist.com/business/2020/12/12/a-formidable-alliance-takes-on-facebook> [Accessed 22 December 2020].

The Economist, 2020. *Already Indicted*. [online] The Economist. Available at: <https://www.economist.com/united-states/2016/05/28/already-indicted> [Accessed 2 October 2020].

The Economist, 2020, *American trustbusters take on Google.* [online] The Economist. Available at: <https://www.economist.com/business/2020/10/21/american-trustbusters-take-on-google> [Accessed 21 November 2020].

The Economist, November 10th 2020, *America's urban-rural partisan gap is widening. Without reforms to its winner-take-all system, this trend will continue to benefit Republicans.* [online] Available at: https://www.economist.com/graphic-detail/2020/11/10/americas-urban-rural-partisan-gap-is-widening [Accessed 12 November 2020].

The Economist, 2020. *Britain Moves To Rein In Data-Analytics.* [online] The Economist. Available at: <https://www.economist.com/britain/2018/03/28/britain-moves-to-rein-in-data-analytics> [Accessed 2 October 2020].

The Economist, 2020. *Changing Nature.* [online] The Economist. Available at: <https://www.economist.com/babbage/2013/02/27/changing-nature> [Accessed 2 October 2020].

The Economist, 2020. *Countries Are Using Apps And Data Networks To Keep Tabs On The Pandemic.* [online] The Economist. Available at: <https://www.economist.com/briefing/2020/03/26/countries-are-using-apps-and-data-networks-to-keep-tabs-on-the-pandemic> [Accessed 1 October 2020].

The Economist, 2020. *Don'T Rely On Contact-Tracing Apps.* [online] The Economist. Available at: <https://www.economist.com/leaders/2020/05/16/dont-rely-on-contact-tracing-apps> [Accessed 1 October 2020].

The Economist, 2020. *Home Of The Brave.* [online] The Economist. Available at: <https://www.economist.com/books-and-arts/2016/06/02/home-of-the-brave> [Accessed 2 October 2020].

The Economist, 2020. *How Science Goes Wrong.* [online] The Economist. Available at: <https://www.economist.com/leaders/2013/10/21/how-science-goes-wrong> [Accessed 2 October 2020].

The Economist, 2020. *How The Internet Has Changed Dating.* [online] The Economist. Available at: <https://www.economist.com/briefing/2018/08/18/how-the-Internet-has-changed-dating> [Accessed 2 October 2020].

The Economist, 2020. *Internet Security: When Back Doors Backfire.* [online] The Economist. Available at: <https://www.economist.com/leaders/2015/12/30/when-back-doors-backfire> [Accessed 1 October 2020].

The Economist, 2021, *Mario Draghi gives Italy another chance. From banker to prime minister (Leader),* [online] The Economist. Available at: https://www.economist.com/leaders/2021/02/20/mario-draghi-gives-italy-another-chance [Accessed 1 December 2020]

The Economist, Nov. 26th 2020, *Poland and Hungary enjoy a physics lesson courtesy of the EU (Charlemagne),* [online] The Economist. Available at: https://www.economist.com/europe/2020/11/26/poland-and-hungary-enjoy-a-physics-lesson-courtesy-of-the-eu> [Accessed 1 December 2020].

The Economist, 2020. *Privacy In A Pandemic.* [online] The Economist. Available at: <https://www.economist.com/europe/2020/04/23/privacy-in-a-pandemic> [Accessed 1 October 2020].

The Economist, 2020. *Public Spending Puzzle.* [online] The Economist. Available at: <https://www.economist.com/buttonwoods-notebook/2012/10/17/public-spending-puzzle> [Accessed 14 September 2020].

The Economist, 2020. *Rise Of The Machines.* [online] The Economist. Available at: <https://www.economist.com/briefing/2015/05/09/rise-of-the-machines> [Accessed 1 October 2020].

The Economist, 2020. *Some Countries Want Central Databases For Contact-Tracing Apps.* [online] The Economist. Available at: <https://www.economist.com/europe/2020/04/30/some-countries-want-central-databases-for-contact-tracing-apps> [Accessed 1 October 2020].

The Economist, 2020. *State Of The Art.* [online] The Economist. Available at: <https://www.economist.com/1843/2016/05/03/state-of-the-art> [Accessed 2 October 2020].

The Economist, 2020, *The art of losing. Accepting a disappointing election result is a key part of democracy.* (Leaders), [online] The Economist. Available at: <https://www.economist.com/leaders/2020/11/21/accepting-a-disappointing-election-result-is-a-key-part-of-democracy>[Accessed 22 December 2020].

The Economist, 2020. *The Battle For Wikipedia's Soul.* [online] The Economist. Available at: <https://www.economist.com/technology-quarterly/2008/03/08/the-battle-for-wikipedias-soul> [Accessed 2 October 2020].

The Economist, 2020. *The Free-Knowledge Fundamentalist.* [online] The Economist. Available at: <https://www.economist.com/technology-quarterly/2008/06/07/the-free-knowledge-fundamentalist> [Accessed 2 October 2020].

The Economist, 2020. *The Sandernistas' Last Hurrah In Philadelphia.* [online] The Economist. Available at: <https://www.economist.com/democracy-in-america/2016/07/26/the-sandernistas-last-hurrah-in-philadelphia> [Accessed 2 October 2020].

The Economist, 2020. *Tracking And Tracing Covid-19: What Are The Promises, Limitations And Risks?.* [online] The Economist. Available at: <https://www.economist.com/podcasts/2020/06/24/tracking-and-tracing-covid-19-what-are-the-promises-limitations-and-risks> [Accessed 1 October 2020].

The Economist, 2020. *Trouble At The Lab.* [online] The Economist. Available at: <https://www.economist.com/briefing/2013/10/18/trouble-at-the-lab> [Accessed 2 October 2020].

The Economist, 2020, *United States of Amoeba.* [online] The Economist. Available at: <https://www.economist.com/united-states/2013/12/05/united-states-of-amoeba> [Accessed 22 December 2020].

The Economist, 2020, *Voter suppression. At risk of losing Texas, Republicans scheme to limit Democratic votes* [online] The Economist. Available at: <https://www.economist.com/united-states/2020/10/10/at-risk-of-losing-texas-republicans-scheme-to-limit-democratic-votes> [Accessed 20 October 2020]>.

The Economist, 2020, Leaders. Who controls the conversation. How to deal with free speech on social media. It is too important to be determined by a handful of tech executives. [online] The Economist. Available at: The Economist. Available at: <https://www.economist.com/briefing/2013/10/18/trouble-at-the-lab> [Accessed 20 October 2020]>.

The Editors of Encyclopedia Britannica, 2020. *Works Progress Administration: Definition & History.* [online] Encyclopedia Britannica. Available at: <https://www.britannica.com/topic/Works-Progress-Administration> [Accessed 30 September 2020].

The New Hampshire State Constitution, 2020. *Bill Of Rights: Right To Revolution.* [online] Nh.gov. Available at: <https://www.nh.gov/glance/bill-of-rights.htm> [Accessed 1 October 2020].

The Week, 2014. *Today In History: The Birth Of Social Security.* [online] Theweek.com. Available at: <https://theweek.com/articles/461094/today-history-birth-social-security> [Accessed 30 September 2020].

The World Economy, 2020. *Europe's Decline From The First To Tenth Centuries.* [online] Theworldeconomy.org. Available at: <http://www.theworldeconomy.org/impact/Europe_s_decline_from_the_first_to_tenth_centuries_100_1000.html> [Accessed 10 September 2020].

The World Economy, 2020. *The Contours Of World Development.* [online] Theworldeconomy.org. Available at: <http://www.theworldeconomy.org> [Accessed 10 September 2020].

Thomas, R., 1992. *Literacy And Orality In Ancient Greece.* Cambridge UK: Cambridge University Press.

Thornton, M., 2010. Hoover, Bush, and Great Depression. *The Quarterly Journal of Austrian Economics*, [online] 13. Available at: <https://www.researchgate.net/publication/228639724_HooverBush_and_Great_Depressions> [Accessed 30 September 2020].

Tocqueville, A., 1840. *De La Démocratie En Amérique, Tome Premier Et Augmentée D'un Avertissement Et D'un Examen Comparatif De La Démocratie Aux États-Unis Et En Suisse.* London: Saunders and Otley.

Tooby, J. and Cosmides, L., 2001. Does Beauty Build Adapted Minds? Toward an Evolutionary Theory of Aesthetics, Fiction and the Arts. *SubStance*, [online] 30(1/2), p. 6. Available at: <https://www.jstor.org/stable/3685502?seq=1#metadata_info_tab_contents> [Accessed 3 September 2020].

Topol, E. J. (2019). *Deep medicine: How artificial intelligence can make healthcare human again.* New York, NY: Basic Books.

Transpacific Project 2020, 2020. *Transpacific Migrations:* [online] Transpacificproject.com. Available at: <http://www.transpacificproject.com/index.php/transpacific-migrations/> [Accessed 4 September 2020].

Trask, R. and Stockwell, P., 2007. *Language And Linguistics: The Key Concepts.* 2nd ed. London: Routledge.

Turner, F., 1921. *The Frontier In American History.* New York, NY: Open Road Integrated Media.

Turkle S., 2005, *The Second Self: Computers and the Human Spirit Twentieth Anniversary Edition*, Cambridge USA, MIT Press

Turner, M., 1998. *The Literary Mind.* Oxford: Oxford University Press.

UCLA, 2020. *Tablet Entries.* [online] cdli.ucla.edu. Available at: <https://cdli.ucla.edu/cdlitablet/showcase> [Accessed 9 September 2020].

UN, 1948. *Universal Declaration Of Human Rights.* [online] Un.org. Available at: <https://www.un.org/en/universal-declaration-human-rights/index.html> [Accessed 9 September 2020].

United States Senate, 1787. *Constitution Of The United States.* [online] Senate.gov. Available at: <https://www.senate.gov/civics/constitution_item/constitution.htm> [Accessed 29 September 2020].

US Buro of Justice Statistics, Justice Expenditure And Employment Extracts, 2016 - Preliminary, [online] Available at: https://www.bjs.gov/index.cfm?ty=pbdetail&iid=6728 [Accessed 2 October 2020].

US Census Bureau, 2020. *E-Stats 2014 Report: Measuring The Electronic Economy*. [online] The United States Census Bureau. Available at: <https://www.census.gov/newsroom/press-releases/2016/cb16-tps108.html> [Accessed 2 October 2020].

US Congress, 1776. *Declaration Of Independence: A Transcription*. [online] Archives.org. Available at: <https://www.archives.gov/founding-docs/declaration-transcript> [Accessed 1 October 2020].

US Congress, 2020. *Amendments To The Constitution Of The United States Of America*. [online] Govinfo.gov. Available at: <https://www.govinfo.gov/content/pkg/GPO-CONAN-1992/pdf/GPO-CONAN-1992-7.pdf> [Accessed 29 September 2020].

US Department of Commerce, 2020. *Digital Economy*. [online] U.S. Department of Commerce. Available at: <https://www.commerce.gov/tags/digital-economy> [Accessed 2 October 2020].

US Supreme Court, 1984, *Court's Ruling in Chevron U.S.A., Inc. v. Natural Resources Defense Council, Inc.*, 467 U.S. 837, [online] https://supreme.justia.com/cases/federal/us/467/837/.

US Supreme Court, 2013. *Court'S Ruling In Riley V. US*. [online] Supremecourt.gov. Available at: <https://www.supremecourt.gov/opinions/13pdf/13-132_8l9c.pdf> [Accessed 1 October 2020].

Van de Mieroop, M., 1999. *Cuneiform Texts And The Writing Of History*. New York: Routledge.

Vergano, D., 2011. *Grapes Domesticated 8.000 Years Ago*. [online] USATODAY.COM. Available at: <http://content.usatoday.com/communities/sciencefair/post/2011/01/domestics-grape-genome-sequenced/1#.X1kFAy17HRY> [Accessed 9 September 2020].

Watson, A., 2006. *Lord Mansfifield; Judicial Integrity Or Its Lack; Somerset's Case*. [online] Digitalcommons.law.uga.edu. Available at: <https://digitalcommons.law.uga.edu/cgi/viewcontent.cgi?referer=&httpsredir=1&article=1386&context=fac_artchop> [Accessed 10 September 2020].

Warrell H., 2019, *Home Office under fire for using secretive visa algorithm. Lawyers warn software could discriminate against applicants based on nationality or race*. In Financial Times 9 June 2019, [online] Available at: <https://on.ft.com/3n35cSk> [Accessed 10 September 2020].

Weisdorf, J., 2005. *From Foraging To Farming: Explaining The Neolithic Revolution*. In *Journal of Economic Surveys*, [online] 19(4), pp. 561-586. Available at: <https://onlinelibrary.wiley.com/doi/abs/10.1111/j.0950-0804.2005.00259.x> [Accessed 4 September 2020].

Wescoat, B. and Ousterhout, R., 2012. *Architecture Of The Sacred: Space, Ritual, And Experience From Classical Greece To Byzantium*. Cambridge: Cambridge University Press;

Wittgenstein L., (1922) *Tractatus Logico-Philosophicus*, New York - Harcourt Brace & Company, London Kegan Trench Trubner & co.

Wittgenstein L., (1953) *Philosophische Untersuchungen*, Berlin Suhrkamp.

Woirol, G., 2012. Plans to end the Great Depression from the American public. *Labour History*, [online] 53(4), pp. 571-577. Available at: <https://www.tandfonline.com/doi/abs/10.1080/0023656X.2012.732760> [Accessed 30 September 2020].

Wood, L., 2008. *The LAN Turns 30, But Will It Reach 40?*. [online] Computerworld. Available at: <https://www.computerworld.com/article/2538907/the-lan-turns-30--but-will-it-reach-40-.html> [Accessed 1 October 2020].

World Bank, GDP Current USD, [online] www.worldbank.org. Available at: https://data.worldbank.org/indicator/NY.GDP.MKTP.CD [Accessed 3 September 2020].

Wozniak, R., 1995. *The 17Th Century*. [online] Serendipstudio.org. Available at: <https://serendipstudio.org/Mind/17th.html> [Accessed 3 September 2020].

Wu, T., 2003. Network Neutrality, Broadband Discrimination. *SSRN Electronic Journal*, [online] Available at: <https://www.researchgate.net/publication/228198900_Network_Neutrality_Broadband_Discrimination> [Accessed 2 October 2020].

Yardley, J., 2020. *Pope Francis Suggests Donald Trump Is 'Not Christian'*. [online] Nytimes.com. Available at: <https://www.nytimes.com/2016/02/19/world/americas/pope-francis-donald-trump-christian.html?auth=login-email&login=email> [Accessed 1 October 2020].

Youtube, 2012. *Merchant Of Venice Act IV*. [online] Youtube. Available at: <https://www.youtube.com/watch?v=_A4Oh3FaHUk> [Accessed 10 September 2020].

Youtube, 2020. *George Floyd "I Can't Breath" - Full Raw Video Of Death - Suffocated By Police Officer In Minnesota*. [online] Youtube. Available at: <https://www.youtube.com/watch?v=UMN35n4UVSA> [Accessed 2 October 2020].

Youtube, 2020. *The Guardian: Tunisian Election 2011: Protesters Demand Freedom Of Speech*. [online] Youtube. Available at: <https://www.youtube.com/watch?v=SVpN312hYgU> [Accessed 2 October 2020].

Youtube, 2020. *Trump Stands In Front Of Church Holding Bible After Threatening Military Action Against Protesters*. [online] Youtube. Available at: <https://www.youtube.com/watch?v=0oRQF68psdY> [Accessed 2 October 2020].

Youtube, 2020. *US National Anthem With Subtitles*. [online] Youtube. Available at: <https://www.youtube.com/watch?v=nCP5r2syjbE> [Accessed 2 October 2020].

Zag'orski, F., Carback, R., Chaum, D., Clark, J., Essex, A. and Vora, P., 2020. *Remotegrity: Design And Use Of An End-To-End Verifiable Remote Voting System*. [online] Chaum.com. Available at: <https://chaum.com/publications/Remotegrity-Design-and-Use-of-an-End-to-End-Verifiable-Remote-Voting-System.pdf> [Accessed 2 October 2020].

Zakaria, F., 2020. *Ten Lessons for a Post-Pandemic World*. New York: W.W. Norton & Company.

Zakaria, F., 2007. *The Future Of Freedom: Illiberal Democracy At Home And Abroad*. New York: Penguin.

Zelazo, P., Moscovitch, M. and Thompson, E., 2007. *The Cambridge Handbook Of Consciousness.* Cambridge: Cambridge University Press, pp. 9-35.

Zhang, X., 2019, *Integration of CCP Leadership with Corporate Governance*, in *China Perspectives,* [Online], 2019-1 Centre d'étude français sur la Chine contemporaine, Online since 19 March 2020, connection on 19 December 2020. URL: http://journals.openedition.org/chinaperspectives/8770; DOI: https://doi.org/10.4000/chinaperspectives.

Zimmer, C., 2016. *In Neanderthals' DNA, Ancient Humans May Have Left Genetic Mark.* [online] Nytimes.com. Available at: <https://www.nytimes.com/2016/02/23/science/ancient-humans-may-have-left-a-genetic-mark-on-neanderthals.html?contentCollection=weekendreads&action=click&pgtype=Homepage&clickSource=story-heading&module=c-column-middle-span-region&region=c-column-middle-span-region&WT.nav=c-column-middle-span-region> [Accessed 9 September 2020].

Zuboff, S., 2019, *The Age of Surveillance Capitalism*, London, Profile Books Kindle Edition.

Zunshine, L., 2006. *Why We Read Fiction.* Columbus: Ohio State University Press.

Wikipedia A, 2020. *Human.* [online] En.wikipedia.org. Available at: <https://en.wikipedia.org/wiki/Human> [Accessed 3 September 2020].

Wikipedia B, 2020. *Feral Child.* [online] En.wikipedia.org. Available at: <https://en.wikipedia.org/wiki/Feral_child> [Accessed 3 September 2020].

Wikipedia C, 2020. *Michael Wilson (Writer).* [online] En.wikipedia.org. Available at: <https://en.wikipedia.org/wiki/Michael_Wilson_%28writer%29> [Accessed 3 September 2020].

Wikipedia D, 2020. *Rod Serling.* [online] En.wikipedia.org. Available at: <https://en.wikipedia.org/wiki/Rod_Serling> [Accessed 3 September 2020].

Wikipedia E, 2020. *Leap Second.* [online] En.wikipedia.org. Available at: <https://en.wikipedia.org/wiki/Leap_second#Insertion_of_leap_seconds> [Accessed 3 September 2020].

Wikipedia F, 2020. *Augmented Reality.* [online] En.wikipedia.org. Available at: <https://en.wikipedia.org/wiki/Augmented_reality> [Accessed 3 September 2020].

Wikipedia G, 2020. *Kony 2012.* [online] En.wikipedia.org. Available at: <https://en.wikipedia.org/wiki/Kony_2012> [Accessed 3 September 2020].

Wikipedia G1, 2020, *Roman Forum*, [online] En.wikipedia.org. Available at: <https://en.wikipedia.org/wiki/Roman_Forum> [Accessed 3 October 2020].

Wikipedia H, 2020. *The School Of Athens.* [online] En.wikipedia.org. Available at: <https://en.wikipedia.org/wiki/The_School_of_Athens#/media/File:Sanzio_01.jpg> [Accessed 10 September 2020].

Wikipedia I, 2020. *Securitisation.* [online] En.wikipedia.org. Available at: <https://en.wikipedia.org/wiki/Securitisation> [Accessed 10 September 2020].

Wikipedia J, 2020. *Stock Exchange*. [online] En.wikipedia.org. Available at: <https://en.wikipedia.org/wiki/Stock_exchange> [Accessed 10 September 2020].

Wikipedia K, 2020. *Right-Wing Dictatorship*. [online] En.wikipedia.org. Available at: <https://en.wikipedia.org/wiki/Right-wing_dictatorship> [Accessed 14 September 2020].

Wikipedia, 2020. *Bitcoin*. [online] En.wikipedia.org. Available at: <https://en.wikipedia.org/wiki/Bitcoin> [Accessed 1 October 2020].

Wikipedia, 2020. *Blockchain*. [online] En.wikipedia.org. Available at: <https://en.wikipedia.org/wiki/Blockchain> [Accessed 1 October 2020].

Wikipedia, 2020. *Buddhism*. [online] En.wikipedia.org. Available at: <https://en.wikipedia.org/wiki/Buddhism> [Accessed 27 September 2020].

Wikipedia, 2020, *Chevron Deference* [online] En.wikipedia.org. Available at: https://en.wikipedia.org/wiki/Chevron_U.S.A.,_Inc._v._Natural_Resources_Defense_Council,_Inc.

Wikipedia, 2020. *Christianity*. [online] En.wikipedia.org. Available at: <https://en.wikipedia.org/wiki/Christianity> [Accessed 27 September 2020].

Wikipedia, 2020. *Classical Demography*. [online] En.wikipedia.org. Available at: <https://en.wikipedia.org/wiki/Classical_demography> [Accessed 27 September 2020].

Wikipedia, 2020. *Confucianism*. [online] En.wikipedia.org. Available at: <https://en.wikipedia.org/wiki/Confucianism> [Accessed 27 September 2020].

Wikipedia, 2020. *Contract*. [online] En.wikipedia.org. Available at: <https://en.wikipedia.org/wiki/Contract> [Accessed 29 September 2020].

Wikipedia, 2020. *David Chaum*. [online] En.wikipedia.org. Available at: <https://en.wikipedia.org/wiki/David_Chaum> [Accessed 1 October 2020].

Wikipedia, 2020. *Declaration And Resolves Of The First Continental Congress*. [online] En.wikisource.org. Available at: <https://en.wikisource.org/wiki/Declaration_and_Resolves_of_the_First_Continental_Congress> [Accessed 1 October 2020].

Wikipedia, 2020. *DigiNotar*. [online] En.wikipedia.org. Available at: < https://en.wikipedia.org/wiki/DigiNotar> [Accessed 29 September 2020].

Wikipedia, 2020. *Employment Contract*. [online] En.wikipedia.org. Available at: <https://en.wikipedia.org/wiki/Employment_contract> [Accessed 29 September 2020].

Wikipedia, 2020. *Feral child*. [online] En.wikipedia.org. Available at: < https://en.wikipedia.org/wiki/Feral_child> [Accessed 29 September 2020].

Wikipedia, 2020, *FRAND*. [online] En.wikipedia.org. Available at: < https://en.wikipedia.org/wiki/Reasonable_and_non-discriminatory_licensing> [Accessed 29 September 2020].

Wikipedia, 2020, *Gesetz zur Verhütung erbkranken Nachwuchses* [online] En.wikipedia.org. Available at: < *https://de.wikipedia.org/wiki/Gesetz_zur_Verh%C3%BCtung_erbkranken_Nachwuchses*> [Accessed 2 October 2020].

Wikipedia, 2020. *Gini Coefficient*. [online] En.wikipedia.org. Available at: <https://en.wikipedia.org/wiki/Gini_coefficient> [Accessed 1 October 2020].

Wikipedia, 2020. *GSM*. [online] En.wikipedia.org. Available at: <https://en.wikipedia.org/wiki/GSM#History> [Accessed 2 October 2020].

Wikipedia, 2020. *Graphology*, [online] En.wikipedia.org. Available at: https://en.wikipedia.org/wiki/Graphology [Accessed 27 September 2020].

Wikipedia, 2020. *Hinduism*. [online] En.wikipedia.org. Available at: <https://en.wikipedia.org/wiki/Hinduism> [Accessed 27 September 2020].

Wikipedia, 2020. *Internet Access*. [online] En.wikipedia.org. Available at: <https://en.wikipedia.org/wiki/Internet_access> [Accessed 1 October 2020].

Wikipedia, 2020. *Islam*. [online] En.wikipedia.org. Available at: <https://en.wikipedia.org/wiki/Islam> [Accessed 27 September 2020].

Wikipedia, 2020. *Lease*. [online] En.wikipedia.org. Available at: <https://en.wikipedia.org/wiki/Lease> [Accessed 29 September 2020].

Wikipedia, 2020. *Life, Liberty And The Pursuit Of Happiness*. [online] En.wikipedia.org. Available at: <https://en.wikipedia.org/wiki/Life,_Liberty_and_the_pursuit_of_Happiness> [Accessed 1 October 2020].

Wikipedia, 2020. *Life, Liberty And The Pursuit Of Happiness*. [online] En.wikipedia.org. Available at: <https://en.wikipedia.org/wiki/Life,_Liberty_and_the_pursuit_of_Happiness> [Accessed 2 October 2020].

Wikipedia, 2020, *Mercantilism*. [online] En.wikipedia.org. Available at: <https://en.wikipedia.org/wiki/Mercantilism> [Accessed 29 September 2020].

Wikipedia, 2020. *Marriage*. [online] En.wikipedia.org. Available at: <https://en.wikipedia.org/wiki/Marriage> [Accessed 29 September 2020].

Wikipedia, 2020. *Medieval Demography*. [online] En.wikipedia.org. Available at: <https://en.wikipedia.org/wiki/Medieval_demography> [Accessed 27 September 2020].

Wikipedia, 2020. *Novella Del Grasso Legnaiuolo (Red. Codice Palatino 200) Ì*. [online] It.wikisource.org. Available at: <https://it.wikisource.org/wiki/Novella_del_Grasso_legnaiuolo_(red._Codice_Palatino_200)> [Accessed 2 October 2020].

Wikipedia, 2020. *Outsourcing*. [online] En.wikipedia.org. Available at: <https://en.wikipedia.org/wiki/Outsourcing> [Accessed 1 October 2020].

Wikipedia, 2020. *Patent Troll*. [online] En.wikipedia.org. Available at: <https://en.wikipedia.org/wiki/Patent_troll> [Accessed 1 October 2020].

Wikipedia, 2020. *Property*. [online] En.wikipedia.org. Available at: <https://en.wikipedia.org/wiki/Property> [Accessed 29 September 2020].

Wikipedia, 2020. *Roman Law*. [online] En.wikipedia.org. Available at: <https://en.wikipedia.org/wiki/Roman_law> [Accessed 29 September 2020].

Wikipedia, 2020. *Speakers' Corner*. [online] En.wikipedia.org. Available at: <https://en.wikipedia.org/wiki/Speakers'_Corner> [Accessed 1 October 2020].

Wikipedia, 2020. *Social networking system*. [online] En.wikipedia.org. Available at: <https://en.wikipedia.org/wiki/Social_networking_service>[Accessed 2 October 2020]

Wikipedia, 2020. *Three Laws Of Robotics*. [online] En.wikipedia.org. Available at: <https://en.wikipedia.org/wiki/Three_Laws_of_Robotics> [Accessed 2 October 2020].

www.ingramcontent.com/pod-product-compliance
Lightning Source LLC
Chambersburg PA
CBHW061129220326
41599CB00024B/4221